Gender in Communication

Third Edition

Gender in Communication
A Critical Introduction
Third Edition

Catherine Helen Palczewski
University of Northern Iowa

Victoria Pruin DeFrancisco
University of Northern Iowa

Danielle Dick McGeough
University of Northern Iowa

Los Angeles | London | New Delhi
Singapore | Washington DC | Melbourne

FOR INFORMATION:

SAGE Publications, Inc.
2455 Teller Road
Thousand Oaks, California 91320
E-mail: order@sagepub.com

SAGE Publications Ltd.
1 Oliver's Yard
55 City Road
London EC1Y 1SP
United Kingdom

SAGE Publications India Pvt. Ltd.
B 1/I 1 Mohan Cooperative Industrial Area
Mathura Road, New Delhi 110 044
India

SAGE Publications Asia-Pacific Pte. Ltd.
3 Church Street
#10-04 Samsung Hub
Singapore 049483

Acquisitions Editor: Terri Accomazzo
Production Editor: Laureen Gleason
Copy Editor: Deanna Noga
Typesetter: C&M Digitals (P) Ltd.
Proofreader: Sarah J. Duffy
Indexer: Marilyn Augst
Cover Designer: Scott Van Atta
Marketing Manager: Allison Henry

Printed in the United States of America

Library of Congress Cataloging-in-Publication Data

Names: Palczewski, Catherine Helen, author. | DeFrancisco, Victoria L. (Victoria Leto), author. | McGeough, Danielle Dick, author.

Title: Gender in communication : a critical introduction / Catherine Helen Palczewski, University of Northern Iowa, Victoria Pruin DeFrancisco, University of Northern Iowa, Danielle Dick McGeough, University of Northern Iowa.

Other titles: Communicating gender diversity

Description: Third Edition. | Thousand Oaks : SAGE Publications, [2018] | Revised edition of the authors' Gender in communication, [2014] | Includes bibliographical references and index.

Identifiers: LCCN 2017034869 | ISBN 9781506358451 (pbk. : alk. paper)

Subjects: LCSH: Sex role. | Gender identity. | Communication—Social aspects. | Communication—Sex differences. | Sexism in language.

Classification: LCC HQ1075 .D43 2018 | DDC 305.3—dc23
LC record available at https://lccn.loc.gov/2017034869

This book is printed on acid-free paper.

18 19 20 21 22 10 9 8 7 6 5 4 3

Brief Contents

Detailed Contents

Sara Miller McCune founded SAGE Publishing in 1965 to support the dissemination of usable knowledge and educate a global community. SAGE publishes more than 1000 journals and over 800 new books each year, spanning a wide range of subject areas. Our growing selection of library products includes archives, data, case studies and video. SAGE remains majority owned by our founder and after her lifetime will become owned by a charitable trust that secures the company's continued independence.

Los Angeles | London | New Delhi | Singapore | Washington DC | Melbourne

Preface

As we worked through the revisions for this third edition throughout 2016 and into the summer of 2017, a number of events transpired that threw into relief the importance of gender in communication: the presidential campaign, the Women's March on Washington, the silencing of Senator Elizabeth Warren, and the scolding of reporter April Ryan and Representative Maxine Waters. All these events have historical antecedents. So first a little more detail on the events.

Events Informing the Third Edition

The 2016 Presidential Election

In the summer of 2016, former senator and secretary of state Hillary Clinton won the Democratic nomination for the presidency, but she later lost the electoral college vote to businessperson and reality TV figure Donald Trump. No single factor explains the election, but research indicated that sexism likely had something to do with the result (Maxwell & Shields, 2017). Although polls indicated many Trump voters prior to the election voiced concerns about Clinton's use of personal e-mail, after the election they indicated they were not concerned about Trump's use of a personal e-mail server, leading one commentator to conclude, "This news proves that Hillary Clinton's loss was about sexism, not her emails" (Strassner, 2017). Even though Clinton testified for more than 11 hours about Benghazi and turned over all her files and nothing was found, criticism persisted. Why?

An experimental study about backlash against female politicians provided one explanation. Male politicians who were perceived as power-seeking were also perceived to be "more assertive, stronger, and tougher" and have "greater competence" while women politicians who were perceived as power-seeking were seen as uncaring and people responded to them with moral outrage (Okimoto & Brescoll, 2010). General resistance to female candidates has been demonstrated in experiments that found 26% of the population express anger at the idea of a female president (Streb, Burrell, Frederick, & Genovese, 2008).

The findings of these predictive studies were confirmed by research on 2016 voters. University of Arkansas researchers found that "modern Sexism did influence the 2016 presidential election for many Americans" (Maxwell & Shields, 2017). *Modern sexism*, defined as hostility or resentment toward working women, generally was more pervasive among White U.S. citizens and southerners and was not exclusive to men. The conclusion of the study: Of White Independents and Democrats, 11 million men and 6.5 million women "feel enough animosity towards working women and feminists to make them unlikely to vote for one of them—even from their own party" (Maxwell & Shields, 2017).

Regardless of your opinion of the electoral outcome, gender in communication played a role in the election. But it is important to remember that this was not the first, or only, election in which gender and sex played a role. For every contemporary example of women in politics, a long history of struggle precedes it.

Clinton was not the first woman to run for the presidency. In 1872, Victoria Woodhull ran, even before women had the right to vote. In 1884, Belva Ann Lockwood was the first woman to actually appear on ballots. In 1964, Margaret Chase Smith was the first woman to receive nomination votes at a major party's convention. In 1972, Shirley Chisholm, the first Black woman elected to Congress, earned delegates at the Democratic National Convention. Patsy Matsu Takemoto Mink and Linda Jenness ran in 1972, Pat Schroeder in 1988, Elizabeth Dole in 2000, and Carol Moseley Braun in 2004. For any contemporary issue related to gender in communication, a long history precedes it. The same is true for this book. Our ability to write this book, and to cite research about gender in communication, is the product of a history of activism, scholarship, and writing by others.

Many of the arguments for Trump and against Clinton hearkened back to arguments originally used to deny women the right to vote. On at least 12 different occasions, Trump's running mate, Mike Pence, commented on how Trump being "broad-shouldered" qualified him for the presidency. For example, Pence indicated he agreed to run with Trump because "he embodies American strength, and I know that he will provide that kind of broad-shouldered American strength on the global stage as well" (as cited in Chait, 2016). Although Pence denied that the comments had anything to do with masculinity (Griffiths, 2016), the repeated references to shoulders and strength sounded similar to comments from 100 years ago.

One of the main arguments against women voting was that their bodies were too weak to enforce their vote. The New York Association Opposed to Woman Suffrage, in a circa 1910 statement presented to both houses of the U.S. Congress, noted: "To extend the suffrage to women would be to introduce into the electorate a vast noncombatant party, incapable of enforcing its own rule" (as cited in Hazard, 1910, p. 88). British-born historian and journalist Goldwin Smith, in his commentary on the question of woman suffrage, explained: "Political power has hitherto been exercised by the male sex . . . because man alone could uphold government and enforce the law" (as cited in "Opinions," 1912, p. 6). Author Rossiter Johnson worried, "To make any party victorious at the polls by means of blank-cartridge ballots would only present an increased temptation to the numerical minority to assert itself as the military majority. . . . If an election is carried by a preponderance of votes cast by women, who is to enforce the verdict?" (as cited in "Opinions," 1912, p. 5). Men's physical strength was foregrounded as central to their political strength. These contemporary comparisons to historical moments did not end with the election.

The Women's March on Washington

On January 21, 2017, the day after the inauguration and 10 weeks after the election, the Women's March on Washington occurred, at which over 470,000 people marched. Across the globe, 999 marches occurred with an estimated 5.6 million people participating, the largest single protest event in history ("Feet," 2017; see also "Sister Marches," 2017). In describing the mission of the March, organizers noted how "the rhetoric of the past election cycle has insulted, demonized, and threatened many of us—immigrants of all statuses, Muslims and those of diverse religious faiths, people who identify as LGBTQIA [lesbian, gay, bisexual, trans, queer, intersex, and asexual], Native people, Black and Brown people, people with disabilities, survivors of sexual assault." The final element of the mission was "HEAR OUR VOICE" ("Mission & Vision," n.d.). For every contemporary example of a march about gender injustice, a long history of marches precedes it.

This was not the first women's march on Washington. On March 3, 1913, the eve of President Woodrow Wilson's inauguration, the first national woman suffrage procession occurred. Five thousand women participated, including a contingent of Black women from Howard University who had to fight for their inclusion, as an estimated 100,000 people watched. The march was important, but the crowd's reaction (first verbally and then physically attacking the suffragists) and the police department's failure to respond together catapulted woman suffrage into national attention. According to the *New York Times*, "for more than an hour confusion reigned. The police, the women say, did practically nothing, and finally soldiers and marines formed a voluntary escort to clear the way"; a police officer designated to guard the marchers was overheard shouting, "If my wife were where you are I'd break her head" ("5,000 Women," 1913, p. 5). Suffrage movement organizers described how marchers were "struck in the face by onlookers, spat upon, and overwhelmed by rabid remarks" (Blatch & Lutz, 1940, p. 196). Our ability to write this book is made possible by the work of activists who made clear women's issues were public issues and fought for women's voices to be heard.

The Silencing of Elizabeth Warren

In February 2017, during Senate debate about attorney general nominee Jefferson Beauregard Sessions, Senator Elizabeth Warren read the words of Coretta Scott King criticizing Sessions for suppressing the vote of Black citizens. Senate majority leader Mitch McConnell interrupted and prevented Warren from completing the remarks, enforcing a senate rule that prohibits one senator from "impugning" another. Commenting on this moment, Megan Garber (2017), a reporter for *The Atlantic*, wrote:

> There are many ways that American culture tells women to be quiet—many ways they are reminded that they would really be so much more pleasing if they would just smile a little more, or talk a little less, or work a little harder to be pliant and agreeable. Women are, in general, extremely attuned to these messages; we have, after all, heard them all our lives. . . . [W]hen Senate majority

leader Mitch McConnell intervened to prevent her from finishing the speech—many women, regardless of their politics or place, felt that silencing, viscerally. And when McConnell, later, remarked of Warren, "She was warned. She was given an explanation. Nevertheless, she persisted," many women, regardless of their politics or place, felt it again. Because, regardless of their politics or place, those women have heard the same thing, or a version of it, many times before. (paras. 1–2)

Instead of recognizing the gender politics at play, other Senators reinforced sex roles. Senator Orrin Hatch agreed that Warren should have been silenced because she was criticizing another senator. Hatch's reason: Warren needed to "think of his [Sessions's] wife" (as cited in Crockett, 2017). In response, a meme was born: "Nevertheless, she persisted" adorned T-shirts, hashtags, and profile pages. For every contemporary example of persistence in the face of gendered opposition, a long history of persistence precedes it.

It is important to remember that in 1917 representatives of the National Woman's Party would be the first group to protest at the White House directly. Even when the United States entered World War I, the Silent Sentinels kept up the protests in front of the White House only to face arrest, violent crowds, and police violence after arrest. Nevertheless, they persisted.

The Scolding of April Ryan and Maxine Waters

At a March 2017 press conference, Press Secretary Sean Spicer thought it was appropriate to tell American Urban Radio Networks' veteran White House correspondent April Ryan to "stop shaking your head" (as cited in Silva, 2017). The same day, Fox News host Bill O'Reilly answered criticisms of Trump made by Representative Maxine Waters by snidely commenting: "I didn't hear a word she said. I was looking at the James Brown wig" (as cited in Taylor, 2017).

These events motivated educator and activist Brittany Packnett to create the hashtag #BlackWomenAtWork, under which Black women noted the range of ways their nonverbal communication and bodies were disciplined in the workplace, for example, by being told their hair was unprofessional or not being recognized as being the owner or manager. Packnett explained:

This idea that a black woman's presence is to be policed or politicized in the workplace is what we're talking about. The idea that Sean Spicer can tell April Ryan what to do with her face, irrespective of her years in journalism, the idea that Maxine Waters' voice is less important than her hair, is what black women are experiencing every single day. (as cited in Taylor, 2017)

For every contemporary example of Black women fighting for their rights, a long history of struggle precedes it.

It is important to remember that when the U.S. Congress was debating whether to extend voting rights to women, congressmen argued that the vote should not be extended to women because, while the South had figured out ways to suppress the

Black man's vote, they would not be able to suppress Black women's vote. Representative Clark (1918) explained that Black women would not be as easily cowed as Black men and would be "fanatical on the subject of voting" and "much more insistent and vicious" in their "demands for social recognition which will never be accorded them" (p. H90).

Why Studying Gender in Communication Is Important

The examples of Clinton, Warren, Ryan, Waters, and the March illustrate four points.

First, gender matters. To be able to understand and explain current events and analyze communication, you need to be able to name and articulate the way in which gender operates in communication. Trump was performing a particular type of masculinity just as much as Clinton and Warren were disciplined for not performing femininity appropriately. Additionally, people's perceptions of the candidates were refracted through expectations tied to the candidate's sex. More than actual differences in communication patterns, perceptions and expectations of other people's behaviors are gendered. In *Same Difference: How Gender Myths Are Hurting Our Relationships, Our Children, and Our Jobs*, psychologist Rosalind Barnett and journalist Caryl Rivers (2004) critiqued social myths of gender differences. They argued that the belief in gender differences has created a self-fulfilling prophecy in which people's stereotypes actually create the differences.

Second, race matters. One is never just a gender, and the communication challenges Black women, Latinas, Asian woman, and Native American women face are distinct from those that White women face. The challenges Black men, and other people of color, face are distinct from those that White men and women face.

Third, masculinity matters. Gender is as much about masculinity as it is about femininity. And being held to a gender binary, masculine *or* feminine, limits all people.

Fourth, protest matters. People using their voices to advocate for issues about which they are passionate makes a difference. The 2017 Women's March on Washington was not the first time women marched for rights in the capitol of the United States, Elizabeth Warren was not the first person to persist in the face of being silenced, and the #BlackWomenAtWork hashtag was not the first attempt to make clear the unique challenges Black people face as a result of how their race and sex intersect. Social change regarding gendered expectations and sex roles does not happen overnight; instead, repeated acts of communication—of public protest, of interpersonal interactions, of small-group discussions—are needed to make change.

Because gender is a constantly evolving concept in individuals' gender identity, in the larger culture's predominant notions about gender, and in continuing research, absolute claims are not possible and would be irresponsible. Instead, our intent is to better equip readers with tools you can use to examine and make sense of gender in communication. As such, this book is not simply a review of communication research but is rather an attempt to place the research in the context of larger theoretical, social, and political issues that influence, and are influenced by, gender in communication. We have attempted to write this book as an extended conversation in which we interact with research and popular discussions of gender in communication that have most excited our own scholarly imaginations.

We study the variety of ways in which communication of and about gender and sex enables and constrains people's identities. We believe that people are social actors and create meaning through their symbolic interactions. Thus, our emphasis is not on how gender influences communication but on how communication constitutes gender. We believe people are capable of being self-reflexive about communication processes and creative in generating new ways to play with symbols.

Core Principles

To study how people construct, perform, and change gender and what factors influence these performances, we draw on seven principles:

1. *Intersectionality*. You cannot study gender or sex in isolation. How a particular sexed body performs gender always intersects with other identity ingredients, including race, ethnicity, social class, age, sexual orientation, physical ability, and more. People are who they are, and act the way they act, not just because of their sex or gender. People are wonderfully complex and form their gendered identities at an intersection of influences from multiple identity ingredients, and the social structures in which people operate are never formed solely along sex lines. Dominance and power also are best understood through an intersectional analysis. Thus, to more accurately study gender, we study gender in the context of other social identities.

2. *Interdisciplinarity*. We seek to fuse and balance social scientific, humanistic, and critical methods. Thus, we cite quantitative, qualitative, rhetorical, critical, and creative scholarship. As coauthors, we have the benefit of drawing on three fields of communication studies that often operate independent of each other but that are inextricably interlinked: rhetoric, social science, and performance studies. Palczewski, trained as a rhetorical scholar, was a college debate coach for 15 years and studies political controversies and social protest. DeFrancisco, trained as a social scientist, uses qualitative research methods to study how gender and related inequalities and acts of resistance are constructed through interpersonal relationships and individuals' identities. Dick McGeough, trained in performance studies and qualitative methods, uses creative approaches to explore scholarly questions. Most texts on gender in communication focus on social science studies of gendered interpersonal interactions and, thus, fail to recognize how broader public discourse can influence gender.

Not only do we bridge methodological chasms within our own discipline, but we do so among disciplines. We purposely reviewed each topic from multiple disciplinary and activist perspectives. Throughout the text, we honor the contributions of Black womanist theory, we celebrate the challenges offered by third-wave feminisms, we gratefully include lessons taught by queer and trans theory, we integrate the insights of men's studies scholars, and we happily navigate the tensions between global and postmodern feminisms. The result is a richer, fuller understanding of the topic that stretches the boundaries of what is commonly considered relevant for a communication text.

We do not present research consistent with our view only. People learn most by stepping outside their academic or personal comfort zones to consider other perspectives. We value engaged and vital disagreement because we believe readers are able to glean more from our presentation of substantiated arguments than they could if we presented the research as if it were all consistent and value free. We express our views of the material, and we hope this encourages you to do the same. Know up front that we believe agreement is neither a necessary nor a preferred requirement for learning from this book, and disagreement is not a sign of disrespect.

3. *Gender diversity, not sex differences.* We do not subscribe to typical conceptualizations of gender as a form of difference. Instead, we problematize the differences view by showing how it engages in essentialism, ignores power, reinforces stereotypes, fails to account for intersectional identities, and is inconsistent with statistical analyses demonstrating that sex does not consistently account for differences in communication. However, our rejection of the differences approach does not mean that we deny differences exist. Instead, we seek to recognize differences within genders as a result of intersectionality. We reject binary ways of thinking. We embrace a gender diversity approach. Research embracing this approach continues to grow, and we make a concerted effort to recognize multiple femininities and multiple masculinities and complex mixtures of them.

4. *Gender is performed.* Gender is something a person *does*, not something a person *is*. Gender is not something located within individuals; it is a social construct that institutions, groups, and individuals maintain (and challenge). Thus, we examine the microlevel (how an individual might perform gender), the mesolevel (how groups within institutions communicate about gender), and the macrolevel (how social understandings of gender are performed on individuals).

5. *Masculinity.* The study of gender is not exclusively the study of women. However, the study of gender has traditionally been considered a "women's issue," hence researchers and textbooks often have focused almost exclusively on women and femininities, underemphasizing men and masculinities. Thanks to the recent growth in men's studies, we have at our disposal a rich literature base that considers gender and masculinity.

6. *Violence.* To study gender in lived experiences means to study the darker side of gender: oppression and violence. In this textbook, we do not shy away from this uncomfortable reality. Ours is not a narrative that says, "We are all just different, and isn't that nice?" To tell the whole story one must go deeper, making visible connections to the realities of gendered violence. This does not mean we are bashing men or that we presume all men have the potential to be violent and all women are victims. Rather, we recognize violence as systemic. That is, who can be violent and who can be a victim and who can be viewed as violent and who can be viewed as a victim are all part of a socially constructed system to maintain differences and inequalities. Gendered violence includes domestic abuse, rape, violence against LGBTQ people, street trafficking, and cyberbullying.

In each chapter, we make visible the connections between presumably innocent gendered practices and a range of specific social injustices connected to the topic. By linking gendered practices to more overt forms of gendered violence, we move beyond superficial generalizations about gender differences and make visible the struggles many people face in their unique contexts.

7. *Emancipation*. Even as we recognize how gendered norms are linked to gendered violence, we also seek to make visible the emancipatory potential of gendered practice. To focus only on the negative would be to reinforce stereotypes and ignore the ways people challenge gendered norms to create spaces for diverse individual and group choices. Gender identity need not be oppressive and limiting. We offer examples of how diverse groups of people have created strategies to free themselves of stereotypical gender restrictions and other cultural expectations.

We do not shy away from complex and controversial subjects. We reject the sex binary of male and female, instead recognizing the existence of intersex, transgender, and gender non-conforming people. We reject the binary-differences approach to studying gender as masculine *or* feminine, instead finding people to be wonderfully diverse and competent at adjusting their behavior according to situational needs. We reject the false assumption that the norm is to be cisgender (meaning one's sex and gender are consistent according to social dictates), instead recognizing most people are far more complex. We reject heteronormativity, instead seeing heterosexuality, homosexuality, bisexuality, and queer sexualities as equally valid sexual orientations.

Organization of the Book

The book is divided into two parts. "Part I: Foundations" includes five chapters that describe the fundamentals of studying gender in communication: definitions and explanations of key terms, theoretical approaches, gender in conversation, gendered bodies, and language. These chapters provide a foundational vocabulary that enables you to study gender in communication with more subtlety and nuance. "Part II: Institutions" includes an introductory chapter to explain a focus on social institutions, followed by five chapters on the institutions that make evident the intersections of gender and communication: family, education, work, religion, and media. Each chapter examines how individuals experience and enact gender within the institution and how institutional structures and predominant ideology influence the experience and performance of gender. The concluding chapter highlights links among the preceding chapters and presents visions for future study.

New to This Edition

The third edition of this textbook is revised and updated to make it accessible to undergraduate students while still challenging them. Graduate students will still find it a strong critical introduction to the study of gender in communication.

The chapters on voices, work, education, and family have been completely rewritten to reflect major shifts in the state of knowledge. New sections on debates over bathroom bills, intensive mothering, humor, swearing, and Title IX have been added. The sections on trans and gender non-conforming people have been expanded and updated to reflect changes in language. All other chapters have been updated with new examples, new concepts, and new research. Over 500 new sources have been integrated. In an effort to be more inclusive, we have replaced the pronouns *his* or *her* with *they* in most cases even if the reference is singular.

We hope our third edition challenges the way in which readers think about gender and sex, as well as how gender and sex intersect with race, ethnicity, class, sexual orientation, and nationality. Instead of providing simplistic answers, we hope we provide guidance on how to ask good questions. We also hope this book will inspire researchers to contribute to the study of gender in communication, further stretching the boundaries of culturally gendered perceptions.

Individual Acknowledgments

This book could not have been written without the assistance of our colleagues. People too numerous to list have helped us as we wrote this book, but a few deserve special note for the extra time they spent sharing resources, reading chapters, and providing invaluable research assistance. The chapters would not have been as grounded in current scholarship, and the examples would not have been as rich, had it not been for the excellent contributions of graduate research assistants and students over the years: Derk Babbitt, Ruth Beerman, C. A. Brimmer, Kiranjeet Dhillon, Danelle Frisbie, Tristin Johnson, Ashley Jones, Christian Kremer-Terry, Jessany Maldondo, Megan Mapes, Emily Paskewitz, and Eric Short. Colleagues, students, friends, and staff served as resources, offering ideas, examples, and other support: Rob Asen, Judith Baxter, Harry Brod, Dan Brouwer, Patrice Buzznell, April Chatham-Carpenter, Jeanne Cook, Melissa Dobosh, Valeria Fabj, Jennifer Farrell, Patricia Fazio, John Fritch, Susan Hill, Kelsey Harr-Lagin, Stephanie Logan, Karen Mitchell, Amymarie Moser, Harrison Postler, Jennifer Potter, Alimatul Qibtiyah, Martha Reineke, Kyle Rudick, Colice Sanders, Montana Smith, Mary Beth Stalp, Leah White, and Nikki Zumbach Harken. We thank the UNI library staff, especially Christopher Neuhaus and Rosemary Meany. We recognize that no book is created in isolation. We thank Julia Wood *(Gendered Lives)*, Diana Ivy and Phil Backlund *(GenderSpeak)*, and Karlyn Kohrs Campbell *(Man Cannot Speak for Her)* for helping pave the way in gender/sex in communication textbooks. We thank our life partners, Arnie Madsen, David Pruin, and Ryan McGeough, for honoring our work.

We thank the SAGE staff. Our SAGE editor, Matthew Byrnie, advocated for this third edition. We also want to thank the skilled SAGE professionals who worked with us through the final stages of the publication process: Terri Accomazzo (acquisitions editor), Erik Helton (editorial assistant), Laureen Gleason (production editor), and Deanna Noga (copy editor). Support for the development of this book was provided in part by the University of Northern Iowa's Graduate College, the College of Humanities and Fine Arts, the Department of Communication Studies, and the Women's and Gender Studies Program.

SAGE Publications gratefully acknowledges the following reviewers: Cynthia Berryman-Fink, University of Cincinnati; Derek T. Buescher, University of Puget Sound; Sandra L. Faulkner, Syracuse University; Lisa A. Flores, University of Colorado Boulder; Jeffrey Dale Hobbs, University of Texas at Tyler; Charlotte Kr 0lkke, University of Southern Denmark; D. K. London, Merrimack College; Linda Manning, Christopher Newport University; M. Chad McBride, Creighton University; Elizabeth Natalle, University of North Carolina, Greensboro; Narissra Punyanunt-Carter, Texas Tech University; Leah Stewart, Rutgers University; and Lynn H. Turner, Marquette University.

Social Acknowledgments

Not only is it important to recognize the individual people in our lives who helped make this book possible, but it also is important to recognize the historical and contemporary movements that made our lives as professors, and the ideas presented in this book, possible. Communication scholars Karma Chávez and Cindy Griffin (2014) were right when they pointed out women's (and gender) studies in communication is "a field of study that emerges from activist efforts and grassroots social movements" (p. 262). We need to acknowledge the contributions of those movements and activists.

This book would not be possible were it not for decades, if not centuries, of social movements and protests that have made clear that gender, sex, and sexuality are public issues and not merely personal expressions. For this reason, we have integrated examples of social movements that have influenced understandings of gender/sex throughout our chapters (e.g., social protest about sexual harassment, fat activism, gender-inclusive bathroom activism, LGBTQ social protests, woman suffrage, equal pay activism, farm worker's rights). We could write an entire book about protests and movements for sex and gender justice, but this is a not a textbook about social movements.

Instead, we want to make clear how this book, about this topic, written by three people who identify as women, was made possible as a result of social activism by those who came before us—activism that challenged sex-based restrictions on who could be educated, who could speak in public, which topics could be spoken about in public, and what evidence counted in debates over those topics. The historical centering of some communicators (e.g., White educated men), and the marginalization of others (e.g., White women, women and men of color, poor people, and LBGTQ people), informs contemporary practices. An understanding of that history can help you understand contemporary communication practices and research.

We could not write a book about gender in communication were it not for activists who struggled for centuries to create space for women to speak publicly as knowledgeable experts. We recognize the work it took in Western countries for anyone other than a White land-owning man to be given the chance to speak. Karlyn Kohrs Campbell (1989), in her germinal two-volume *Man Cannot Speak for Her*, outlined the history of exclusion that women speakers faced even as "public persuasion has been a conscious part of the Western male's heritage from ancient Greece to the present" (Vol. I, p. 1). For decades in public address classes, the speeches of great men were studied, from Pericles's funeral oration to the most recent presidential state of the union. Unfortunately, "women have no parallel rhetorical history" (Vol. I, p. 1). In fact, for much of Western history, women were explicitly prohibited from speaking publicly by social mores and law.

Kathleen Hall Jamieson (1995), in *Beyond the Double Bind*, collected some of the religious, cultural, and legal statements prohibiting women's speech. We reproduce only a few of them here to make clear how communication, when it emanated from bodies coded as female, was disciplined. Public punishment was used against the speaking woman: "In seventeenth-century colonial America, the ducking stool held a place of honor near the courthouse alongside the pillory and the stock. After being bound to the stool, the 'scold,' 'nag,' 'brabling *(sic),'* or 'unquiet' woman was submerged in the nearest body of water, where she could choose between silence and drowning" (pp. 80–81). Philosophers, such as Søren Kierkegaard, proclaimed in 1844, "Silence is not only woman's greatest wisdom, but also her highest beauty" (as cited in Jamieson, 1995, p. 80). Biblical injunctions, repeated through the early 1900s, reinforced these social restrictions: "I am not giving permission for a woman to teach or tell a man what to do. A woman ought not to speak, because Adam was formed first and Eve afterwards, and it was not Adam who was led astray but the woman who was led astray and fell into sin. Nevertheless, she will be saved by childbearing" (1 Timothy 2:12–15). To even conceive of a book about gender in communication, pathbreakers had to create the possibility of people other than White men communicating.

Even as we write about how silence was the right speech of White womanhood, we want to recognize that silence was resisted. Scholar and educator bell hooks (1989) cautioned against reading the history of silence as universal:

> Within feminist circles, silence is often seen as the sexist "right speech of womanhood"—the sign of woman's submission to patriarchal authority. This emphasis on woman's silence may be an accurate remembering of what has taken place in the households of women from WASP backgrounds in the United States, but in black communities (and diverse ethnic communities), women have not been silent. Their voices can be heard. Certainly for black women, our struggle has not been to emerge from silence into speech but to change the nature and direction of our speech, to make a speech that compels listeners, one that is heard. (p. 6)

hooks's warning about reading history in too absolute a way also encourages a rereading of the history of women. Just because women have been exhorted to silence, and punished for speaking in public, does not mean they actually have been silent. A book that recognizes that gender is diverse and intersects with ethnicity, class, citizenship, religion, and other identity ingredients would not be possible were it not for the work of people of color who have made clear that gender norms concerning what it means to be a good woman and a good man have long assumed only White women and White men.

In the early 1830s, Maria Miller Stewart, an African American woman, became the first U.S. woman to speak to audiences in the United States that included both women and men (Sells, 1993). In the mid-1830s, Sarah and Angelina Grimké, daughters of a slave-owning family, began writing about abolition and spoke to small groups of women in parlor meetings (Japp, 1993; Vonnegut, 1993). As their renown as abolitionists grew, they began to speak to mixed-sex audiences and expanded their advocacy to include women's rights. All three faced rebuke and scorn because of their speaking. Yet they paved a pathway for others to follow: Elizabeth Cady Stanton, Lucretia Mott, Susan B. Anthony, Sojourner Truth, Mary Church Terrell, Ida B. Wells, Frances Ellen Watkins Harper, Emma Goldman, Voltairine de Cleyre, Lucy Parsons, Mary Harris "Mother" Jones, to name only a few. Our voices in this book would not have been possible were it not for the voices of those who opened space for people other than White men to speak.

We could not write a book about gender in communication were it not for activists who struggled for centuries to challenge the sexualization of women in public. Sex and sexuality were intertwined with the admonitions against women's public communication. Jamieson (1995) argued that "since silence and motherhood were twinned, a corollary assumption was formed of the alliance: Public speech by a woman is the outward sign of suspect sexuality" (p. 14). Although women's actual public participation is far more rich and complex than the narrative of men's and women's separate spheres would indicate (Eastman, 2009; Matthews, 1992; Piepmeier, 2004; Ryan, 1992), women faced discipline for violating social dictates concerning separate spheres. As strange as it might now sound to contemporary ears, the very term *public woman* was synonymous with *prostitute* through the 1800s in the United States. Thus, if a woman ventured outside the private sphere into public spaces, the assumption was that she was sexually available.

Two stories illustrate this. First, in May of 1862, the commander of the Union forces in New Orleans issued the following General Order:

> As the officers and soldiers of the United States have been subject to repeated insults from the women (calling themselves ladies) of New Orleans . . . it is ordered that hereafter when any female shall, by word, gesture or movement, insult or show contempt for any officer or soldier of the United States, she shall be regarded and held liable to be treated as a woman of the town plying her vocation. (as cited in Ryan, 1992, p. 3)

Second, in December of 1895, New York City police arrested young, White, working-class Lizzie Schauer for engaging in disorderly conduct. Her crime? She was out in public at night and asked for directions from two men. She was what was then considered a "'public woman,' or prostitute" (Matthews, 1994, p. 3). We want to make clear the centuries of work that people completed just to carve out a public space where women could communicate and not fear loss of their virtue. As these examples make clear, it is impossible to talk about gender in communication without also talking about sex and sexuality.

We could not write a book about the multiplicity of genders, and the way people are never just a sex, were it not for the activists who made clear the importance of ethnicity. In 1866, Frances Ellen Watkins Harper challenged White woman suffrage activists when they argued against enfranchising Black men before White women, saying "the white women all go for sex, letting race occupy a minor position" (as cited in Bacon, 1989, p. 35). In 1974, the Combahee River Collective Statement made clear,

> There have always been Black women activists—some known, like Sojourner Truth, Harriet Tubman, Frances E. W. Harper, Ida B. Wells Barnett, and Mary Church Terrell, and thousands upon thousands unknown—who have had a shared awareness of how their sexual identity combined with their racial identity to make their whole life situation and the focus of their political struggles unique.

Gender is never only about sex. Feminist scholar Chandra Talpade Mohanty (2003) wrote, "To define feminism purely in gendered terms assumes that our consciousness of being 'women' has nothing to do with race, class, nation, or sexuality, just with gender. But no one 'becomes a woman' . . . purely because she is female" (p. 55). Arguments against essentialism and for intersectionality are not new, although the language to talk about them might be.

In 1863, poor women made clear that neutral government policies did not affect everyone equally. As the Civil War raged, and the Union forces needed public support for conscription, poor women protested because the draft impacted them more because "the loss of a male wage earner was the most devastating fate to befall the poor wives and mothers of New York, a sure sentence to poverty given the dearth of women's employment opportunities and the paltriness of their wages" (Ryan, 1992, p. 149). These women, along with men, engaged in riots to protest the forced conscription of working men on whom families depended. In response, the city of New York suspended its draft and only reinstated it after it had set aside $2.5 million to purchase exemptions for the poorest families (Ryan, 1992, p. 150). Studying gender only by thinking about its relationship to sex would offer an incomplete analysis.

We could not write a book about gender in communication were it not for activists who struggled to make clear gender is not biologically determined. Even after achieving some degree of legal recognition of equality, activists had to struggle for social equality. To do that, they had to challenge the idea that men and women were naturally different. The work of activists in women's movements made clear that many of the differences between men and women were the result of socialization, not an innate characteristic. The work of activists in the Civil Rights Movement, the Red Power Movement, and the United Farmworkers Movement made clear that many of the differences between White people and people of color were the result of socialization and unequal social relations, not an innate characteristic. We honor the work of the Black Women's Club Movement of the 1890s, the Woman Suffrage Movement whose work spanned from 1848 to 1919, and the feminist and Civil Rights movements of the 1960s through the 1970s.

To be able to write a book that explores gender diversity requires not only that gender not be biologically determined, but also that we could imagine a range of ways to do gender. Trans activist Leslie Feinberg (1998) used the metaphor of poetry to explain the possibilities of gender:

> That is why I do not hold the view that gender is simply a social construct— one of two languages that we learn by rote from early age. To me, gender is the poetry each of us makes out of the language we are taught. When I walk through the anthology of the world, I see individuals express their gender in exquisitely complex and ever-changing ways, despite the law of pentameter. (p. 10)

Although there are prosaic constraints on how each person performs gender, we hope this book allows the poetry of each person's individual gender artistry to sing.

We could not write a book about gender in communication were it not for activists in the trans and intersex communities who have pushed scholars to think about gender *and* sex in more complex and nuanced ways. Feinberg (1998) made clear the need to consider gender, and not just sex, when fighting for liberation: "Women's oppression can't be effectively fought without incorporating the battle against gender oppression. The two systems of oppression are intricately linked. And the population of women and trans people overlap" (p. 17).

We could not write a book about gender in communication were it not for activists who struggled to make clear the importance of sexuality to understanding sex and gender and the reality that families come in many forms. The Mattachine Society (founded in 1950) and the Daughters of Bilitis (founded in 1955) laid the groundwork so that when in 1969 the police again harassed the Stonewall Inn, the patrons there, including drag queens and trans people of color who high kicked their way against the police line, would catalyze a wave of activism (Duberman, 1993; Vaid, 1995). The innovative protest actions of ACTUP in the 1980s continue to guide contemporary protest (Westervelt, 2017) and marriage equality was not realized until the 2015 Supreme Court decision in *Obergefell v. Hodges*. The political imagination of lesbian, gay, and queer people offered new ways of world-making and expanded the understanding of gender beyond the masculine/feminine binary.

We could not write a book about gender in communication were it not for activists who struggled to make clear we need new ways to think about able-bodiedness, neuro-typicality, and gender. To write a book that celebrates diversity requires that we think about those who are disabled and able-bodied, about those who are neuro-typical and neuro-atypical. Alison Kafer (2013), in *Feminist, Queer, Crip*, offered the idea of "crip futurity" as a way to imagine new futures "that might be more just and sustainable. In imagining more accessible futures, I am yearning for an elsewhere—and, perhaps, an 'elsewhen'—in which disability is understood otherwise: as political, as valuable, as integral" (p. 3). In thinking about the way in which able-bodiedness and contemporary conceptions of femininity intersect, Kafer began to question "the naturalness of femininity" and then to "question the naturalness of disability, challenging essentialist assumptions about 'the' disabled body" (p. 14).

We could not write a book about gender in communication were it not for the masculinity studies scholars who made clear gender is never just about women and femininity. Those people who have, across time, challenged the way in which all people were confined by the limits of binary gender restrictions made clear gender in communication is as much about masculinity's expectations placed on men as it is about femininity's expectations placed on women.

We could not write a book about gender in communication about and in education were it not for those who worked to make education accessible to people of color and women. Women's right to receive an education was not freely given, but had to be fought for. After Sor Juana Inés de la Cruz (1651–1695), a Mexican nun, poet, and theological writer, distributed an essay, she was chastised by a bishop. Her response, *La Respuesta*, defended women's rights to education, presaging the U.S. women's demands for educational and social equality by almost a century.

In the United States, after White women were given access to education, African American enslaved people were denied education and even the right to meet, not just in public but also in private. The Virginia Revised Code of 1819 declared

> that all meetings or assemblages of slaves, or free negroes or mulattoes mixing and associating with such slaves at any meeting-house or houses, &c., in the night; or at any SCHOOL OR SCHOOLS for teaching them READING OR WRITING, either in the day or night, under whatsoever pretext, shall be deemed and considered an UNLAWFUL ASSEMBLY; and any justice of a county, &c., wherein such assemblage shall be, either from his own knowledge or the information of others, of such unlawful assemblage, &c., may issue his warrant, directed to any sworn officer or officers, authorizing him or them to enter the house or houses where such unlawful assemblages, &c., may be, for the purpose of apprehending or dispersing such slaves, and to inflict corporal punishment on the offender or offenders, at the discretion of any justice of the peace, not exceeding twenty lashes.

Thus, even before those who were not land-owning White men could participate in movements for abolition of slavery, workers' rights, equal suffrage regardless of race, or equal suffrage regardless of sex, they had to create conditions whereby their communication would not be met with punishment.

We could not write a book about gender in communication about and in work were it not for a history of women who blazed the way into workplaces and challenged unfair practices. Women mill workers in the early 1800s were, according to historian Glenna Matthews (1992), "pioneers of changing gender roles" because they were the first group of women to live away from home for work (p. 97). They also "went on strike and publicly protested what they deemed to be unjust treatment by their bosses" (p. 98). In 1834, 800 women struck, one of the first all-woman strikes in U.S. history. By 1860, cotton textile manufacturing companies in New England employed more than 60,000 women. Although many originally were native-born, starting in the 1850s most were immigrant women. Women have worked for as long as the United States has existed. The fact that women can work at paid labor can be traced to the pioneering efforts of others who entered the realm of work and made clear paid labor is "women's work."

As these vignettes should demonstrate, there was never one single "women's movement" that flowed along one single path in three waves. Instead, a broad range of social forces ebbed and flowed, reshaping the contours of how we understand sex and gender, and how sex and gender interact with communication. We acknowledge the importance of all these, and other, movements that made it possible for us to do this work.

PART I

Foundations

CHAPTER 1

Developing a Critical Gender/Sex Lens

Gender, the behaviors and appearances society dictates a body of a particular sex should perform, structures people's understanding of themselves and each other. Communication is the process by which this happens. Whether in a person's communication or in how others interpret and talk about the person, gender is "always lurking" in interactions (Deutsch, 2007, p. 116). Gender is present in an individual's gender performance and in other messages that create, sustain, or challenge gender expectations. To illustrate this, consider an example from popular culture: the seemingly innocent custom of assigning infants pink or blue based on the baby's biological sex.

- When parents announce the birth of a child, typically what is the first question asked? "Is it a boy or girl?" or "Is the baby healthy?" "Is the baby eating and sleeping well?" "Is the birth mother okay?"
- What do birth celebration cards look like? Spend some time in the greeting card section of a store, and you will find two main choices: pink or blue, and the pink cards are decorated with flowers and docile girls while the blue cards are decorated with animals or transportation vehicles (planes, trains, automobiles, and ships) and active boys.
- What mistake tends to cause people the most embarrassment when complimenting new parents on the birth of their child? What happens if you say, upon seeing a baby boy, "Isn't she pretty" instead of "He is so big"? Or what happens if you say, upon seeing a baby girl, "Wow, what a bruiser" instead of "She is so cute"?

At the moment of birth (before, if sex identification happens *in vitro*), people differentiate children on the basis of sex and begin to impose gendered expectations on them with clothing, activities, and interactions (Zosuls, Miller, Ruble, Martin, & Fabes, 2011).

In case you think pink and blue color designations have been practiced forever or exist across cultures, consider this:

- Color segregation on the basis of sex is primarily a U.S. and Western European custom, although Western commercialization spread it globally.
- Sex-based color assignments did not appear until the early 1900s. When first assigned, the generally accepted rule was pink for the boy and blue for the girl. Pink was thought to be a more decisive and stronger color while blue was seen as delicate and dainty (*Ladies Home Journal*, June 1918, as cited in Frassanito & Pettorini, 2008).
- The colors assigned to babies did not switch until the 1950s. No one seems to know why. Advice books and magazines targeted at White, upper-class people in the United States stipulated pink was for girls and blue was for boys.
- Although sex-segregated colors lessened in the 1970s, by the 1980s their dominance returned, as is evidenced by the fuchsia pink and cobalt blue aisles of toys at major retailers (McCormick, 2011; Paoletti, 2012).

The color-coding of children inspired artist JeongMee Yoon's "The Pink and Blue Project." Noting the international sex-targeted marketing, Yoon photographed children in the United States and South Korea. The results were visually astounding. Rooms awash in blue for boys and pink for girls (visit "The Blue Project" *Jake and His Blue Things*, 2006 and "The Pink Project" *Dayeun and Her Pink Things*, 2007 at http://www.jeongmeeyoon.com/aw_pinkblue.htm).

If you look at babies dressed in blue or pink, you may see an unremarkable cultural practice. But if you look at the practice through a *critical* gendered lens, you might begin to ask some questions: Why do we need to assign sex to infants? What does it mean that pink is seen as passive and blue is seen as strong? Why does it seem that a cultural choice is made to appear as a biological necessity?

Obviously, the colors are not biologically caused or universally gendered the same way. The color designations result from the communication practices of specific time periods in commercialized cultures and a particular set of political beliefs about differences between women and men. Further, the color designations indicate how people are conditioned to differentiate between sexes and genders. Although babies may now wear green, yellow, and purple, few parents are daring enough to dress a boy baby in pink or a girl baby in blue. The symbols people use to describe the sexes (pink or blue, pretty or strong), and the way they interact with others on the basis of their sex, matter.

This example reveals that gender is communicated in a variety of forms, even those as mundane as greeting cards. Communication scholar Bren Murphy (1994) made this clear in an analysis of holiday cards targeted at children, noting cards are "part of a social discourse that constructs everyday gender patterns and perceptions" (p. 29). A variety of cultural texts "construct our understandings of gender and gendered relationships" (Keith, 2009, p. iv). Thus, to study gender in communication, you need to study not only how gendered bodies communicate, but also how gender is constructed through communication in cultural texts.

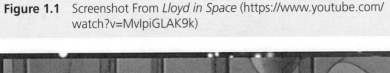

Figure 1.1 Screenshot From *Lloyd in Space* (https://www.youtube.com/watch?v=MvlpiGLAK9k)

Source: Lloyd in Space. Disney.

Tellingly, many people do not know how to talk to or about a person without first categorizing that person as female or male. This very conundrum was the focus of one episode of the Disney Channel's animated series *Lloyd in Space*, about the adventures of a group of teenage aliens (see Figure 1.1).

In the ninth episode of season three, "Neither Boy Nor Girl," the main characters argue over the relative merits of two bands, the girls advocating for Aurora and the boys for Total Cosmic Annihilation. They decide the tie-breaking vote belongs to the new kid: Zoit. After Zoit's answer praising both bands, the boys and the girls each claim Zoit was their sex. Given this is a world populated by aliens, you might assume the human sex binary no longer applied, but it did. As this screen shot illustrates, even alien bodies can be marked in ways that sex and gender them. Body size and shape, hair length, clothing, lip coloration and plumpness, eyelashes, and posture mark some of the bodies as boy and others as girl, except for Zoit. Zoit is purple, does not wear clothes, and has expressive eyes. Visually, no explicit clues are provided about sex.

Demonstrating the obsession with categorizing people by sex, the remainder of the episode is spent trying to box Zoit into one sex. The characters try observing Zoit's preference in notebook design (Zoit likes monsters *and* rainbows), whether Zoit rides a "boy bike" or "girl bike" (Zoit rides a unicycle), and which restroom Zoit uses after imbibing an extra-large 640 fluid ounce drink (Zoit claims to be absorbent). Like many, the characters conflate sex and gender, assuming that by observing things Zoit says and does, they can figure out Zoit's biological designation.

Eventually, the boys and girls decided to ask Zoit: "OK, we gotta know. What the heck are you, a boy or a girl?" Zoit explained that their species is neither boy nor girl until their 13th birthday, when they are free to choose either. On Zoit's 13th birthday, Zoit decided but kept it to themselves, again sending the friends into a flurry of questions, concluding with: "So we'll never find out if you're a boy or a girl?" To this, Zoit replied: "You'll find out some day when I get a crush on one of you." Here, another conflation occurred: between sex and sexual orientation.

To say that most gender and sex differences are socially constructed rather than biological does not mean that no differences exist or that perceived differences do not matter. Our argument throughout this textbook is that a range of differences exists. We celebrate human beings' wonderful diversity. To limit one's understanding of diverse human communication to only two choices, feminine or masculine, reinforces stereotypes. Still, that is often how people think about gender in communication—as a description of the differences between how women and men communicate. If you start from the assumption that women and men communicate differently, then you tend to see only differences between them rather than the more common similarities (Dindia, 2006).

More than actual differences in communication patterns, cultural and individual *perceptions* of women's and men's behaviors are gendered. People see baby girls and baby boys as different because people code them that way; girls are pink, sweet, and pretty, and boys are blue, agile, and burly. This leads people to interact differently with babies, coddling ones they think are girls and playing more roughly with ones they think are boys (Frisch, 1977; Rubinstein, 2001). Emphasizing sex differences reinforces separate expectations about how women and men should behave. In doing so, it restricts what is considered acceptable behavior for all people, and it puts rigid limitations on children's potential.

In *The Truth About Girls and Boys: Challenging Toxic Stereotypes About Our Children*, journalist Caryl Rivers and psychologist Rosalind Barnett (2011) argued that gendered social myths are growing out of control, supported by popular media and consumer demand. As a result, a new biological determinism is emerging supported by questionable data that human beings are born with "brains in pink and blue" (p. 10). This social myth creates a self-fulfilling prophecy to which parents and teachers contribute by maintaining assumptions of sex-based gender differences. Instead, "human beings have multiple intelligences that defy simple gender pigeonholes. Unfortunately, the real (and complex) story line is generally missing from the popular media. It is buried in scholarly peer-reviewed journals and articles that seldom see the light of day" (p. 2). We exhume some of the complexity in this textbook.

Although the predominant culture continues to assume that women and men are different, and therefore communicate in different ways, actual research does not support this (e.g., Anderson & Leaper, 1998; Burleson & Kunkel, 2006; Edwards & Hamilton, 2004; Holmstrom, 2009). Researchers have found that gendered behavior variances *among* women and *among* men are actually greater than those *between* women and men (Burleson & Kunkel, 2006; Dindia, 2006; Goodwin & Kyratzis, 2014; Hyde, 2005, 2007; Mare & Waldron, 2006; Ye & Palomares, 2013). Many other factors affect behavior, such as social roles, ethnicity, individual differences, and purpose of the interaction (Aries, 2006; Deutsch, 2007; Goodwin & Kyratzis, 2014). The focus exclusively on sex differences is too simplistic. Consider the following question: Do all women around the world and across ethnic groups and generations communicate the same way? Do all men?

People believe in universal sex and gender differences for a variety of reasons. For starters, sex is a primary way in which people categorize themselves and others, and people have a great deal invested in maintaining these categories. Because society expects everyone to be heterosexual unless proven otherwise, early on, girls and boys are encouraged to see each other as the "opposite" sex and to vie for the other's attention. Heterosexual dating is a primary means to popularity for many in U.S. middle and high schools. And heterosexual weddings are the ultimate heterosexual social ritual (Ingraham, 2008), so much so that some states amended their constitutions to bar marriage among gays and lesbians. It took the 2015 U.S. Supreme Court decision in *Obergefell v. Hodges* to make clear that the Constitution requires states to recognize marriage between same-sex individuals.

The continued cultural insistence on differences despite a massive amount of research that disconfirms this view is *political*. Subscribing to a differences perspective maintains the status quo, and in that status quo particular groups are privileged (heterosexuals, men, Whites) while others are marginalized and subordinated (homosexuals, women, people of color). This is not to blame individual White men or individual heterosexuals for power differentials but to recognize *all* people are complicit in the process when they fail to question it. Linguist Mary Crawford (1995) explained that if communication problems were due solely to gender differences and not to group power or status, women and men could borrow each other's communication styles with similar effectiveness. Instead, the same communication styles do not perform equally well for all people. What style works depends on the situation, the social status of the speaker, and the power relations between the speaker and listener.

Another reason why the culture continues to embrace (empirically disproved) gender and sex differences is that it sells. If you are not convinced, check out how retail sellers target specific sexes in toy aisles, cosmetics, wedding planning, sports, music, and gaming. Yoon's (n.d.) "The Pink and Blue Projects" provides visual evidence of "the influence of pervasive commercial advertisements aimed at little girls and their parents."

In this book, we summarize research on gender in communication and equip you with critical analytical tools to develop your own informed opinions about that research, society's gender expectations, and prevailing cultural views. To accomplish this, it is necessary to understand how predominant cultural views about gender and sex create a gendered lens through which people view reality. This lens can become so embedded that people do not realize how it limits their perceptions of reality. We hope to help you construct a more *critical* gendered lens by providing analytic tools with which you can examine common assumptions about gender, sex, and communication.

A precise vocabulary is needed to develop a critical gendered lens; intersectionality, communication, and systemic violence are the central components of that vocabulary. Together these concepts provide a more complete understanding of gendered cultural identity and how one does gendered identity work through communication.

Generally speaking, the term **identity** refers to how people see themselves, *and how others see them*, as individuals and as members of groups. *Identity* includes concepts such as personality; the multiple group identities one holds—for example, gender, sex, ethnicity, class, sexuality, nationality; and contextual role identities—for example, friend, lover, student, supervisor, community member. A person's identity has multiple interacting, and sometimes contradicting, facets (Kroløkke & Sørensen, 2006; Tracy, 2002). For example, the social expectations of a person who identifies as a man may seem to contradict with the role that person plays as a teacher or day care provider.

Although people may prefer to box others into set categories, identity is not fixed and unchanging. Rather it is constantly negotiated through intrapersonal communication with oneself, interpersonal communication with others, and public communication circulating in mass media and popular culture. This does not mean that people can change their identities on a whim. Although identity is in constant flux, it is perceived as stable. As such, individuals and groups have some control over their identity construction, but much of the predominant cultural assumptions extend beyond one's awareness or control (Butler, 2004; Tracy, 2002).

Intersectionality

Gender and sex are woven into a person's identity and are axes along which social power is organized. But writing a book that focuses only on gender in communication would be reductive. It is impossible to separate gender/sex from other facets of identity or other social categories along which power is organized. Communication scholar Bernadette Marie Calafell (2014) explained: "Like many women of color before me, I have never been able to be just a woman. . . . My womanhood is messy" (p. 267).

Ethnicity, class, sex, sexual orientation, citizenship status, religion, and gender all intersect to form a person's identity and to inform social relations. Before you can understand gender in communication, you first need to understand that how a person's gender identity is performed is not separable from the person's ethnicity, class, sex, sexual orientation, citizenship status, and religion. Additionally, to study how gender is an arena in which power is exercised, you need to understand how gender intersects with other axes along which social power is exercised.

Intersectionality is a theory of identity *and* of oppression. Women's and gender studies professor Vivian M. May (2015) explained that intersectionality "approaches lived identities as interlaced and systems of oppression as enmeshed and mutually reinforcing" (p. 3). Thus, intersectionality enables analysis of communication both at the "micropolitical level of everyday life and at the macropolitical level of social structures, material practices, and cultural norms" (p. 5). An intersectional approach should inform how people understand interpersonal communication, organizational cultures, pay inequity, and mass-mediated messages.

Legal scholar and critical race feminist Adrien Wing (1997) explained the theory of intersectionality as the idea that identity is "multiplicative" rather than additive (p. 30). Instead of understanding identity as the addition of one independent element to another and another, like in a pop-bead necklace, identity makes more sense if you think of each element as inextricably linked with the others. An intersectional approach makes clear that all facets of identity are integral, interlocking parts of a whole.

African American women were the first to make this point clear. Activists in the late 1800s and early 1900s, such as Sojourner Truth, Frances E. W. Harper, Ida B. Wells Barnett, and Mary Church Terrell, all noted how sex and race intersected in a way that made Black women's social location and struggles unique. Recognizing the contribution of their foremothers, a group of Black feminists wrote the Combahee River Collective Statement in 1974 in which they outlined how "the major systems of oppression are interlocking." In the Statement, they explained:

> We believe that sexual politics under patriarchy is as pervasive in Black women's lives as are the politics of class and race. We also often find it difficult to separate race from class from sex oppression because in our lives they are most often experienced simultaneously. We know that there is such a thing as racial-sexual oppression which is neither solely racial nor solely sexual, e.g., the history of rape of Black women by white men as a weapon of political repression.

Author Audre Lorde (1984) offered a description of how an intersectional approach is necessary to fully understand and accept your own identity:

> As a Black lesbian feminist comfortable with the many different ingredients of my identity, and a woman committed to racial and sexual freedom from oppression, I find I am constantly being encouraged to pluck out some one aspect of myself and present that as the meaningful whole, eclipsing or denying the other parts of self. But this is a destructive and fragmenting way to live. My fullest concentration of energy is available to me only when I integrate all the parts of who I am, openly, allowing power from particular sources of my living to flow back and forth freely through all my different selves, without the restrictions of externally imposed definition. Only then can I bring myself and my energies as a whole to the service of those struggles which I embrace as a part of my living. (p. 120)

Lorde's metaphor *ingredients* is useful when explaining intersectionality. For example, a cake is an object with ingredients such as flour, eggs, oil, sugar, and milk that can exist separately from each other but, once combined, each element influences the others. Even though the cake contains all the ingredients, none are recognizable in their separate forms. A cake is not just flour and eggs and sugar and oil and milk. A cake is a cake only when the ingredients are so fused together that they cannot be separated again. Like a cake, human identity is the result of a fascinating alchemic process in which ingredients are fused in such a way that each is influenced by the others, to the point where you cannot extricate the flour from the cake once it is baked. The flour is not simply flour (and gender is not simply gender) once fused with other ingredients.

Because identity ingredients interact, you cannot understand how a person does gender unless you also consider how that person's gender, sex, sexual orientation, ethnicity, national identity, and socioeconomic class interact to demand a particular gender performance. Researchers who take only gender into account do not recognize that identity actually occurs as a complex, synergistic, infused whole that becomes something completely different when parts are ignored, forgotten, and unnamed (Collins, 1998).

Kimberlé Crenshaw (1989), a lawyer and legal scholar, was the first to use the word *intersectionality* to describe how the oppression faced by Black women was distinct from oppression solely from race or sex. Crenshaw analyzed how employment nondiscrimination law that used the discrete categories of sex and race (as well as color, religion, and national origin) failed to protect Black women who face forms of discrimination that emanate from the intersection of race and sex. Crenshaw's insights allowed scholars to articulate how "major axes of social divisions in a given society at a given time, for example, race, class, gender, sexuality, dis/ability, and age operate not as discrete and mutually exclusive entities, but build on each other and work together" (Collins & Bilge, 2016, p. 4). The interactions matter.

Intersectionality as a theory of identity is helpful because it prevents reducing complex identities down to a single ingredient, and then attributing to the ingredient causal power to explain why a person acts in a particular way. Intersectionality as a theory of power is helpful because it shifts attention away from "preoccupations with intentional prejudice and toward perspectives grounded in analysis of systemic dynamics and institutional power" (Chun, Lipsitz, & Shin, 2013, p. 922). With this overarching understanding of intersectionality, we now turn to a consideration of the ingredients.

Gender and Sex, Gender/Sex

If you have ever filled out a survey, you likely have been asked about your gender and then given the options of male or female. In this example, the words *sex* and *gender* are used interchangeably, even though they refer to two analytically distinct things. *Sex* refers to biological designations (e.g., female, male, intersex, trans), while *gender* refers to the social expectations attached to how particular bodies should act and appear and, thus, is socially constructed. It is important to understand the distinction between the two terms while, at the same time, recognizing their inextricable interconnection.

Before the 1970s, most people assumed people's sex determined their behavior; no concept of gender as distinct from sex existed. In the late 1970s, researchers began using the term *gender* as distinct from *sex* to identify personal attributes of women and men (Unger, 1979). Gender referred to one's identity and self-presentation—that is, the degree to which a person associated themselves with what society had prescribed as appropriate behavior given their sex. You can probably brainstorm expected sex-specific stereotypical gender attributes. Feminine attributes are to be emotional, a caretaker, sensitive, compassionate, revealingly dressed; masculine attributes are to be rational, independent, tough, aggressive, comfortably dressed

Figure 1.2 Gender Continuum

(Coates, 2004; Eagly & Koenig, 2006; Eliot, 2009b; Lorber & Moore, 2007). When researchers embraced the concept of gender, sex and gender were seen as distinct; one's sex did not determine one's gender, but social structures linked particular gender presentations with particular sexed bodies.

These early understandings of gender placed variances in human identity on a continuum rather than casting them as two binary or opposite categories where one is *either* male/masculine *or* female/feminine. The continuum helped make visible that instead of two independent categories, degrees of gender are possible (see Figure 1.2).

One could be more masculine (and less feminine) or more feminine (and less masculine). Because researchers saw gender as socially prescribed rather than biologically caused, they assumed that people identify to varying degrees with masculinity *and* femininity rather than just one *or* the other. This was heralded as an important breakthrough. No longer were authors saying all men acted one way and all women another, based solely on their biological sex. However, the continuum still set up masculine and feminine as opposites and as trading off with each other; as you were more of one, you were less of the other.

Further developing this idea, psychologist Sandra Bem (1974) coined the term **androgyny** by combining two Greek words: *andros* meaning "male" and *gyne* meaning "female." Bem developed a questionnaire called the Sex-Role Inventory (SRI) to identify a person's gender orientation on a continuum from highly feminine to highly masculine, androgynous (high in both), or undifferentiated (low in both masculine and feminine traits). Androgynous persons are believed to have more behavioral flexibility. Instead of seeing masculinity and femininity as a zero-sum tradeoff on a continuum, Bem believed one could exhibit characteristics of both (see Figure 1.3).

Figure 1.3 Gender Diversity

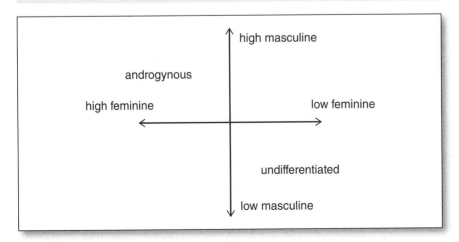

Now, people talk not just about one form of femininity and one form of masculinity, but about feminini*ties* and masculini*ties*. Many ways to be feminine and masculine exist, and many ways express gender that are neither masculine nor feminine.

> W. Kamau Bell, comic and host of *United Shades of America*, reflected on their early career in comedy:
>
> Black comedy clubs . . . felt like public school but grown up. It's like, these are the same kids when I was a kid where I felt like I was being made fun of because I wasn't listening to the right music or I wasn't being a black man in the right way. (as cited in Gross, 2017)

Although focusing on gender instead of sex was meant to be a step away from overgeneralizing people's identities based on their sex, masculinity and femininity are still stereotypes, prescribing how women and men are supposed to behave (Crawford & Fox, 2007). Because of this criticism, researchers have dropped the terms *masculine* and *feminine*, relying instead on measures of dominance, nurturance, orientation toward self versus others, and so forth, but the stereotypical inferences are still present. There is no ideal social science means to study gender identity that avoids reinforcing the very characteristics it is trying to study.

If you use the term *gender* when you mean *sex*, you are not alone. Researchers and popular media often do not use the concept of gender correctly or consistently (Muehlenhard & Peterson, 2011). If you read published research, many claim to have found gender differences or similarities, when in actuality they never asked for or assessed the participants' gendered self-identities. They merely asked participants to label themselves as biologically female or male and then assumed that by studying females they could determine what was feminine and that by studying males they could determine what was masculine. Most people unintentionally conflate *sex* and *gender*.

However, some intentionally rethink the relationship between sex and gender, claiming sex, too, is socially constructed. Gender theorist Judith Butler (1990a) posited that "perhaps this construct called 'sex' is as culturally constructed as gender; indeed, perhaps it was always already gender, with the consequence that the distinction between sex and gender turns out to be no distinction at all" (pp. 9–10). Butler's argument is that the only way a person can come to understand anything, even biology, is through language and cultural experience. The understanding of the body and its relationship to identity is always mediated by the words and symbols people use to talk about the body. In the words of Butler (1993), "There is no reference to a pure body which is not at the same time a further formation of that body" (p. 10). Thus, sex is as much a social construction as gender, and bodies have no meaning separate from the meaning language gives them. The argument that people's biological sex is influenced by communication is not to deny the existence of a material body "but to insist that our apprehension of it, our understanding of it, is necessarily mediated by the *con*texts in which we speak" (Price & Shildrick, 1999, p. 7; italics in original).

When the predominant culture names the sex of a body female *or* male (and nothing else), the culture engages in an act of communication that has "normative force" because it recognizes some parts of a person but not all (Butler, 1993, p. 11). Even as the body is referenced, a particular formation occurs—a formation of the body as *either* female *or* male. Butler identified the binary linguistic framing of bodies as an act of power because it refuses to recognize the existence of those who do not fit into the male/female binary. The reality, however, is that many bodies do not fit the binary of female *or* male.

As early as 1993, developmental geneticist Anne Fausto-Sterling argued that people should recognize at least five sexes, with an infinite range in between: "Biologically speaking, there are many gradations running from female to male; and depending on how one calls the shots, one can argue that along that spectrum lie at least five sexes [female, ferm, herm, merm, male]—and perhaps even more" (p. 21). If language names only two sexes, then only two will be seen and any body that does not fit into the two sexes will be forced to fit, or be considered an "it"—not human. The power of language to construct social reality is illustrated by what has been done to those bodies.

Intersex "is a general term used for a variety of conditions in which a person is born with a reproductive or sexual anatomy that doesn't seem to fit the typical definitions of female or male" (Intersex Society of North America, 2008). Lest you think this is an extraordinarily rare medical phenomenon, from 1,000 to 15,000 intersex babies are born a year in the United States (Greenberg, 2012, p. 7). In a study that reviewed medical literature from 1955 to 2000, the authors concluded that intersex babies may account for as many as 2% of live births (Blackless et al., 2000).

An infant born who did not fit into the male/female binary used to be considered a "medical emergency" (Fausto-Sterling, 2000, p. 45) and, until new policies were proposed in 2005, in European countries, parents were told to decide within the child's first day of life if the baby will be male or female (Pasterski, Prentice, & Hughes, 2010). The rate of infant genital surgery is still high, and a tendency persists to surgically alter infants' genitals to female because the vagina is supposedly easier to construct surgically. Butler (2004) pointed out that this practice shows how narrowly defined "normal" is in society, and the failure to recognize that intersex persons are part of the human continuum prevents them from being treated humanely.

Despite the biological reality of more than two sexes, the way U.S. society talks about and legislates sex constantly reinforces the idea that there are only two sexes (and that one's sex determines one's gender). Law professor Julie Greenberg (1999) explained how "despite medical and anthropological studies to the contrary, the law presumes a binary sex and gender model. The law ignores the millions of people who are intersexed" (p. 275). The language of law has structured the reality of sex and gender in such a way that the grand diversity of human existence is stifled.

In addition to the recognition that sex is as socially constructed as gender, scholars recognize that social constructions (like gender) can be as difficult to change as things people consider biological. Butler (2004) argued that gender is often as immutable as sex, given how social institutions and language constantly reiterate and reinscribe it. One of the primary ways sex and gender discipline bodies is through the enshrinement of **binary** views (meaning you have either one choice or another) of one's sex, gender, and sexuality. A person who did not fit in the sex/gender binary (wherein you are *either* a man *or* a woman and men are masculine and women are feminine) was unintelligible; people lacked the language to name and understand them. This is why new terms have entered into vocabulary, such as **genderqueer,** a term used to "defy all categories of culturally defined gender"; it is "gender free" or "gender neutral," claiming an identity "outside gender" (Ehrensaft, 2011, p. 531). New terms enable people to think outside the binary. English professor Jordynn Jack (2012) offered *copia,* the classical rhetorical concept of inventing as many terms as possible for a concept, as an alternative to the binary and the continuum. Included in Jack's copia: "*genderqueer, transgende[r], femme, butch, boi, neutrois, androgyne, bi-* or *tri-gender, third gender,* and even *geek*" (p. 3).

We see gender and sex as something you *do,* not something you *are,* and gender is done by you, between individuals, and by institutions. Gender scholar A. Finn Enke (2012) explained that "there is no natural process by which *any*one becomes woman, and . . . *every*one's gender is made: Gender, and also sex, are made through complex social and technical manipulations that naturalize some while" making others seem unnatural (p. 1). Linguist Lal Zimman (2012) complicated the term *gender* even further based on research with transgender men, suggesting distinctions between gender assignment at birth, gender role socialization, the gender identity one claims at any given time, gender presentation, and the variety of ways an individual may perform their gender in a given context "rather than treating gender as a simple binary or even a singular continuum" (p. 161).

If sex and gender are something you do rather than something you *are* or *have,* they can be done in a wide variety of ways. If, in your doing, you are performing social scripts, then gender and sex are never just individual quirks, but instead are social institutions. To be able to see how gender and sex are done by and to people, you first need to recognize neither is natural or biologically determined. Gender and sex are not things that belong to an individual. Rather, gender and sex are done by people interacting in accordance with institutional and cultural demands. Gender and sex are social institutions that individuals express. People experience their gender and sex together, and sex and gender are both socially constructed, and hence changeable, while at the same time being difficult to change.

We use the term **gender/sex** in this textbook to emphasize the interrelation between the concepts of gender and sex. When we discuss gender in communication, we always discuss sex in communication because communication that is about gender, that is influenced by gender, and that differentiates gender also always is about sex, is influenced by sex, and differentiates sex.

To summarize, researchers in the field of communication studies began by focusing on sex, visualizing it as a binary. They progressed to using the term *gender* as two culturally imposed opposite identities located on one continuum. This approach was nuanced to recognize gender as not necessarily a zero-sum game; androgynous people could have characteristics of both masculinity and femininity. This allowed the recognition of more variances of behavior and identity (Slesaransky-Poe & García, 2009). However, even as scholars studied gender, they sometimes conflated it with sex. As scholars began to theorize gender as cultural, they also began to theorize sex as cultural. Thus, the distinctions between sex and gender were intentionally complicated. Now researchers are moving toward a much more diverse, realistic portrayal of gender/sex.

Transgender and Gender Non-Conforming

Transgender or **trans** is "used to describe individuals whose gender expression and behavior do not match the usual expectations associated with the male-female binary system" (Gherovici, 2010, p. xiii). Susan Stryker (2008), in *Transgender History*, noted how the term only came into "widespread use" in the last 20 years and is "still under construction," but refers to

> people who move away from the gender they were assigned at birth, people who cross over (*trans-*) the boundaries constructed by their culture to define and contain that gender. Some people move away from their birth-assigned gender because they feel strongly that they properly belong to another gender in which it would be better for them to live; others want to strike out toward some new location, some space not yet clearly defined or concretely occupied; still others simply feel the need to get away from the conventional expectations bound up with the gender that was initially put upon them. In any case, it is *the movement across a socially imposed boundary away from an unchosen starting place*—rather than any particular destination or mode of transition—that best characterizes the concept of "transgender." (p. 1)

Trans and gender non-conforming people include those who identify as trans men (people assigned female at birth, AFAB, who identify as men); identify as trans women (people assigned male at birth, AMAB, who identify as women); reject the gender/sex binary or see themselves as nonbinary; choose to take hormones or not; or have surgical sexual organ changes or not. Thus, *trans* refers to "a constellation of practices and identities variably implicated in sexual and gender normativities" (West, 2014, p. 10).

The concept of *normativity* is helpful because it makes clear that some things are treated as the norm, or as normal, when they are statistically or diagnostically neither. Often that which is labeled *normal* is not really the most common; instead, it is normative, meaning it is the standard by which people are judged. Communication scholar Gus Yep (2003) defined **normativity** as the "process of constructing, establishing, producing, and reproducing a taken-for-granted and all-encompassing standard used to measure goodness, desirability, morality, rationality, superiority, and a host of other dominant cultural values" (p. 18).

Normativities tied to the sex/gender binary result in those who do not fit the binary being labeled as bad, undesirable, immoral, irrational, and inferior. So the sex binary has been normalized, made to appear right, even though it is not the only way to organize understandings of sex.

The cultural disciplining of transgender persons is an example of the way the sex/gender binary constructs sex and gender. Until 2012, the standard diagnostic manual used by U.S. mental health practitioners identified persons who desire to be "another sex" or participate in the pastimes of the "other sex" as having a disorder (American Psychiatric Association, 2000, pp. 576–577). Gender identity disorder was the label given to this "dysfunction." It was also used for individuals with homosexual or bisexual tendencies, and some practitioners attempted to alter the individuals' gender identities. However, psychotherapy rarely changes gender identity (Gherovici, 2010; Reiss, 2009; Unger & Crawford, 1992). Intersex and transgender activists raised the question of how medical professionals can ascertain a person's "real" gender/sex identity. They argued that gender should be a matter of personal choice (Schilt, 2011). As a result of this activism, the American Psychiatric Association decided in 2012 to change its diagnostic manual so that it no longer referred to gender identity disorder but instead to gender dysphoria (Lennard, 2012). In the most recent revision, *DSM-5*, gender dysphoria is diagnosed when there is incongruence between a person's assigned sex and their gendered behaviors, and it causes significant distress (American Psychiatric Association, 2013).

To provide a language that lets people think outside the binary, activists have introduced new terms, like *genderqueer, genderfluid,* and *trans,* into the public vocabulary. The *New York Times* added the sex/gender-neutral Mx. as an alternative to Mr. and Ms. (Curkin, 2015). To provide a term parallel to *trans, cis,* short for *cisgender* or *cissexual,* was introduced in 1994 and popularized in the first decade of the 2000s (Enke, 2012, pp. 60–61). **Cis** refers to those whose gender self-identity and gender expression match the sex they were assigned at birth. However, even those who introduced this term still worry that it reinforces the very binary that trans folk challenge (Enke, 2012).

Transgender studies scholars note the importance of language and communication to trans people. Susan Stryker (2015) explained:

> Transsexuals such as myself were then still subordinated to a hegemonic inter-locking of cissexist feminist censure and homosexual superiority, psycho-medical pathologization, legal proscription, mass media stereotyping, and public ridicule. The only option other than reactively saying "no we're not" to every negative assertion about us was to change the conversation, to inaugurate a new language game. (p. 227)

To make trans people intelligible, to make them recognizable, new language was required.

Existing language also has been stretched because old terms have seen their meanings shift. For example, in 2015 the *Washington Post* changed its style guide to allow the singular third person pronoun *they* (which typically was used when referring to more than one person) and in 2016 the American Dialect Society named the singular *they* as its word of the year (Guo, 2016). Why? It is an alternative to *he* or *she*, terms that unnecessarily tend to sex/gender people.

Sexuality and Romantic Attraction

Sexual orientation describes the gender/sex of the people to whom you are physically attracted. *Heterosexual* refers to people who are sexually attracted to a person of the other sex. *Homosexual* refers to people who are sexually attracted to others who share their sex. *Bisexual* refers to people who are sexually attracted to both sexes. You might notice that these sexual orientations depend on a sex binary (same or other); if there are five sexes, which is the "other" sex? Again, the sex/gender binary limits human understanding, in this case, an understanding of sexuality.

New language has emerged, such as *pansexual*, which refers to those who are capable of being attracted to a person of any sex/gender. Celebrity Miley Cyrus declared they were pansexual, explaining, "I don't relate to being boy or girl, and I don't have to have my partner relate to boy or girl" (as cited in Petrusich, 2015).

Sexual orientation is about physical attraction while romantic orientation is about emotional attraction. Recognizing this distinction makes it possible to recognize those who are *asexual* and *aromantic*. **Asexual** (Ace) refers to those who are not sexually attracted to others; approximately 1% of the U.S. population identifies this way (Emens, 2014). **Aromantic** (Aro) refers to people who are not romantically attracted to others, meaning there is no desire to form an emotional relationship (Bogaert, 2015).

The way culture communicates about sexual orientation constructs and maintains the sex/gender binary and maintains heterosexuality as the norm (Rich, 1980). **Heteronormativity** describes how social institutions and policies reinforce the presumption that people are heterosexual and that gender and sex are natural binaries (Kitzinger, 2005). Persons who are discriminated against due to their sexual orientation are subordinated because they are perceived as sexual deviants. Sociologist Gayle Rubin (1984) stated, "The system of sexual oppression cuts across other modes of social inequality," such as racial, class, ethnic, or gendered inequality, "sorting out individuals and groups according to its own intrinsic dynamics. It is not reducible" (p. 293). Conversely, discussions of gender and sex are intricately tied to sexual orientation and sexuality. They are not separable. In the study of gender/sex, people must recognize the role of heteronormativity, sexual identity, and romantic identity.

Race and Ethnicity

We want to be clear from the outset: Race is a social construction. Biologically, there is only one race: the human race. However, humans have long used race as a social construct to divide people from one another, to place them in categories and claim one category is better than another. Scientists have known for some time that race is not an accurate means by which to categorize human beings in terms of ancestry or genetics (Blakey, 1999; Long & Kittles, 2003; "Race," 2011).

Society holds on to this false assumption that race is a meaningful category because believing in such differences is easy and it benefits those in power. We use the term *race* to recognize that many people self-identify with a particular ethnic identity and take great pride in it. However, to be clear, when we use the term *race*, we mean the *social construction* understood as race; we do not mean *race* as some biological designation.

Race, like gender/sex, has a socially constructed meaning that has real consequences. Sociologist Estelle Disch (2009) explained why and how we use the term in this book:

> The term race is itself so problematic that many scholars regularly put the word in quotation marks to remind readers that it is a social construction rather than a valid biological category. Genetically, there is currently no such thing as "race" and the category makes little or no sense from a scientific standpoint. What is essential, of course, is the meaning that people in various cultural contexts attribute to differences in skin color or other physical characteristics. (p. 22)

To illustrate, consider that Germans, Irish, Italians, and Russians are now considered White in the United States, but after the great migration of the early 1900s up to the 1960s, they were considered "colored or other" (Foner & Fredrickson, 2005).

Ethnicity, too, is a contested term; identifying one's ethnic origins is not as clear as researchers once thought, given the increasingly transnational world and how cultural labels are subject to change. **Ethnicity** is a term commonly used to refer to a group of people who share a cultural history, even though they may no longer live in the same geographic area (Zack, 1998).

One way to more clearly see the power of arbitrary social constructions of groups is to consider White identity. Whiteness is a socially constructed racial and ethnic category even if society typically does not recognize it as such. The central position of Whiteness in predominant U.S. culture allows it to be normalized to the extent that it almost disappears; it is deraced and nonethnic. Many who identify as White do not even recognize it is a category. They can readily list characteristics of other peoples, such as the expectation that Asians should be smart and that African Americans should be good at sports, but they have difficulty naming a quality that applies to Whites (Nakayama & Krizek, 1999). When race is conceptualized as natural rather than as culturally created, the power of this category is hidden (Kivel, 2002).

It is important to recognize Whiteness in the study of gender because, if one does not, race remains a concern only for those considered non-White, and gender, when studied alone, remains implicitly an identity belonging solely to Whites. What is important to remember is that, like gender/sex, when society constructs arbitrary racial and ethnic categories, these categories are rarely different and equal. Rather, race and ethnicity are tools of social oppression.

Throughout this book, we capitalize *Black* and *White* to clarify that we are referring to socially constructed racial categories and the politics of skin color rather than to hues on the color wheel. We hope to move beyond thinking just about differences, whether gender or ethnic differences, and instead induce thinking about power. As Patricia Hill Collins (1995) explained: "Difference is less a problem for me than racism, class exploitation, and gender oppression. Conceptualizing these systems of oppression as difference obfuscates the power relations and material inequalities that constitute oppression" (p. 494). Thus, when it comes to thinking about the category called *race*, our question is not "How are the races different?" but instead "Who benefits from the belief in difference?"

National Identity

National identity refers to a person's immigration status, citizenship, and country allegiance. Interdisciplinary feminist scholars and global human rights activists were the first to explore how national cultural identities are gendered/sexed and how citizens tend to experience their national rights differently based on gender/sex (Enloe, 1989; Moghadam, 1994; Yuval-Davis, 1997, 2003). International studies scholar Tamar Mayer (2000) posited that "control over access to the benefits of belonging to the nation is virtually always gendered" and that "the ability to define the nation lies mainly with men" (p. 2). The feeling of belonging to a nation and the privileges and oppressions contained therein are gendered/sexed in unique ways according to cultural norms, histories of religion, ethnic and class conflicts, economics, and much more.

Gender/sex issues around the world *are* extremely relevant to any study of gender in communication. Placing the study of gender in the context of national identity prevents assuming universal differences between women and men or, worse yet, assuming that research primarily conducted in the United States represents gendered lives around the world. Gender and ethnic studies scholar Nira Yuval-Davis (1999) explained, "Essentialist notions of difference . . . are very different from the notions of difference promoted by those of us who believe in the importance of incorporating notions of difference into democracy. In the first case notions of difference replace notions of equality—in the second case they encompass it" (p. 131). Recognizing national identities is an important part of a gender diversity approach to the study of gender/sex in communication.

When national identity is included in the study of gender/sex, the focus has usually been on citizens of economically disadvantaged countries. The influence of the United States as a nation has not been a primary focus in gender/sex in communication research. Instead, most of the research has focused on the one-to-one relationship level, as if it existed independently of national identity. Yet U.S. national identity and its economic power have had a profound influence on carving out gender identities worldwide. Gender/sex and national identity are related, not just for persons in economically disadvantaged countries, or in countries with more visible internal violence, but for U.S. citizens as well (Mayer, 2000; Mohanty, 2003).

Socioeconomic Class

In the United States, **socioeconomic class** refers to the social position people enjoy as a result of their income, education, occupation, and place of residence. The class to which a person belongs influences the expectations of how gender should be performed. When children are told to "act like a lady" or "act like a gentleman," the underlying message is usually about class. They are being told to act like a particular type of gender/sex, one that knows the upper-class gentile norms of politeness and identity performance. The message goes even further when children of color receive this message. They are being told to act like White upper-class people do. This command carries class-prescribed expectations of gendered/sexed behaviors that White upper-class people have controlled.

The field of communication studies has been slow to examine the ways in which class may affect communication in the United States. Yet it is clear class often determines how much leeway one is allowed in gender performance. For example, historian Glenna R. Matthews (1992) explained how working-class women were able to enter the public realm as labor activists more easily than upper-class women prior to the 1930s because they were already present in the economic sphere. Economic necessity required them to work and, hence, to violate the social demands of the time requiring that wealthy White women remain domestic. Being politically active presented no unique violation of gender/sex expectations for the working-class women. As a result, the history of labor activism is full of women leaders: Mary Harris "Mother" Jones (Tonn, 1996), Emma Goldman (Kowal, 1996; Solomon, 1987), Voltairine de Cleyre (Palczewski, 1995), and Lucy Parsons (Horwitz, 1998).

Class affects how gender is performed and how gender/sex is perceived. Men of lower classes face the stereotype that they are less intelligent, immoral, and prone to criminality. Women of lower classes are stereotyped as sexually promiscuous, easily duped, and dependent on state assistance. This discrimination and related stereotypes help maintain oppression (Ehrenreich, 1990), which can be multiplied by oppressions due to racism and sexism.

Intersectionality Conclusion

An intersectional approach has many implications for the study of gender. First, intersectionality prevents scholars from falling into a specific type of generalization called essentialism. **Essentialism** is the presumption that all members of a group are alike because they have one quality in common. If researchers study only the fragment of a person called *gender* or *sex*, they reduce a person's complex identity to one dimension. Sexuality, ethnicity, nationality, and class also must be considered.

Second, intersectionality recognizes assumptions about gender, sexual orientation, race, nationality, and class influence the way individuals view the world and the social realities and inequalities they produce (Jordan-Zachery, 2007). Thus, the study of gender in communication is not about quirks of personality but is about the way broad social patterns privilege some people and disadvantage others. Intersectionality makes clear how oppressions of groups interrelate. Just as any analysis of gender in communication is incomplete without taking one's intersectional identity into account, so, too, is any analysis of the cultural tools used in power and privilege (Davis, 2008). Educator-consultant Heather Hackman (2012) explained that one cannot accomplish social justice by addressing one form of oppression in isolation. Oppressions are not independent. A part of the power of oppressions is the ways they intersect, supporting each other.

Third, intersectionality recognizes that *all* people are labeled with and internalize multiple group identities: "It is not just the marginalized who have a gender, race, and so on" (Harding, 1995, p. 121). Whiteness is part of identity, as is heterosexuality and being a man. People do not always recognize these ingredients because they are considered the norm. So even as intersectionality enables the understanding of complex forms of subordination, it also makes visible how dominant groups have an ethnicity, sex, gender, and class.

Intersectionality renders a more complex, realistic portrayal of individuals' gendered/sexed experiences. Sociologist Leslie McCall (2005) termed it the "intra-categorical approach to complexity" that "seeks to complicate and use [identity categories] in a more critical way" (p. 1780). Like McCall, we seek to "focus on the process by which [categories of identity] are produced, experienced, reproduced, and resisted in everyday life" (p. 1783). As you explore your own intersectional identity, your list of ingredients can be quite lengthy, including religious or faith affiliation, age, physical and mental abilities, immigration status, marriage status, and region of country. Keep in mind that gender, sex, sexuality, ethnicity, national identity, and socioeconomic class influence your perceptions, but they are not innate, permanent, or universal categories.

Intersectionality of identities and oppressions highlights the way cultural identities and inequalities are embedded in political systems and social structures, not only in people. Philosopher Sandra Harding (1995) explained that sexual and racial inequalities "are not *caused* by prejudice—by individual bad attitudes and false beliefs." In fact, Harding believed that focusing on "prejudice as the cause of racial (or gender, class, or sexual) inequality tends to lodge responsibility for racism on already economically disadvantaged whites who might hold these beliefs." It keeps the focus on individuals rather than on the larger culture in which their attitudes were created. Clearly, prejudice does contribute to racism, sexism, and other forms of inequity, but Harding argued that people should view inequalities as "fundamentally a political relationship" that manifests itself through cultural strategies or norms that privilege some groups over others (p. 122).

Communication

Communication constructs, maintains, and changes gender/sex. It is how group and individual differences and inequalities are created and sustained. Fortunately, because of its dynamic nature, communication also makes social change possible. For these reasons, it is particularly beneficial to focus on communication when examining gender.

We define **communication** broadly as a meaning-making process, consistent with a social construction perspective (Gergen, 1994). People are not passive receivers of meanings but are actively engaged in the meaning-making process.

As the title of this book suggests, one of those meanings being continually constructed through and *in* communication is gender (Taylor, personal correspondence, January 2003). For us, communication is an action (not a reflex). Given gender is communicated, it, too, is an action or something people do.

If we had to summarize the thesis of this entire book in one sentence, it would be this: Communication creates gender, gender does not create communication. Instead of examining how gender influences communication, we explore how communication constrains, perpetuates, stimulates, ignores, and changes gender (Rakow, 1986). We hope to spotlight the profound role communication plays in the construction of gender/sex identities.

Focusing on communication offers important benefits. First, it reminds you that individual gender identities and cultural assumptions about gender change over time. Second, it clarifies that gender does not simply exist on the individual level. Rather, gender is a cultural *system* or *structure* of meaning constructed through interactions that govern access to power and resources (Crawford, 1995). Third, it reveals that individuals play an active role in maintaining and/or changing gender constructions.

A communication approach helps prevent essentializing gender because it treats gender as a verb, not a noun. Gender is a process, not a thing or a universal product. Accordingly, in this book we examine how people "do" (West & Zimmerman, 1987) or "perform" (Butler, 1990a) gender. Gender emerges in the seemingly apolitical, routinized daily behaviors you enact in conscious and nonconscious ways. This, however, does not mean that your performance is without gendered intent or goals. Communication is goal driven. Through repeated stylizations such as gender performance, the communication may become automatic, but it is no less strategic (Brown & Levinson, 1978; Kellerman, 1992). We use the word *strategic* in its broadest sense to refer to how people use components of communication in an attempt to accomplish their multiple, simultaneous interactional goals.

Our reference to cultural *systems* and *structures* highlights the point that communication never happens in a void. It always takes place in multiple contexts, including physical, relational, cultural, and temporal. Cultural systems and values play major roles in constructing meanings. Studying gender as a cultural system or structure makes visible how gender is constructed on at least three communication levels covered in this textbook: individual, interpersonal, and societal (Crawford, 1995).

At the individual or intrapersonal communication level, a person develops personal gendered identities. At the interpersonal communication level, people influence each other's gender identities. At the societal level, social institutions contribute to the construction of gender/sex—both by imposing gender expectations and by liberating persons from them. This is why we dedicate the second half of the textbook to an analysis of the ways in which family, education, work, religion, and media contribute to the construction of gender/sex.

Individuals experience these communication levels simultaneously. For example, rape is an attack on the individual, but it happens in an interpersonal context, and the reason for the sexual assault, the meaning it is given, and even the laws that define the attack as a crime are gendered. (Note, for example, that not until 2012 did the FBI definition of rape recognize the possibility that men could be raped.) Rape is a crime of gendered and sexual power and domination. It is not a coincidence that women as a group have historically been the most frequent victims of rape, that men as a group have historically been the most frequent aggressors, and that when individual men are the victims, they are emasculated intrapersonally, interpersonally, and culturally. A phrase from the 1960s U.S. women's movement makes the three levels of gender in communication clear: "The personal is political." This maxim explains that what happens to people on a *personal* level is inherently tied to social norms supported by *political* social structures, such as norms about masculinity and femininity. In the study of gender/sex, analyses of communication enable close examination of how gender/sex is socially constructed, maintained, and changed.

The most comprehensive way to study gender in communication is to study all three of these levels—individual, interpersonal, and societal. Doing so makes it easier to recognize how the gender/sex norms that influence individual and interpersonal communication also influence the range of rhetorical choices available to people in public contexts. Similarly, the way politicians or popular culture stars communicate in public contexts may influence one's expectations of how people will interact in daily life.

Systemic Gendered Violence

You cannot adequately study gender in communication without addressing its dark side: violence, including interpersonal physical and emotional violence as well as structural violence. A full understanding of violence requires an understanding of how it is gendered/sexed (Johnson, 2006). Around the world, violence disproportionately affects women and gender non-conforming people.

Regarding women and girls, a United Nations report, *The World's Women 2015*, found:

> In all societies, to varying degrees, women and girls are subjected to physical, sexual and psychological abuse that cuts across lines of income, class and culture. . . . In some cases, violence against women can lead to death; about two thirds of the victims of intimate partner/family-related homicide are women, in contrast to all cases of homicide, of which 20 per cent of the victims are women. Whereas other forms of homicide have shown significant declines over time, rates of intimate partner/family-related female homicide have remained relatively stable. (UN Statistics Division, 2015, pp. 139–141)

Women and girls, as a result of living in systems that devalue them, face violence as a result of their sex.

Figure 1.4 UN Statistics on Violence Against Women

Source: UN Statistics Division, 2015. "The World's Women 2015: Trends and Statistics" by United Nations (CC By-NC 4.0_, https://creativecommons.org/licenses/by-nc/4.0).

Homosexual people, and people who are gender non-conforming, also are targeted for violence. A 2015 report from the UN High Commissioner for Refugees found:

> In addition to "street" violence and other spontaneous attacks in public settings, those perceived as LGBT remain targets of organized abuse, including by religious extremists, paramilitary groups and extreme nationalists. LGBT and gender non-conforming youth are at risk of family and community violence. Lesbians and transgender women are at particular risk because of gender inequality and power relations within families and wider society. Violence motivated by homophobia and transphobia is often particularly brutal, and in some instances characterized by levels of cruelty exceeding that of other hate crimes. (pp. 7–8)

The reality is that regardless of the sex of the victim, masculine men tend to be the perpetrators of violence. Typically, those targeted for violence tend to be gendered feminine (or at least not masculine). The term *systemic gendered violence* makes clear that across cultures, gender is a predictor of who is likely to be a perpetrator, and who a victim, of violence.

Gendered/sexed violence is institutionalized. Systems or social structures maintain the notion that being violent is a legitimate part of heterosexual masculinity, whether through war between nations or verbal aggression between individuals. Violence becomes a normalized, accepted behavior for men. Predominant expectations of masculinity tend to enable men to dominate other men, women, children, animals, and their environment. Men's studies scholar Harry Brod (1987) explained,

> Whether learned in gangs, sports, the military, at the hands (often literally) of older males, or in simple acceptance that "boys will be boys" when they fight, attitudes are conveyed to young males ranging from tolerance to approval of violence as an appropriate vehicle for conflict resolution, perhaps even the most manly means of conflict negation. From this perspective, violent men are not deviants or *non*conformists; they are *over*conformists, men who have responded all too fully to a particular aspect of male socialization. (p. 51)

If violence is equated with proving one's masculinity, it becomes difficult for young men to be nonviolent and maintain their masculinity. Worse yet, society struggles to recognize boys and men as victims of psychological or physical abuse by other men, let alone by women. Men who are victimized are emasculated. Furthermore, when women are violent (e.g., suicide bombers or murdering their spouses or children) society struggles to recognize the acts as violence. They are typically explained as acts of self-defense (Johnson, 2006; Stuart, Moore, Hellmuth, Ransey, & Kahler, 2006), acts of martyrdom, or a form of mental desperation. They are viewed as unusual or unnatural acts for women.

Gendered violence cannot simply be explained by examining an individual person's violent behaviors. Placing blame only on individual men ignores the social structures that enable and even encourage such behavior. People are taught from an early age to view men's violence as the natural effect of testosterone. But if the hormone causes aggression, all people with higher levels of testosterone would be violent, and they are not. In actuality, men are socialized to act aggressive to become men. There is a hierarchy of masculinity, and those at the bottom due to factors such as body size, racism, sexual orientation, or classism must work harder to prove their masculinity (Kimmel, 2012b).

Countless social practices contribute to a culture that normalizes the violence committed by many men against others. These practices include the seemingly innocent standard that girls and women should be more polite, ladylike, and willing to smile and that they should take sexist remarks, street calls, and whistles as innocent jokes or flattery (Kramarae, 1992). Those who speak up risk criticism or physical retaliation. Such gendered social practices also include the expectation that all men should be aggressive, sexually active, and unemotional or risk abuse of some kind.

We introduce you to the interconnections between gender/sex and violence in this chapter, but this is only the start of the conversation. Throughout the rest of this book, we return to this theme by exploring, for example, domestic violence in family settings, bullying in educational settings, sexual harassment in work settings, and sexualized violence in media.

Conclusion

This chapter demonstrates why a gender diversity approach is necessary. Gender does not exist in isolation from other identity ingredients, nor does it exist in isolation from social pressures and structures that maintain it. Anthropologist Nancy Henley and communication scholar Cheris Kramarae (1992) explained that "cultural difference does not exist within a political vacuum; rather, the strength of difference, the types of difference, the values applied to different forms, the dominance of certain forms—all are shaped by the context" (p. 40). When two people communicate, there are never just two parties present in the interaction; instead, multiple social groups (ethnicity, class, and gender) are represented, each with varying degrees of privilege and oppression.

Given people's intersectional identity, it makes sense that there are far more than two gendered styles of communication. And given the intersections of forms of dominance, a study of gender in communication also requires the study of diverse social categories' relative power. Studying gender diversity in communication calls for an analysis of more than just masculine and feminine styles of communication.

In many ways, this textbook is a "how to" book. It explains *how* to study gender/sex more than it explains what already has been discovered in gender/sex research (although we do a good bit of that as well). Given that researchers' understandings and people's performances of gender/sex continually evolve, it is more important to know how to read, hear, understand, and critique gender in communication than it is to know what has already been discovered. Our goal is not to tell you the way things are, for the state of knowledge changes. Instead, our goal is to teach *how* to see *why* things are the way they are. That way, you can consciously choose to embrace that which is liberatory and work against that which denies the full measure of your wonderfully unique, distinct, and idiosyncratic humanity.

KEY CONCEPTS

androgyny 11	gender 3	race 18
aromantic 17	genderqueer 14	sex 10
asexual 17	gender/sex 14	sexual orientation 17
binary 14	heteronormativity 17	socioeconomic class 19
cis 16	identity 8	trans 15
communication 21	intersectionality 8	transgender 15
essentialism 20	intersex 13	
ethnicity 18	normativity 15	

DISCUSSION QUESTIONS

1. Identify five key ingredients that make up your intersectional identity. Reflect on how they interact with each other, creating your gender identity. Consider how power relations influence them.

2. What does it mean to "do gender"? In what ways is the study of communication central to the study of gender?

3. In your own life, you do gender. Think of examples where you were rewarded for gendered behavior appropriate to your sex or punished for gendered behavior that did not fit your sex. How did this affect how you do gender?

CHAPTER 2

Theories of Gender/Sex

Although people often think of theory as an abstraction far removed from day-to-day living, theories about gender/sex constantly circulate through public and interpersonal discussions. For example, in April 2011, controversy erupted about an e-mail advertisement showing J. Crew president and creative director Jenna Lyons with her son, whose toenails are painted neon pink. The advertisement about how to be stylish during weekends includes a quotation indicating how happy Jenna is to have a son whose favorite color is pink (see Figure 2.1).

Figure 2.1 April 2011 J. Crew E-mail Advertisement

Media reactions appeared on all the major news networks and across the Internet. Responses ranged from Jon Stewart on *The Daily Show* calling the controversy "Toemageddon" to the following:

> "It may be fun and games now, Jenna, but at least put some money aside for psychotherapy for the kid—and maybe a little for others who'll be affected by your 'innocent' pleasure. . . . [A]lmost nothing is now honored as real and true. . . . [T]his includes the truth that . . . it is unwise to encourage little boys to playact like little girls. . . . [E]ncouraging the choosing of gender identity, rather than suggesting our children become comfortable with the ones that they got at birth, can throw our species into real psychological turmoil."

> Dr. Keith Ablow, psychiatrist and Fox News contributor

> The J. Crew ad is a "marketing piece that features blatant propaganda celebrating transgendered children."

> Erin R. Brown, Culture and Media Institute

> "I can say with 100 percent certainty that a mother painting her children's toe nails pink does not cause transgenderism or homosexuality."

> Dr. Jack Drescher, psychiatrist (as cited in S. D. James, 2011)

Embedded within these statements are theories about where a person's gender/sex comes from and whether it is acceptable for a person (even a 5-year-old) to engage in actions that violate the norms of gender socially assigned to the person's sex. Dr. Ablow's declaration that psychotherapy will be needed is premised on a theory that children's early experiences may be suppressed in their unconscious and that this particular experience will cause harm requiring therapy. Ablow also asserted that the natural "truth" about one's gender identity is "got at birth" and it is harmful for parents to manipulate it through social interactions. In contrast, Dr. Drescher argued that a single gender nonnormative action will not cause a change in gender/sex or sexual orientation. To completely understand the controversy, one has to be aware of the different underlying theories at work that explain formative influences on gender/sex.

In this chapter, we examine theories that explain where gender comes from. Researchers generally identify one of three influences as central: biological, psychological, or cultural. **Biological theories** define gender as biologically tied to sex, and distinctive hormones, brain structures, and genitalia typify each sex. **Psychological theories** emphasize the internal psychological processes triggered by early childhood experiences with one's body and interpersonal interactions with primary caregivers. **Critical/cultural theories** emphasize the role broad cultural institutions and norms play in the construction and maintenance of gender.

Any research done on gender in communication is premised on some set of theoretical assumptions. Theories guide what questions researchers ask. For example, research that begins with a question about *how* men and women communicate differently makes sense only if one believes that men and women are biologically different. If you resist the biological approach, then you might instead ask: *Do* men and women communicate differently? or How do *diverse people* communicate? In many ways, research that begins with the assumption that differences exist reinforces those very differences by not asking questions about similarities or about whether the differences might be a result of some other variable, such as social power, rather than sex.

In this chapter, we review biological, psychological, and critical/cultural theories of gender/sex. By the end of the chapter, whenever you hear a statement about gender/sex in communication, or read research about it, you should be able to identify the theoretical assumptions supporting that research or statement.

Biological Theories

Biological theories of gender/sex show up everywhere, including in popular culture. An October 6, 2011, *Grey's Anatomy* episode, titled "What Is It About Men," opened with the male doctors in the show offering the following declarative statements:

> There are distinct differences between male and female brains. Female brains have a larger hippocampus, which usually makes them better at retention and memory. Male brains have a bigger parietal cortex, which helps when fending off an attack. Male brains confront challenges differently than female brains. Women are hard-wired to communicate with language, detail, empathy. Men—not so much. It doesn't mean we are any less capable of emotion. We can talk about our feelings. It is just that most of the time, we'd really rather not. (McKee, 2011)

Research, theories, religious doctrine, and popular literature that describe the gender binary as "hard-wired," and place an emphasis on "differences between male and female brains," rely on biological explanations for gender. The researcher attributes *primary* causation to genetics, and the assumption of two "opposite" sexes leads to an emphasis on two "opposite" genders (Fausto-Sterling, 1992; Tavris, 1992).

Recent scientific research has made clear "human brains cannot be categorized into two distinct classes: male brain/female brain" (Joel et al., 2015). *Grey's Anatomy* got it wrong when it referred to "male brains" and "female brains." Researchers analyzed over 1,400 MRIs and found "extensive overlap between the distributions of females and males for all gray matter, white matter, and connections assessed" (Joel et al., 2015, p. 15468). In particular:

> Analyses of internal consistency reveal that brains with features that are consistently at one end of the "maleness-femaleness" continuum are rare. Rather, most brains are comprised of unique "mosaics" of features, some more common in females compared with males, some more common in males compared with females, and some common in both females and males. . . . Our study

demonstrates that, although there are sex/gender differences in the brain, human brains do not belong to one of two distinct categories: male brain/female brain. (Joel et al., 2015, p. 15468)

Much previous research only looks at one element of the brain, like those identified by *Grey's Anatomy*. Thus, research that focuses on only one element might be interesting, but it alone does not prove sex differences.

Most biological research focuses on two areas of difference: chromosomes (which in turn produce hormones and genitalia) and brain development. As we review this research, you will note that it is far more complex, contradictory, and unsettled than the *Grey's Anatomy* characters would have you believe.

Chromosomes (Hormones and Genitalia)

One determinant of the sex of a fetus is its chromosomes (usually XX for female and XY for male). We say *one* determinant because some people have sex chromosome combinations of XO, XXX, XXY, or XYY. The existence of intersex persons demonstrates there are more than two sexes. The existence of trans persons demonstrates chromosomes alone are not determinative of sex.

Males' and females' chromosomes are more alike than different. Males and females share 22 of 23 of the pairs of chromosomes in humans. Furthermore, a fetus's sex is undifferentiated through the 6th week of gestation; anatomically and hormonally all fetuses are alike (Carroll, 2005; Strong, DeVault, & Sayad, 1999). The genes present in the chromosomes begin to induce gonadal (or reproductive gland) differences in about the 6th or 7th week, leading to hormonal and anatomical differences among the sexes.

Anatomical differences linked to the X and Y chromosomes have long been used to explain gender/sex identity. Artists, journalists, historians, and religious leaders have heralded the penis as an outward sign of men's virility and right to assert their strength over others. The virile penis has become an essential characteristic of masculinity. Communication studies scholar Diana Ivy (2011) suggested that the more obvious, external nature of males' sex organs makes the strength of it more overt than females' less overt sex organs: "The social interpretations of women's sexual organs identify them as reactors, receivers, followers, and beneficiaries of men's decisions" (p. 49).

Male and female genitalia are distinct, but what the penis (and clitoris) means is socially constructed. Power has been linked to the penis because of its visible size in comparison to the clitoris. But that size assessment is open to contest. Pulitzer Prize–winning science author Natalie Angier (1999) noted, "The clitoris is simply a bundle of nerves: 8,000 nerve fibers, to be precise. That's a higher concentration of nerve fibers than is found anywhere else on the body, including the fingertips, lips, and tongue, and it is twice the number in the penis" (pp. 63–64). So is a woman's clitoris smaller than a man's penis? In terms of external exposed tissue, yes. But regarding its function as a pleasure organ, is the clitoris smaller? Not if you measure size by the number of nerve endings. The meaning of sexual organs is socially constructed.

Regarding hormones, testosterone tends to occur in larger proportions in males, and estrogen tends to occur in larger proportions in females. However, both hormones appear in male and female bodies. Biology professor Anne Fausto-Sterling (2000), after reviewing a year of articles in major newspapers, noted that "despite the fact that both hormones seem to pop up in all types of bodies, producing all sorts of different effects, many reporters and researchers continue to consider estrogen the female hormone and testosterone the male hormone" (p. 179). Fausto-Sterling urged people to remember, when thinking about hormones, "social belief systems weave themselves into the daily practice of science in ways that are often invisible to the working scientist" (p. 194). The question is "How do hormones interact with *all* people's bodies?" Not "How do hormones determine sex?"

Testosterone appears to be related to aggression and risk taking (Archer, 2006; Hermans, Ramsey, & van Honk, 2008; McAndrew, 2009). Although many people think there is a simple relationship wherein testosterone induces violent and aggressive behavior, the reality is much more complicated. Research makes clear that situational factors strongly influence how testosterone affects behavior. In their book *Heroes, Rogues, and Lovers: Testosterone and Behavior*, social psychologists James Dabbs and Mary Dabbs (2001) reviewed over two decades of research indicating that in certain circumstances (usually those relating to competition for social dominance), testosterone tends to motivate rebellious, aggressive, delinquent, and violent behavior. Under other conditions (where a person is in a protective position like a firefighter), testosterone tends to motivate altruistic and prosocial heroic behaviors. In other words, the social situation influences testosterone's effects. There is no simple biological cause but a complex interplay of biology and culture. Quite simply, testosterone does not determine one's gender or one's behavior.

Not only may social circumstances influence how testosterone's influence is expressed, but social circumstances can affect one's level of testosterone. Scientists had long known that fatherhood tended to reduce testosterone in nonhuman species whose males care for young, and so they hypothesized that would happen in human males, too. In a longitudinal study that followed 624 men in the Philippines, researchers found that when single nonfathers became partnered fathers, they experienced a larger decline in testosterone compared to the modest declines that occurred in nonfathers, and those who spent the most time parenting had the lowest levels (Gettler, McDade, Feranil, & Kuzawa, 2011).

Brain Development

Research about whether male and female brains differ has been conducted for well over a century. In the 1900s, scientists believed that because females' brains were smaller, women were intellectually inferior. The fact that this would also mean that smaller males were intellectually inferior to larger males did not seem to register (Boddice, 2011). The debate about brain difference was reignited in 2005 when then Harvard president Lawrence Summers, in a speech about diversifying the science and engineering workforce, offered the explanation that women were underrepresented because of "different availability of aptitude at the high end" (para. 2).

Embedded in Summers's statement is a biological theory of gender/sex differences in development.

In the last decade, investigators have found functional, chemical, and structural variations between male and female brains. Thus, you can see why Summers might have felt comfortable making that statement. However, before we detail this research, we want to offer a few caveats—caveats Summers might have been wise to consider.

First, the existence of structural differences does not mean they are biologically caused. Because of brain plasticity (the fact the brain changes depending on a person's experiences over a lifetime), little can be inferred from the identification of differences (Vidal, 2011). Psychologist Cordelia Fine (2010) explained that the idea that dominates the popular press of "brain development as a gene-directed process of adding new circuitry" is just plain wrong; the most recent research makes clear how "our brains . . . are changed by our behavior, our thinking, our social world" (pp. 176–177; see also Hyde, 2007). Differences are not caused by sex but are caused by experiences over a lifetime (Maguire et al., 2000).

Second, discussing stereotypical sex differences can actually create them because the people to whom the stereotypes apply may believe them and, as a result, perform according to the stereotype instead of according to their skills. **Stereotype threat** was defined by the research that initially identified it as "being at risk of confirming, as self-characteristic, a negative stereotype about one's group" (Steele & Aronson, 1995, p. 797). Simply being "awar[e] of stereotypes about their group's underperformance" in a specific task, like math, nurturing, or navigating, may induce people in that group to perform that task less well even if they have the skills and ability to do it (Smith & Cokley, 2016, p. 145). Although stereotype threat can affect everyone, it "is a phenomenon that primarily affects individuals belonging to stigmatized groups" (Smith & Cokley, 2016, p. 157). Thus, Summers's mentioning of sex differences in the sciences actually may have helped cause or maintain them.

Stereotype threat is so powerful that the message need not be linked specifically to an upcoming task. Instead, general cultural messages can influence performance. However, the good news is that messages countering the stereotype can mitigate its effects. In a study of performance in an upper-level university math course, one class was given a test under normal circumstances and another group was told that "this mathematics test has not shown any gender differences in performance or mathematics ability" to nullify the stereotype that males perform better than females in math (Good, Aronson, & Harder, 2008). In the first case, women and men performed equally well. In the second, women not only performed as well as the men in the class, but their performance "was raised significantly to surpass that of the men in the course" (p. 17). The study concluded, "Even among the most highly qualified and persistent women in college mathematics, stereotype threat suppresses test performance" (p. 17). This demonstrates how powerful communication about gender/sex can be. Messages about who is good at what influence who is good at what.

Stereotype threat can influence people's communication patterns just as much as it influences their math test performance (McGlone & Pfiester, 2015). One study placed participants in a communication situation that required conflict. When told the simulation was about leadership, women's communication was "less fluent and used more tentative language" (p. 111); when told the simulation was about relationship maintenance, men's communication was less fluent and more tentative. In other words, the way we talk about gender/sex communication in this textbook may cause the very effects we are describing. Thus, we want to be very clear: We note the differences in brain structure, but there is *no* evidence they actually affect performance or communication.

Scientists have examined brain structure to identify sex (and then infer gender) differences. Males' brains do tend to be larger than females' by about 100 grams (Ankney, 1992), but brain size is relative to body mass, and males tend to have more body mass than females. Contemporary neuroscience finds that animals need a larger brain in proportion to their body's mass; thus, larger brains have more to do with larger mass than with superior brain functioning. Normal variation in human brain size is not related to IQ (Heymsfield, Muller, Bosy-Westphal, Thomas, & Shen, 2012).

Some argue that women tend to be better at using both sides of the brain because the corpus callosum, which bridges the two hemispheres, tends to be larger in women. This has been used to explain many women's tendency toward stronger language skills, the ability to identify others' emotions more quickly (Begley & Murr, 1995), and the ability to use both hemispheres for listening. However, neurons travel quickly across the two hemispheres regardless of the size of the corpus callosum. Psychologist David G. Myers (2004) cautioned against assuming that people use only one hemisphere for individual tasks. Instead, they almost always use both hemispheres because there is a constant exchange of information. Social psychologist Carol Tavris (1992) explained, "The two hemispheres of the brain do have different specialties, but it is far too simple-minded (so to speak) to assume that human abilities clump up in opposing bunches" (p. 49). The two hemispheres have the ability to compensate for each other and to cooperate. For example, if one hemisphere is damaged, the other hemisphere takes over its tasks. This demonstrates that each side has the neurological ability to perform the other side's tasks. Even though this plasticity decreases with age, the two hemispheres are interdependent (Myers, 2004).

Researchers have found more consistent links between sex differences and responses to mental disorders, stress, hormones, and memory (Cahill, 2005). These findings have raised awareness that research and medical treatment procedures performed on men cannot be generalized to women or even to all men.

Additionally, the National Academy of Sciences reported that sexual orientation may be influenced by brain differences (Allen & Gorski, 1992). A band of fibers called the anterior commissure, which connects brain hemispheres, tends to be larger in gay men than in heterosexual people. Other researchers have found that twins raised apart tend to have the same sexual orientation (Whitam, Diamond, & Martin, 1993), and lesbians are consistently different from heterosexual women in self-reported sexual orientations across cultures (Whitam, Daskalos, Sobolewski, & Padilla, 1998). Yet researchers do not know whether the fiber band's size is affected by use and whether it can change. In addition, cognitive researcher William Byne

(2005) pointed out that quantitative size differences in brain structure alone cannot tell about qualitative differences in sexual orientation.

Although some evidence of biological influences exists, biology alone cannot determine gender identities, and it certainly cannot predict gendered communication. Otherwise, all women and all men in all cultures and all countries across the world would express masculine and feminine gender in identical ways. Biological links to gender are probably more realistically described as influences rather than as sole or direct causes (Reiss, 2000).

When researchers do not start from the assumption that the sexes differ, and instead sort people based on gender, interesting results emerge. Researchers at the University of Iowa studied the relationship among sex, gender, and social cognition. Given studies found women are more adept than men at social perception and the interpretation of nonverbal social cues, the researchers wondered whether the brain might give some clue about why. They studied 30 men and 30 women matched for age and IQ. The researchers used a magnetic resonance imaging (MRI) scan to measure gray matter volume and surface area of the ventral frontal cortex (VFC). However, instead of just comparing people based on sex (comparing males to females), they sought to compare people based on gender (as determined by the answers to the Personal Attributes Questionnaire, the PAQ, a scale of femininity and masculinity). They found "identification with more feminine traits on the PAQ correlated with greater SG [straight gyrus] gray matter volume and surface area. In addition, higher degrees of femininity correlated with better performance on the IPT [Interpersonal Perception Test]" (Wood, Heitmiller, Andreasen, & Nopoulos, 2008, p. 534).

This begs the question: Why is the SG larger in adult women? The researchers did a second study to look at 37 girl and 37 boy children to see if the size difference was innate (meaning programmed from birth). They found the SG was actually *larger* in boys, yet the same test of interpersonal awareness showed that skill in this area correlated to a smaller SG (Wood, Murko, & Nopoulos, 2008). In commentary on these studies, neuroscience professor Lise Eliot (2009a) explained,

> This finding—that brain structure correlates as well or better with psycho-logical "gender" than with simple biological "sex"—is crucial to keep in mind when considering any comparisons of male and female brains. Yes, men and women are psychologically different and yes, neuroscientists are uncovering many differences in brain anatomy and physiology which seem to explain our behavioral differences. But just because a difference is biological doesn't mean it is "hard-wired." Individuals' gender traits—their preference for mas-culine or feminine clothes, careers, hobbies and interpersonal styles—are inevitably shaped more by rearing and experience than [by] their biological sex. Likewise, their brains, which are ultimately producing all this masculine or feminine behavior, must be molded—at least to some degree—by the sum of their experiences as a boy or girl. (para. 10)

The studies by Wood and colleagues are important because theirs are some of the very few studies that do not look solely for sex differences.

Biological Theories Conclusion

Biological theories should be approached with skepticism. If something is presented as caused by biology, this creates the impression it is unchangeable. **Biological determinism**—the idea that biology (sex) determines gender differences—means that inequalities are natural and, hence, cannot be changed by social action. Biologist Fausto-Sterling (2000) urged people to never "lose sight of the fact that our debates about the body's biology are always simultaneously moral, ethical, and political debates about social and political equality and the possibilities for change. Nothing less is at stake" (p. 255).

Psychological Theories

When you read research, theory, or popular material that assumes gender is an innate part of one's personality, the authors are likely drawing from the field of psychology. They focus on how one's identity becomes gendered through early childhood experiences, as when Ablow warned of the "psychological turmoil" caused by a young boy having his toenails painted. Some argue that a child's gender identity is generally set as early as 1 to 3 years of age (A. Campbell, 1993). Although psychological theories vary, they focus on linking one's sex to gendered personalities via the influences of close relationships. Later theories also recognize the influences of culture in developing one's gender.

Psychoanalysis and Psychoanalytic Feminism

Psychoanalytic theories call attention to how unconscious thoughts and memories influence a person's identity, actions, and beliefs. Thus, to truly understand why a human being is the way they are, psychoanalysis demands attention to "early bodily and emotional experience in infancy and early childhood" as central elements forming the unconscious ways people do gender (Minsky, 1998, p. 6).

Sigmund Freud originated psychoanalysis as a psychological treatment technique. Central to psychoanalysis was the study of gender and sex identity formation. Freud (1975) theorized that children develop gender identity personalities based on their perceptions of sex differences in biological genitalia. Freud theorized that until age 4, sex difference is irrelevant to the child. At around 3 to 4 years of age, "the sexual life of children usually emerges in a form accessible to observation" when they enter the phallic stage, during which they become aware of their genitals (pp. 42–43). From the phallic stage till puberty (the genital stage), Freud argued children see themselves in terms of having, or not having, a penis. While little boys initially assume everyone has a penis like theirs, Freud argued that little girls recognize their genitals are different and "are overcome by envy for the penis—an envy culminating in the wish . . . to be boys themselves" (p. 61). When boys do notice girls lack a penis, they experience "castration complex" wherein they recognize the possibility that the penis can be removed, and they begin to fear castration as punishment (p. 61). In Freud's view, for girls to develop normally, they must be heterosexual and associate with their mother to compensate for their failed masculinity. For boys to develop normally, they must ultimately identify with their father. According to Freud's original theory, boys who do not make a complete break in their dependence on their mothers will not become fully masculine (Brannon, 2011). Thus, successful gender and sexual development in girls and boys is marked by their willingness to identify with the parent of their sex (instead of seeing that parent as competition for the affections of the other parent).

Much of Freud's work has been criticized for reflecting a heteronormative and masculine bias and a misunderstanding of women's psyche. A contemporary of Freud, Karen Horney, initiated the criticism. Horney argued that for girls, penis envy did not represent a literal envy for the physical penis but rather represented a symbolic envy for the social power and prestige men and boys experienced. In addition, Horney argued that men experienced "womb envy," in which men sought social and material accomplishments to compensate for their inability to give birth. Horney (1967) wrote, "From the biological point of view woman has . . . in the capacity for motherhood, a quite indisputable and by no means negligible physiological superiority. This is most clearly reflected in the unconscious of the male psyche in the boy's intense envy of motherhood" (pp. 60–61).

In addition to the near universal rejection of the theory that all women experience "penis envy" (Tavris, 1992), Freudian psychoanalysis is criticized because it essentializes gender/sex when it dictates only two sex-based paths for successful gender identity development (Bell, 2004). The reality is children respond to gender identity in highly idiosyncratic and individual ways. Further, Freud's early theory recognized only heterosexual identities and did not consider cross-cultural variations.

Although many rightly critique Freud's work, the attention to the unconscious and the role of early experiences in gender identity formation were revolutionary. For feminists, Freud helped make clear that gender was not biologically determined but was influenced and formed by social experiences. One could understand gender from a psychoanalytic perspective by focusing on the way adults impose gender/sex norms on infants and, in the process, structure the human mind. Psychoanalysis generated multiple strands of psychoanalytic feminism (e.g., interpersonal psychoanalytic feminism [Gilligan, 1982], Lacanian theory [Lacan, 1998], and object relations theory).

In object relations theory, feminist psychologist Nancy Chodorow (1978) built on Freud by arguing that the mind (and gender identity) is formed in childhood, not in response to children discovering their genitalia but rather by the relationships children have with others—particularly their primary caregivers, who tended to be women. According to Chodorow, because the mother is a gendered person herself, she interacts with boy and girl children according to her gender, forming distinct relationships. At the same time, each child experiences internal conflict in trying to construct a separate identity from the mother. Because the mother and daughter are overtly similar, the daughter resolves her conflict by identifying with the mother and thus emulates a feminine gender identity. The girl develops intimacy and relationship as a primary part of who she is. According to Chodorow, the mother tends to treat a boy child differently from a girl child. The mother encourages independence in the boy earlier than in the girl and is less intimate in her talk with the boy. The boy child also recognizes that he is not like his mother in basic ways. To resolve his internal conflict, the boy must reject the mother as a part of his independent identity development. The boy develops an orientation toward independence and activity as a primary part of who he is and thus finds relationships potentially smothering.

Object relations and other strands of feminist psychoanalysis agree with Freud that all gender identity, conscious and unconscious, has its origins in early bodily and emotional experiences and the fantasies associated with them (Minsky, 1998). They also suggest gender is influenced by one's sex identity and vice versa. Persons do not experience these in isolation but rather as related parts of the self (Bell, 2004). However, this does not mean that sex *causes* gender. Psychoanalytic theorists since Freud have emphasized the role of culture in gender development.

By combining the influences of culture and the unconscious self, theorists are better able to explain why some individuals do not conform to cultural pressures of gender/sex expectations; why gender, sex, and sexuality are more fluid and diverse than cultural stereotypes suggest; and how race, class, and culture create multiple variations of gender, sex, and sexuality (Bell, 2004). Social learning theorists offer examples of this explanatory power.

Social Learning

Social learning theory posits gender is a learned behavior, learned by observing, analyzing, and modeling others. When gender behavior is modeled consistent with sex identity, it is rewarded; if done incorrectly, it is punished. Particularly with children, this process of modeling, reinforcement, and punishment shapes gender/sex identities. Originally developed by Walter Mischel (1966) and later modified by Albert Bandura (2002; Bandura & Walters, 1963), this theory explains the socialization process whereby children internalize many identity ingredients and norms of behavior, not just gender. When children are positively rewarded for mimicking preferred behaviors, the behaviors attached to prescribed social roles become internalized habits (Addis, Mansfield, & Syzdek, 2010). Young girls tend to be rewarded for being polite, neat, emotionally expressive, and well behaved. Young boys tend to be rewarded for being independent, emotionally controlled, and physically active. Thus, girls tend to develop feminine qualities, and boys tend to develop masculine qualities.

As with object relations theory, in the initial research on social learning theory, the parents' and/or primary caregivers' behaviors were considered most influential. However, more recent uses of social learning theory have highlighted three things. First, observational learning occurs not only in relation to immediate family but also through media sources such as video games (Wohn, 2011). Second, social learning is situational; a variety of ways to do gender in different situations are rewarded. Third, relationships with peers also are influential.

Understanding the role media play in social learning is necessary. For example, given most people do not directly observe others' sexual activity, social learning theory recognizes people can learn from, and model, mediated gender and sexuality performances. This also demonstrates why "increased exposure to media is associated with more sexually permissive behaviors and attitudes" (Petersen & Hyde, 2010, p. 23). Given that sex scenes on television doubled from 1998 to 2003, and that they increased most dramatically in depicting sexually active women, based on social learning theory, researchers predicted that women would report engaging in more sexual behaviors. These predictions proved true (Petersen & Hyde, 2010). Mediated communication practices contribute to the formation of gendered expression related to sexuality.

Recent research on social learning also encourages scholars to recognize that learning is far more situational than previously thought. The same action might be rewarded by one group in one setting but punished by a different group in a different setting. Psychologists Addis, Mansfield, and Syzdek (2010) explained:

> Social learning is situated learning; particular actions are followed by particular consequences in specific contexts. Young boys, for example, often learn that expressing soft vulnerable emotions like sadness will be followed by punishment and other forms of ridicule, particularly when this behavior occurs in the context of other dominant males. These same consequences may be less likely to occur among close confidants, or around one's mother versus one's father. Over time, what emerge are relatively differentiated or discriminated repertoires of activity that are highly sensitive to context. (p. 80)

As a result of their research, they argue that researchers and theorists should "embrace the contextual nature of gendered social learning" and "avoid metaphors that locate gender as an internal property of individuals" (p. 83). Again, gender is something one does, not something one has.

Recent research has focused on the role of relationships in identity development. The **relational theory** approach "starts from the premise that our perceptions of, and subsequently our knowledge about, our selves and our world are inextricably embedded within and influenced by our interpersonal relationships as well as our social and cultural contexts" (Chu, 2014, p. 3). Chu (2014) intensively studied 4- and 5-year–old boys over a 2-year period to explore the ways in which their relationships with each other interact with gendered social expectations. Chu's conclusion was that characteristics labeled "boy behavior" are not inherent to boys, but are learned behaviors. In commenting about the results, Chu noted:

> I am wary of the whole "[just] boys being boys" thing because . . . if you expect boys to be a certain way, you'll say, oh, it's boys being boys when they're rowdy or rambunctious or whatever, but never "boys will be boys" when they're being sweet or sensitive or smart or insightful. So I am wary of those kinds of stereotypes or gender roles.
>
> Especially because . . . when you take the whole range of human capabilities and qualities, and you say one half is masculine, and one half is feminine, and only boys can be masculine, and only girls can be feminine, then everybody loses, because you're asking everyone to cut off and deny a part of their humanity. (as quoted in Berlatsky, 2014)

Chu argued that the perception that boys are worse at relationships than girls is likely the result of two factors: (1) because people do not expect boys to have relationships skills, they do not look for them, and (2) boys' relationship skills may not be apparent especially as they get older because they have been socialized to hide that capacity so they do not appear feminine (Chu, 2014, p. 200). For Chu (2014), "becoming 'boys'—namely by aligning with prevailing norms of masculinity—is neither automatic nor inevitable" (p. 204).

Social learning theory fares better than the psychoanalytic approaches in its ability to help explain communication influences and because it is much easier to directly observe and test. However, it still tends to dichotomize gender/sex, and it cannot explain why some boys and girls do not conform to social expectations.

Psychological Theories Conclusion

Psychological approaches suggest that gender identity is not naturally set at birth but instead developed through early childhood interaction. The psychological approaches we reviewed presume that all children are raised in Western, two-parent, heterosexual, nuclear, bourgeois families. Psychologist Janet Hyde (2005) conducted a review of 46 meta-analyses on gender and psychology research. Hyde concluded that there is no foundation for the continued belief in prominent psychological gender differences: "The gender similarities hypothesis holds that males and females are similar on most, but not all, psychological variables. That is, men and women, as well as boys and girls, are more alike than they are different" (p. 581).

Critical/Cultural Theories

Writing in 1949, French philosopher Simone de Beauvoir questioned how the natural and social sciences had depicted womanhood as mysterious when justifying women's inferiority. Beauvoir argued that these supposedly objective sciences were biased in the presumption of women's inferiority to men and, in turn, reinforced that bias and justified patriarchy (the institutionalized maintenance of male privilege). Beauvoir recognized biological differences exist, but challenged the social value attached to those differences. To make clear the cultural, and not innate biological or inherent psychological, causes of gender, de Beauvoir (2011) declared,

> One is not born, but rather becomes, woman. No biological, psychic, or economic destiny defines the figure that the human female takes on in society; it is civilization as a whole that elaborates [what] is called feminine. Only the mediation of another can constitute an individual as an *Other*. (p. 283)

Although social inequality between the sexes had been questioned for decades, if not centuries, de Beauvoir's book marked a turning point in the critical analysis of the cultural foundations of gender. The *Stanford Encyclopedia of Philosophy* declared, "Beauvoir's *The Second Sex* gave us the vocabulary for analyzing the social constructions of femininity and a method for critiquing these constructions" ("Simone de Beauvoir," 2014, part 6, para. 6). To fully understand where gender/sex comes from, critical attention to cultural constructions of gender/sex is necessary.

The emphasis on gender as something a person *does* and not something a person *is* emerged from this perspective. A critical/cultural approach calls for people to understand gender as something that is done—by individuals, groups, and institutions. Gender cannot be understood by examining a single individual's biology or psychology. Instead, the broader situations in which an individual lives—the social meanings embedded within communication—must be studied. West and Zimmerman (1987), the scholars who wrote the germinal essay "Doing Gender," explained,

> Doing gender involves a complex of socially guided perceptual, interactional, and micropolitical activities that cast particular pursuits as expressions of masculine and feminine "natures."
>
> When we view gender as an accomplishment . . . our attention shifts from matters internal to the individual and focuses on interactional and, ultimately, institutional arenas. . . . Rather than as a property of individuals, we conceive of gender as an emergent feature of social situations: both as an outcome of and a rationale for various social arrangements and as a means of legitimating one of the most fundamental divisions of society. (p. 126)

Thus, studying gender is about more than studying how an individual person acts. Instead, to study gender, one needs to analyze how it is culturally and socially constructed. One's gendered lens should focus on how social interactions and institutions do gender by gendering people and practices (see also West & Zimmerman, 2009). Thus, the idea of *doing gender* "de-emphasized socialization as the basis for gendered difference between men and women" (Deutsch, 2007, p. 107).

If gender is done, then it can be *un*done as well. Psychology professor Francine Deutsch (2007) clarified: "If gender is constructed, then it can be deconstructed" (p. 108). Thus, when examining how gender is done, you should also look for places where it is undone, where other ways of doing and undoing arise. Exploring other ways of doing gender requires attention to individual examples of resistance and to institutions because power differentials are always in play (Collins, 1995, p. 493).

A range of critical/cultural approaches to gender/sex exist, including postmodernism, deconstructionism, poststructuralism, postcolonialism, queer theory, and cultural studies. We outline some of the common assumptions these approaches share and then focus on two of them to give a better sense of how critical/cultural approaches explain gender/sex.

Shared Assumptions

1. *Social reality is communicatively constructed.* **Social reality** is reality as understood through the symbols humans use to represent it. Social reality is created as people name objects, actions, and each other. Although a material world from

which human beings receive sensory data exists, people do not know how to interact with that world until their sensory data is given meaning through symbolic action.

The centrality of communication to social reality is explained by communication scholar Barry Brummett (1976), who argued "experience is sensation plus *meaning*" and "*reality is meaning*" (pp. 28, 29). All symbolic action participates in the creation of meaning. The power of symbols to make meaning explains why communication scholars note a distinction between reality and *social* reality. Critical/cultural theorists emphasize the power of discourse to shape social reality and study the processes by which this is accomplished.

Communication is more than a means to transmit information. When people communicate, they participate in the construction of social reality. Introduced in Berger and Luckmann's (1966) book *The Social Construction of Reality*, social construction theory informs much contemporary communication research (Leeds-Hurwitz, 2009). Although you may know things exist apart from your symbol systems, you cannot know what those things mean, or how you are to react to them, except through the symbol system. In terms of gender/sex, critical/cultural approaches examine gender as a social construction, communicatively constituted, and ask how a particular construction of gender and sex privileges some and disempowers others.

No biological entity exists that humans can access without socially constructing it in some way. Critical/cultural scholars emphasize the role communication plays in forming people's understandings of the world. Even the seemingly simple terms of *female* and *male* illustrate the power of communication to create social reality. As long as these were the only terms available to refer to the human body, bodies were forcibly fit—through sex assignment surgery at birth—into one of those binary categories. Until the language for intersex emerged, bodies could only be one of two things.

Imagine if you had to find a way to present your gender to the world, but you could not use any form of communication. You could not speak, wear clothes (which carry with them symbolic messages), or move. How would others know your gender? For critical/cultural theorists, gender is something one does, not something one is, *and* gender is something that is socially created, not biologically or individually created.

Given this, English professor Jordynn Jack (2012) pointed out how "the formation of gender identities themselves . . . constitutes a rhetorical process" in which gender "provid[es] a range of available discourses through which individuals make sense of, model, and perform a gendered identity" (p. 2). Thus, critical/cultural scholars tend to focus on the rhetoric of gender and sex.

2. *Categories such as sex, gender, sexuality, and race become the focus of criticism.* Because reality is socially constructed, critical/cultural theorists conceive of sex, gender, sexuality, race, and other categories not as neutral designations of "the way things are" but as ways people structure what is. Philosopher Judith Butler (1992) explained how the critical/cultural theory of poststructuralism highlights how "power pervades the very conceptual apparatus" that people use to understand the world and themselves (p. 6).

Critical/cultural theorists note how the categories just listed tend to be mutually exclusive binaries (if you are *either* male *or* female, then intersex people do not exist) or create differences where none exist (the single human race has been artificially divided into races). The categories determine whose lives are recognizable and intelligible—which people exist socially. Thus, instead of starting from the assumption that males and females indicate the two sexes that exist, a critical/cultural theorist would question and investigate how those categories were created, who those categories benefit, and how the categories are placed in a hierarchical relation to each other.

3. *One cannot study gender/sex unless one also studies power and systems of hierarchy.* Systems of hierarchy refer to the patterns and institutional structures that maintain inequality between groups. Critical/cultural scholars emphasize the broad cultural patterns at play to highlight that gender/sex is not simply located within individuals but is sustained throughout the culture, in its symbol systems, institutions, and rituals. In other words, gender is not something you were born with or learned only from interactions with your parents; socialization is an insufficient explanation for gender. Saying that you learned gender from only your parents begs the question: Where did your parents learn gender? Gender/sex, together with ethnicity, class, sexual orientation, and other cultural identities, lives in the ideology, norms, laws, worldviews, traditions, popular culture, and social institutions that sustain a culture. Critical/cultural approaches argue that you cannot understand gender only by studying individuals' performance of it. Instead, one must study the systems of hierarchy that privilege some sexes over others and some performances of gender over others.

Critical/cultural scholars make clear that the issue is not just whether one person exerts power over another. Instead, one needs to critique systems. Systems of hierarchy, embedded within social, economic, and political institutions, explain the existence of ethnic and gender/sex inequality; biology and personal bias are not the central foundations of inequality. Critical/cultural scholars understand discrimination as a system of hierarchy, "fundamentally a political relationship, a strategy that" as a system, gives social, economic, political, psychological, and social privileges to one group and denies them to another (Harding, 1995, p. 122).

Privileges are unearned freedoms or opportunities. Often, privileges are unconscious and unmarked. They are made to appear natural and normal through cultural hegemony, which makes them easy to deny and more resistant to change. When violence prevention educator Jackson Katz (2003) asked men in his workshops what they do to prepare to walk alone on campus at night, most of them responded with an unknowing stare. When Katz asked women this question, they readily offered several strategies they used to keep safe, such as phoning roommates ahead to tell them they are leaving, carrying their keys pointed out between their fingers as a weapon against would-be attackers, or looking in their cars before they open the doors. Gay, lesbian, bisexual, and transgendered persons often try to pass as straight to avoid possible verbal or physical violence. Heterosexuals usually do not have to consider such acts.

For critical/cultural scholars, gender/sex is never just a simple difference. Instead, to study gender/sex, one must study power. Power is a social phenomenon. People have power in relationship to others. Social power is embedded in the communicative negotiations of gender/sex, race, class, sexual orientation, and other identity ingredients. For each of these social groups, multiple differences are socially created, and differences are rarely constructed equally. Rather, the groups that have more say about the construction are privileged over others.

Power can simply mean "the ability to get things done" (Kramarae & Treichler, 1992, p. 351). It is not an innately evil concept. However, feminist theorists make an important distinction between "power to" and "power over" (Freeman & Bourque, 2001, pp. 10–11). *Power to* is the ability to get things done that does not infringe on others' rights and may actually lead to the emancipation of others. *Power over* refers to coercive misuses of power. If one is in a position of power over others, then one can dominate and coerce others and, in the process, subordinate or oppress them. If one lacks power over, one is more likely to be in a subordinate position. The interesting point is that to respond to any instance of power over, or to get out of a situation in which one is subordinated by those who have power over, one needs power to.

In their book on intersectionality, sociology professors Patricia Hill Collins and Sirma Bilge (2016) identified four "distinctive yet interconnected **domains of power**: interpersonal, disciplinary, cultural, and structural" (p. 7). Interpersonal power can be found in one's ability to control or dominate others in the negotiation of personal or professional relationships. Thus, it is important to recognize "power relations are about people's lives, how people relate to one another, and who is advantaged or disadvantaged within social interactions" (p. 7). However, power also is systemic. Disciplinary power can be found in how "informal social rewards and punishments get distributed in everyday interactions" (p. 27). For example, when parents punish boys for showing emotion and reward girls for being agreeable, disciplinary power is at work. Cultural power can be traced in socially accepted ideas and messages transmitted across media. For example, cultural norms of masculinity and femininity, reinforced by media representations, are a form of cultural power as is the privileging of the nuclear family over other family forms. Finally, structural power can be traced through how groups, institutions, and laws are organized (p. 12). For example, the disproportionate incarceration of men of color is an example of how racism is embedded within structures of law.

4. *Oppositional critical views are necessary to critique hegemonic norms.* Hegemony designates the systems of hierarchy maintained by the predominant social group's ideology (Gramsci, Rosenthal, & Rosengarten, 1993). Philosopher Rosemary Hennessy (1995) explained that hegemony is not a form of power that controls through overt violence. Rather, it controls subtly by determining what makes sense: "**Hegemony** is the process whereby the interests of a ruling group come to dominate by establishing the common sense, that is, those values, beliefs, and knowledges that go without saying" (pp. 145–146). People willingly belong to cultures for the protection and order those cultures provide, even though predominant

cultural ideology may control them in some ways. By following society's norms of behavior, members uphold the culture's ideology.

When analysts of gender talk about **patriarchy**, they are not talking about the domination of one man over one woman but are talking about a hierarchical system that exercises hegemonic control wherein men are privileged over women, and some men are privileged over men, and in which even some of those who are subordinate in the hierarchy accept it because such an ordering appears to make sense.

Sociologist R. W. Connell introduced the concept of **hegemonic masculinity** in 1982. Connell noted there is not one single way to perform masculinity; instead, a range of masculinities exists. But not all forms of masculinity are equal; some forms of masculinity are privileged (White, upper-class, wage-earning, hetero-sexual, athletic) over other forms, and masculinity is privileged over femininity. Although Connell recognized that a plurality of masculinities exists, the focus was on the normative form of masculinity, the type that has been the most honored way to be a man, even if it is not the type that is most prevalent (or the norm). Hegemonic masculinity does not require all men to engage in overt toxic practices, but it does encourage men to remain silent to protect their own masculinity when others commit such practices. In doing so, they become complicit in the violence (Katz, 2003). Thus, hegemonic masculinity constitutes a "pattern of practices . . . that allowed men's dominance over women to continue" (Connell & Messerschmidt, 2005, p. 832).

To see hegemony at work, one needs to be critical of taken-for-granted cultural norms, to take what media scholar Stuart Hall (1993) identified as an opposi-tional, or counterhegemonic, reading of cultural texts (pp. 98–102). Instead of "*operating inside the dominant code*" (p. 102, italics in original), an oppositional reading challenges the social meanings. Thus, one finds critical/cultural scholars critiquing the way blood donation, as "a performative act of civic engagement," constructs sex, sexuality, and citizenship in a way that disempowers gay men (Bennett, 2008, p. 23); how *Knocked Up*, *Juno*, and *Waitress*, three 2007 films that all centered around a White pregnant woman, "reframe unplanned pregnancy as women's liberation" and present a model of family that serves only the needs of White, economically privileged women (Hoerl & Kelly, 2010, p. 362); and how media stories about Black male athletes accused of domestic violence construct understandings of them as "naturally aggressive due to their sporting background and black rage" and, in the process, reinforce hegemonic White masculinity (Enck-Wanzer, 2009, p. 1).

To see how specific critical/cultural approaches enact these four assumptions, we offer two examples: Multiracial and Global Feminisms and Queer Theory.

Multiracial and Global Feminisms

Scholars and activists studying gender/sex through the lens of *global feminist theory* and *multiracial feminist theory* have crystallized the reasons that gender/sex must be studied from an intersectional critical/cultural perspective. They note how the category of woman often has represented the concerns of White, economically privileged women from Western countries and, as a result, has reinforced hierarchies that emphasize the concerns of the privileged. Thus, they make clear how the category of *woman* itself is inflected with race, nationality, and class.

Their position is that no singular gendered experience defines women or men, and the norms of one culture should not be imposed on another in an attempt to improve women's and children's human rights. Law professor Isabelle Gunning (1997) put the challenge this way: Instead of being "arrogant perceivers" of the world who judge other cultures based on the ethnocentric view of their own culture as the norm, people should strive to be "world travelers" (p. 352). To be world travelers means to be ethnographers, to try to view other cultures from their members' perspectives rather than one's own. To be world travelers also means to recognize the interconnections between cultures. This requires not only observing the other culture but also being willing to turn that same critical lens back on one's own culture, including examining how one's cultural practices contribute to the oppression of other cultures. These scholars call for an oppositional perspective.

Authors from this perspective emphasize the experiences and voices of multiple gendered/sexed people, particularly racial minorities living in the West and those living in non-Western, nonindustrialized, noncapitalist countries. They argue that White, Western, educated feminists have had the most to say in defining women's experiences and have falsely assumed that their worldview represents all women, consequently portraying other women as passive, backward, unenlightened, oppressed, undereducated, and needing help (Kapur, 2005). These scholars make clear the role of privilege.

Chandra Talpade Mohanty (2003) outlined the failures of White Western feminists' studies of third-world women and women of color:

> To define feminism purely in gendered terms assumes that our consciousness of being "women" has nothing to do with race, class, nation, or sexuality, just with gender. But no one "becomes a woman" (in Simone de Beauvoir's sense) purely because she is female. Ideologies of womanhood have as much to do with class and race as they have to do with sex. Thus, during the period of American slavery, constructions of white womanhood as chaste, domesticated, and morally pure had everything to do with corresponding constructions of black slave women as promiscuous, available plantation workers. It is the intersections of the various systemic networks of class, race, (hetero)sexuality, and nation, then, that positions us as "women." (p. 55)

Mohanty (2003) urged everyone to recognize "the application of the notion of women as a homogeneous category to women in the Third World colonizes and appropriates the pluralities of the simultaneous location of different groups of women in social class and ethnic frameworks; in doing so it ultimately robs them of their historical and political agency" (p. 39). An intersectional approach to understanding gender/sex is necessary.

Global feminists urge a consideration of all hierarchies and how they interact. A sex-only approach misidentifies third-world men as the root cause of third-world women's oppression, not capitalist colonial systems. This creates a dynamic that English professor Gayatri Chakravorty Spivak (1988) described as "white men saving brown women from brown men" (p. 297). This is not a dynamic confined only to colonial times. Dana Cloud (2004) provided a trenchant analysis of images circulated by Time.com of Afghan people while the U.S. administration was building public support for the 2001 invasion of and war in Afghanistan. Focusing on the women as veiled and oppressed, the images appealed to White men to save Brown women from Brown men and evoked a paternalistic stance toward the women of Afghanistan. Power is at the center of their analysis.

So-called third-world people and the colonization of them can exist in any country, including the United States. Chicana author and activist Gloria Anzaldúa (1987) explored the ways in which living on the U.S.-Mexican border shapes mestiza (mixed-race) women in *Borderlands/La Frontera*. Throughout this work, Anzaldúa moved between English and Spanish, detailing the process and purpose of communication, constantly reminding the reader of their role as a person positioned on the border between two cultures. As part of the exploration of political and personal borderlands, Anzaldúa, like other Chicana feminists, created a space in which to perform multiple identities (Flores, 1996; Palczewski, 1996).

Rhetorician Raka Shome (1996) explained why the study of communication and imperialism is important. **Postcolonialism**, as a theoretical orientation, examines the social, gendered, economic, and environmental impacts of colonization and the ways in which colonial ideologies have continued to exist in contemporary institutions in the form of neocolonialism. In the United States, this also means attention to settler colonialism, or how the settling of the lands that became the United States displaced Native peoples. As "a critical perspective that primarily seeks to expose the Eurocentrism and imperialism of Western discourses," it asks two related questions:

> How do Western discursive practices, in their representations of the world and of themselves, legitimize the contemporary global power structures? To what extent do the cultural texts of nations such as the United States and England reinforce the neo-imperial political practices of these nations? (Shome, 1996, p. 41)

Shome explained that a focus on communication is necessary because "discourses have become one of the primary means of imperialism" (p. 42). Although "in the past, imperialism was about controlling the 'native' by colonizing her or him territorially, now imperialism is more about subjugating the 'native' by colonizing her or him discursively" (p. 42) by forcibly changing gender and national identities and values. The tremendous reach of Western media, the universality of English (a legacy of earlier territorial imperialism), the way in which academics have named and defined the "native" as "other," and the creation of economic dependency all mean that attention to communication patterns is central to understanding how colonialism persists (see also Shome & Hegde, 2002). They note the role of communication to construct social reality.

Queer Theory

Queer theorists challenge noncritical approaches' use of binary categories such as gender (feminine/masculine), sex (female/male, woman/man), and sexuality (homosexual/heterosexual); contest heteronormativity; and offer a politics that is not tied to stable identity categories (McDonald, 2015). Queer theorists do not deny that identity categories exist. Instead they argue that the categories should be analyzed because identity is, in the words of Heather Love (2011), "spoiled, partial, never fully achieved, but sticky, familiar, and hard to lose completely" (p. 185).

Queer theory argues that social categories artificially restrict people's perceptions. Thus, when communication scholars use the word *queer*, they do so "to denote bodies, identities, and enactments that challenge and/or reimagine normative gender and sexual arrangements" (LeMaster, 2015, p. 170). Queer theorists operate with an oppositional perspective.

As a form of study, queer theory is the "process by which people have made dissident sexuality articulate," meaning "available to memory, and sustained through collective activity" (Warner, 2002, pp. 17, 203). Queer theory creates a language that names and makes present those who live outside the binaries. Queer theory critiques the categories used to understand gender, sex, and sexuality as part of the very hierarchies that maintain privilege for some groups over others. Queer theorists "contest and deconstruct identity categories by conceptualizing identities as multiple, fluid, unstable, changeable, and constantly evolving" (McDonald, 2015, p. 319). Queer theory is one of the clearest locations where the categories themselves become the subject of study.

Queer theory questions all forms of sex and sexuality categorization because it addresses "the full range of power-ridden normativities of sex" (Berlant & Warner, 1995, p. 345), particularly heteronormativity. Queer theory makes clear the variety of ways in which heterosexuality is composed of practices that have very little to do with sex (Warner, 2002, p. 198). When it comes to thinking about sex, sexuality, and gender, queer theory calls for a "rethinking of both the perverse and the normal" (p. 345). For queer theorists, desire is a focus of study, including the "categorization of desiring subjects" and what allows some desires to "pass as normal, while others are rendered wrong or evil" (Giffney, 2004, p. 74). Queer theorists challenge hegemonic understandings of sex, gender, and sexuality.

By recognizing and examining connections among sexual desire, gender, sex, and sexual orientation, this approach broadens the study of gender/sex in communication in important ways. For example, English professor J. Halberstam (1998) showed that studying women performing masculinity may reveal more about cultural assumptions of masculinity than studying men, for whom society assumes the relationship is normal. Halberstam's (2005) study of drag kings (women and men who expressly perform masculinity, like Mike Myers in *Austin Powers*) exposed some of the absurdity of gender norms and how gender functions as "*a kind of imitation* [or copy] *for which there is no original*" (Butler, 1991, p. 21, italics in original). Halberstam's oppositional perspective made hegemonic norms more visible.

In communication studies, queer theory critiques the heteronormativity of much research in family and interpersonal communication. The family, for example, is not a neutral or natural institution, but "a primary vehicle through which hetero-normative ideologies are mobilized" (Chevrette, 2013, p. 173). But emerging research offers an alternative. As Roberta Chevrette (2013) compellingly argued in their *Communication Theory* essay, "Queering communication, and 'feminizing' queer theory, requires scholars to be theoretically diverse, to utilize mixed methods, and to frame research questions with power, language, sexuality, and difference in mind" (p. 185).

Cultural Critic Wesley Morris reflected on the effect of three pop culture icons: Prince, David Bowie, and George Michael, all of whom died in 2016. All three rose to prominence in a time of hyper-masculinity during the 1980s: "Arnold Schwarzenegger's career as an action hero began. Sylvester Stallone moving from *Rocky* not just to *Rambo*, but to things like *Cobra* and *Over the Top*. This was a time when Michael Douglas was the sexiest man alive." In assessing their impact on understandings of masculinity, Morris said the following about the three performers:

Prince: "And so you have this tension between straight culture—and you have, in somebody like Prince, this person who is really queering the difference between these two. He was singing about heterosexual sex while looking anything but conventionally heterosexual."

George Michael: "I think that by the time the 'Faith' video came around—it was his first solo album—he wanted to have a look that separated him from Wham! And this very sort of butch, rockabilly thing that he went for was so different than the other George Michael that it was arresting. That video just completely eroticized him: I mean, the camera is rising up his body as moving around this contraption that's spinning. It's great."

David Bowie: "He made every aspect of what was normal about being human seem foreign. I think that *Ziggy Stardust* period was probably the most obviously queer period that he performed in. He was interested in this makeup and these platforms and this hair, and it was neither male nor female, and I think that was what was so disconcerting about him.

"But also, if you were a kid, it was kind of weirdly exciting, because these ideas of gender and masculinity and femininity are these acquired notions. I think that if you're ignorant of what they signify, you see this person signifying none of it and it kind of blows your mind."

(as cited in Shapiro, 2016)

Critical/Cultural Theories Conclusion

Despite the range of approaches, critical/cultural approaches theorize that one can never understand gender and sex unless one studies broad cultural systems that sustain power differences. Critical/cultural approaches emphasize that reality is constructed through communication and that social reality contains systems of hierarchy and power differentials. Thus, gender differences are never seen just as differences but always as possible patterns that expose relations of power.

Applying Gender Theory: Some Useful Criteria

In this chapter, we outlined three primary approaches (biological, psychological, critical/cultural) used by researchers, popular media, and laypeople to explain gender in communication. They have different underlying assumptions about how people conceptualize, study, and explain gender/sex. Our goal has been to help you better identify and examine your own and others' assumptions before our upcoming chapters present more specifics about gender in communication.

After reviewing these approaches to studying gender/sex in communication, we find the multiple theories and research practices useful, depending on the precise question studied. Given that gender is complex and diverse, it makes sense that complex and diverse theories are necessary, and that the influence of biology, psychology, and social hierarchies are likely interrelated. To make clear the way the theories interact, we offer the diagram shown in Figure 2.2.

Figure 2.2 Theory Chart

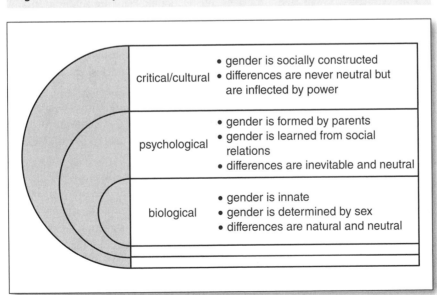

The three approaches differ in the expansiveness of their assumed cause of gender, with the critical/cultural approach being the most encompassing.

We now offer some fundamental criteria for, and questions to empower, you to do your own critical thinking about gender/sex in research and popular culture.

Criterion 1: Is an intersectional approach being used?

An intersectional approach is needed to avoid stereotypes and to more accurately reflect the diversity that exists in gender/sex identities. Because many other identity ingredients intersect with gender, gender diversity makes more sense than gender differences tracked along a single axis. There is not just one femininity or one masculinity. Given the multitude of variables that influence who persons are, it makes sense that there would never be just two gendered types of communication. Like Jordynn Jack (2012), we embrace moving beyond binary gender differences and toward gender copia.

Communication studies professor Celeste M. Condit (1998) outlined the benefits of a **gender diversity perspective**. First, "the gender diversity perspective advocates respect and care for persons of all genders and gender types (as long as those types do not directly harm others or infringe on the human rights of others)" (p. 177). It is inclusive. Second, it reorients research in an invigorating way: "Instead of trying to describe how men and women speak differently, we can begin to explore the range of gendered options available to people" (p. 183). It diverts attention from the study of how women's gender limits communication and directs it to the study of how a range of people have used diverse gender styles to speak passionately, ethically, and effectively to their audiences. A gender diversity approach provides a more realistic, more interesting, and wider scope for analyzing gender/sex in communication.

How will you know if an approach is intersectional? Here are some questions you can ask:

- Does the source study sex or gender or both? Research that identifies only the sex of each person in the study, and then draws conclusions about gender, may be unintentionally conflating these concepts.
- Does the gender/sex analysis include other possible interdependent influences on one's behavior, and on how others perceive that behavior, such as how one's gender intersects with ethnicity, age/generation, social class, physical or mental ability, and nationality?
- Does the analysis consider gender/sex differences *and* similarities?
- Does the source offer nuanced conclusions? For example, claiming gender/sex differences exist does not tell *how much* difference was found. In a study of sex and self-disclosure, Dindia and Allen (1992) claimed statistically significant differences, but in looking closer they admit only about 1% of the differences in self-disclosure could be attributed to sex differences (Dindia, 2006).
- Does the source account for power differences? Intersectionality is not about identity alone; it also explains power. Does the source account for how the same act of communication might be interpreted differently depending on

how the body communicating is perceived and where the person is placed in social hierarchies of power? For example, anger when expressed by a White male body might be perceived as righteous indignation and passionate defense of an idea, while anger expressed by a Black male body is perceived as incipient violence and anger expressed by a Black woman is perceived as mental imbalance (Hugenberg & Bodenhausen, 2003). Keep in mind that descriptions of behavior alone tell little about why the behaviors exist or what the social consequences might be. Others might interpret the same behaviors very differently depending on the sex, ethnicity, age, and so on of the person doing them.

To examine how people communicate, one needs to look beyond gender/sex. Communication differences *and* similarities between people are rarely, if ever, determined solely by the sex of the speaker.

Criterion 2: Is the focus on communication?

We suggest placing communication at the center of analysis. Communication creates, maintains, and alters identities and relationships. Communication creates gender/sex; gender/sex is not a static identity that produces communication. Gender/sex is a communicative process, not a fixed attribute.

This does not mean things like economics, politics, psychology, or biology are irrelevant to gender/sex. Indeed, we have demonstrated the value of combining information from diverse fields. We emphasize communication because it is important to recognize people have degrees of agency in creating and communicating their gendered/sexed identities, *and* people are compelled to follow social norms through communication in relational, institutional, or cultural interactions.

Here are some questions you can ask:

- Are claims about gender based on specific observations of communication, mere generalizations, or anecdotal experiences? Many popular publications and media products are based on cultural assumptions, not careful analysis of particular data collected.
- Are the communication process and the possible patterns it creates the focus? People create meaning by practicing recognizable patterns of interaction (such as norms of taking turns to speak) or unique interpersonal patterns (such as both parties using a particular emoticon in text messages). These patterns create meanings. Claims based on an isolated example may only serve to maintain stereotypes.

Criterion 3: Does the source recognize unique context-dependent influences on behaviors?

Surprisingly, most of the research on gender in communication has not traditionally taken into account unique situational influences (Dindia & Canary, 2006; Eckert & McConnell-Ginnet, 1992, 2011). This is problematic because any act of communication can have multiple meanings and serve a variety of functions (Tannen, 1994). Without context, researchers fall back on stereotypical cisgender norms to simply label behaviors as masculine *or* feminine. Communication context includes the physical, social (West & Turner, 2014), cultural (Campbell, Martin, & Fabos, 2015), and psychological elements of a given interaction (Palomares, 2012).

Here are some questions you can ask:

- How might the physical context influence behavior? Consider the immediate setting, time, place, and so on.
- How might the social context influence behavior? This refers to the type of relationship such as interpersonal, small group, organizational, public speaking, or social media.
- How might larger cultural influences, such as social norms, values, languages, inequalities, and violence, influence communication?
- How do the participants view their own interactions? What is going on for a person in the moment can be very telling. People can play active roles in creating, maintaining, and/or challenging their gendered identities. The lesson here is that you should not assume a person always talks the same way regardless of context.

Criterion 4: Are there possible power implications?

Power can take many forms, and it exists on many levels. The pervasiveness of power is a part of the reason it is difficult to recognize and so influential.

Here are some questions you can ask:

- What roles do the participants play and is power embedded in these roles (e.g., parent/child, boss/worker, friends)?
- Are there signs of some people trying to control others or trying to resist control?
- Do the participants seem free to be themselves?
- Can you identify ways in which power might be embedded in the context (e.g., cultural expectations, standard organization policies or procedures)?

We note power separately to mark its importance. When studying groups defined by their gender, ethnicity, class, and so on, identity distinctions are rarely different and equal. The nature of the distinctions, the values assigned, and the power attributed to those distinctions are culturally determined and decidedly unequal most of the time.

Conclusion

A more productive way to study the topic of gender in communication is to use a broader lens of analysis that recognizes that theory and knowledge construction are rhetorical and political acts, as are people's efforts to interpret, embrace, and reject them. This does not mean that there is no objective reality but rather that reality means nothing until people give that reality meaning as they play active roles in its construction and deconstruction. People's perceptions are their reality. This is no less true for researchers. Understanding the link between expectations and reality brings with it an awesome ethical responsibility to attend to how one communicates and how one studies gender in communication. It also represents an exciting adventure through which we travel in the remainder of this book.

KEY CONCEPTS

biological determinism 37

biological theories 30

critical/cultural theories 30

domains of power 45

gender diversity perspective 52

hegemonic masculinity 46

hegemony 45

patriarchy 46

postcolonialism 48

privileges 44

psychoanalytic theories 37

psychological theories 30

queer theory 49

relational theory 40

social learning 39

social reality 42

stereotype threat 34

DISCUSSION QUESTIONS

1. What expectations do you have for appropriate gender-related behaviors? Where do you think these expectations come from? What are your underlying theories about gender given what you have identified as the sources of gender?

2. How do biological theories explain the formation of gender and its role in communication? Identify examples from popular culture that embrace this theory.

3. How do psychological theories explain the formation of gender and its role in communication? Identify examples from popular culture that embrace this theory.

4. How do critical/cultural theories explain the formation of gender and its role in communication? Identify examples from popular culture that embrace this theory.

CHAPTER 3

Gendered/Sexed Voices

*T*ime magazine and *Huffington Post* wrote about it. Kim Kardashian and *This American Life* host Ira Glass do it. Linguists and speech pathologists study it. What is it? Also known as "creaky voice" or glottal fry, **vocal fry** occurs when speakers lower their vocal pitch at the end of sentences to the lowest register they are capable of producing. This creates irregular vibrations of the vocal cords resulting in a creaky, gravelly sound. If you are still unsure of what it sounds like, for an example visit https://www.youtube.com/watch?v=R6r7LhcHHAc (or search "Faith Salie on speaking with vocal fry" on YouTube).

Although women receive the most negative attention for the use of vocal fry (Anderson, Klofstad, Mayew, & Venkatachalam, 2014; Blum, 2016), linguist Penelope Eckert found men are its most frequent users: "So the disparity in people's noticing is very clear to me. People are busy policing young women's language, and nobody is policing older or younger men's language" (as cited in NPR, 2015). People perceive sex/gender differences in voice that simply do not exist.

Voice researcher Cate Madill (2015) explained that everyone uses some vocal fry, usually when stressed or tired, and it is actually a normally occurring feature in many tonal languages such as Vietnamese, Wu Chinese, and Burmese. Madill reported that lower voices are perceived almost universally as more authoritative or higher status. Thus, vocal fry is fine if you are a man, an older woman, or a person with a position of higher status, meaning "all this commentary about vocal fry is not actually about the voice, but about power and status, and who is allowed to have it." Differences in perception also depend on who is hearing the voice. The listener's age (Anderson et al., 2014), sex, and region (Yuasa, 2008) affected their judgment of vocal fry.

Vocal fry illustrates a number of points about gendered/sexed voices. People often perceive gendered difference in voices that are not actually there. Power rather than sex explains perceived difference in communication styles. And no universal gender assessment of voice makes sense because gendered talk varies according to the topic being discussed, speaker status, how salient gender is in the interaction, and other people present (Ye & Palomares, 2013). When you take into account a speaker's intersectional identities and how a context calls for unique norms of behavior (such as legal court testimony or a chat with a friend), what were presumed to be gender/sex differences in behavior are often better explained by other influences (Dindia & Canary, 2006; Hinde, 2005; Schleff, 2008).

This chapter helps you think about how you do gender, and how others do gender to you, in your daily conversations. Mundane interactions—conversations—are the most pervasive micro-process during which people perform gender. **Conversation** is the process of two or more parties working interactively to create meanings through the exchange of verbal and nonverbal cues within a given context. Conversations include content (i.e., verbal and nonverbal vocalizations) and structure (e.g., social expectations for turns at talk that build and end conversations).

Conversations require work. The concept of **conversation work** makes clear that some degree of intent, effort, and cooperation is required in the seemingly easy turn-taking process of talking to others (Brown & Levinson, 1987; Tracy & Robles, 2013). For example, when Sam says, "Thanks for going to the movie with me. I really liked it," Casey will likely feel compelled to build on that comment in some way. Casey might say, "Sure, I wasn't doing anything," or "I liked it, too." Each speaker has taken a conversational turn and, if they continue to respond to each other, they will build a conversation. The topic may change, their roles in carrying the conversation may shift, but they each work to keep the conversation going.

People do gender through conversation. Thus, we first examine how conversational work itself can have gendered expectations by focusing on three linguistic forms people use in everyday talk: politeness norms, humor, and swearing. They are by no means the only components of conversation used to do gender, but they offer compelling examples of how conversational work is often done to construct and deconstruct gender.

Next, we examine how people do gendered **identity work** through conversation as they present who they are and negotiate that identity with their conversational partners (Brown & Levinson, 1987; De Fina, Schiffrin, & Bamberg, 2006; Tracy & Robles, 2013). Individuals do not have exclusive control over constructing their identities. Identities also are constructed when people respond to each other in conversation. Social psychologists call this **altercasting**, a concept that "highlights how the way we talk to and act toward others (alters) puts them in roles (casts them)" (Tracy & Robles, 2013, p. 28). Conversational partners may reinforce your identity, restrict it, contest it, and/or embellish it. Altercasting plays a central role in maintaining stereotypical gender role expectations. Altercasting does not mean people have to accept the roles in which they are cast, but the potential for negative judgments exists should they violate expected roles. To illustrate gendered identity work, we examine stereotypical masculine and feminine identity markers in conversation, as well as more recent research on trans and LGBQ identity markers.

Finally, we examine how conversations are central to **relationship work**. Relationships take continuous effort by all parties involved. Conversations enable people to create, sustain, negotiate, and/or end their interpersonal connections with others (Baxter, 2011). Interpersonal communication scholar Steve Duck (2002) explained that by the time two parties exchange their second utterance, they have a shared history and that history will influence what comes next in their interactions. Cultural norms informed by age, gender, ethnicity, and power influence how relationships are negotiated. To demonstrate this, we examine children's play, ineffective conflict management in adult romantic relationship, and verbal aggression and abuse in relationships.

Conversation work, identity work, and relationship work occur simultaneously. Together they reveal the realistic, context-specific ways in which intersectional gender identities are constructed in unique social contexts. This chapter demonstrates that

- popularly presumed gender/sex differences in talk are not innate but socially constructed,
- stereotypic expectations can lead to gendered perceptions and judgments of behaviors,
- people have more agency and diversity in actual talk than simple binary stereotypes suggest, and
- behaviors are often more about power and other intersecting identities than gender/sex alone.

Conversation Work

People do conversation work when they follow (or violate) socially recognized patterns and rules, including rules about politeness, what is considered funny and who gets to be funny, and who gets to swear and when. Women, children, and upper-class men have typically been expected to follow politeness rules more carefully. In fact, polite behaviors and feminine behaviors are seen as synonymous (Mills, 2003). In contrast, humor and swearing have traditionally been seen as more crude, reserved for men performing hegemonic masculinity (Coates, 2013).

Politeness

Feminist linguist Sara Mills (2003) noted, "Linguistic politeness lies implicitly at the heart of a great deal of gender and language research" (p. 1; see also Baxter, 2011; Brown & Levinson, 1978). **Politeness** is commonly and historically thought of as having good manners, saying "please" and "thank you," and apologizing to avoid offending others. It has traditionally been relegated to (White) women's domain. It is associated with stereotypical feminine conversation qualities tied to women's traditional responsibilities as caregiver and nurturer, including keeping harmony; showing interest in others; listening; and being supportive with verbalized expressions "oh," "aha," and "mmm." Politeness has also been associated with the manners of sophistication needed to fit into upper- or middle-class society (Eelen, 2014). Politeness can be used to regulate gender, social class, and race, but the cues of politeness may vary by culture.

Identifying and interpreting politeness behaviors is complex because interpretations must account for context. Everyone is capable of using a range of politeness skills to negotiate social situations; your gender/sex does not determine your level of politeness. Thus, one cannot assume politeness or any other conversational component is innately, consistently, or universally gendered/sexed, even though traditionally some women have been held to higher expectations of politeness than some men (e.g., Coates, 2013; Mills, 2003). Furthermore, politeness is too narrowly defined, limited to upper-class expectations, and its performance is not always genuine. More research is needed on gendered links to politeness behaviors.

Humor

In a 2007 issue of *Vanity Fair* magazine, columnist Christopher Hitchens asked: "Why are men, taken on average and as a whole, funnier than women?" Answering his own question, Hitchens explained that men use humor to attract women and "loosen" them up, whereas "women have no corresponding need to appeal to men this way. They already appeal to men, if you catch my drift." Hitchens's question and response is sexist and heterosexist (and not very funny). But he is not the first to make such a declaration: "The idea of the humorless female has been embedded in Western culture for at least the past century" (Crawford, 1995, p. 135).

A traditional assumption has been that humor is a part of the culture of masculinity. Various explanations exist for why humor is perceived as a masculine trait: Humor is associated with public figures and White men have traditionally dominated public life; and humor is often vulgar or rough, traits associated with masculinity and working-class identities (Coates, 2014). Conversely, it is simply not considered ladylike to be funny (Kotthoff, 2006).

Expressed verbally and/or nonverbally, **humor** is a quality that usually leads to positive feelings expressed by laughter or a smile from the observer. Although most everyone uses humor, the concept of humor is gendered, raced, classed, and culturally defined. Humor is about power and can be effective in getting another person to comply, conform, or submit.

Helga Kotthoff (2006) identified four dimensions of humor as especially gender-, power-, and relationship-sensitive. First, status: People of higher status seem to be at more liberty to use humor, sometimes teasing persons of lower status. Status humor can reinforce and/or reduce hierarchies, as when a boss shows their more human side by making fun of themselves. Second, aggressiveness: defined as teasing, mocking, parody or ridicule. Boys have been found to display more aggressive humor than girls, and ritualized humorous attacks on each other have been more common among boys' and men's groups. Third, body politics/sexuality: Across cultures people used humor to talk about taboo topics, such as sex. A wide range of body politics/sexuality humor exists, from shared sexual banter to sexual harassment, and from innuendo to overt graphic claims. Whether or not these behaviors are received as humorous depends on the gender/sex of the participants, age, nature of their relationship, and context. Fourth, social alignment: This is the giving and receiving of social support, cooperative conversational style, and teasing among close friends. Some women have been found to prefer the use of collaborative humor to create intimacy and solidarity (Coates, 2014). Some men have been found to use humor as social support in nonromantic relationships, in the form of teasing, friendly competition, playful punches, or backslaps (Swain, 1989; Wood & Fixmer-Oraiz, 2017).

Although there is evidence of stereotypical gendered roles and styles in humor, Rod Martin (2014) found more similarities than differences between men and women "in self-reported tendencies to perceive, enjoy, and create humor in daily life" (p. 144). The rigid gendered expectations around humor seem to be lessening, enabling all to more fully explore the productive uses of humor.

Women's use of humor, especially for political ends, has a robust history. From Anna Howard Shaw and Sojourner Truth to Ann Richards and Flo Kennedy, humor has played an integral role in women's political activism. For example, journalist Marie Shear offered this simple definition of feminism in 1986: "Feminism is the radical notion that women are people." The phrase became enormously popular and appeared on T-shirts, posters, and mugs, providing a way to poke fun at those who unnecessarily fear feminism.

We identify four common functions of feminist humor. First, it creates a space for marginalized voices. Humor suspends predominant social arrangements so that roles may be tried on and voices may be exorcised and exercised. Second, as space is opened, challenges to taboo emerge. In feminist humor, women are allowed to recognize their bodies and not be ashamed. They are allowed to be simultaneously intellectual and sexual, even aggressively sexual, as seen in Eve Ensler's (1998) award-winning play *Vagina Monologues* and its more gender-inclusive versions today (Brighe, 2016). Third, feminist humor challenges stereotypes (Kaufman & Blakeley, 1994). Comedian Ellen DeGeneres models this approach by playing the role of the innocent nice White butch girl next door while she challenges assumptions about comedy as men's domain and marriage as heterosexuals' domain (Mizejewski, 2014). Fourth, by breaking taboos and challenging stereotypes, funny feminists are politically subversive (Barreca, 1991). Humor challenges power relations, standards of who may speak, and who may speak about what. It is powerful as a subversive tool because, unlike traditionally rational attacks on systemic uses and abuses of power, humor works on a nonrational level as well.

Swearing

Former U.S. secretary of state Madeline Albright noted she nearly gave then Joint Chiefs' chair Colin Powell an aneurysm with her bad language. In one instance, as she watched a video of Cuban pilots celebrating the downing of two civilian U.S. planes, Albright responded, "That's not cojones, that's cowardice" (cited in Mills, 2003, p. 193). Even in this highly emotional moment and with her power as a world leader, she was expected to speak lady-like and refrain from directly expressing anger. Swearing does not serve all users equally to express emotion.

Perhaps more than any other conversational tool, swearing has a history of being considered men's talk. In fact, several states once had laws regulating swearing. A Michigan law required, "Any person who shall use any indecent, immoral, obscene, vulgar or insulting language in the presence or hearing of any woman or child shall be guilty of a misdemeanor." The law suggested that swearing was reserved for the company of men. It took until 2015 to repeal this archaic and unconstitutional law (Feldscher, 2015).

Swearing uses expletives or offensive language to express strong emotion, whether anger at specific others or simply general frustration. As potent language, it can sometimes achieve impressive effects (Eckert & McConnell-Ginet, 2013). Today, many adults and children swear, regardless of gender/sex, social class, or ethnicity. And yet swearing is still perceived as more acceptable for men given "swearing has historically been used by men in the company of other men as a sign of their toughness, manhood" and for group bonding (Coates, 2003, p. 46). Ample evidence proves that taboo language has been a defining part of all-male subcultures, including the military, fraternities, and sports, "as well as in male peer groups on the street as a way of constructing solidarity" (Coates, 2013, p. 153).

Swearing serves multiple functions. First, it can provide emotional release. Second, people use swearing to perform identity that is gendered, classed, generational, and sometimes raced. Third, people use swearing to create conversations and unique relationships. Fourth, swearing can assert and/or resist power. A speaker can accomplish many of these functions in the same utterance (Eckert & McConnell-Ginet, 2013).

Robin Lakoff (1975) long ago claimed swearing was a privilege reserved for men to exert power and express emotion while women were expected to speak indirectly and politely. Lakoff's work has since been challenged by evidence that many women use profanity and many men do not (e.g., Charteris-Black & Seale, 2009; Mendoza-Denton, 2008) and that swearing's effectiveness depends on a person's relative power and the social context.

Research on swearing and illness makes clear the relationship between swearing and gender/sex is complicated, as rules surrounding masculinity and femininity limit possible forms of expression. In interviews with British male cancer patients, researchers found a younger, higher socioeconomic class of men commonly used the word *fucking* to discuss their illness (Charteris-Black & Seale, 2009). The researchers suggested the relationship between swearing and masculinity may not simply be about the right to use profanity, but about their frustration that hyper-masculine expectations did not allow them to express their fear or grief in other ways (such as crying). In contrast, in a study of women dealing with illness, some swore as a form of emotional release, but the expression often came at the cost of losing the emotional support of others. People did not want to hear them swear. The researchers pointed out that swearing for women in their 50s might have been perceived by others as taboo, which reinforced the notion that swearing has age and gender connotations (Robbins et al., 2011).

Who is allowed to swear where and when are forms of social control and reveal the potential power of swearing. Some of what can make swearing powerful are (1) the nonverbal way in which it is said, (2) the words used, (3) its link to masculinity and aggression, (4) swearing as a form of violence, and (5) swearing to empower a speaker or group.

First, a part of the power of profanity is that when expressed in anger, the speaker usually increases their volume and vocal inflection, and adds facial and bodily gestures for emphasis. When expressed this way, particularly in cultures where relative inexpressiveness is the norm, swearing can be a strategy to demand compliance to a request by attempting to frighten or intimidate others.

Second, not all swear words are equally powerful. Kristy Beers Fägersten (2012) found students and nonstudents used a wide range of swear words, but eight were most common: *ass, bitch, cunt, damn, dick, fuck, hell, shit,* and possible inflections and derivations such as *asshole* or *motherfucker.* Of these, "the single most important contributor to the swearing paradox is the word 'fuck.' It is consistently cited among the most frequently used swear words and consistently rates among the most offensive" (p. 108). Other swear words have misogynist connotations, as in *bitch* (referring to a female dog), *son of a bitch,* and *motherfucker.* It is difficult to think of strongly offensive words that are not homophobic or misogynistic.

Third, swearing has been relegated to the realm of aggressive masculinity. Fägersten (2012) found African American and White men tended to disapprove of women swearing, particularly using the more offensive word *fuck.* This meant the more powerful swear words were reserved for men's use. However, Fägersten found fewer gender differences than previous research in the actual use of swearing.

Fourth, swearing is powerful because it can be a form of aggression and violence. The seemingly habitual, less overt forms of violence create a context in which physical forms become normative in a culture (Kissling, 1991; Kramarae, 1992). Swearing can be used to convey aggression and commit verbal abuse.

Fifth, some women and men use swearing to seek empowerment (unfortunately, sometimes at the expense of others). This is visible when some young adolescents and teens attempt to assert their independence by swearing. In a study of Irish college students who identified themselves as drinking friends, the researcher did not find gender/sex differences in swearing and concluded the women used profanity not to try to talk like men, but because it was a fun part of the pub culture. They enjoyed the shock value swearing sometimes had on others, and they wanted to model other women they admired who did not follow the predominant norm that women should not swear (Stapleton, 2003).

In sum, politeness, humor, and swearing offer three examples of the ways in which conversational work has been gendered/sexed in binary, stereotypical ways and how individuals and groups attempt to strategically use these tools to accomplish their conversational goals.

Identity Work

People use conversation to assert individual, interpersonal, and group identities. This can be accomplished in overt ways such as introducing yourself as Ms., Mrs., Mx., Mr., Senorita, Professor, Doctor, or by your name. But identity is more commonly accomplished in the myriad, subtle ways you speak—your conversational style.

For example, communication scholar Karla Scott (2013) studied how young Black professional women used conversation to perform competence while faced with the double, intersecting oppressions of race and gender/sex in predominantly White work environments. The 33 participants' reflections revealed that the "'preferred outcome' of their communication strategies is to construct an alternate identity of a Black woman and redefine Black womanhood" (p. 318). They were well aware of the stereotypes of Black women's conversational style as "overbearing, too outspoken, strong, angry" (p. 319). One of the participants, Cathy, described:

> When I step into a setting where . . . I'm the only Black, I'm feeling like all eyes are upon me, for my entire race, especially Black women. My tone changes, the way I speak, I speak properly, following the rules of language arts [laughter from other women]—not that I don't do it anyway, but I'm more alert, making sure that I don't stumble over certain words. (p. 319)

The research concluded, "These young Black women perceive themselves as having some measure of control in dispelling myths about Black women through the use of specific communicative strategies that are immediately available and well developed from a field of experience" (p. 325). They perform identity work through their conversational style.

Conversational style refers to a person's tendency to communicate verbally and nonverbally in a particular way, such as being assertive, indirect, argumentative, collaborative, polite, or animated (Norton, 1983). Your style is created through your rate of speech, vocal inflection, vocal pitch, pronunciation of words, volume, amount of talk and silence, how you tend to take turns in conversation, and even topic preferences. Put simply, "style is a combination of what we do and how we do it" (Eckert & McConnell-Ginet, 2013, p. 248). As the above example illustrates, it can also include tone, grammar, and enunciation.

The presumption of opposing feminine and masculine conversational styles has dominated popular culture and media across many cultures for some time, even though actual research does not support such claims (e.g., Canary & Hause, 1993; Dindia & Canary, 2006; Goldsmith, & Fulfs, 1999; Hyde, 2005; Leaper & Robnett, 2011). Holding on to these stereotypes discredits the behavioral flexibility of all genders/sexes and fails to recognize what the research actually shows. Unique contexts and intersectional identities such as race, ethnicity, social class, national origin, and language have far more influence on conversational styles than gender differences (e.g., Carbaugh, 2002; Hall, 2009; Kikoski & Kikoski, 1999; Kochman, 1990; Ye & Palomares, 2013). We describe feminine and masculine conversational styles, gay and lesbian conversational styles, and trans and gender non-conforming conversational styles here. One caveat: We know that by describing them, we risk reifying their normative power. However, it is helpful to understand the norm against which most gendered performances tend to be judged. Research has shown *perceived* gender/sex differences in conversational style far exceed any *performed* ones (Kirtley & Weaver, 1999).

Feminine Conversational Style

The primary characteristic attributed to feminine style is **rapport talk**: talk that focuses on building relationships, connecting collaboratively with another person, and showing empathy. Speakers using this style are said to view talk as the primary means of negotiating and maintaining relationships. To build rapport, speakers use verbal and nonverbal cues that convey support to the other person (offering affirmations or questions that convey interest) and seek cooperation rather than competition (Coates, 1997; Johnson, 1996; Tannen, 1990; Wood & Fixmer-Oraiz, 2017).

A second characteristic attributed to feminine style is **indirect communication**, which includes hedges ("I am sort of thinking . . ." rather than "I think what we should do is . . ."); qualifiers ("Well, I may be wrong, but . . ."); tag questions ("I think we should do this, don't you?"); and indirect requests ("There is a hole in my glove" rather than asking "Could you buy me some new gloves?"). Indirectness softens the claims or requests being made and is perceived as more polite (Mills, 2003). In what was considered a groundbreaking article, feminist linguist Robin Lakoff (1975) argued women strategically learn to use indirectness to better accomplish their goals as relatively powerless speakers in a patriarchal culture.

Third, feminine talk is said to be more collaborative than masculine talk (Aries, 2006; Coates, 1996; Holmes, 1997). One person's story becomes the group's story or an invitation for others in the group to share their stories (Coates, 1997). The goal is to catch up on each other's lives by sharing intimate details (Holmes, 1997). As such, simultaneous talk is seen more as collaboration and enthusiasm, not as interruption, making the organization of the story less linear.

Masculine Conversational Style

The primary characteristic attributed to masculine style is **report talk**: talk that focuses on instrumentality or task orientation, asserting oneself, and competitiveness. Those who use a masculine style are said to use talk as a tool to accomplish a goal. The goal can be to complete a task, solve a problem, exert control, assert oneself, or gain independence and status (Cameron, 1997; Coates, 1997; Wood & Fixmer-Oraiz, 2017). Masculine style avoids personal disclosure and vulnerability, which is typically associated with feminine style. The focus on using talk to accomplish tasks also indicates masculine speakers will talk less than feminine speakers; talk is a means to an end, not an end in itself as when using talk to do relational work.

Second, masculine talk is described as direct and assertive (Mulac, 2006; Wood & Fixmer-Oraiz, 2017). **Direct communication** straightforwardly states what a person wants, thinks, or feels. Being direct and assertive fits well with a speaker who is task-oriented rather than relationship-oriented and with one who uses communication to establish and maintain control or status.

Third, masculine talk such as storytelling is characterized as being largely about status. Men studied tend to prefer to tell stories in ways that helped enhance their status and masculinity (Coates, 1997; Holmes, 1997). In an extensive study, linguist Jennifer Coates (2003) identified five prominent features in young British men's stories: (1) the stories were about stereotypical masculine topics such as cars, sports, drinking, and technology, and these topics helped detour the conversation away from personal self-disclosure and vulnerability; (2) the stories were told as a series of monologues, not interactively; (3) the organization of stories was chronological or linear; (4) the men used profanity heavily; and (5) the men's stories stressed achievement or bragging rights. The men engaged in competitive storytelling, seeing who could tell the bigger "fish story." Storytelling became a competitive sport in a way Coates did not observe in the women's conversations.

Gay and Lesbian Conversational Styles

Although sexual orientation and gender are different identity ingredients, Western cultures conflate them. Traditionally, the worst name a boy or man can be called is *woman*, *fag*, or *femme*. The stereotypic expectation that gay speech is highly feminine is a constant source of ridicule, rebuke, and prejudice, even though studies demonstrate observers cannot distinguish gay from straight speakers (Smyth, Jacobs, & Rogers, 2003). Just as heterosexuals might emphasize masculine or feminine speech styles to convey their identities, some gay men choose a flamboyant feminine style when performing drag, to celebrate gay pride, or to protest for gay rights. In using this style, Eckert and Sally McConnell-Ginet (2013) argued gays are not "doing female," but "they are extracting expressiveness from the gender binary" (p. 270).

In contrast, lesbian speech style receives little ridicule or attention. Researchers have not been able to identify common features in lesbian speech. This may be because society tends to tolerate a wider range of speaking styles from women than men. Women's adoption of masculine style is more tolerated than men's adoption of feminine style. Patriarchal culture mandates closer compliance with hegemonic masculinity for those fighting for the top of a social hierarchy. Also, lesbians are subject to the double oppression of being a woman and being homosexual, so they may simply have less safety to experiment with expression (Cameron, 2011).

Trans and Gender Non-Conforming Conversational Styles

The claim that the voice is integral to constructing gender identities is clearly illustrated in the voice of a person transitioning genders. If a transwoman has a body that reads woman to others but speaks with a deeper voice, her voice may belie her body, and others may reject her identity as a woman. This seems to be the case, even though the majority of people have a conversational style that is not extremely masculine or feminine. For those who are gender non-conforming, "there is great variation in the extent to which voice and communication changes are undertaken or desired" (Davies, Papp, & Antoni, 2015, p. 120).

Scholars have not completed a great deal of research on transgender voices (Davies et al., 2015), but the work that does exist made a few things clear. Many (not all) transitioning individuals feel vocal change is essential for their new identities. Vocal change is attainable with practice; no surgery is needed. Vocal change involves more than simply raising or lowering pitches. People use a combination of speaking patterns to sound more feminine or masculine. There is no single ideal pitch level that sounds feminine or masculine; rather a range of pitches exists.

The instructions given to sound more masculine or feminine reveal much about cultural stereotypes of binary gendered voice expectations. People who are transitioning often use these stereotypes strategically to attain their desired vocal gendered identities. Together, these findings reveal not only that trans individuals are able to successfully adjust their voices, but that everyone, cis and trans, adapts their voices over time to convey preferred gendered voices.

YouTube Voice Training for Trans Women

Caroland, a trans woman, provided videos in fluent Spanish and English. Her three disclaimers are found in other tutorials as well:

1. You don't have to alter your voice at all to be a woman.
2. There is no set pitch that you have to reach to have the woman's [or man's] voice you want.
3. There are many ways to achieve the voice you want.

—Caroland (2014) Volume 1, with more than 27,000 hits.

To conclude, "speakers who cross the gender divide in this way [vocally] can help us better understand the relationship between gender and the voice as it functions for all speakers" (Zimman, 2012, p. 49). People literally speak themselves and others into a gender identity. Although much of gender is done in subtle, habitual ways, all doing of gender is strategic and has potential social consequences. The question remains: How do these gendered conversational style expectations affect relationships?

Relationship Work

Relationships do not just happen. Like communication, relationship work is an ongoing, ever-changing process. Like conversation work and identity work, relationship work requires some degree of cooperation from all parties involved. The work is complex because the individuals involved are simultaneously negotiating their individual and relationship identities (Baxter, 2011). Gender/sex is not a primary component of all relationships, but because gender/sex is a component of how people categorize themselves and others, it makes sense that it commonly plays a role in relationship development and maintenance. The following are examples of how gendered identities and gendered interpersonal (one-to-one) or small-group relationships are negotiated through conversation.

Children's Play

Gender/sex, along with intersecting identities such as social class and ethnicity, is central to children's and teen's relationships due to hegemonic influences (Goodwin & Kyratzis, 2014). Children often help create each other's identities through relationship play: imitating adults' speech, creating unique greetings for each other, singing, telling stories, and creating verbal competitions or other power plays. Such play allows children to try on and explore social roles, such as gender/sex. Children's play is not merely a form of passive socialization where binary gendered identities are imposed on them. Instead, play is a means by which children push back, explore multiple identities, have fun, insult, and negotiate relationships (Goodwin & Kyratzis, 2014).

In relationships, peers monitor each other's behaviors through communicative strategies such as bullying or gossip to sanction those who do not conform to identity and relationship expectations (Goodwin & Kyratzis, 2014). In a study of working-class boys in Sweden, the researcher observed a pattern of gossiping in front of the targeted boy as a way for the speaker to solicit support and solidarity from other boys (Evaldsson, 2002). This research countered the stereotype that only girls gossip and demonstrated how the boys taunted each other about perceived failures to perform masculine expectations. For example, boys were much more likely to be teased when they expressed anxiety about not being included, cried, wet their pants, or told on others. Similarly, in a study of preschool middle-class Turkish girls, researchers observed sanctioning of other girls for failure to comply with feminine, collaborative play expectations (Kyratzis & Tarim, 2010).

Unfortunately, much of the research on gender in children's interactions is older and focuses on White children, but in a more recent review of studies looking at children's talk in diverse ethnographic settings, Goodwin and Kyratzis (2014) found communication behaviors and relationships differed more by age and class than by gender/sex. Older children used more complex communication strategies (e.g., teasing and storytelling), and younger children used less variety (e.g., song or pretend games). In working-class contexts or other social contexts that required one to be tough due to minority group membership or difficult economic situations, girls and boys used more argumentativeness. Although earlier gender research suggested girls' play focused on creating symmetrical relationships (Tannen, 1990), a multitude of studies showed working-class and middle-class girls built asymmetrical relationships of exclusion, such as by indicating who can and cannot be the leader of a game or by comparing each other in terms of material possessions (Goodwin & Kyratzis, 2014).

Children's play often occurs in sex-segregated groups. Researchers have observed tendencies toward single-sex play in studies of preschool children from Australia, Italy, Japan, Norway, the Peruvian Aymara, the United States, and Wales. You can probably speculate some of the causes of such segregation: binary gender socialization, fear of perceived differences, gendered toys, anxieties toward the other sex tied to cultural expectations of romance and sexual activities, and gender identity competitions. Some sociolinguistic researchers argued segregation encourages children to develop limited binary masculine or feminine conversation styles because the rules of interaction differ. Boys' stereotypical play teaches competition and assertion; girl stereotypical play teaches relationship nurturance and collaboration (Maltz & Borker, 1982; Tannen, 1990; Wood & Fixmer-Oraiz, 2017). Although many girls learn the rules and play so-called boys games such as soccer and wrestling, many boys consider playing so-called girls' games taboo, not because they do not know the rules but because they are afraid of retribution or are attempting to distance themselves from anything considered girly (Eliot, 2009b).

Regardless of the gender/sex make-up of friendships, children know how to do relationship work. The giving and receiving of **social support**—providing emotional support and showing care and concern—is a central element of relationship work. Social support fulfills an innate human need for the help of others, and people use multiple strategies to assist each other (Burleson & MacGeorge, 2002). Having social support is linked to personal well-being and relationship well-being (Goldsmith, 2004). Recent research showed girls and boys in stressful situations provided necessary social support to each other by listening and sympathizing, but with a gender/sex twist. The girls talked about the problem longer and the boys used more humor with age, but the boys and girls all felt closer to their friend after their talk (Rose, Smith, Glick, & Schwartz-Mette, 2016).

Research on children's conversations demonstrates how children play active roles in simultaneously constructing individual and relationship identities even as diverse gendered approaches are used.

Ineffective Conflict Management

Conflicts in long-term relationships are inevitable, and the more interdependent two people are the more likely they are to have conflicts over shared resources, values, needs, and so on (Kelley et al., 1983; Wilmot, 1995). Thus, experts suggest one's communication goal should not necessarily be to end conflicts, but to learn to manage them effectively through conversational work (Guerrero, Andersen, & Afifi, 2018).

Most interpersonal conflict research is on married heterosexual couples. A particularly ineffective communication pattern of heterosexual marital conflict is the **demand/ withdrawal conflict pattern.** The partner who most wants a change demands (through requests, complaints, criticisms, coercion, or other forms of pressure), and the one who does not want that change withdraws (by changing the topic, avoiding eye contact, leaving the room, or just never doing as asked), resulting in a failure to resolve the conflict (Papp, Kouros, & Cummings, 2009). One behavior triggers the other, and soon the conflict escalates. For example, if Jo wants Bernie to stop playing the video game to talk, and Bernie does not want to, Bernie withdraws from Jo, and Jo makes more demands. This is an example of how conversational and relationship patterns of interaction are the work of both parties, even if the result is not positive.

Researchers repeatedly have found wives tend to demand (e.g., for closeness) and husbands tend to withdraw (e.g., Christensen, Eldridge, Catta-Preta, Lim, & Santagata, 2006; Gottman, 1994; Walker, 1999). Researchers link these findings to traditional gender roles. The woman demands because feminine relationship-orientation is toward talk and connection, and the man withdraws because he is socialized to value unilateral problem solving. Men are expected to be able to fix problems alone, and if a problem cannot be repaired, they may not see value in discussion (Tannen, 1990).

This explanation contains several flaws. First, the person who raises the topic tends to be the demander regardless of gender/sex in heterosexual and same-sex couples, and the one who withdraws may be exercising the power of the least-interested rather than, for example, because they cannot fix the problem (Baucom, Snyder, & Gordon, 2009; Holley, Sturm & Levinson, 2010). Researchers have found, regardless of the topic, individuals are more demanding for their own issues and withdraw more when it is their partner's issues (Papp et al., 2009). Second, the demand/withdrawal pattern is not likely to become an endless cycle if the two parties use more effective communication such as cooperation. Competitiveness and indirect fighting lead couples to get stuck in demand/withdrawal patterns (Heavey, Christensen, & Malamuth, 1995). Third, power can reside with the demander or the withdrawer, depending on the relationship. Parents and children display this pattern as well, with parents demanding more than children, regardless of the gender/sex of the parent. In this context, the one who has the most power is demanding (Caughlin & Ramey, 2005). Thus, the tendency to demand or withdraw during conflict is not consistently or innately tied to a person's gender/sex.

However, gender/sex can explain why heterosexual couples in distressed relationships over time seem to lock into stereotypical gender roles of wife demanding/husband withdrawing (Eldridge, Sevier, Jones, Atkins, & Christensen, 2007). People tend to adhere to rigid binary gender roles when there is stress in the relationship and, once adopted, these roles are difficult to change. Regardless of gender/sex, sexual orientation or relationship type, and which partner plays which role, falling into a pattern of demand/withdrawal can lead to negative emotions, lower levels of conflict resolution, spousal depression, break-ups, and what is known as common reciprocal domestic violence (Papp et al., 2009). To break the cycle, the partner who wants a change needs to step back, be patient, and avoid becoming aggressive or violent. The person who does not want the change needs to listen and try to understand the other's position. Thankfully these are skills people can learn, regardless of gender/sex.

Conversational Aggression

We cannot end this chapter without acknowledging that conversation can do harm to individuals and relationships, whether intentional or not. Some of that harm can result in physical and sexual violence. We use the phrase **conversational aggression** to recognize the multiple forms of verbal aggression people may use to inflict pain on another (Aloia & Solomon, 2017; Spitzberg, 2011). Verbal aggression refers to communication in which a person "uses language to attack the self-concept of a message recipient" (Aloia & Solomon, 2017, p. 1). Verbal aggression can include verbal attacks, blaming, and name-calling, but it does not include physical contact. Communication scholar Brian Spitzberg (2011) indicated verbal aggression does not require the receiver to perceive the behavior as hurtful nor does it require intentionality from the sender.

From a legal perspective, domestic or intimate partner violence is more severe than verbal aggression and includes a degree of intentionality. **Intimate partner violence,** also known as domestic violence, is harm to someone "in an ongoing interdependent or close relationship with the perpetrator" (Spitzberg, 2011, p. 328). It includes physical, psychological, and/or sexual abuse. Violence then is a subset of aggression. Violence almost always includes some form of aggression, but aggression does not always include violence.

Communication scholar Julia Wood (2006) observed, "An increasing number of researchers assert that intimate partner violence is a heavily gendered phenomenon . . . given the greater number of male perpetrators of intimate partner violence and the greater severity of their violence" (p. 402). Intimate partner violence is the most common form of violence against women in the United States; 28% to 50% of women experience physical, mental, emotional, and/or verbal abuse from an intimate partner (Catalano, 2012). About four in five reported victims of intimate-partner violence are female. Males are less likely to report or file charges (Catalano, 2012); some suggest it is because men have a harder time realizing and then admitting they are victims of domestic violence (Oliffe et al., 2014; Stiles-Shields & Carroll, 2015). The pervasiveness of violence in intimate relationships indicates it is a common part of the predominant culture. Violence likely exists in all forms of intimate relationships: queer, gay, lesbian, and heterosexual romantic partners, as well as siblings, parents, grandparents, and friends. Here, we focus on couple violence as tied to gender/sex.

People tend to assume all domestic violence is basically the same. Feminist scholars Joan Kelly and Michael Johnson (2008) were among the first to challenge this idea. They identified three types of domestic couple violence: coercive controlling violence, violent resistance, and situational couple violence.

Most early research focused on intense wife battering from husbands, which Kelly and Johnson called *coercive controlling violence* or *intimate terrorism*. Johnson (2006) suggested this type of violence is fed by traditional gender expectations that men should be the head of the household. This leads some men who feel they are not meeting this expectation to perform their masculinity through dominance and control. It has been tied to the demand/withdrawal conflict pattern (Olson, 2002). Coercive controlling violence generally combines physical abuse with verbal and emotional abuse, destroying the partner's self-esteem with repeated messages such as "No one else would have you," "You are worthless," "You are ugly," "What would you do without me?"—all comments that might boost the speaker's self-esteem by derogating the partner. Among heterosexual couples, the primary perpetrators are men, and misogyny and traditional gender roles are contributing factors (Johnson, 2011).

Johnson (2006) argued the cultural rhetoric of romance plays a powerful role in coercive controlling violence. Communication scholar Julia Wood (2001) discovered this link between abuse and romantic myths. Wood interviewed women from abusive relationships and found they were strongly invested in predominant heterosexual gender expectations and fairy-tale notions of romance. Many spoke of failing in their responsibilities as women to care for their partners, or they insisted the abuse was out of character for the Prince Charming who had originally swept them off their feet. They would not leave the relationships because they felt they needed men to feel complete. Wood (2001) and several masculinity studies scholars (Kimmel, 2012b; Messner, 2016) suggested men who batter their partners (gay or straight) are overly complying with cultural expectations of masculinity, even as they may profess to feel it is their responsibility as men to protect the ones they love.

Gay and lesbian couples report this type of domestic violence at similar or higher rates than heterosexual couples. This demonstrates the link between violence and gender is complex and that there are always other contributing influences, such as the social stress of being a sexual minority (Stiles-Shields & Carroll, 2015). For example, one qualitative study of gay men who had been victims of such violence revealed that some of the violence was about them engaging in masculinity competitions with their partners. Given gender is not the same as sexual orientation, it makes sense that gay men may experience hegemonic masculinity just as heterosexual men do, and violence may be a response when one's masculinity feels threatened (Oliffe et al., 2014). Similarly, there are lesbian, heterosexual, bisexual, and trans women who identify as highly masculine and may be more inclined toward violence (Baker, Buick, Kim, Moniz, & Nava, 2013). Some research suggested lesbian couples experience slightly less violence as compared to gay couples (e.g., Bartholomew, Regan, White, & Oram, 2008), but more research is needed.

What we do know is coercive controlling violence should not be understood as an aberration in an otherwise well-functioning relationship. Instead, it ought to be seen as a possible outcome of the cultural gendered/sexed pressures brought to bear on couples. Coercive controlling violence is not the result of inherent sex differences but of socialization practices that tend to socialize some people who identify strongly with a form of aggressive masculinity to see violence as a solution to problems.

A second type of domestic violence is *violent resistance* in which a person tries to protect themself by resisting the other's abuse. This type of domestic violence is not reported as often, but the resistance situation that receives the most media attention is women who murder their partners. In a study of women on trial for, or convicted of, attacking their intimate partner, the women reported frequent violent attacks from their partner, and most murders were not preplanned but took place during an attack from their partner (Ferraro, 2006). There is not enough research, however, to make any gender/sex claims regarding this type of violence (Spitzberg, 2011).

The third type of domestic violence is the most common form of aggression: *situational couple violence*. This type of violence is perpetrated by both partners in heterosexual or same-sex relationships, married or cohabitating. It is not typically tied to relationship-wide patterns of control and coercion. Either partner is likely to initiate the violence in specific situations; it does not seem influenced by gender expectations. Causes are more unique, such as observing one's partner flirting with another person or stress due to finances or concerns about children. The violence typically happens with less frequency and partners are not afraid of each other as in coercive controlling violence. In teen and young adult research, the women tended to initiate the violence against their partner more frequently than the men (Kelly & Johnson, 2008).

Not all domestic partner violence is the same. These distinctions are important because they prevent readers from overgeneralizing claims such as "only men abuse" or "women are violent only when abused." Men do tend to inflict more serious physical injuries when they are violent and participate in all the listed forms of domestic violence more than women. Violence is inflicted on women and other men (Kelly & Johnson, 2008).

Conclusion

Conversation is a primary means by which people and groups continually negotiate identities and relationships. Contrary to popular assumptions, any presumed gender differences in conversational style cannot be aligned with a person's sex. Stereotypical cultural expectations and perceptions of gender/sex behavior do have the potential to strongly influence how people do gender and construct group identities and inequalities through talk. But people also make choices of behaviors according to their goals in unique situations.

Because the construction and perceiving of gender are cultural, they are also potentially political. Understanding the power embedded in conversation helps answer the question of why differences rather than similarities are culturally emphasized. After reviewing a large volume of research on gender in communication, researcher Kathryn Dindia (2006) noted that with all the pressure for people to conform to different gender/sex expectations in communication styles, it is amazing how similar the sexes are in their communication. The similarities between women and men, and the variances among women and among men, offer evidence that differences are not innate or universal. Yet people still impose expectations on others based on perceived universal differences, so communication problems may emerge not from actual style differences in how people *do* talk but in different expectations of how people *supposedly* talk.

Individuals and groups must continually negotiate gender/sex tensions to assert their identities and specific communication goals in diverse cultural contexts. The selective use of feminine and masculine styles in politics, management, and cultures should help make clear that patterns of communication often emerge as a particular way to respond to a particular situation. However, as situations, people, and cultures change so, too, does the utility of the styles and their labels.

Thus, rather than asking whether a person's speech is feminine or masculine, we advise people to ask: What wide variety of ways of speaking allows each person to communicate more clearly, effectively, ethically, and humanely? Rather than asking how women and men communicate differently, researchers should explore how the range of gender options might be a resource for everyone, whether in interpersonal, group, or public settings.

KEY CONCEPTS

altercasting 58

conversation 58

conversation work 58

conversational aggression 70

conversational style 64

demand/withdrawal conflict pattern 69

direct communication 65

humor 60

identity work 58

indirect communication 65

intimate partner violence 70

politeness 59

rapport talk 64

relationship work 58

report talk 65

social support 68

swearing 62

vocal fry 57

DISCUSSION QUESTIONS

1. Why is it useful to study conversation?

2. Have you observed the construction of gender through conversations in classrooms? At work? In social groups? In church? In your family? Describe them.

3. Describe your own conversational style and ask a friend to describe it as well. Look for similarities and differences in your descriptions. Do either of you include assumptions about gender, ethnicity, or class? If so, which identity ingredients are noted and which are not? Why not? What can you learn from this activity about your gender identity and performance in conversation?

4. How might employing diverse gendered styles become a communication resource for individuals? What are examples of this?

CHAPTER 4

Gendered/Sexed Bodies

With the 2017 Australian Open, Serena Williams won 23 Grand Slam single titles, the most for any player in the Open era. Yet Maria Sharapova makes nearly twice as much in commercial endorsements. Why? Kareem Abdul-Jabbar (2015), six-time NBA champion, explained, "Because endorsements don't always reward the best athlete. They often reward the most presentable according to the Western cultural ideal of beauty." Despite Williams being arguably the greatest tennis player ever, people criticized Williams's body in ways "that perpetuate racist notions that black women are hypermasculine and unattractive. Imagine being asked to comment at a news conference before a tournament because the president of the Russian Tennis Federation . . . has described you and your sister as 'brothers' who are 'scary' to look at" (Rankine, 2015). Author Jenée Desmond-Harris (2016) reviewed the media coverage of Williams and found three themes: stereotypes that attributed Williams's success to race rather than hard work, sexualization of Williams's body's size and shape, and violent animalistic descriptions of William's strength.

The focus on Williams's body illustrates a range of points we make in this chapter. The body is political—a site of social contest where consumer markets, predominant cultural norms, and medical practices police the boundaries of appropriate behavior and appearance (Langman, 2008). Bodies are disciplined by norms of attractiveness, size, and appropriate movement. Perceptions of bodies are informed by intersections of sex, gender, ethnicity, religion, nationality, age, and ability. Embodied communication is a primary place for the doing of sex/gender.

We prefer the term **embodied communication**, instead of *nonverbal communication*, because it calls attention to the body in and as communication, specifically highlighting body politics, the disciplining of the body, and the body as a locus of agency. To explore embodied communication, we focus on three points. First, the body is political; the body is a powerful social tool in which intersectional identities and inequalities are created through performativity and objectification. Second, the body is disciplined through cultural norms about appearance, the use of space, and gendered movement. Third, bodies can be a locus of agency. Bodies not only are acted upon but also can act. We offer multiple examples of how people strategically use their bodies to resist the command performance of prescriptive gendered behaviors.

Body Politics

Although biology and ethnicity contribute to a wide variety of distinctive sizes and shapes of bodies, social norms constrain bodily forms and expressions and your very relationship to your body. People who identify as women are encouraged to be continually aware of their bodies as they prune, pose, provide sexual gratification, menstruate, give birth, and nurse children. People who identify as men tend to experience their bodies as a double bind: They dare not pay too much attention to their bodies for fear of appearing effeminate (Gill, Henwood, & McLean, 2005), but they must work to present their bodies in a masculine way or risk ridicule from appearing feminine. Gender studies professor Rosalind Gill (2017) noted how, in just a matter of years, men have joined women in what she calls the "body culture"—an obsession with shaping "the body beautiful":

> Look around at the pierced, tattooed, scarred, dyed, muscled bodies in any western urban environment and it seems clear that the look of the body is increasingly central to identity. . . . [W]e are experiencing a phenomenal fetishisation of muscles and muscularity among young men at precisely the moment that fewer than ever of them are working in traditionally male manual jobs that require physical strength. In fact, the man building muscles at the gym . . . is more likely to be working in an office than in heavy industry. Highly developed muscles have become semiotically divorced from the previous connotations of social class and manual labour. (Session 1)

Men, like women, increasingly define themselves through their bodies, and gay men tend to be more aware of this than straight men (Gill, 2017). For some time, men's bodies were barely (pun intended) noticed by critical researchers, but they are increasingly being used in advertising to sell products. Although men's poses differ from women's (Gill, 2017; Jhally, 2009), all tend to represent idealized young adult images of binary masculinity and femininity, and all are increasingly eroticized.

Men's bodies are the unspoken norm to which women's bodies often are compared and devalued (Weitz, 2017). Men are to be strong, women weak; men should be tall, women short; men should be substantial, women slender; men should be sexually aggressive, women passive. When men are presented as vulnerable (young, clean-shaven, soft-looking skin, big eyes), viewers notice because the image is playing against the macho gendered norm. The result is not just gendered/sexed bodies but a system that requires particular groups of bodies to dominate over other bodies (Lorber & Martin, 2011).

Gender Performativity

Doing gender involves a continuous process of identity negotiation through verbal and bodily communication (West & Zimmerman, 1987). In this chapter, we focus on philosopher Judith Butler's (2004) concept of **gender performativity** as the stylized repetition of acts. Butler's work built on doing gender to point out not only that people *do* gender in interaction, but also that the repeated style of interaction genders people.

Each person learns a script about how to act, move, and communicate gender. If gender is "a practice of improvisation within a scene of constraint" (Butler, 2004, p. 1), then it is a command cultural performance. Although some variation occurs, and gradual broadening of constraints is happening, it is always within set limits. Through the repetition of gendered behaviors over time, people continually construct and constrict their gender identities. Butler argued this is how binary genders and compulsory heterosexuality were formed. The repetition is largely guided by social expectations of dominant groups and habit, not free will.

We agree with Butler. People do not get up each morning and consciously decide how they will perform their gender that day. Instead, people internalize predominant cultural norms that gender their bodies. However, we also believe people are goal oriented, and they can play with gender performativity to challenge gender/sex norms.

Drag shows demonstrate that gender is a prescribed set of actions. In the staged performance of drag queens and kings (see Figure 4.1), the performers act in often exaggerated ways to appear as another sex as they sing, dance, model, or act on stage. By doing so, they challenge normative gender performances. The exaggerated performance of femininity opens up the possibility of questioning gender/sex prescriptions. When drag "mimics dominant forms of femininity" it can, at the same time, "produce and ratify alternative drag femininities that revel irony, sarcasm, inversion, and insult" (Halberstam, 2005, p. 130). Mimicking femininity is not the same as praise. At its core, doing drag recognizes the *performance* of gender.

Some people who are transitioning have commented on the need to *over-*perform their preferred gender while they seek public approval of their new identity

Figure 4.1 Drag Queen (Left) and Drag Kings (Right)

Sources: iStockphoto.com/karens4 and ZUMA Wire Service/Alamy.

(Zimman, 2012). They may have long identified internally as their desired gender/sex, but when they begin publicly to claim that identity, they may look to stereotypes on how to behave and pass. This is an initial phase in the process of settling into a newly claimed identity rather than a long-term ideal (Caroland, 2014).

Overt gender performance is not reserved for those who practice drag or trans identities. Sociologists Richard Majors and Janet Billson (1992) observed how some young African American men challenged racial stereotypes through the performance of a cool pose. Street pimps originally created the pose that included a specific stance, walk, posture, handshake, and speech pattern, which all suggested a relaxed, confident, and cocky masculinity. The walk was similar to a slow stroll, with parts of the body moving together. By posing, the men presented themselves as a spectacle of self-expression, detachment, and strength. Majors (2001) argued that many learned to use posing as a strategic tool to convey control and toughness when other resources of power and autonomy were not available to them. The pose has become more mainstream for some young African American men facing the intersecting threats of racism and homophobia in predominantly White universities (Harris, Palmer, & Struve, 2011). Their ritualized acts were directed at the dominant culture and other Black men to assert pride and masculine, heterosexual identity. However, others caution the pose may further prevent Black men from full participation by no longer passing in a privileged White masculine culture (Johnson, 2010).

The concept of performativity points out that when people internalize social expectations about gender tied to their body's sex, it becomes difficult for them to realize gender/sex expectations construct their gendered/sexed identities. Objectification theory explains a more specific way society disciplines the performance of gendered bodies.

Objectification

Objectification occurs when people are viewed as objects existing solely for the pleasure of the viewer, rather than as agents capable of action. The person being objectified often is reduced to body parts: breasts, genitalia, muscles, curves, buttocks, and hair. The person is no longer human but commodified—turned into a commodity like other inanimate products, free to be bought and fondled (even if only by others' eyes). **Self-objectification** occurs when people internalize the objectifier's view of their body and "participate in their own objectification" by seeking to exert a limited power linked to their ability to attract the gaze of others (Lynch, 2012, p. 3).

People who internalize objectification engage in heightened **body surveillance**; they critically look at and judge themselves. Objectified people's perceived physical and sexual attractiveness may become more important to them than their morality, honor, intellect, sense of humor, or kindness. Researchers have linked objectification to low self-esteem, depression, anxiety, disordered eating/eating disorders, muscle dysmorphia (obsession with building muscles), and suicide (Moradi & Huang, 2008; Travis, Meginnis, & Bardari, 2000), particularly for puberty-age children and teens (Grabe, Hyde, & Lindberg, 2007; Grogen, 2017; Tiggermann & Slater, 2013).

Researchers continue to identify women and girls, across ethnicity and race, as particularly vulnerable to objectification (Moradi & Huang, 2008; Ramsey & Hoyt,

2014; Velez, Campos, & Moradi, 2015). Sexual objectification has become a part of feminine gender socialization, as evidenced by some women's recollection of the first time they were sexually objectified and how that experience became a part of their identity growing up (Valenti, 2016). Sexual objectification does not come only from the gaze of strangers. In a study of heterosexual college women, several reported their boyfriends at times looked at their bodies in sexually objectifying ways, and those women reported feeling more sexual pressure from their partners (Ramsey & Hoyt, 2014).

Sexual objectification happens earlier and is more pervasive than you might think (Levin & Kilbourne, 2009). Beauty pageants, such as Dream Girls U.S.A. and Real Girls U.S.A., start at age 4; others start even younger. The Learning Channel (TLC) broadcast a highly successful reality show called *Toddlers and Tiaras* that followed young pageant competitors and their parents to competitions (Mirabello, 2009–2013, 2016). Television scholar and filmmaker Christina Hodel (2014) found that although "the negative aspects of child pageants is exaggerated" to "boost viewership with its shock value," the show did depict the sexualization of the youngsters through distinctive constructions of gender (p. 114). By studying the first five seasons, Hodel found "gender and identity is prescribed" to the girls in the show (p. 126).

Girls do not have to be in a beauty pageant to internalize sexualization. A study of 60 6- to 9-year-old girls in the Midwest found the girls chose a sexualized paper doll as their ideal self (68%) and the doll that would be popular (72%; Starr & Ferguson, 2012). Researcher Christy Starr said, "Although the desire to be popular is not uniquely female, the pressure to be sexy in order to be popular is" (cited in Abbasi, 2012, paras. 6–7). Not all the girls chose the sexualized doll as their ideal self: Girls who took dance classes, had maternal influences that did not self-objectify, had been taught to view media critically, and/or were raised with strong religious beliefs were more likely to choose the doll with more clothing as their ideal self.

Increasingly, men and boys are victims of sexual objectification (Davidson, Gervais, Canivez, & Cole, 2013; Moradi & Huang, 2008), but this tends to be less frequent (Harris, 2016) and is less likely to be internalized (Grabe et al., 2007; Grogen, 2017). Indicators of this trend are the growth in a $50 billion cosmetic market for men (Whipp, 2017), greater stigma for men perceived as fat (Monaghan, 2015), and hair transplants for balding heads (Shapiro, 2010). Men and masculinities scholar David Buchbinder (2013) argued a difference in men's self-objectification is that it is not for women's pleasure as much as it is to compete with other men.

Men who are members of oppressed groups due to race, ethnicity, and/or sexual orientation are most often the male

Figure 4.2 Eden Wood, from *Toddlers and Tiaras,* promotes her new LOGO docu-series *Eden's World*.

Source: Anthony Behar/Sipa Press (Sipa via AP Images).

Figure 4.3 Paper Dolls Used in Starr and Ferguson Study

Source: Starr & Ferguson (2012).

recipients of objectification (Teunis, 2007; Whitehead, 2002). The objectification marks them as not quite men, or certainly not as normative White fit men. The dominant White culture has a history of objectifying African American men's bodies, reducing them to being violent, sexual, aggressive, naturally talented, and athletic (Bordo, 1999; hooks, 1992; Jackson & Dangerfield, 2003). African American gay men may become sexual objects of desire by some White gay men because of the stereotype that they are endowed with larger penises, and Asian and Hispanic American men may be labeled exotic objects of sexual pursuit. When "the sexual objectification of men of colour forces them to play specific roles in sexual encounters that are not necessarily of their choosing" (Teunis, 2007, p. 263), gay communities uphold normative White masculine domination (McKeown, Nelson, Anderson, Low, & Elford, 2010).

The embodied performance of gender is far from natural. For more than 50 years, researchers have documented the negative effects of cultural norms that objectify bodies and command particular gendered performances. Bodies are disciplined to perform gender in particular ways.

Disciplining Gendered Bodies

Communication scholar John Sloop (2004) used the term **disciplining gender** to make visible the multiple ways in which people and cultures consciously and unconsciously maintain rigid norms of binary, heteronormative, and cisnormative gender performance. Common body practices, or signifiers, are so intertwined with gender expectations that it is difficult to recognize these are socially constructed practices. Sloop explained,

> Just as with a child's clothing and hairstyle, a single set of signifiers (gait, gestures, body movements, rough-and-tumble play, and the stance for urination) are used to illustrate masculinity and femininity in binary fashion regardless of whether gender is posited as a product of socialization or the materiality of the body, that is, its sex. In terms of gender culture, we clearly see . . . the signifiers that are employed in the judgments people make about one another and themselves in their evaluations of gender performance. . . . Heterosexuality is signified, indeed emphasized, as a norm in the performance of gender. (pp. 36, 40)

What follows are three examples of how heteronormativity disciplines the gendered body.

Attractiveness

People speak of natural beauty, but most human beauty is constructed, perceived, and regulated through a narrow cultural lens of what is defined as **gendered attractiveness**: normative physical appearance that is seen as pleasing, beautiful, and sexually appealing. The norm of attractiveness that merges beauty and sexuality "moves sexuality into the public realm . . . and thereby [makes it] amenable to inspection, definition, social monitoring, and control" (Travis et al., 2000, p. 239). People's sexualities are not private; through attractiveness norms, they become public, social property. Gendered attractiveness norms reinforce and privilege White heterosexual gender expectations and help maintain women as objects (Felski, 2006).

Attractiveness norms are maintained and changed through consumer markets. The dominance of Western capitalism and commercialization has imposed a narrow definition of attractiveness worldwide (Bordo, 2003). Consumers, particularly women, spend millions of dollars annually to buy cosmetics, diets, hair products, beauty advice, plastic surgeries, clothing, and accessories. The demand for beauty products continues to increase annually (see Figure 4.4).

Attractive Men

Feminist sociologists Judith Lorber and Patricia Yancey Moore (2007) described a "hot" man's body:

> In Western contemporary cultures, a sampling of popular images would suggest that the ideal male body is over six feet tall, 180 to 200 pounds, muscular, agile, with straight white teeth, a washboard stomach, six-pack abs, long legs, a full head of hair, a large penis (discretely shown by a bulge), broad shoulders and chest, strong muscular back, clean-shaven, healthy, and slightly tanned if White, or a lightish brown if Back or Hispanic. Asians . . . are rarely seen. (p. 114)

Size matters. Social norms dictate that attractive men are big—but muscular, not flabby. They are tall. Lorber and Martin (2011) noted, "We may say that intelligence

Figure 4.4   Revenue in the Cosmetics and Personal Care Market

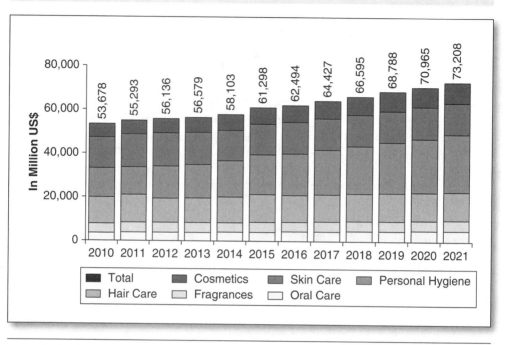

Source: Statista (2017).

and competence count for much more than physical appearance, but only a few presidents of the United States have been shorter than 6 feet tall, and research on corporations has shown that approximately 10% of a man's earnings can be accounted for by his height" (p. 282). Interpersonally, many women who marry men shorter than they are consciously choose to wear flat shoes on their wedding day to deemphasize their height. Men's studies scholar R. W. Connell (1995) explained the social significance of expecting men to be bigger than women: "Visions of hegemonic masculinity help to legitimize a patriarchy that guarantees the dominant physical position of men and subordination of women" (p. 77).

Consider the well-known G.I. Joe action figure (see Figure 4.5), who turned 50 in 2014. In its years on toy shelves, the doll's size has ballooned, from its 1960s life-size equivalent of 5′10″ tall (unchanged for 40 years) with biceps of 12″ and a chest of 44″ to 2011's biceps of 27″ and chest of 55″. Given these measurements, "GI Joe would sport larger biceps than any bodybuilder in history" (Pope, Olivardia, Gruber, & Borowiecki, 1999; see also Olivardia, Pope, Borowiecki, & Cohane, 2004). Barbie celebrates her 60th anniversary in 2019. The size did not change until 2016. If the original Barbie was life-size, it would have a height of 6′9″, with only a 20-inch waist but a 41-inch bust and she would not be able to stand up. The odds of a woman having these proportions are 1 out of 100,000 ("As G.I.," 1999; BBC, 2009).

When you compare current cultural norms of men's attractiveness to current cultural norms of women's attractiveness, an interesting insight emerges: As women are encouraged to become smaller, men are encouraged to become larger. Even as children, size matters. Shorter boys are bullied more (Voss & Mulligan, 2000).

Figure 4.5 G.I. Joe, 1964 (Left), and G.I. Joe, 1992 (Right)

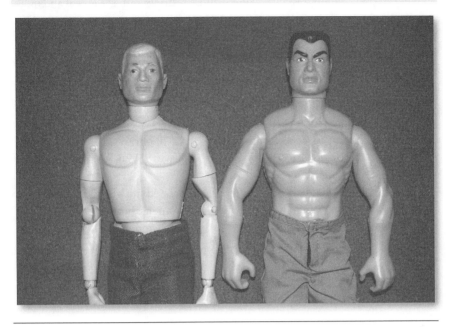

Source: Photograph by Catherine Palczewski. G.I. Joes from the collection of Tom Stewart.

Negative body image is affecting men in increasing numbers (Gill, 2017; Grogen, 2017). One study found the percentage of men dissatisfied with their overall appearance almost tripled in 25 years (to 43%), and the men reported being nearly as unhappy with how they look as women reported (Pope, Phillips, & Olivardia, 2000). Men are concerned about being underweight and lacking body muscularity. Muscle dysmorphia is a preoccupation with muscularity and the misperception of one's physique as small, often despite distinct muscularity and size (Pope, Gruber, Choi, Olivardia, & Phillips, 1997). This psychological disorder leads to compulsively working out, weight lifting, and rigid low-fat diets. The causes are attributed to increasing social pressures for boys and men to be large, muscular, and athletic: "For many men today, muscles—literally—make the man" (Olivardia, 2000, p. 11).

Some segments of the LGBTQ community have been identified as having greater tendencies toward eating disorders. The National Eating Disorders Association (n.d.) attributed this to multiple stressors, including coming out, threats of violence, and bullying. Some gay men report stressors similar to those heterosexual women report regarding making themselves attractive to men (Olivardia & Pope, 1997). The more a person's value is reduced to their sexual attractiveness, the more they are likely to engage in self-destructive practices.

Attractive Women

Cultural ideals of attractiveness are impossible to attain because they keep changing. In the 1910s and 1920s, when women entered the U.S. workforce in larger numbers and gained the right to vote, women's fashion trends seemed to counter this political progress by becoming more restrictive of movement and more revealing of the body. Sexual appeal became about external appearance, with short flapper-style dresses. Pale complexions, slender legs, narrow hips, and flat breasts were the ideal, causing many women to bind their breasts and shave their legs and armpits. In the 1950s, Marilyn Monroe became a beauty icon. As the first woman to be featured naked in *Playboy*, Monroe exhibited breasts and hips that became sexy. Her size 12 is considered large by today's beauty standards. The ideal woman's body type has become increasingly thinner, both in reality and as a result of photo alteration. According to advertising analyst Jean Kilbourne (2010), only 5% of today's women fit the preferred body type, which leaves 95% of women wondering what is wrong with their bodies.

The thin, White, blonde Barbie doll physique dressed in tight-fitting, revealing clothing captures predominant expectations of women's beauty. In a survey of 4,000 people, results echoed this narrow definition (Brumbaugh & Wood, 2009). This beauty ideal is normative, even though it is not the norm. The White upper-class ideal of beauty is impossible for most women, but the ideal particularly disciplines women who have disabilities, darker skin, larger bodies, kinky hair, or limited money (Gerschick & Miller, 2004; Kramer, 2005; Lorber & Martin, 2011; Shapiro, 2010).

Body size, especially for girls and women, tends to affect popularity (Parker-Poke, 2008), employment, and pay (Levine & Schweitzer, 2015). Women who do not comply with social demands regarding beauty regularly experience humiliation, harassment, and discrimination. They are called lazy, mentally ill, unfeminine, and asexual (Lorber & Martin, 2011; Travis et al., 2000). In acknowledgment that Barbie is not the norm and stirred by slumping sales, Mattel redesigned the dolls to look more like the kids who play with them (Abrams, 2016). Barbie is now available in tall, petite, and curvy as well as a variety of ethnicities.

A clear indication that women's attractiveness is a social construction is apparent when comparing Western ideals to other cultures' traditional notions of beauty. Azawagh Arabs of Niger defined ideal femininity as extreme fatness (Popenoe, 2004). Latinx and African American cultures traditionally defined larger-sized women as voluptuous and physically and emotionally strong (Patton, 2006). Traditional Asian Hmong culture valued sturdy women who could work hard, making larger waists and hips attractive. But Hmong immigrants in the United States are assimilating to Western notions of thinness (Lynch, 1999).

White skin, round eyes, and thin bodies are now markers of social status around the world. In a study of 3,300 females from 10 countries, aged 15 to 64, 90% said they would like to change at least one thing about their bodies. Most wanted to lose weight, and 67% said they withdrew from life-sustaining activities because of their perceived bodily flaw (Etcoff, Orbach, Scott, & D'Agostino, 2004). Women and girls' body anxiety has become a global problem (Calogero, Boroughs, & Thompson, 2007). Skin-whitening products, plastic surgeries, and weight reduction are believed to help women's earning potential and marital prospects in countries such as Hong Kong, India, Japan, and South Korea (Glenn, 2008; Li, Min, Belk, Kimura, & Bahl, 2008).

Figure 4.6 Barbie's Redesign

Source: Barbie®.

The message is clear: The natural body is sick or unacceptable, and altering feminine bodies through products or surgery is the way to fix it. Western beauty ideals have become a tool to colonize women around the world (Hegde, 1995).

Clothing

Beyond protecting you from the elements, clothing constructs personal and group identities. Researchers in textiles and apparel understand clothing as an overt form of gender performance (Lynch & Strauss, 2007). Given Butler's (1990a) description of gender performance as operating in a scene of constraint, how you clothe yourself is not necessarily freely chosen. Even though you may choose what to wear each day, the closet you choose from likely has a limited range of gendered options. Western clothing designated for girls and women tends to be restrictive, following the contours of the body. Men's clothing tends to be loose fitting, has practical pockets, and allows movement.

Sociologist Ruth Rubinstein (2001) argued that gendered clothing reinforces heteronormative gender/sex differences in society when it serves to "alert an approaching individual about suitability for sexual intercourse" (p. 103). When you are socialized into wearing binary clothing, you perform your gender/sex and sexual identity through apparel.

Clothing's maintenance of binary gender and sexuality becomes more obvious at Halloween. In a study observing 828 students' costumes on a state university campus, researchers found women were three times more likely to dress sexually, and men were three times more likely to dress comically or scarily. They concluded, "Although Halloween is a time when the imagination can run wild and people can engage in extreme forms of self-presentation, the young men and women in this study choose to address gender, as opposed to other aspects of the construction of self" (MacMillan, Lynch, & Bradley, 2011, p. E23).

The continued disciplining of gender attractiveness through dress is apparent in responses to cross-dressing and some trans people. People in the United States tend to be uncomfortable with and ridicule cross-dressers because they do not conform to the norm. Transgender youth are heavily bullied in school (Gattis & McKinnon, 2015), likely in large part because of their clothing. Why does the vision of anyone other than a person assigned female at birth in a skirt make some people uncomfortable? In many places, men wear skirts in the form of kilts, sarongs, caftans, or djellabas. Ridicule is an indication of the disciplining power of clothing to dictate social norms for gender/sex and sexual orientation.

Fashions change and with them gender transformations occur because "fashion allows us to embody our desire, buy our identity, in the most intimate sense and the most linked to the performance of everyday life" (Lynch & Strauss, 2007, p. 120). Women no longer have to cover their ankles as they did prior to the invention of bicycles in the 1890s. Unisex clothing—known for its loose fitting, comfortable style, in neutral black, white, and gray colors, and designed not to call attention to binary gender/sex—has been available in the United States since the 1960s. The T-shirt and jeans popular for casual U.S. dress is an example even though most do not see it as unisex. More clothing companies have begun to advertise (and make money) from "gender fluid" looks (Sharkey, 2016).

Figure 4.7 Jaden Smith in *Vogue Korea 01*

Celebrities seem to be given more flexibility with clothing. Entertainer Jaden Smith has received mixed reviews for wearing dresses (Abeydeera, 2016; Goldstein, 2016). Smith is a self-identified 17-year-old African American heterosexual man. Megan Mapes (2016) suggested his celebrity status, youth, and the unique ways in which he combines masculine (bare-chest and crossed arms) and feminine (flower, head tilt, and skirt) fashion enable him to push back on rigid expectations for African American men's dress: "His character as the carefree black boy seems like a reaction to the cool but hypermasculine and hypersexualized black man" image (p. 15–16).

As some gendered distinctions in dress are challenged or disappear, others reappear. Women's stiletto high-heel shoes, a marker of sexiness, are still popular, even though they are more restrictive and harmful than flat shoes (Peck, 2016). For women in higher status positions in law, finance, administration, and consulting, they are expected. One attorney explained: "Everybody wears heels. . . . It's just a convention. It's like wearing a tie" (Meya Laraqui as cited in Peck, 2016). Neckties remain a requirement for men in most formal and semiformal situations, but while uncomfortable, they do not risk injury or exaggerate sex-specific traits of the male body. In contrast, "placed atop those teetering spikes, a woman's butt and breasts jut out just so" (Peck, 2016) and researchers found "high heels exaggerate sex specific aspects of female gait" (Morris, White, Morrison, & Fisher, 2013, p. 176).

Embodied Space

Embodied space refers to the holistic way in which people experience their bodies in physical spaces, often in relation to others (Low, 2003). The study of embodied space is referred to as **proxemics**, the analysis of the invisible area around a person that is considered their private territory (Hall, 1966). The size of personal space with which a person feels comfortable varies greatly by culture, situation, status, and type of relationship (Hall, 1966). In general, people from what are called *contact cultures* (e.g., South American, Middle Eastern, southern European) tend to stand or sit close together, hold hands with friends, and touch frequently. People from noncontact cultures (e.g., North American, European, Japanese) tend to maintain more space and touch less (Low, 2003).

In the United States, taking up personal space with your body, gestures, or property is commonly associated with unspoken claims of power and status. Who is permitted to invade another's space also can reveal intimate relations and/or power differentials (Khan & Kamal, 2010).

Feminists recently coined the term *manspreading* to recognize the tendency of many men to spread their legs widely apart and take up more than their fair share

Figure 4.8 Manspreading on Public Transport

of space in public transit (Burchette, 2017). Conversely, heightened awareness of the body as an object for others' observations has explained some women's discomfort in taking up space around others (Kwan, 2010). While large, muscular men are rarely judged as taking up space illegitimately, women and men considered obese are (Buchbinder, 2013).

Obviously, the relative size of your body influences the amount of personal space you take. Thus, the cultural norm that masculinity be signaled by more muscular and taller bodies makes the larger use of space more legitimate for men, even if many men are not larger than many women. Great variances in size among women and among men exist, but social expectations persist. For example, from the 1950s to 1990s, U.S. doctors prescribed the sex hormone synthetic oestrogen to treat what was called an "abnormality of tall stature in females" (Rayner, Pyett, & Astbury, 2010, p. 1076). Although there is no evidence to suggest tallness hurts women's health or reproductive ability, tallness was diagnosed as a psychological threat.

Women and men with large, less muscular bodies experience discrimination from what sociologist Samantha Kwan (2010) called **body privilege**: "an invisible package of unearned assets that thin . . . individuals can take for granted on a daily basis" as they navigate public space in their daily life (p. 147). Critical studies scholar Samantha Murray (2008) argued that fatness has become gendered; men who are seen as fat are feminized. Their masculinity is stripped away from them, meaning they cannot be fat and manly, too. In interviews with 42 overweight women and men, participants noted discrimination and humiliation when doing such basic things as trying to sit in classroom chairs, buying clothing, ordering food, and publicly enjoying food. White and Hispanic women seemed to especially internalize these negative experiences.

Given that women tend to be disciplined more severely for how they look, it is no surprise obese women report being the target of frequent ridicule from strangers and acquaintances alike. In a critical review of research, Janna Fikkan and Ester Rothblum (2012) found discrimination against obese women, and particularly obese poor women and women of color, exists in workplaces, education, health care, media representations, and opportunities for romantic relationships.

Taking up physical space with your body can be gender inclusive and has psychological advantages. **Power posing** occurs when a person adopts a stronger, more spread out posture that is often associated with masculinity. Psychological evidence suggested that such poses act on innate physiological mechanisms to increase self-confidence (Cuddy, Wilmuth, Yap, & Carney, 2015), willingness to take risks (Carney, Cuddy, & Yap, 2010), and positive peer ratings (Carney, Hall, & Smith LeBeau, 2005). Cuddy et al. (2015) found that men and women who adopted a power pose for two minutes before going into a job interview were rated as more competent and confident by the interviewer, who had no knowledge of their power posing prior to the interview. This effect was found after accounting for the gender and ethnicity of the interviewer and interviewee. Taking up space during the interview was not what helped the applicant; how they prepared with their mind and body prior to the interview gave them more confidence.

Embodied Movement

Embodied movement refers to how people ambulate, flow, travel, move in their bodies in daily life, and feel their movement. It includes your demeanor, which sociologist Nancy Henley (1977) defined as how you physically carry yourself. People tend to think of demeanor as something unique to an individual, but Henley (1977) pointed out that demeanor can have gender/sex and power/status attributions. Sociologist Erving Goffman (1963) found that demeanor can be used to mark upper and lower status and that higher-status persons tend to have more latitude in their behavior. They may carry their bodies more loosely. Persons of lower status may be tighter or more attentive to their physical demeanor. Philosopher Iris Marion Young (1990) observed how this might affect some girls' movements:

> walking like a girl, tilting her head like a girl, standing and sitting like a girl, gesturing like a girl, and so on. The girl learns actively to hamper her movements. She is told that she must be careful not to get hurt, not to get dirty, not to tear her clothes, that the things she desires are dangerous for her. Thus she develops a bodily timidity that increases with age. (p. 154)

Bodies are disciplined to conform to gendered expectations. The disciplining often happens in seemingly innocent messages of encouragement. Boys are told to "man up," meaning "don't be a pussy, brave it, be daring," put your body in harm's way (Urban Dictionary, n.d.). And boys and girls are told, "Don't throw like a girl," making the point that the worst athlete is one whose demeanor is feminine.

The social importance of this phrase is further demonstrated by academic research. In 1966, psychologist Erwin Straus examined a series of photographs of young girls and boys throwing baseballs and was struck by the perceived differences in how they used space and motion:

> The girl of five does not make any use of lateral space. She does not stretch her arm sideward; she does not twist her trunk; she does not move her legs, which remain side by side. . . . A boy of the same age, when preparing to throw, stretches his right arm sideward and backward; supinates the forearm; twists, turns and bends his trunk; and moves his right foot backward. From this stance, he can support his throwing almost with the full strength of his total motorium. (pp. 157–160)

In an attempt to explain these differences, Straus considered biological origins, but the children had not reached puberty so possible sex differences in muscle mass and bone size were not likely, and the girls did not have breasts that might inhibit their throwing. Straus had to dismiss the idea that the girls were simply weaker, because a weaker person would likely throw the whole body into the movement to compensate. Instead, Straus concluded that the difference in style came from a "feminine attitude." Straus did not consider the possibility that the boys had been taught to throw and the girls had not, or that girls who throw like a boy may be ridiculed as unfeminine tomboys, and boys who throw like girls often are ridiculed as feminine and gay.

Twenty-four years after Straus's work, Iris Young (1990) examined what it meant to "throw like a girl." Young compared the assumption of gender/sex differences in throwing to other presumed gender/sex differences in body movement to make clear children are taught how to move.

> Not only is there a typical style of throwing like a girl, but there is a more or less typical style of running like a girl, climbing like a girl, swinging like a girl, hitting like a girl. They have in common first that the whole body is not put into fluid and directed motion, but rather . . . the motion is concentrated in one body part; and . . . tend not to reach, extend, lean, stretch, and follow through in the direction of her intention. (p. 146)

While current generations of girls are challenging Young's description of gendered expectations, the key point is that people tend to experience their bodies in uniquely gendered/sexed ways. Many girls and women experience their bodies in more guarded ways than boys and men because of how they are *taught* to use and relate to their bodies.

Figure 4.9   U.S. Softball Olympian Jennie Finch's Book *Throw Like a Girl* (Triumph Books)

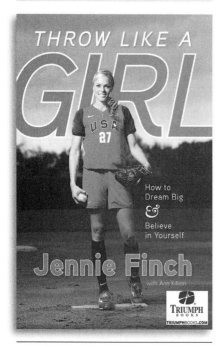

Source: Jennie Finch's *Throw Like a Girl: How to Dream Big and Believe in Yourself* (9781600785603) was published by Triumph Books.

What does it now mean to "throw like a girl"? Traditionally it was a criticism, meaning the person threw with little force. Recently, the meaning was resignified as girls and women came into their own successes in competitive sports and displayed "throw like a girl" and "I am one" on T-shirts as a badge of honor (see Figures 4.9, 4.10, and 4.11).

Masculinities scholars observed that most men do not experience their bodies in the guarded way girls and women tend to (Buchbinder, 2013; Forth, 2008; Whitehead, 2002). In fact, boys are taught that their bodies are to be used and abused. Stephen Whitehead (2002) described masculine bodily experiences: "The male/boy/man is expected to . . . place his body in aggressive motion . . . in so doing posturing to self and others the assuredness of his masculinity" (p. 189). Social norms of masculinity encourage boys and men to physically exert their bodies to extremes. Men's studies scholar David Buchbinder (2013) explained the demands placed on men's bodies:

> Traditionally women have been constructed as coextensive with their bodies (they are bodies), whereas men are deemed to *use* their bodies. . . . [T]he motto, "No gain without pain" makes explicit the secondary and subordinate nature of the body. Even where the aim is the enhancement . . . of the body itself, the [man's] body must be subjected to a rigorous discipline in the cause of achieving an idealized goal outside and beyond it. (p. 123)

Figure 4.10   Erin DiMeglio, the first girl to play high school quarterback in the state of Florida, warmed up before a preseason game on August 24, 2012, and showed that throwing like a girl can be strong, accurate, and powerful.

Figure 4.11   Megan Schachterle at age 11, a softball pitcher from Iowa. She opened her body widely and grunted every time she pitched. Megan took "you throw like a girl" as a compliment.

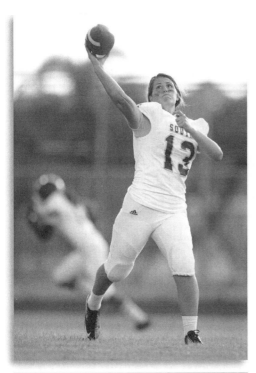

Source: Jim Rassol/Sun Sentinel/MCT via Getty Images.

Source: Victoria DeFrancisco.

The social significance placed on men's bodies as large, strong, and agile influences many men's gender identities (Connell, 1995). While there is increasing recognition of embodied gender diversity, Whitehead (2002) noted, "We should not allow the exceptions to deny the differing realities of the lived experiences of most women's and men's bodily existence" (p. 190). Social pressure to conform to gendered embodied movement persists.

Refusing the Command Performance

People push at the disciplinary norms placed on bodies. That pushing by individuals and groups helps propel social change. The very tools used to discipline people's bodies also can be used to challenge these restrictions. Ways of **refusing the command performance** include using norms against each other, making norms visible, overtly challenging norms, and revaluing the body.

To explore the multiple ways people resist and change the command performance, we first introduce the concept of agency. Even as people use embodied communication to differentiate and oppress, people also can be agents and use the body to bring about self-empowerment and social change. We then turn to specific strategies people use to challenge the constraints within which they improvise.

Agency

Even in the face of social constraints on gendered bodies, people exert agency in diverse ways. **Agency** is the ability to act or the degree to which people can control their experience or identities in a given situation through creative communication strategies and/or the manipulation of contextual circumstances (Campbell, 2005). People are not helpless; even people in oppressed groups find ways to survive, make needed changes, and gain some control over their own destiny (Scott, 1992). Resistance is not easy, and only a fine line separates actions that exert individual agency and those that comply with cultural pressures to conform. For example, do men who body build constitute agents in control of their own bodies? Do breast cancer survivors who have had mastectomies and opt for breast implants show self-empowerment? As gender/sex is reiterated through performance, the reiteration also creates "gaps and fissures," instabilities and something that "escapes or exceeds the norm," that allow agency and resistance of the command performance (Butler, 1993, p. xix). No repetition is a perfect reproduction of gendered body expectations. These seeming imperfections provide avenues for oppositional performance, or what Judith Butler (1993) called "working the weakness in the norm" (p. 237).

Using Norms Against Each Other

One of the most traditional norms about women's bodies is that of being a mother. Over time and across cultures, women have used the role of mother as their foundation for public advocacy. They manipulate the expectations of being caretakers to seek social justice. The Mothers of Plaza de Mayo formed in 1977 to protest the "disappearance" of their children under the repressive military regime that ruled Argentina from 1976 to 1983. Communication scholar Valeria Fabj (1993) explained that a verbal response by men was not possible because the society was repressive, yet women as mothers were valued and could protest the state's murder of their grown children. Wearing their children's cloth diapers as headscarves (embroidered with the children's names and dates of disappearance) and carrying pictures of their disappeared children, the mothers marched around the

Figure 4.12 Mothers of Plaza de Mayo plead their case with men politicians in 1977.

Source: Presidencia de la Nación Argentina.

Figure 4.13 Mothers of Plaza de Mayo protest in 2006.

Source: Photo by Roblespepe.

plaza at a time when public protest was prohibited. Fabj argued it was the very "myth of motherhood," the social beliefs attached to the women's bodies, that allowed them "to draw from their private experiences in order to gain a political voice, discover eloquent symbols, and yet remain relatively safe at a time when all political dissent was prohibited" (p. 2).

Because they were fulfilling social expectations attached to devoted motherhood, they were able to violate social and legal norms when men could not. In a situation where verbal argument was not an option, embodied communication linked to women's traditional role was necessary.

In Nigeria, women also used the threat of their public bodies as a form of silent protest. From July 2002 to February 2003, thousands of Nigerian women ranging in age from 30 to 80 peacefully seized Chevron-Texaco's terminals, airstrip, docks, and stores, disrupting oil production (Agbese, 2003; Turner & Brownhill, 2004). The women demanded jobs for their sons, schools, scholarships, hospitals, water, electricity, and environmental protection. They wanted some of the wealth being pumped out of the ground to be pumped back into their communities. As part of the protests, a group of women threatened public nudity if their demands were not met, an act that was culturally understood to shame men. The women explained, "Our nakedness is our weapon" (quoted in Wysham, 2002).

Nigerian and Argentinian women used social norms and prohibitions to pressure those in power to meet with them and meet their demands. The social norms demanding that women be good mothers were used to violate other social norms. When social norms concerning how one should be in one's body contradict or conflict, as in the earlier examples, the gaps and fissures that emerge can be productive places to explore new ways to be in one's body.

Making Norms Visible

The Guerrilla Girls, a New York–based group formed to protest the exclusion of women from the art world, employ the tactic of "zap actions"—placing posters around New York City (Demo, 2000). Their first action was in 1985 and focused on the absence of women in the major museums and galleries in New York. "Using mass-media techniques and advertising world savvy" (Guerrilla Girls, 1995, p. 10), they quickly gained notoriety.

Their emblematic poster, which appeared in 1989 on buses in lower Manhattan, refigured Ingres's *Odalisque*,

> a reclining figure whose sinuous nude back and hips have long stood for idealized female beauty. Rather than meeting the classical profile of Ingres' original, however, our eyes confront a large shaggy gorilla head, mouth open, teeth glistening. Twisted to meet us eye to eye, it challenges instead of seducing. (Guerrilla Girls, 1995, p. 7)

Challenging the objectification of women's bodies and positioning women as artists, the poster made visible the naked body of a real woman, challenging the

Figure 4.14   Guerrilla Girls 1989 Poster

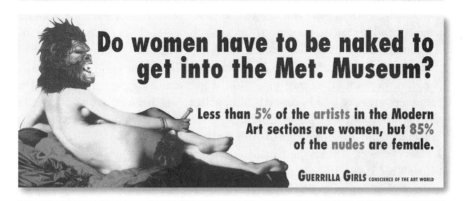

fetishized, artistically rendered bodies in museums. It refigured what it means for women to be present, and it blocked the ability of museum defenders to claim that women are present as more than bodies on canvases (Demo, 2000). The poster made visible the norm of women as objectified bodies even as the alternative of women's bodies as artists was offered (see Figure 4.14).

Communication scholar Bonnie Dow (2003) analyzed feminists' protest against the 1968 Miss America Pageant, which made the extreme social expectations of women's attractiveness visible. Women threw into trash cans bras as well as "girdles, high heels, cosmetics, eyelash curlers, wigs, issues of *Cosmopolitan, Playboy,* and *Ladies Home Journal*—what feminists termed 'instruments of torture' to women" (pp. 130–131). Although media coverage of the event referred to bra burning, *no bras were burned.*

This event provides an interesting example of how those who attempt to make oppressions visible often are disciplined. Dow explained how, in a society obsessed with breasts, the false claim of bra burning was a way of sexualizing and trivializing the women's demands. For example, 2 years after the protests, Senator Jennings Randolph described feminists as "braless bubbleheads" in his response to the Women's Strike for Equality in 1970 (as cited in Dow, 2003, p. 130). More than 35 years after this initial protest, it is clear that many of the women's movements' challenges to attractiveness have taken hold (girdles, anyone?) even as new norms have replaced them (breast implants, anyone?).

Overtly Challenging Norms

The sex binary is a norm that organizes and codes bodies: Discrete clothing exists for women *or* men, and prohibitions restrict women's bodies from participating in events that are reserved for men's bodies. In 1967, Kathrine Switzer became the first woman to run the Boston Marathon and overtly challenged the norm that marathons were only for men. When signing up for the race, Switzer used only the initial K, and the application was accepted. After the race started, the race director realized a woman was running, and jumped off a press bus and tried to rip off Switzer's race bib: #261. In response, the male runners around Switzer blocked the race official, and Switzer was able to complete the race. To celebrate this norm breaking, Switzer ran the marathon (for the ninth time) in 2017, at age 70 (breaking another norm about aged bodies), and the race retired #261 (Lyons, 2017).

The sex binary norm also is "reflected in our built environment" (Herman, 2013, p. 65) in the form of separate public toilets for women *or* men. In most homes, bathrooms are used by all sexes; it is just public toilets that tend to be separated as *men's* or *women's*. Public policy scholar Jody Herman (2013) noted "the concept of gender that underlies the design of these facilities ignores people who do not fit into a binary gender scheme, particularly transgender and gender non-conforming people" (p. 65).

In most of Europe, public bathrooms (often called toilets) are traditionally gender inclusive. The sex-segregated bathroom is neither natural nor the only way to organize public spaces. Instead, "sex-segregated public toilets are a thoroughly modern invention" (West, 2014, p. 61). The segregation of U.S. public bathrooms can be traced to the Victorian notion that men and women should inhabit different spheres and, thus, different physical locations. Separate spaces were supposedly "safe spaces ... tucked in a world in which women were vulnerable" (Gerson, 2016). Not until the late 1800s did U.S. law require separate public bathrooms; but by 1920, 40 states had mandated that bathrooms be segregated by sex.

Much as Victorian society grappled with changing gender/sex roles, so, too, does contemporary U.S. society. Current consternation over gender/sex roles may explain why society is "experiencing a resurgence of paternalist concern about women's sexual vulnerability.... [I]t is no surprise that there would also be a new emphasis on the Victorian phenomenon of separate restrooms" (Gerson, 2016). A *New Yorker* article asked a series of interesting questions:

> Today, men and women, not assumed to be only heterosexual, are expected to function at work alongside one another, eat at adjacent seats in restaurants, sit cheek by jowl in buses and airplanes, take classes, study in libraries, and, with some exceptions, even pray together. Why is the multi-stall bathroom the last public vestige of gendered social separation? When men, gay or straight, can stand shoulder to shoulder at urinals without a second thought, is there much to back up the view that men and women must not pee or poop next to one another, especially if closed stalls would shield them from view? Women may have some distinctive sanitation needs, but why does that require a wholly separate space from men? (Gerson, 2016)

The answer: "Perhaps the point is precisely that the public restroom is the only everyday social institution remaining in which separation by gender is the norm, and undoing that separation would feel like the last shot in the 'war on gender' itself" (Gerson, 2016).

Although toilets might seem like an odd location to overtly challenge norms that organize bodies, the reality is that they have long been central in struggles for equality. In a comprehensive analysis of the 1980s debates over the Equal Rights Amendment, political scientist Jane Mansbridge (1986) noted how the specter of unisex toilets "fed the fervor of the anti-ERA forces by giving them something absolutely outrageous to focus on" (p. 113): Unisex toilets played on fears of predatory rapists, symbolized the stripping away of special protections for women, and reminded White audiences of the racial integration of toilets. Communication scholar Isaac West (2014) noted that even though polling indicated the "'potty issue' may not have been decisive in the defeat of the ERA," the mere fact that it was an issue "speaks to gendered and racialized anxieties associated with public restrooms" (p. 63).

These anxieties show concern for the wrong group. Ciswomen are not at risk in restrooms; trans people are. The statistics are clear: A trans person has never assaulted someone in a bathroom (Maza & Brinker, 2014); however, cismen and ciswomen have harassed 70% of trans people using public restrooms (Herman, 2013).

People in Search of Safe and Accessible Restrooms (PISSAR) is "a genderqueer and disability coalition composed of college students and staff dedicated to providing safe and accessible bathrooms" for nonbinary people, families, and people with disabilities and their attendants. They first overtly challenged the norm of sex-segregated public restrooms at the University of California-Santa Barbara (West, 2014, p. 68). PISSAR engaged in patrols, composed of three members of varying gender identities and able-bodiedness, during which they assessed bathrooms' accessibility to disabled people, gender safety, supply of tampons and pads, and whether changing tables were present.

A number of states have enacted "bathroom bills." Kansas and North Carolina require a person to use the public bathroom that corresponds to the sex marked on their birth certificate. Public bathrooms include "public K–12 schools, state colleges and universities, parks and historic sites, some hospitals and airports, libraries, state and county courthouses and offices buildings, and more" (Maurer, 2017). On May 13, 2016, the Obama administration offered a federal government interpretation of Title IX that advised public schools that they must allow transgender students to use bathrooms that correspond with their gender identity. Dozens of states filed lawsuits against the administration (Beech, 2016) and, in February 2017, the Trump administration rescinded that presidential directive (Kohli, 2017).

As actor and activist George Takei (2017) recently tweeted, "It's not about bathrooms . . . as it was never about water fountains [in race segregation]." Cisgender people in the United States typically take bathroom access for granted when out in public. For those who are transgender, "using a restroom is a major safety concern and a daily struggle" (Maurer, 2017; see also Herman, 2013). It might take some political imagination for cisgender folks to understand this: Would you be able to make it through a school day, or a work shift, or shopping at a mall if you did not have access to a bathroom? Would you go out in public as much? How much effort would have to go into planning your daily activities? Scholar Luca Maurer (2017), coauthor of *The Teaching Transgender Toolkit*, argued "bathroom bills" are not about bathrooms at all. It is about whether transgender people will be fully recognized as human beings or banished from the public sphere.

During other periods of American history, the focus of who is granted full humanity, who is deemed worthy of dignity and respect, has rested squarely on allowing or denying access to public facilities. History contains other examples of public restrooms as a focus of oppression and legislation against marginalized groups. Segregation, discussions to move forward the ERA and the Americans with Disabilities Act, attempts to curtail people living with HIV from society—all have been times when laws carved out access for some to have the right to use public facilities, while others did not. (para. 6)

Overtly challenging gender/sex norms requires people to literally put their bodies on the line. The resistance they experience can reveal a great deal about how invested the dominant culture is in established norms.

Revaluing the Body

Cultural norms dictate that an attractive person should be able-bodied and neurotypical. That criteria eliminates 32.4% of the adult population (CDC, 2017b), who have some physical disability, and 18.5% of the adult population, who experience mental illness in a given year (National Alliance on Mental Illness, 2017). The linkage of able-bodiedness and neurotypicality to attractiveness is particularly injurious to those whose challenges are visible even when doing seemingly simple things such as eating, walking, and controlling defecation.

When mundane bodily tasks are a challenge, imagine the challenge rigid notions of femininity and masculinity impose. Women who go through mastectomies must find new ways of valuing their bodies as feminine, whether they choose reconstructive surgery or not. Men who use wheelchairs must find new ways of valuing their bodies as masculine in ways not tied to physical strength. Communication studies scholar Julie-Ann Scott (2014) explained, "In U.S. patriarchal culture, the physically disabled man body is often feminized, seen as incapable of autonomy, bodily strength and aggressiveness associated with dominant Western Masculinity."

Exploring how the embodied experience of disability is gendered, Scott (2014) interviewed 14 men living with physical disabilities. Scott found a range of masculine gender identities: "mourning, resisting, accepting, and/or embracing their daily performances of physically disabled masculinity." One person Scott interviewed named Kale performed resistance to the stereotype that a person with a disability is asexual:

This guy, we work together and have for awhile. And one day out of the blue he asks, "Who is the semi-attractive woman with you all the time? Is that your nurse?" And I said, "No ha, ASSHOLE, that's my wife." She comes and meets me for lunch some days.

Kale revalued the body with a disability as a body with sexuality.

Bodies with disability also enable a revaluing of masculinity. Herman accepted his disability and noticed a shift in his gender identity. Before his accident, he

"embodied dominant cultural expectations of masculinity and personal autonomy."
He described his relationship with his wife:

> Well I was a real redneck. (laugh). A guy's guy you know. It's easier to talk with
> each other [now]. She never was a partier and I was and I actually probably
> respect her more now. . . . The relationship is . . . deeper now. (as cited in
> Scott, 2014)

Although no one right way to negotiate disability and gender identities exists,
Herman and another man named Travis "embrace diminished autonomy, force and
intimidation and a personal performance of a 'softer man' rather than resisting the
change to their bodies" (Scott, 2014). Travis said his new identity has allowed him
to work more collaboratively with others and not engage in the constant power
struggles he fought before his life changed.

Conclusion

For every norm concerning embodied communication, locations of resistance
arise. Yet that resistance will face a response. Although the Mothers of Plaza de
Mayo faced fewer reprisals than other activists, the government punished many
of them. Although the Guerrilla Girls have been active for over 30 years, women
continue to be underrepresented in major galleries and museums. Although
dress standards have changed remarkably in the last 100 years, the range of individual expression regarding dress really is quite limited (look around your classroom if you are unconvinced). Even as the most marginal of bodies are made
visible, that does not mean they are accepted. Even if one recognizes that bodies'
performances of gender are not natural, that does not mean it is easy to change
the performance.

Social norms train people to throw, sit, walk, move, dress, and be in ways appropriate to what a person's gender/sex is perceived to be. Cultures label particular
movements of the body as gender/sex specific, and members of the culture then
ridicule those who do not follow the prescribed behaviors. Over time, routinized
movements of the body in gendered/sexed ways appear natural. The body is an
important location on which gender/sex identities are communicated, constructed,
maintained, and challenged.

KEY CONCEPTS

agency 92

body privilege 88

body surveillance 78

disciplining gender 80

embodied communication 75

embodied movement 89

embodied space 87

gender performativity 77

gendered attractiveness 81

objectification 78

power posing 88

proxemics 87

refusing the command performance 92

self-objectification 78

DISCUSSION QUESTIONS

1. Do you agree with Whitehead that cisgender men do not tend to experience their bodies in the guarded way women do? Why or why not?

2. Why is Butler's notion of gender performativity particularly relevant here?

3. Identify examples of how objectification is present in your everyday life.

4. What are the primary ways in which persons have refused the command performance? Are there any ways you have refused a command performance?

CHAPTER 5

Gendered/Sexed Language

On January 8, 2016, the American Dialect Society (ADS, n.d.), an organization "dedicated to the study of the English language in North America," overwhelmingly voted to recognize *they* as 2015's "Word of the Year" and its "Most Useful" word. What led to this recognition for a simple pronoun? The ADS (2016) explained: "*They* was recognized by the society for its emerging use as a pronoun to refer to a known person, often as a conscious choice by a person rejecting the traditional gender binary of *he* and *she*." The ADS honored the singular *they* because it provided an alternative to pronouns that assign a sex to a person. *They* symbolizes "how mainstream culture has come to recognize and accept transgender and gender fluid people, some of whom reject traditional pronouns" (Guo, 2016).

The ADS is not the only entity to recognize the singular *they*. In 2014, Facebook gave its users the option to choose their pronouns, including the singular *they* (Zimman, 2015). In 2015, the *Washington Post* changed its style rules. In a memo to its staff, the *Post* explained *they* is useful not just when referencing nonbinary people, but generally when one is in need of a non-sex-specific singular pronoun (Poynter, 2015). In March 2017, the Associated Press announced it changed its Stylebook to allow the use of singular *they* (Berendzen 2017), and in April 2017, the *Chicago Manual of Style* announced a similar change. All this points to the fact that English speakers "are in the midst of some kind of shift in the way pronouns are used and understood" (Zimman, 2015, p. 141). You are living through a moment where the fact that languages are living becomes recognizable.

The singular *they* is not new (Zimman, 2015). Since the 14th century, "singular *they* has been used ubiquitously to fill the place of the gender-neutral, sex-indefinite, third-person singular pronoun" (LaScotte, 2016, p. 63) and authors, including Jane Austen, William Shakespeare, and Geoffrey Chaucer, used a singular *they* (Zimmer, 2015). Nor is the use of a singular *they* a radical departure from how people actually talk. In an empirical study, LaScotte (2016) found that 68% of the time people use *they* to refer to a person when they do not know their sex.

The recognition of singular *they* has some big implications for how language organizes the world. With sex-specific pronouns, communicators marked people's sex even when it was irrelevant to the sentence. Writer and research associate at the Harvard Business School Silpa Kovvali (2015) argued that because people were limited to using *he* or *she* when referring to friends, coworkers, and students

> our language . . . forces us to immediately characterize people as male or female, associates other aspects of their personalities with their sex and, in doing so, makes it an inseparable part of how we perceive ourselves and each other, far more so than any other random biological feature or accident of birth.

The singular *they* allows you to reference a person without designating their sex, not just because a person may not fit the sex binary, but also because a person's sex usually is irrelevant to the point you are making.

If you are thinking one pronoun makes no difference, consider this: How would you feel if someone called you by the wrong name, not just once but repeatedly? How would you feel if you asked to be called one name and another person refused to recognize that as your name? How would you feel if a boss decided to call all their workers *Cog* because they could not bother to learn everyone's names? You likely would feel disrespected. This explains *Washington Post* etiquette writer Steven Petrow's (2014) advice to someone who resisted using singular *they* because they found it "odd and grammatically incorrect":

> Language is about respect, and we should all do our best to recognize how people wish to be identified, whether it is using their preferred name or a pronoun spelled any which way. In other words, do your best to adjust to changing times and terms, and address people the way they ask you.

If you think rules are rules, and people should follow them, consider the fact that other pronouns, such as *you*, can be both singular and plural. So why is there resistance to a singular, sex-neutral *they*? The controversy over pronouns demonstrates that language does, indeed, matter when it comes to gender/sex. There would be no controversy if language had no effect on the world and how people perceive it.

For example, when Merriam-Webster tweeted, "The astute may have noticed a difference in our feed. Our witty and fabulous social media manager is away. But don't worry, they'll return," Maryland State Board of Education member Andy Smarick responded, "I won't be baited into a pronoun agreement fight I won't be baited. . . ." A minor tweetstorm ensued. The dictionary defended the usage given they are "descriptivists" who "follow language, language doesn't follow us." Smarick declared, "Language rules are all that separate us from the animals" (as cited in Crum, 2016). Although Smarick meant for the exchange to be "lighthearted ribbing," it generated some intense responses. Commenters argued words needed to describe all people, including those who do not fit the gender binary. Smarick's (2016) response?

> So in the spirit of humility, after getting this feedback, I researched the topic and talked to a number of colleagues about the way the "singular they" has evolved,

how it's now being used, and why more organizations are adopting it. I've learned a great deal, and I'm much more aware. For example, I better understand and appreciate why those for whom the "singular they" is already an integral part of an identity-sensitive lexicon interpreted my response as a provocation.

Though I didn't mean to wade into such a sensitive issue, in some eyes, I did. It's a very good reminder to those of us who write: Words have enormous meaning, always manifest but often latent as well. And those meanings can vary dramatically from one person or group to the next.

As someone who trades in words, that's a reminder I'll take with me. (paras. 17–19)

Language matters, even a simple pronoun. And changing pronouns has implications for other words. For example, if one wants to move away from a rigid sex binary, then *Mx.* is a useful replacement for *Ms.* and *Mr.*, and *Latinx* can replace *Latino* or *Latina* (Scharrón-del Río & Aja, 2015).

The element of sexist language that has received the most attention is the use of sex-exclusive language (e.g., generic *he* or *man* used to refer to any person or to all people). Research conclusively demonstrated that sex-exclusive pronouns and nouns influence people's perceptions (Martyna, 1980a, 1980b, 1983; McConnell & Fazio, 1996; McConnell & Gavanski, 1994; Miller & James, 2009; Newman, 1992; Ng, 1990; Wilson & Ng, 1988). People do not read and hear *man* as a noun referring to all human beings, and people do not read and hear *he* as a pronoun for those who are not men. Every major style manual (APA, MLA, Chicago, Turabian, *New York Times*) requires sex-inclusive language that does not exclude over half the population. It is clear *he* as a pronoun does not refer to everyone; not everyone identifies as a man. Similarly, *he or she* does not refer to everyone; not everyone identifies as a man or a woman.

Enter singular *they*. Petrow (2016) declared, "In 2016, 'they' became singular, and everyone learned more about gender." We agree that this example of language change has much to teach about gender/sex. It illustrates the power of language to make some gender/sexes visible and others invisible if not impossible. It illustrates how language can be used to suppress and subordinate by marking some groups and not others, by providing language for some people and not others, and by denying vocabulary to some groups and not others. In addition, the resistance to these evolutions in language demonstrates that controversies over language are important. Finally, the singular *they* demonstrates how language can be used as a form of resistance and how new language can be developed or old language put to new uses.

Language is more than a tool used to transmit information or a mirror to reflect reality. Words *do* things. Saying something is as much an action as moving something. However, people do not always recognize that every time they communicate, they engage in symbolic action constructing social reality.

Language structures people's understanding of social reality, and insofar as gender/sex is part of social reality, language about gender/sex structures understandings of gender/sex and hence structures gender/sex. People speak and perform their bodies and identities into being. Australian scholar Dale Spender (1985) described language as "our means of ordering, classifying and manipulating the world. It is through language that we become members of a human community, that the world becomes comprehensible and meaningful, that we bring into existence the world in which we live" (p. 3).

This chapter focuses on patterns of communication embedded in language that speak to how sex and gender have been structured and, in turn, have structured the world. Sex is not a thing (even though the word is used to describe the human body), and gender cannot be held in your hands. Instead, when you study sex and gender, you study the trace evidence of them in language. To understand this, we first explore theories explaining the power of language. We then identify ways in which language is used to subordinate and to liberate.

The Power of Language

Rhetoric scholar Kenneth Burke (1966) argued that human beings are "symbol-using (symbol-making, symbol-misusing)" creatures (p. 16). He did not stop at this description. Instead, he asked, "Do we simply use words, or do they not also use us?" (p. 6). Linguist Robin Lakoff (1975) answered this question: "Language uses us as much as we use language" (p. 3). Burke's question and Lakoff's answer direct students of language to consider how words circumscribe people's interactions with each other and the world.

Words do not exist in isolation but combine to form **terministic screens**, filters composed of language that direct people's attention away from some things and toward others. Burke (1966) highlighted the "necessarily *suasive* nature of even the most unemotional scientific nomenclatures" (p. 45). For example, even the language used in a world geography textbook, a subject that seems relatively objective, is persuasive. In 2015, Roni Dean-Burren received a text from their teenage son, Coby, of a photo of the ninth-grade textbook used in Coby's class (Wang, 2015). A caption on the map of the eastern United States indicated, "The Atlantic Slave Trade

Figure 5.1 Map Caption From McGraw-Hill World Geography Ninth-Grade Textbook

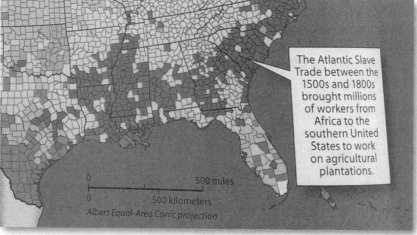

The Atlantic Slave Trade between the 1500s and 1800s brought millions of workers from Africa to the southern United States to work on agricultural plantations.

between the 1500s and 1800s brought millions of workers from Africa to the south-ern United States to work on agricultural plantations" (see Figure 5.1).

One word in particular directs attention: *workers*. The word *workers* selects out for attention the idea that Africans willingly emigrated to the United States for work, and it deflects the reality of slavery. White slavers forcibly brought Africans to the United States not as workers who received pay, but as enslaved people whom Whites violently forced to toil in forced labor. The publisher quickly admitted the error, corrected the caption in digital versions, and offered schools corrected versions or stickers to cover up the caption.

This example illustrates how all communication is persuasive because "even if any given terminology is a *reflection* of reality, by its very nature as a terminology it must be a *selection* of reality; and to this extent it must function also as a *deflection* of reality" (Burke, 1966, p. 45). A single word can direct the way you see the world. In addition, words interact with one another to form a screen through which you view the world. Thus, because language directs people's attention to see some things about gender/sex and not others, terministic screens are sexed and gendered.

Another example clarifies Burke's point about how language directs atten-tion. Reproductive freedom and abortion are rhetorically charged issues in the United States. Two main sides have long dominated the controversy: pro-life and pro-choice. People who are pro-life tend to refer to the "reality" as a *baby*, whereas those who are pro-choice tend to refer to the "reality" as a *fetus*. Each term selects, deflects, and reflects reality in a particular way and calls forth dif-ferent clusters of terms that accompany it.

Baby accurately reflects reality insofar as some people often ask, "When is the baby due?" and some people perceive miscarriage as the loss of a baby. *Baby* also selects a particular aspect of reality to highlight; it focuses attention on how the real-ity is a fully formed human being separable from its gestational location. A person could leave a baby in a room unattended (but of course safely ensconced in a crib). However, when in the womb, it cannot be separated from its location. *Baby* also selects a particular type of relationship to other human beings; babies have mothers and fathers, not women and men. *Baby* also calls forth positive associations because U.S. culture is pronatal; it celebrates the arrival of babies. People think of babies as innocent and pure. Once people think of the "reality" as a separate and distinct human being, to terminate its existence means that someone has committed murder.

In the process of selecting some parts of reality to highlight, *baby* also deflects that the "reality" is located within a person's body, and it deflects the possibility that women can be something other than mothers; if there is a baby, there is a mother. It also deflects the fact that people recognize stages in development in the human as it undergoes gestation, from zygote to embryo to fetus.

In the same way that *baby* reflects, deflects, and selects parts of reality, so does the term *fetus*. *Fetus* selects those very parts of reality that the term *baby* deflects. It selects the reality that is described in medical and scientific terms, that gestational stages exist, and that a fetus cannot exist without a person to carry it. In fact, *fetus* reverses the relationship: Babies *have* mothers, whereas women *carry* fetuses. In selecting the medical reality, *fetus* highlights a not-yet-complete human being. Although people may fondly imagine cuddling a baby while sitting in a rocking chair, imagining cuddling a fetus is not quite the same. *Fetus* highlights the incompleteness of the human.

In the process of selecting, *fetus* also deflects attention away from the very things *baby* selects. *Fetus* deflects the emotional attachments people tend to have to small human forms, and it deflects the possibility that the fetus can be murdered. Fetuses are not murdered; instead, pregnancies are terminated.

Ultimately, words contain implicit exhortations to see the world one way rather than another. Words "affect the nature of our observations" (Burke, 1966, p. 46). However, Burke (1966) went even further, positing that "many of the 'observations' are but implications of the particular terminology in terms of which the observations are made" (p. 46). People see only that for which they have words.

Lexicographer Julia Penelope (1990) extended this analysis from a gender/sex perspective to highlight how systems of sexism have influenced the words available:

> Language draws our attention to only some experiences in some ways, making it difficult to grasp and articulate those it doesn't provide labels or descriptions for. We can describe feelings and perceptions English doesn't provide words for, but finding an accurate description takes time and patience and some fluency with the language. Because English foregrounds only some aspects of experience as possibilities, we have a repertoire of specific gestures, sounds, words, sentence structures, metaphors, that focus our attention on just those activities named by patriarchy. (p. 204)

Given this, it is important to understand the patterns present in language that privilege some views of the world, while displacing others. One way to track power's presence in language is to identify when some groups' perspective can be found in language and other groups' cannot.

In 1963, when Betty Friedan identified women's discontent caused by sexism as "the problem that has no name" (p. 11), she recognized that the English language does not serve all its users equally. Language is created, maintained, and changed by its users, but not all users have equal access to influencing the language. Those who belong to dominant groups within a culture have more influence over the language and, hence, over the terms that form a culture's terministic screen.

Some oppressed and subordinated groups attempt to speak to the challenge presented by problems without names. In the United States in the 1960s, consciousness-raising groups were used by many White, middle-class women to talk about subjects considered taboo, such as their sexuality (Campbell, 1973). Writers such as Gloria Anzaldúa, a scholar of Chicana and feminist theory, used poetry, slang, multiple languages, unique forms, and profanity in academic writing (Palczewski, 1996). Sociolinguist Braj Kachru (1982) documented ways in which second-language speakers of English adapt the language to better reflect their worldviews, resulting in multiple world Englishes.

Rules of language usage mute people, too. Penelope (1990) focused on the grammatical rules that govern language use, as well as the words, and argued that the English language is not neutral but supports patriarchy insofar as English creates a **patriarchal universe of discourse (PUD):**

A "universe of discourse" is a cultural model of reality that people use daily to decide how to act and what to say in specific contexts. . . . It is the same thing as "consensus reality," and those who accept its terms assume that it is an accurate description of reality. . . . In fact, people can be so attached to "consensus reality" that its assumptions and predictions override contradictory evidence. (pp. 36–37)

When the model of reality is one in which a patriarchal system dominates, then that model tends to hide the exercise of male privilege.

The existence of a consensus reality explains why thinking critically about gender/sex can be so difficult. The language system pushes people to see things in a particular way. For example, according to the existing consensus reality, there are only two sexes, the sexes are opposite, and the words used to describe those sexes are not semantic equivalents.

Penelope's analysis made clear that once people accept that language has power, then they need to start thinking about how those with power deploy language to maintain and extend power: by denying access to it (e.g., refusing education or public speaking forums), by stripping others of their languages (e.g., the forced suppression of Native American languages in Bureau of Indian Affairs schools beginning in the 1880s and continuing until passage of the Native American Languages Act of 1990), by generating rules of proper usage (e.g., proper English as a class and race marker), and by structuring the language in such a way that it masks power.

Language Can Be Used to Oppress and Subordinate

Thus far, we have described how dominant groups structure reality through language. We now identify some specific examples of language-based gender/sex privilege. Some of the examples may seem natural, unremarkable, or insignificant. This is part of the power of language. Linguist Deborah Cameron (1998) noted,

Language is ideological. The same reality can be represented in any number of ways, and the power of linguistic conventions lies precisely in the selectiveness with which they represent the world, making one way of perceiving reality seem like the only natural way. (p. 161)

Our hope is that by learning to recognize the language patterns that reinforce sex and gender inequality in U.S. American English, you will develop the critical faculties to think more politically about all language use, your own included.

He/Man Language

He/man language refers to the use of masculine pronouns and nouns to refer to all people. Style manuals are in universal agreement that the universal *he* or *man* is not an acceptable neutral term to describe all people. This is consistent with informal conversation. Most people forgo sex-exclusive language in regular conversation. In a study of the use of the generic *he*, researchers Jeffrey L. Stringer and Robert Hopper (1998) found that the "generic he occurs rarely, if at all, in spoken interaction" (p. 211). In an analysis of scholarly writings and the *New York Times* from 1970 to 2000 and a comparison of personal writing from 1990 to 2008, cognitive scientist Brian D. Earp (2012) found "he/man language is increasingly less used, and nonsexist alternatives are on the rise" (p. 15). The conclusion? "We may be well on our way to seeing the ultimate extinction of masculine generics in the English language. It would be about time" (p. 16).

Although people no longer use the generic *he* in conversation, and style manuals discourage it in written communication, it is common, even acceptable, for *guys* to be used to describe all people. *Urban Dictionary* takes a dig at the phrase by defining it as, "Proof of America's sexist bias. Although it's obviously designed to address the male sex, this phrase is used just as often by girls between girl[s]" (aleclair, 2006). Why does something as seemingly benign as the phrase *you guys* matter? Sherryl Kleinman (2002) explained that "male-based generics are another indicator—and, more importantly, a *reinforcer*—of a system in which 'man' in the abstract and men in the flesh are privileged over women" (p. 300; emphasis in original). Kleinman referred to male-based generics as "symbolic annihilation," which simultaneously makes women less visible and objectifies them: "If we [women] aren't even deserving of our place in humanity in language, why should we expect to be treated as decent human beings otherwise?" (p. 302). So is the debate over sex-inclusive language resolved? It is our position that sex-exclusive language should not be used. Sex-inclusive language should be used.

Semantic Derogation

Semantic derogation occurs when two terms ought to represent parallel concepts, but one term is derogatory while the other is not (Schulz, 1975). Penelope (1990) described these terms as "semantically symmetrical (paired), but conceptually asymmetrical" (p. 48). Some scholars argue that derogation is sex based: "Because naming and defining is a prerogative of power, semantic shifts in vocabulary have been determined largely by the experience of men, not women" (Miller & Swift, 1993, p. ix).

Consider the degree college students earn: the bachelor's degree. The parallel term for bachelor is *spinster*, yet spinsters are thought of as dried-up old women who never married. The etymology of *spinster* indicates that positive meanings were once attached to it but have atrophied over time. Originally, *spinster* referred to women who spun fibers into thread and yarn. When men began to spin, the term referred to men, too. In the 17th century, the term began to refer to unmarried women (although some resisted this usage because *spinster* also was a colloquial term for *harlot*); the term became sexualized and derogated. Whereas *bachelor* referred to any unmarried man, a *spinster* was an unmarried woman beyond the marriageable age, making clear that men are never too old to marry but women can be. Other examples include *mistress/master; lady/lord; womanly/ manly; tramp* (sexually active woman)/*tramp* (homeless man); *to mother children/ to father children; governess/governor;* and *madam/sir.*

An interesting pattern emerges in the derogation of nouns: Sexuality is used to derogate women. *Bachelor* and *spinster* ought to be equal, but *spinster* connotes someone who cannot get any sex. *Lord* and *lady* ought to be equal, but *lord* designates a ruler, whereas *lady* contains a prescription for how women should act. *Master* and *mistress* ought to be equal, but a *mistress* is a kept woman who gets sex by "stealing" it from another woman. *Governor* and *governess* ought to be equal, but again the masculine term connotes political power, whereas a *governess* is a person who takes care of others' children.

Semantic Imbalance

Semantic imbalance refers to an overabundance of terms to describe something related to one group but few terms existing to describe the other. Answer this:

How many terms can you think of that describe a sexually active woman? A sexually active man?

The number of terms available that negatively describe women swamps the list of terms that describe men. Only recently have terms like *player*, referring to men, come to carry negative connotations typically associated with *slut*, referring to women, but even now *player* is not nearly as bad a name as *slut*.

Semantic imbalance is created not only when there are too many words but also when there are too few. Women often are referred to as *hysterical* (*hysteria*, derived from the Greek word for women's reproductive organs), yet men are not referred to as *testerical*. Similarly, men may be referred to as *womanizers*, but women are not *mannizers* (Penelope, 1990, p. 187).

Peggy Orenstein (2017) interviewed 70 young women, age 15 to 20, to understand how they understood their sexuality and physical intimacy. The main finding: Girls lack a language to talk about their body parts. Orenstein noted how parents, when naming body parts (nose, toes, belly button, etc.), typically will name boys' genitals, but not girls' (p. 61). Why might this be of concern? Orenstein explained: "Leaving something unnamed makes it quite literally unspeakable: a void, an absence, a taboo" (p. 61). That void continued as the girls got older, impacting how the young women understood sexuality.

Semantic Polarization

Semantic polarization occurs when two parallel concepts are treated as though they were opposed, like "opposite sexes." In case you had not noticed, we avoid that phrase because it structures a perception of the world that we find problematic. The sexes are not opposite; all are human and may have more in common with those who are a different sex than with some who are the same sex. However, by framing the sexes as opposite, language reentrenches the notion that there are two and only two sexes and that the characteristics of one cannot be possessed by the other. Communication scholar Barbara Bate (1988) explained, "If you see women and men as polar opposites, you are likely to believe that any features or quality of men should be absent from women, and vice versa" (p. 16).

Marked and Unmarked Terms

Marked and unmarked terms occur when someone combines an indicator of a person's sex (or race, or other identity ingredient) with a noun in some cases, but not all. When one sex or race tends to dominate a category, people may sex or race mark the category only when a nondominant person fills it. Because the nursing profession is dominated by women, people tend to refer to "the nurse" (unmarked) when the nurse is a woman but refer to "the male nurse" (marked) when the nurse is a man. Similarly, you often see references to "female police officer" but not "male police officer," "male slut" but not "female slut," and "Black professor" but not "White professor." In all these examples, the race and sex of the person are incidental or irrelevant to the job being performed. Marking creates the impression that a person is violating a norm. This construction is not as common as it once was, but it still is an interesting tendency to track. It reveals a great deal about cultural expectations and designated roles, which may explain why it is most persistent in university sports teams: The men's team is the "Bears," and the women's team is the "Lady Bears."

Trivialization

Trivialization refers to the use of diminutives to refer to a disempowered group member. Historically, Black men's masculinity was demeaned by the use of the term *boy*. Although *boy* does not initially seem like a derogatory term, when used by a White person (often younger) to refer to a Black man (often older), it exposes the power dynamic at play. No matter how old, wise, or respected, a Black man was forever diminished as an immature person—a boy. Women also often are referred to in ways that strip them of stature. Women are referred to as desserts: *honeybun, cupcake, sweetheart, tart*. Linguist Caitlin Hines (1999) argued that this is no accident, insofar as dessert metaphors refer to women not just as "objects, but sweet (that is compliant, smiling), and not just desserts, but *pieces* or *slices*" (p. 148).

To correct semantic imbalance and derogation, trivialization, and marked terms, it is not enough simply to erase them from our vocabularies. Cameron (1998) pointed out,

> The crucial aspect of language is meaning: the point of non-sexist language is not to change the forms of words just for the sake of changing, but to change the repertoire of meanings a language conveys. It's about redefining rather than merely renaming the world. (p. 161)

Therefore, attention to the vocabulary people have—or lack—becomes important.

Naming

Naming refers to the practices surrounding how proper nouns (names) are assigned to people. A power imbalance exists between the sexes in relation to naming practices after heterosexual marriage. Historically in the United States, women lost their names after marriage, becoming "Mrs. John Smith." Women's marriage status was embedded in their names; married women were addressed differently than unmarried: *Mrs.* versus *Miss.* As early as the 1600s, the alternative of *Ms.* was proposed as a way to make designations parallel: Men were *Mr.* whether married or unmarried and so women, too, could be *Ms.* whether married or unmarried. In addition, the option of keeping one's name after marriage was introduced. In the 1970s, only 1% of women kept their name, in the 1980s it was 9%, and in the 1990s a high of 23% kept their name. Then, in the 2000s, the percentage leveled off at 18% (Kopelman, Shea-Van Fossen, Paraskevas, Lawter, & Prottas, 2009). Even when women keep their birth names or hyphenate it with their spouse's last name, an overwhelming majority still give their children their husband's last name (Emens, 2007).

Scholars who study naming practices see it as a "window into gender attitudes" (Hamilton, Geist, & Powell, 2011, p. 145). Of respondents in one study, 72.3% agreed that "it is generally better if a woman changes her last name to her husband's name when she marries" (p. 156) and 49.9% thought states should "legally require a woman to change her name" (p. 157). Despite this, some women keep their names after marriage. As an intersectional approach might predict, other factors than sex influence one's naming practice. Kopelman et al. (2009) found that women with high-level jobs like CEO, professional occupations like doctor, and those in the arts or entertainment fields tended to keep their name more often.

Mr. and *Ms.* are not the only honorifics related to naming. Another honorific has emerged: *Mx.*—a sex-neutral alternative to *Mr.* and *Ms.* The *Oxford English Dictionary* added the term to its lexicon in May 2015 to account for changes in social understandings of sex and gender. In explaining the change, OED assistant editor Jonathan Dent explained, "This an example of how the English language adapts to people's needs, with people using language in ways that suit them rather than letting language dictate identity to them" (as cited in Segal, 2015). The interesting challenge, however, is when to use the term. If the goal is to not needlessly reference sex and reinforce the sex binary, if you only use Mx. when referencing gender/sex non-conforming people, then that goal is not achieved. It is for that reason that many advocate the use of gender/sex-inclusive terms like *they* and *Mx.* for everyone (Kovvali, 2015; Rosman, 2015).

Lack of Vocabulary

Lack of vocabulary refers to the dearth of words to describe some elements of reality. Friedan's writing about problems without names highlights feminism's struggle to talk about sexism, sexual harassment, date rape, and marital rape, all terms feminists created to recognize these offenses. It is impossible to develop solutions to a problem when it has no name and, hence, is neither identifiable nor observable.

Spender (1985) argued, "Historically, women have been excluded from the production of cultural forms, and language is, after all, a cultural form—and a most important one" (p. 52). Its import stems from language's ability to "form the limits of our reality" (p. 3). Because of women's exclusion from the "production of the legitimated language, they have been unable to give weight to their own symbolic meanings, they have been unable to pass on a tradition of women's meanings to the world" (p. 52). The fact that women have not had *the same* opportunity does not mean they have had *no* opportunity. One example of language development occurred during the debates over pornography that dominated women's movements in the 1980s.

Although men (as religious figures and political leaders) historically controlled the definition of *pornography*, they no longer monopolize its meaning. Historically, *pornography* possessed two meanings: speech and (in the 1500s) images used as an insult to the church and state (Hunt, 1993). These interpretations dominated pornography's meaning until feminism began to challenge the way women's sexuality was defined. Andrea Dworkin and Catharine A. MacKinnon (1988; among many others) focused on pornography's effect on women and redefined *pornography* as an act of sex discrimination, in the process rejecting a focus on pornography's effect on society's moral fiber (Palczewski, 2001). Although the municipal ordinance they wrote did not survive judicial scrutiny, they influenced Canadian law regarding sexually explicit, violent, and sexist materials.

Developing a vocabulary when one is lacking enables you not only to name your experience but also to critically reflect on it—an important component of coming to political agency. African American feminist theorist bell hooks (1989) explained how "simply describing one's experience of exploitation or oppression is not to become politicized. It is not sufficient to know the personal but to know—to speak it in a different way. Knowing the personal might mean naming spaces of ignorance, gaps in knowledge, ones that render us unable to link the personal with the political" (p. 107). For hooks,

> Politicization necessarily combines this process (the naming of one's experience) with critical understanding of the concrete material reality that lays the groundwork for that personal experience. The work of understanding that groundwork and what must be done to transform it is quite different from the effort to raise one's consciousness about personal experience even as they are linked. (p. 108)

In other words, the development of a vocabulary with which to accurately describe one's experiences is an important process during which one needs to reflect on the political implications of that experience.

The Truncated Passive

Grammatical patterns provide evidence of sexism in language because they enable speakers to deny agency and perpetuate oppression (Penelope, 1990). The prime culprit is the **truncated passive**, in which the use of a passive verb allows the agent of action to be deleted (or truncated) from the sentence. Anti-violence educator Jackson Katz used this example to illustrate Penelope's point:

John beat Mary. [active voice]

Mary was beaten by John. [passive voice]

Mary was beaten. [truncated passive]

Mary was battered. [truncated passive]

Mary is a battered woman. (as cited in Keren, 2012)

Each sentence is grammatically correct but operates very differently in its depiction of the event. Sentence constructions using the truncated passive enable blaming the victim because the victim is the only one present in the sentence. Katz explained, "The political effect has been to shift the focus from John to Mary" (as cited in Keren, 2012). The final sentence completely removes the agent from attention.

Individuals who attempt to avoid explicit responsibility for the consequences of the power they exercise often use truncated passives. The result of "agent-deletion leaves us with only the objects of the acts described by the verbs. Passives without agents foreground the objects (victims) in our minds so that we tend to forget that some human agent is responsible for performing the action" (Penelope, 1990, p. 146), as in the phrases "mistakes were made," "Hanoi was bombed," or "the toy got broken." Penelope (1990) explained, "Agentless passives conceal and deceive when it doesn't suit speakers' or writers' purposes to make agency explicit" (p. 149). As a result, "this makes it easy to suppress responsibility" and enables "protection of the guilty and denial of responsibility, . . . the pretense of objectivity, . . . and trivialization" (p. 149).

The Falsely Universal *We*

Political scientist Jane Mansbridge (1998) identified the **falsely universal *we*:** Rhetors use the collective *we* in political discourse to make it seem as though they are speaking about everyone when really they are representing a particular few and making invisible a distinct other. Mansbridge explained, "'We' can easily represent a false universality, as 'mankind' used to" (p. 152). Thus, "the very capacity to identify with others can easily be manipulated to the disadvantage of" a subordinated group because "the transformation of 'I' into 'we' brought about through political deliberation can easily mask subtle forms of control" (p. 143).

One often hears politicians talk about how *we* need to do something or that *we* as a nation believe in particular values, when in reality they are referencing a particular segment of the population who they hope will vote for them. It is extremely easy to fall into using *we*, especially when you want to create a sense of identification and community. However, as Burke (1969) pointed out, any time identification is used, one must "confront the implications of *division*. . . . Identification is compensatory to division" (p. 22). When a group says, "We are alike," it also necessarily implies that others are *not* like them.

The Deverbing of *Woman*

Semantic imbalance and derogation also occur in verbs. The distinctions between the meanings of the verbs *to man* and *to woman*, which ought to be parallel, are intriguing (Palczewski, 1998). The *Compact Edition of the Oxford English*

Dictionary (1971) listed the primary definition of the verb *man* as "to furnish (a fort, ship, etc.) with a force or company of men to serve or defend it" (p. 1711). Its definitions of the verb *woman* included "to become woman-like; with *it* to behave as a woman, to be womanly.... To make like a woman in weakness or sub-servience.... To make 'a woman' of, deprive of virginity.... To furnish or provide with women; to equip with a staff of women" (p. 3808). *Man* carries implications of acting, typically in battle and on ships. *Woman* carries implications of being acted upon, typically to become womanlike, to be made a woman, or to be deprived of virginity. The **deverbing of *woman*** occurs because today, in contrast to the verb *man*, the word *woman* is seldom thought of as a verb at all.

The pattern described between *woman* and *man* also is present in other verb forms, such as *lord* and *lady* and *master* and *mistress*. *Lord's* primary definition is "to exercise lordship, have dominion" (p. 1664). In contrast, the definition of the verb *lady* is "to make a lady of; to raise to the rank of lady ... to play the lady or mistress" (p. 1559). Female verbs deny agency. Male verbs highlight it.

Master's primary verb form means "to get the better of, in any contest or struggle; to overcome defeat ... to reduce to subjection, compel to obey; to break, tame (an animal)" (p. 1739). *Mistress* means "to provide with a mistress ... to make a mistress or paramour of ... to play the mistress, to have the upper hand ... to dominate as a mistress" (p. 1820). Again, mastery involves agency, getting the better of, subjecting, compelling others to obey. *Mistress*, in contrast, is passive. A woman is provided for as a mistress; she does not mistress. Or she is made a paramour. Or she merely plays at being mistress. Or, if one focuses on the latter definitions in which agency is expressed, one realizes that it is often a false agency, for when a woman dominates as a mistress, she dominates (typically) "servants or attendants ... household or family" (p. 1820). Agency is rarely involved; rarely is control possible and never over masters.

Language as Violence

The previous sections focused on how specific parts of language (pronouns, nouns, and verbs) construct sex privilege. However, particular forms of language are not the only way in which subordination is manifested. People use language itself as a form of violence. Critical race theorists examine the function of hate speech, recognizing the "relationships between naming and reality, knowledge and power" (Matsuda, Lawrence, Delgado, & Crenshaw, 1993, p. 5). They argue that people should recognize **language as violence**, forms of speech like hate speech (racist, homophobic, sexist, anti-Semitic language) that cause harm. Although the First Amendment has protected such speech, legal scholar Mari Matsuda (1993) argued that "an absolutist first amendment response to hate speech has the effect of perpetuating racism: Tolerance of hate speech is not tolerance borne by the community at large. Rather it is a psychic tax imposed on those least able to pay" (p. 18).

The distinction between words and actions may not be as clear as once thought. Matsuda (1993) explained, "The deadly violence that accompanies the persistent verbal degradation of those subordinated because of gender or sexuality explodes the notion that there are clear lines between words and deeds" (p. 23). Although First Amendment absolutists argue that the appropriate response to "bad" speech is more speech, such an alternative is not always viable for those targeted by hate speech. Critical race theorist and legal scholar Charles R. Lawrence III (1993) demonstrated how words are more than what they denote:

> Like the word "nigger" and unlike the word "liar," it is not sufficient to deny the truth of the word's application, to say "I am not a faggot." One must deny the truth of the word's meaning, a meaning shouted from the rooftops by the rest of the world a million times a day. The complex response "Yes, I am a member of the group you despise and the degraded meaning of the word you use is one that I reject" is not effective in a subway encounter. (p. 70)

Of course, just because one recognizes that language acts does not mean that one automatically accepts the need for legal redress. Debate over hate speech dominated the 1990s. Those working against sexism, racism, religious intolerance, and homophobia disagree on the appropriateness of legal prohibitions against words that wound, noting the danger of collapsing a word into an action (Butler, 1997). However, all agree that we must respond to, answer, deny, reject, and condemn the use of language as a mechanism of violence.

Language as Resistance

If language has the power to create inequality and injustice, it also has the power to resist them. We do not dismiss the importance of economics, politics, and law to social change, but recognize language is a precursor to recognizing the need for and the possibility of change. Penelope (1990) argued, "Changing our descriptions won't immediately change reality or eliminate white supremacy or male dominance, but it will change the way we perceive power imbalances and the conceptual structures that make them appear to make sense to us" (p. 214). Through language, people can rename, reenvision, and reimagine the world because "language is power, in ways more literal than most people think. When we speak, we exercise the power of language to transform reality" (p. 213).

Talking Back

In *Talking Back*, bell hooks (1989) outlined how simply speaking can function as an act of resistance. For those who have been named subordinate, speaking rejects that naming:

> True speaking is not solely an expression of creative power; it is an act of resistance, a political gesture that challenges politics of domination that would render us nameless and voiceless. . . . Moving from silence into speech is . . . a gesture of defiance that heals, that makes new life and new growth possible. (p. 8)

Talking back is not talking for talk's sake but "is the expression of our movement from object to subject—the liberated voice" (p. 9). Language includes the words themselves, and who is authorized to use them, on which subjects, from which social locations, and with what critical perspectives.

For hooks (1989), talking back is not simply the screaming of frustration, nor do all people speak as subjects and with a liberated voice every time they speak. hooks clarified that "to speak as an act of resistance is quite different than ordinary talk, or the personal confession that has no relation to coming into political awareness, to developing critical consciousness" (p. 14). The distinction between ordinary talk and talking back is necessary for three reasons. First, it avoids trivializing or romanticizing the process of finding a voice; coming to voice is difficult political work. Second, it avoids privileging "acts of speaking over the content of the speech" (p. 14); when talking back, what is said matters. Third, it prevents the commodification of oppositional voices; when one recognizes the oppositional element of talking back, one can no longer treat it as mere spectacle. Talking back is not mere talk but talk with a political consciousness.

Developing a New Language

If existing language does not provide names for a person's experiences, then one of the most profound acts of resistance is to develop new language. **Developing a new language** refers to the creation of vocabulary, phrases, and idioms to describe social reality. Philosopher Mary Daly (1987) explained, "New Words themselves are Mediums, carriers of messages" (p. 10). New words enable people to see new social realities.

Philosopher Sandra Harding (1995) outlined the power of naming for a marginalized group—in this case, women:

> For women to name and describe their experiences in "their own terms" is a crucial scientific and epistemological act. Members of marginalized groups must *struggle* to name their own experiences *for* themselves in order to claim the subjectivity, the possibility of historical agency, that is given to members of dominant groups at birth. (p. 128)

To become agents, or people who act rather than people who are acted upon, a language on and of one's own terms is essential: "For marginalized people, naming their experience publicly is a cry for survival" (p. 129).

Examples of developing language abound. Feminist lexicographers have made efforts to create alternative dictionaries to reclaim the English language, using concepts and definitions that reveal and reflect the diverse experiences and oppressions of women, persons of color, working-class people, LGBTQ people, and people with disabilities (e.g., Daly, 1987; Kramarae & Treichler, 1992; Mills, 1993). Going beyond the creation of new words, Suzette Haden Elgin (1984/2000, 1987/2002b, 1993/2002a) developed an entire language, Láadan, for her fictional *Native Tongue* trilogy ("Suzette Haden Elgin," 2004).

Women in other nations and in other times also have developed languages to come to voice. Communication scholar Lin-Lee Lee (2004) studied how, more than 1,000 years ago in China, women developed *Nüshu*, a female discourse used in "texts sung and chanted by rural woman over their needlework on pieces of red fabric, handkerchiefs, and fans" (p. 407). Chinese women were excluded from formal education in *Hanzi*, the official Chinese script that "was created by men for the use of men." Nüshu offered an alternative as "an oral phonetic transcription passed from generation to generation by women" (pp. 408–409). It developed in an area governed by patriarchal Confucian systems, in which men dominated women and subservience to superiors was morally required. Nüshu texts describe the details of a woman's life and express feelings about "sexual inequality, low social status, and bad treatment" (p. 411). No one trained in ordinary Chinese can read Nüshu. Men who heard it could "understand it when performed, but they could not perform it, read it, or speak it themselves" (p. 409). This distinctive language "allowed women to have a voice, to create an individual and collective subjectivity that enabled them to confer value on and give importance to their lives" as it "transformed the hardships of women into tales that validated their lives and experiences" (p. 410).

Resignification

A word has both a denotation (the thing to which it refers) and connotation (the emotional resonances embedded within a term's meaning). When thinking about a word's meaning, you need to consider not only the thing denoted, but also the cultural baggage attached to and emotional responses embedded within the term. Thus, when you seek to change a sign's meaning, or resignify it, you need to think about the connotational *and* denotational meanings. **Resignification** refers to the linguistic practice in which you reject a term's existing meaning's normative power, expose how the term's meaning was constructed, and attempt to change its connotation. Instead of unreflexively using language, you would "seek to recite language oppositionally so that hegemonic terms take on alternative, counter-hegemonic meanings" (Lloyd, 2007, p. 129).

SlutWalks are an example of resignification because they embrace the term *slut* and seek to change its meaning (Kapur, 2012). How and why do SlutWalks work to resignify the word *slut*? In January 2011, a police officer at a York University panel on campus safety said women, to avoid sexual assault, should not "dress like sluts" (implying that women who do are "asking"—or deserve—to be raped). Historically, the word *slut* referred to a slovenly girl; in contemporary usage, it refers to a sexually promiscuous woman and has risen to the status of being a "four-letter word" (Nunberg, 2012). People could have responded to the police officer by saying "I am not a slut" or "we don't dress like sluts," but such a response would have "affirm[ed] the stigmatic division of women operative in rape logic" (Hill, 2016, p. 32). Instead, local activists responded by embracing the term and planning what they called a SlutWalk. Instead of accepting the division of women into good and bad, slut and pure, the planners refused victim-blaming and slut-shaming (Hill, 2016). As a result, "the young women who sparked this movement have performed a semantic sleight of hand in appropriating the word 'slut,' making it impossible to tell the 'good girls' from the 'bad girls'" (Carr, 2013).

Starting with a Facebook page and Twitter account, Toronto residents Heather Jarvis and Sonya Barnett organized the April 3, 2011, event that drew between 1,000 to 3,000 people. By the end of 2011, tens of thousands of people had marched in 200 cities and 40 countries. The July 2014 SlutWalk in Reykjavík, Iceland, drew over 11,000 people (Mendes, 2015, pp. 2–3). Organizers of SlutWalk Seattle made clear the importance of the term: "One of the most effective ways to fight hate is to disarm the derogatory terms employed by the haters, embracing them and giving them positive connotations" (as cited in Thompson, 2011, p. 14). On their website, Slut Walk NYC (n.d.) explained: "Some SlutWalk supporters have co-opted the term as a means of reclaiming the insult and defusing it of its sting by wearing it as a badge of pride to indicate sexual self-awareness and humanity." Annie Hill's (2016) analysis concluded, "SlutWalk subverts the meaning of 'slut' by resignifying the term and proliferating parodic performances of its stigmatized referent" (p. 31).

However, not all agree that *slut*, as a term, is something to be embraced (Dow & Wood, 2014). Professors Gail Dines and Wendy J. Murphy (2011) described the attempt to change *slut*'s meaning as a "waste of precious feminist resources" given how the term is "so saturated with the ideology that female sexual energy deserves punishment" (p. 25). A group of Black women also challenged the SlutWalk movement to rename and rebrand itself. Calling for an intersectional approach, they argued,

> As Black women, we do not have the privilege or the space to call ourselves "slut" without validating the already historically entrenched ideology and recurring messages about what and who the Black woman is. We don't have the privilege to play on destructive representations burned in our collective minds, on our bodies and souls for generations. ("An Open Letter," 2011, para. 1)

The debates about SlutWalks provide insight into the problems that face resignification. As HuffPost writer Zeba Blay (2015) clarified, "Reclaiming the word 'slut' is an entirely different beast for Black women."

However, Blay argued that Amber Rose's October 2015 SlutWalk in Los Angeles marked a turning point in the debate because that event was organized by a woman of color for women of color and, thus,

> was crucially inclusive of women from all backgrounds. . . . Rose's SlutWalk and the women and men of varied gender expressions who attended were a beautiful reminder of the nuances and complexities inherent in the ongoing issue of slut-shaming and victim blaming. There are women of color in *need* of that kind of solidarity and understanding. There *is* room for women of color in the SlutWalk movement—and it has to be on our terms.

Resignification is not easy, nor always the best strategy. Even if a subordinated group resignifies a term for counter-hegemonic use, that does not mean those who are part of the dominant group can use the term with impunity.

Scholars and activists have written about the need to resignify words. Inga Muscio's (2002) *Cunt*, as well as Eve Ensler's (2000) *The Vagina Monologues*, reclaim *cunt*. Politicized sex workers resignified *whore* in Gail Pheterson's (1989) *A Vindication of the Rights of Whores*. In 1968, Jo Freeman offered the "Bitch Manifesto," Elizabeth Wurtzel's (1998) *Bitch* praises difficult women, *Bitch* magazine offers a feminist response to pop culture, and Meredith Brooks's song "Bitch" proclaims "I'm a bitch / I'm a lover / I'm a child / I'm a mother / I'm a sinner / I'm a saint / I do not feel ashamed. . . . So take me as I am / This may mean / You'll have to be a stronger man." Yet, in 2015, YouTube vlogger Laci Green questioned whether *bitch* could be *re*claimed given it never had a positive meaning.

Many of these examples were cited in a case that went all the way to the Supreme Court in 2017. The Asian-American band The Slants fought to have its name recognized by the U.S. Patent and Trademark Office (PTO). In the legal brief, they argued they were

> following in the long tradition of "reappropriation," in which members of minority groups have reclaimed terms that were once directed at them as insults and turned them outward as badges of pride. In recent times, the most conspicuous examples have been words such as "queer," "dyke," and so on— formerly derogatory terms that have been so successfully adopted by members of the gay and lesbian community that they have now lost most, if not all, of their pejorative connotations. . . . [Band leader Simon] Tam aimed to do the same for Asian-Americans. "We want to take on these stereotypes that people have about us, like the slanted eyes, and own them," he explained. (Brief for Simon Shiao Tam, 2016, p. 2)

Dykes on Bikes Women's Motorcycle Contingent of San Francisco, a group that faced its own problems with the PTO, wrote an *amicus curiae* brief in support of The Slants, explaining how the group "purposefully and intentionally adopted the term 'dykes' as part of its trademark in order to highlight and confront the controversial history of that term and dispel the notion that it is disparaging" (Brief for San Francisco, 2016, p. 2).

But all this raises the question of *who* gets to use the resignified term. The group to whom it is applied or anyone? One might argue that only those to whom the label is applied can use it in a way that resignifies. This is the difference between the Asian music group using the name *The Slants* and the Washington football team using a derogatory term for Native Americans. Why is this different? When a group has used a term to injure another, then a repetition of that term by the dominant group can repeat that injury. However, this does not necessarily mean that some terms should be legally banned. Instead, it means people need to think carefully about what it means for them to use a term. Are you the group to whom the term is applied? Or are you part of the group that has repeated that term as a way to injure another? Judith Butler (1997) explained, "The resignification of speech requires opening new contexts, speaking in ways that have never been legitimated, and hence producing legitimation in new and future forms" (p. 41). This means bodies that have been used by language need to be the ones to use it in new ways.

As an illustration, many of those who participated in the 2017 Woman's March made signs in response to President Donald Trump's 2005 hot-mic comment about how "when you're a star, they let you do it. You can do anything. . . . Grab them by the pussy. You can do anything" (as cited in Fahrenthold, 2016). Trump used *pussy* in a way that injures, reducing women to a body part that he could grab without their consent. During the Women's March on Washington, and around the country and globe, many wore pink "pussy hats" (knit and stitched to look like cat ears) and held up signs declaring, "This pussy grabs back." Ashley Judd recited 19-year-old Nina Donovan's poem "Nasty Woman" that declared, "And our pussies ain't for grabbing. . . . Our pussies are for our pleasure. They are for birthing new generations of filthy, vulgar, nasty, proud, Christian, Muslim, Buddhist, Sikh, you name it, for new generations of nasty women" (as cited in Rosen, 2017). In response to the signs, TV host and lawyer Michael Smerconish asked documentarian Michael Moore (2017), "Has the word been normalized?" Moore commented, "Women have normalized it and owned it," to which Smerconish said, "But not us," to which Moore emphatically replied, "No! No! I think that's not a good idea. I think women have had enough of us and our language that it's time to show some respect but let them own the word. The word has power now that they're going to use with it."

Resignification is a difficult and complicated process. Even when words are reclaimed, they might (intentionally or unintentionally) create other exclusions. At the 2017 Women's March on Washington, the reclaiming of *pussy*, for example, was perceived by some as reasserting the assumption that having a vagina is essential to womanhood. As a result, many trans-women felt excluded from the event. However, others saw *pussy* not as referring to a specific body part, but as a metaphor used to describe all feminine people. For them, the term was inclusive.

Interestingly, when a derogatory word's history is researched, it often (but not always) turns out that the word originally had a positive meaning and only recently came to carry negative connotations. Muscio's (2002) research on *cunt* uncovered how its precursors originally were related to titles of respect for women or names of goddesses and that

> the words "bitch" and "whore" have also shared a similar fate [to *cunt*] in our language. This seemed rather fishy to me. Three words which convey negative meanings about women, specifically, all happen to have once had totally positive associations about women. (p. 6)

Urvashi Vaid (1995), in an analysis of LGBTQ rights, found that *queer* originally was used as a form of self-naming by homosexuals. By the 1910s and 1920s, men who thought of themselves as different because of their homosexual attraction to other men rather than because of their feminine gender appearance called themselves *queer* (p. 42). *Queer* later developed the negative connotation still heard as an epithet in playgrounds and streets. This meaning did not develop overnight, but, as Butler (1993a) explained, "'Queer' derives its force precisely through the repeated invocation by which it has become linked to accusation, pathologization, insult" (p. 172).

This hints at the difficulty involved in resignifying a term. People cannot simply wish a term's connotation to change. Butler's theory on the performativity of gender explains why this is the case: People tend to be "ventriloquists, iterating the gendered acts that have come before them" (Hall, 2000, p. 186). How does one get out of this repetitive loop? By resignification—the repeated invocation of a term that links it to praise, normalization, and celebration. Unfortunately, even when a term may be resignified within a group of people, that does not mean the new meaning carries beyond that group. Butler (1993a) noted, "As much as it is necessary to . . . lay claim to the power to name oneself and determine the conditions under which the name is used, it is also impossible to sustain that kind of mastery over the trajectory of those categories within discourse" (p. 173). However, that may be one's only option.

Butler (1997) noted that people sometimes "cling to the terms that pain" them because they provide "some form of social and discursive existence" (p. 26). Guided by Althusser's theory of interpellation (whereby one becomes a subject because one is recognized by another), Butler posited, "The act of recognition becomes an act of constitution: the address animates the subject into existence" (p. 25). Thus, it is understandable that one might prefer being known as a *queer* or a *bitch* to not being known at all. Additionally, even as dominant naming may disempower, it also creates locations for resistance, for "opening up of the foreclosed and the saying of the unspeakable" (p. 41).

Psychology research supports the liberatory potential of self-labeling. In a series of experiments, researchers tested the effect on marginalized people and on others' perception of marginalized people when the marginalized reappropriated a derogatory slur used by the dominant culture. The researchers found that reappropriation can "weaken the label's stigmatizing force" (Galinsky et al., 2013, p. 2020). However, one of the central variables was the feeling of group power. Reappropriation of a term was easier when an individual felt the group to which they belonged was powerful. In other words, resignification requires collective action, not just a personal decision.

Strategic Essentialism and Rhetorics of Difference

Often, those who are most marginalized are those most strongly denied a language with which to speak. Yet when challenging oppressions, many people choose to speak from the very identity ingredient that has been the basis of their oppression. When people speak as women, as people of color, as queer, as third-world women, as indigenous people, they thematize their named identities as a legitimizing force of their rhetoric.

The relationship between identity categories and political action is complex. Although we are wary about claims of some innate or biological sense of identity, we also recognize that each person is categorized and that those categories have real effects. Even if there is no biological foundation to race, people categorized as Black, Hispanic, Arab, Asian, and Native American are subjected to stereotypes on the basis of that categorization. Regarding sex, even if the differences between women and men are infinitesimal, people treat men and women as different. Identity categories might be artificial, but they have real, material effects. Given that linguistic categories of identity difference do exist, how might they be challenged? One way is to be constantly vigilant about whether the perception of differences is warranted. Another way is to engage in what Gayatri Spivak (1996) called *strategic essentialism* (pp. 159, 214).

Strategic essentialism refers to the intentional embrace and foregrounding of an identity ingredient as definitive of a group's identity for a political purpose and has two important characteristics: (1) the so-called essential attributes of the group are defined by the group members themselves, and (2) even as group members engage in essentialism, they recognize that it is always an artificial construct. They do not deny they are a group but, instead, seek to control what it means to be part of that group. This reclaims agency. Jaqui Alexander and Chandra Talpade Mohanty (1997) explained: "Agency is . . . the conscious and ongoing reproduction of the terms of one's existence while taking responsibility for this process" (p. xxviii). Marginalized people become actors instead of the acted upon.

Even as scholars recognize that identities are fluid and contingent, and that clinging to them carries danger, scholars also understand "'identities' as relational and grounded in the historically produced social facts which constitute social locations" (Moya, 1997, p. 127). Identities matter insofar as they determine where a person fits within the social order as it presently exists. When one is positioned at the margin, this does not mean that one automatically articulates counterdiscourses but that such a person can provide a location from which a group oppositionally can "provide us with a critical perspective from which we can disclose the complicated workings of ideology and oppression" (p. 128). English professor Paula M. L. Moya (1997) argued that the external construction of identities influences experiences, and those experiences then inform what people know and how they know it. Moya urged everyone to remember that although "people are not *uniformly* determined by any *one* social fact, . . . social facts (such as gender and race)" *do* influence who we are (p. 132).

Communication scholar Lisa Flores's (1996) study of Chicanas' development of a rhetorical homeland illustrated strategic essentialism in the form of rhetorics of difference. Flores examined how Chicana feminists' creative works participated in **rhetorics of difference** by creating a discursive space, distinct from the liminal borderlands in which they live—the space between the United States and Mexico that Chicana lesbian feminist Gloria Anzaldúa (1987) described as where the "Third World grates against the first and bleeds" (p. 3). Flores explained that because Chicana feminists live between worlds—physically unwanted in the United States and not wanting to return to Mexico, emotionally seeking the safety of family while seeking respect as women—they must create their own homeland.

The development of a space of belonging, where they can assert agency in relation to their identity, cannot occur in the public sphere given their limited access to it, so Chicana feminists turn to what Flores (1996) called private discourse: "Through the rejection of the external and creation of the internal, marginalized groups establish themselves as different from stereotyped perceptions and different from dominant culture" (p. 145). Importantly, Chicana feminists do not remain an insular group. After they "carv[e] out a space within which they can find their own voice . . . they begin to turn it into a home where connections to those within their families are made strong" (p. 146). Once the homeland is firmly established, "recognizing their still existing connections to various other groups, Chicana feminists construct bridges or pathways connecting them with others" (p. 146).

Even as people strategically appeal to essential identities as locations from which to develop knowledge, create solidarity, and resist dominant definitions, the identities should always be critically examined. Sometimes the identities are strongly embraced to create a sense of belonging. Other times, some identity ingredients are deemphasized so that alliances can be built on the basis of other ingredients. Gloria Anzaldúa (1990) elegantly described this multilayered process as creating bridges, drawbridges, sandbars, or islands. Even as groups build bridges to others, sometimes moments of separation are needed, and the drawbridge is raised.

Although many attempt to use strategic essentialism, its political success is not guaranteed. Spivak (1993) claimed the strategy "has served its purpose" (p. 17), but others still advocate it. One of the concerns is that even if people are conscious of their participation in essentialism, "strategic essentialism keeps alive the image of a homogeneous, static, and essential third-world culture" and can also limit people to only claiming knowledge about the identity they embrace (Lee, 2011, p. 265). The question remains: Do the short-term political benefits outweigh the long-term costs of accepting reductive definitions of self (Eide, 2010, p. 76; Lee, 2011, p. 265)?

Moving Over

Building alliances and creating solidarity across identity categories is a good thing. However, whenever one seeks to represent others, one must be attentive to how one speaks for, about, or in solidarity with that other. The issue of who can speak for whom is complex. Those working in solidarity with marginalized groups have long grappled with it. English professors Judith Roof and Robyn Weigman (1995) edited a collection of essays that address this very issue, *Who Can Speak? Authority and Critical Identity*. In it, scholars explored the problems presented by the act of speaking for others. When a White, college-educated, middle-class, Christian ciswoman who is a U.S. citizen claims to speak for all women, she potentially erases most other women. This woman's concerns are probably not identical to those of a third-world, poor, Muslim transwoman of color. Members of a privileged group also may erase others when they seek economic advantage by passing themselves off as members of a marginal group. People need to be wary of instances of speaking for others, because it

> is often born of a desire for mastery, to privilege oneself as the one who more correctly understands the truth about another's situation or as the one who can champion a just cause and thus achieve glory and praise. The effect of the practice of speaking for others is often, though not always, erasure and a reinscription of sexual, national, and other kinds of hierarchies. (Alcoff, 1995, p. 116)

However, this should not be taken as an excuse to not speak: "Even a complete retreat from speech is of course not neutral since it allows the continued dominance of current discourses and acts by omission to reinforce their dominance" (Alcoff, 1995, p. 108). Sometimes, when a group cannot speak for itself (e.g., due to political repression, lack of time or resources), then those with power have a responsibility to speak. Philosopher Linda Alcoff (1995) explained,

> A retreat from speaking for will not result in an increase in receptive listening in all cases; it may result merely in a retreat into a narcissistic yuppie lifestyle in which a privileged person takes no responsibility whatsoever for her society. (p. 107)

People need to carefully reflect on when, and for whom, they speak, yet speak they must.

Moving over refers to the conscious choice to silence oneself and create space for others to talk. An interesting case exists in which a race-privileged person stepped aside when asked by those for/as whom she was speaking. Anne Cameron, a well-known White Canadian author, wrote first-person accounts of the lives of Native Canadian women. Lee Maracle, a Canadian author of Salish and Cree ancestry and a member of the Stó:lō Nation, was sent as a spokesperson for a group of writers who met and decided to ask Cameron to "move over" at the 1988 International Feminist Book Fair in Montreal. When asked, Cameron did, indeed, move over (Maracle, 1989, p. 10).

The Native women's concern was that as long as Whites writing as Native women filled stores' bookshelves, no room was left for Native women. Maracle (1989) explained, "So few Canadians want to read about us that there is little room for Native books. . . . If Anne takes up that space there is no room for us at all" (p. 10). This example is fascinating because of the deep level of respect everyone involved had for each other. Maracle and the other Native Canadian women did not see Cameron as their enemy, and Cameron understood the basis of the request and honored it. The point is that sometimes material realities (monies for publishing, contracts, space on bookstore shelves) can inhibit the possibilities of the marginalized to be heard. People with privilege, whether race, class, sex, nationality, or religion, may need to step aside, move over, and make space when others wish to speak.

Conclusion

This chapter is not about being politically correct but about being an ethical, conscious, critical, and inventive communicator. Language is fun, fascinating, and of real consequence. Learning to speak clearly, vividly, passionately, and with joy is not drudgery. However, even as we play with language, we still must recognize that rules exist. Almost everyone is familiar with Robert Fulghum's (2004) book *All I Really Need to Know I Learned in Kindergarten* and its list of rules. The first few are "Share everything. Play fair. Don't hit people. Put things back where you found them. Clean up your own mess. Don't take things that aren't yours. Say you're sorry when you hurt somebody" (p. 2). Although most people may have learned these rules in kindergarten, translating them into language rules may not happen until later (college, maybe?).

Here is our playful reinterpretation of the rules. Like Anne Cameron, share, even if it means moving over. Be fair in the way you describe the world, giving all people recognition of their existence by avoiding the falsely universal *we* and sexist language. Do not use violent language. When you use words borrowed from another, make sure you make clear where you found them. If your language is messy, imprecise, or causes messes because it is violent or uses truncated passives, clean up your language. If a term has a specific meaning as part of a coculture, do not use it unless granted permission. And should you ever hurt someone with your language, apologize. Sticks and stones may break bones, and words may break spirits.

Understanding the power of language requires all language users to be more conscious of the words they use and the worlds they construct. Native Canadian author Jeanette Armstrong (1990) outlined a powerful language ethic held by Native people:

> When you speak, . . . you not only have to assume responsibility for speaking those words, but you are responsible for the effect of those words on the person you are addressing *and* the thousands of years of tribal memory packed into your understanding of those words. So, when you speak, you need to know what you are speaking about. You need to perceive or imagine the impact of your words on the listener and understand the responsibility that goes with *being* a speaker. (pp. 27–28)

Even though Armstrong described one nation's ethic, Armstrong believed responsibility is shared by all who use language:

> We are all responsible in that way. We are all thinking people. We all have that ability and we all have that responsibility. We may not want to have that responsibility or we may feel unworthy of that responsibility, but every time we speak we have that responsibility. Everything we say affects someone, someone is hearing it, someone is understanding it, someone is going to take it and it becomes memory. We are all powerful, each one of us individually. We are able to make things change, to make things happen differently. We are all able to heal. (p. 29)

Sometimes, a person may use a term and not recognize that its meaning may have moved on. Mistakes do happen, but as Alcoff (1995) was quick to remind, "a *partial* loss of control does not entail a *complete* loss of accountability" (p. 105).

So speak, speak out, speak loudly, speak softly, speak kindly, speak kindness, play with what you speak, speak playfully, speak in solidarity with others, speak with power, speak truth to power, speak back to power, talk back, talk.

KEY CONCEPTS

DISCUSSION QUESTIONS

1. Why is recognizing both the liberatory and oppressive potential of language important?

2. What is the ethical debate regarding "speaking for others"? How do the authors suggest we address the debate? Do you agree or disagree and why?

3. For each language form that constrains outlined in the chapter, find one example in contemporary discourse.

4. Do you think resignification is possible? Why or why not? Why would some groups or people choose such a strategy?

PART II

Institutions

CHAPTER 6

An Introduction to Gender in Social Institutions

Thus far, we have focused on a person's performance of gender through conversation, body, and language. We tried to make clear that even though gender/sex differences are not biological, perceptions of differences persist and have real consequences, both positive and negative, for individuals and groups. Which raises this question: What are the sources of these differences? Gender/sex differences exist because of larger social forces, particularly institutions and the communication that exists within and between them. Institutions push particular sexes to perform gender in particular ways.

Multiple social institutions operate in a given culture and serve specific functions. Families provide safety and childrearing, educational institutions create and pass on knowledge and rules, work provides income and identity, religions teach beliefs by which members should live, and media inform and entertain. Thus, to understand gender in communication, you need to study not only the micropolitics of personal gender performances and interpersonal interactions, but also the meso- and macrolevel communication within and from institutions that normalize particular understandings of gender through cultural expectations of patterned behaviors.

Sociologist Patricia Yancey Martin (2004) outlined 12 characteristics of **social institutions**. Institutions

(1)   are social,

(2)   persist across time and space,

(3)   have distinct social practices that are repeated,

(4)   constrain and facilitate behavior,

(5)   designate social positions characterized by expectations and norms,

(6)   are constituted by people,

(7)   are internalized as part of people's identities,

(8)   have a legitimating ideology,

(9)   are contradictory,

(10) continually change,

(11) are organized and permeated by power, and

(12) are not separable into micro and macro phenomena. (pp. 1256–1258)

These characteristics foreground how people compose institutions and how "institutions define reality for us" (Andersen, 2015, p. 30). They also help explain why studying the role of institutions in gender communication is challenging. First, institutions are amorphous. They are not reducible to specific organizations or groups but are composed of the practices and beliefs that link groups and organizations together. Second, they are large, pervasive, and interdependent. They support each other. Third, they normalize rules and values and related rights and responsibilities—making them seem natural and universal. Fourth, institutions change constantly and embrace contradictory values and norms. This makes them difficult to grasp and also makes them powerful.

Institutions' hegemonic power to normalize is why analysis of their communicative practices is essential. Sociology professor Kathleen Gerson (2004) explained that "private choices are rooted in social arrangements over which individual women and men have only limited control" (p. 164). For example, consumers tend to think of their purchases of particular brands of jeans, shoes, or cars as personal selections, but they are influenced by manufacturers and advertisers. Capitalism is a social institution that creates consumer needs (Sorrells, 2016). Even when it comes to gender/sex identity, to assume you act completely independent of external influence is to ignore the larger elephant in the room—the institutional forces that influence how people perform their gender. Sociologist Margaret Andersen (2015) explained,

> *Gender is not just an attribute of individuals; instead, gender is systematically structured in social institutions.* . . . Gender is created, not just within families or interpersonal relationships . . . but also within the structure of all major social institutions, including schools, religion, the economy, and the state. . . . These institutions shape and mold the experiences of us all. (p. 30; italics in original)

Institutions, like individuals, communicate gender and are gendered through communication. Thus, to more fully understand gender in communication, you should study how predominant social institutions' communication influences individuals' life choices and, conversely, how individuals can affect the policies, procedures, and practices of social institutions.

To describe institutions' influence, we distinguish between micropolitics, mesopolitics, and macropolitics. **Micropolitics** refers to the negotiations over power in everyday interactions between people. **Mesopolitics**, *meso* meaning middle range, refers to the power exerted by groups within institutions (e.g., specific families, schools, workplaces, religions, or media sources) to ensure that individuals follow the institutions' rules or to challenge those rules (Turner, 2017). **Macropolitics** refers to laws', policies', and culture's power to enforce social norms.

Researchers talk about the micro-, meso-, and macropolitics as theoretically distinct, but they overlap in practice. This means the relationships between the levels and influences are difficult to outline in a clear, cause-and-effect fashion. We devote the remainder of the textbook to some key institutions that normalize particular understandings of gender: family, education, work, religion, and media. Before we explore them, we want to first make clear the relationship between communication and institutions.

Prejudice Versus Institutionalized Discrimination

We embrace the critical cultural approach to interrogate the interrelations among micro- (interpersonal), meso- (group), and macro- (institutional) practices of gender. To do so, we must first make clear that personal prejudice is distinct from institutionalized discrimination. Prejudice in the form of individuals' false or bad beliefs does not *cause* inequalities. Instead, **institutionalized discrimination** is maintained at the macrolevel through complex sets of social institutions that interact with, structure, and influence individual beliefs and prejudices. Institutionalized discrimination creates **systemic inequalities**—patterns of differential group treatment repeated across time even in the absence of overt discrimination. For example, the fact that African Americans are underrepresented among military officers but overrepresented in U.S. prisons is not due to individual acts of discrimination or failure to achieve; it is due to systemic racism. To think of sexism or racism as exclusively lodged within individuals misdirects attention and fails to make visible macrolevel changes that are needed.

The pink tax is another example of a systemic inequality resulting from institutionalized gender/sex discrimination. *Pink tax* is a term recently coined to name arbitrary price markups placed on women's clothes, menstrual products, personal care items, and services. An editorial by Candice Elliot (2015) of *Listen Money Matters* argued that women on average not only make less, but they also pay more for certain products, compared to men. For example, Old Navy charged $10 to $15 more for women's plus-size jeans, while men's jeans were priced the same regardless of size, and products used by all sexes (e.g., deodorant, razors, shaving cream, lotion) are arbitrarily marked up when marketed to women. In New York City, women paid about 7% more than men for similar products, and 13% more for personal care items (deBlasio & Menin, 2015). Women also may pay more for car repairs. Researchers Busse, Israeli, and Zettlemeyer (2017) found men were charged roughly the same for an auto repair regardless of their perceived knowledge about what the repair should cost, while women were charged much higher rates than men unless the women customers proved they knew better. Interestingly, women who asked for a discount were more likely to get it than men who asked but, even when women received a discount, they still were likely to pay a higher rate than men. The fact that women are paying more for the same products and services cannot be explained by extra manufacturing or service costs, and the fact that there is a pattern in such price differences shows this is about systemic sexism, not an individual retailer's prejudice.

Obviously, individual prejudice contributes to the maintenance of systems of discrimination. Still, the most powerful engines that drive and sustain racism, sexism, heterosexism, and cissexism (and hence construct race, gender, sexuality, and sex) are embedded in a society's institutions. Philosopher Sandra Harding (1995) argued that one should view inequality as "fundamentally a political relationship," as a strategy that "privileges some groups over others" (p. 122). Because discrimination is made normal and unconscious through institutionalization, to end discrimination people must identify how it operates on an institutional level via its communicative practices. Attention must turn to the institutions that structure people's relationships to themselves, each other, and society.

Sexism, racism, homophobia, classism, and cissexism are not institutions in and of themselves, but they become so embedded in institutional communicative practices and norms that it becomes almost impossible to identify them as forms of discrimination. When someone hurls an epithet at another human being, it is easy to identify the presence of prejudiced attitudes. However, when one looks at systemic inequalities, it is difficult to identify who is responsible (because no one single person is), and it is impossible to locate the intent to discriminate (because no single person is behind the discrimination). Who is responsible for the fact that only 20% of disabled U.S. children are Black, yet they account for 42% of disabled students put in restraints or seclusion? Black and Hispanic students as young as preschool make up more than half of those suspended, even though they are not half of the student population (Nesbit, 2015).

Subtle forms of sexism occur when a person's gender performance conflicts with institutional expectations. For example, why do males continue to be statistically underrepresented in the professions of registered nurses (10%) and elementary and middle school teachers (21.5%) (U.S. Census Bureau, 2017)? No one is barring men from nursing or elementary education classes. Because these professions are considered caring professions, the gendered expectations attached to sex may make it seem as though men are unfit to perform these roles. The few men who enter caring professions often experience discrimination.

Institutional practices can result in inequality. Just because one cannot directly identify and locate intent does not mean that no discrimination occurred. Communication analyses of institutional practices and norms reveal possible contributors to inequality. For example, political communication scholars studied the news media's objectification of female political candidates and its impact on voters (Funk & Coker, 2016). Communication education scholars studied how enhanced considerations for diversity in students' race, class, and gender may improve equal opportunities in learning (Rudick & Golsan, 2016). A media scholar studied how some women use social media to close the gender gap in political engagement (Bode, 2017). An organizational communication scholar studied how technology companies developed social identities that exclude women and people of color, similar to product branding, and how these brands might be challenged (Aschcraft, 2016). To identify the communicative practices that maintain gender and sex norms, norms that often dictate different and unequal treatment, one must examine how institutions maintain and perpetuate gender/sex.

Institutional Control

Institutions wield a great deal of power via social control. They distribute cultural resources, constrain and facilitate actions, allocate power, assign rights and responsibilities, and define truth and knowledge (Ballantine & Hammack, 2015; Lorber, 1994; Vannoy, 2001). Institutions' maintenance of presumed gender/sex differences is why they remain widely believed and accepted as truisms, in spite of the growing evidence disproving this simplistic notion (e.g., Dindia & Canary, 2006; Ehrlich, Meyerhoff, & Holmes, 2014). How many times have you heard, "Men and women are just different"? Institutions normalize this idea. Our central point is the differences that are noted, viewed as significant, and praised are those sanctioned by institutions. Institutions are not apolitical or universally positive.

Social institutions are created and maintained by the predominant groups within particular historical, cultural, and political environments. As such, the institutions help to maintain the values, ideology, and worldview of the predominant groups. Sexism and racism in language demonstrates this. The fact that people still use marked terms to identify doctors and judges who are women and people of color, as in the "woman doctor" or "Black judge," reveals the White male cultural norm implicit in traditional career labels. Social institutions, communicating through the dominant language, sustain and create cultural hegemony, whereby the beliefs and interests of dominant groups dictate what is considered common sense. Institutions' power comes not from a single act of enforcement but through subtle forms of social control of which people may not be aware.

Social institutions use **cultural ideology**—the predominant ideas, values, beliefs, perceptions, and understandings known to members of a society that guide their behaviors—even if they do not personally subscribe to some of them. Antonio Gramsci's concept of hegemonic or ruling ideology (Zompetti, 1997) is useful here. Gramsci argued that social control, **hegemony**, is accomplished primarily through the control of ideas. People are encouraged to see an idea or ideology as common sense, even if it conflicts with their own experiences. By recognizing how gender is embedded within social institutions and cultural ideology, one is better able to recognize the falsehood of seemingly commonsense binary assumptions and instead realize the diversity of gender/sex experiences (Buzzanell, Sterk, & Turner, 2004).

Here are a few U.S. examples of compliance with hegemonic norms that people believe to be voluntary. Can you identify which social institutions benefit from each?

- In heterosexual marriages, women tend to adopt their husband's name.
- School holidays are structured around Christian holy days.
- Boys are not allowed to play with dolls (but action figures are okay).

(Continued)

(Continued)

- Shopping is considered an acceptable leisure activity, particularly for women.
- Men do not wear skirts.
- Women shave their legs.

Can you think of more?

Institutions enforce and sustain gender expectations. Enforcement mechanisms can appear less coercive for those who abide by socially sanctioned gender roles. But for those who are gender non-conforming, the coercive power of institutions becomes overt. When men exhibit femininity or violate heteronormativity, they are disciplined, sometimes through overt violence, as was army private Barry Winchell, who was murdered by two other soldiers because of his relationship with a trans-woman (Sloop, 2004). When biological women exhibit masculinity, they, too, face violence, as is made clear by the murder of Brandon Teena, a story cinematically told in *Boys Don't Cry* (Sloop, 2004). Challenges to gender norms usually do not pass unremarked and unnoticed by dominant institutions.

Institutionalized Gendered/Sexed Violence

Institutionalized violence occurs when overt and subtle forms of violence become normalized as a result of institutional rules and norms. In the United States, gendered/sexed violence and violent thinking are part of hegemonic masculinity, meaning that men are expected to be violent and women are not. Masculine violence has become so normalized that people often do not recognize the violence when they speak or hear it. Men's studies scholar Michael Kimmel (2012a) said violence is so ingrained in daily life that it is commonplace in the closest relationships, including families, friends, and lovers.

Does this mean that all men are violent? No. But because masculine men need not devote time and energy to thinking about how to avoid violence, all masculine men benefit from the institution of gender that normalizes violence. Does this mean that all women are victims? No. But as long as masculinity is predominantly defined as being aggressive and femininity is defined as being submissive, all women and feminine people potentially can be victimized. Does this mean men cannot be victims, too? Men absolutely can be victims of other people's hypermasculinity. What does this mean for men who work to prevent violence? Their efforts often are not counted, and they are emasculated. What does this mean for women who are violent? Women, too, are socialized in a world in which violence equals power and many enact it.

The institutionalization of violence has effects beyond the microlevel of interpersonal relationships. The fear of sexual violence triggered by street harassment affects many women's mobility and, thus, ability to shop, attend school, work, or participate in civic life. A national survey by a volunteer group, Stop Street Harassment (2006), reported 77% of the women surveyed had been followed during the past year and more than 50% had been groped, fondled, or assaulted by passing men (Chemaly, 2016). Political scientist Amy Caiazza (2005) analyzed factors affecting men's and women's levels of civic participation, including fear of potential violence. Caiazza found that

> for women as a group, a sense of perceived safety is strongly related to involvement in the community, while a lack of perceived safety is linked to disengagement. In contrast, among men as a group, safety plays a relatively insignificant role in encouraging or discouraging engagement. (p. 1608)

This conclusion is moderated when one recognizes that safety is not experienced equally by all women; poor women tend to be less safe, and so their participation is not influenced by the perceived loss of safety (which they normally lack anyway) but by other factors. Caiazza's research made clear that "gender-based violence is an issue relevant to political and civic participation" (p. 1627). Some women participate less than men in politics, city councils, and legislatures not because they are disinterested in politics but because their fear of violence functions as a deterrent to participation.

When sexual violence is examined in this way, antiviolence measures are no longer just a way to decrease crime or maintain law and order. They are a means to fortify democracy and everyone's access to it (Caiazza, 2005). This exposes how gender/sex affects something as taken-for-granted as citizenship. Although every person is equal under the law, the reality is that gender, and the institutionalization of gender/sex violence, make participation unequal.

Understanding the complex ways in which violence is normalized by communication practices across social institutions reveals the sources of gender/sex oppression and social control for all people and identifies paths toward cultural change (Kimmel, 2012a). Individual pathologies cannot explain why violence is so pervasive or why it disproportionately affects some groups. By examining violence as a part of gendered institutions, you can begin to identify how it is socialized into such things as raising boys not to cry, sexual harassment in the workplace, bullying in schools, honoring martyrdom in religions, and the wide variety of violence and pornography in commercial media.

As you confront the multiple forms of violence in society on a daily basis, remember that most are not isolated cases. Rather, they are systemically related to institutions and the communicative acts that maintain those institutions. In the chapters to follow, we help you identify the links among gender, violence, social institutions, communication, and cases of successful resistance.

Preview

Every major social institution in a culture affects the construction of gender/sex, and gender/sex influences the functioning of every institution. Martin (2003) pointed out, "Gendered practices are learned and enacted in childhood and in every major site of social behavior over the life course, including in schools, intimate relationships, families, workplaces, houses of worship, and social movements" (p. 352).

We begin our discussion of specific social institutions by examining the one immediately experienced by most—family. Family communication is heavily influenced by gendered/sexed cultural expectations, and these, in turn, affect the gender identity development and communication of individuals. Understanding the family as an institution makes clear that the family you came from was determined not only by the individuals who populated it but also by the institutional structure of family itself.

Education is another institution that affects persons from childhood on. When you graduate from college, you will likely have spent over 16 years in this institution—your most formative psychological, physical, moral, and intellectual developmental period. What you learn in textbooks is not value-free or objective. Educational influences stem from classroom and extracurricular interactions with teachers, administrators, and peers. These interactions have historically covertly taught heteronormativity as well as racism and sexism.

Work includes the gendering of paid and unpaid labor, organizational cultures, and gendered/sexed barriers such as sexual harassment. In the United States, the almost unquestioned belief that work is good and the demonization of those on welfare demonstrates the way rhetorical constructions of work maintain its function as a social institution (Schram, 1995). Work expectations are not consistent across sexes. Work is not a gender- or sex-neutral institution. Work is a masculine institution that helps uphold caretaking in the family as a feminine trait and responsibility.

We turn next to religion. While most gender research fails to address religion, few other social institutions rival the power of religious doctrine, culture, and practice in establishing and controlling one's identity and values. Religious institutions participate in the construction of sex, gender, and sexuality, and while much of this influence imposes rigid binary gender/sex behaviors and beliefs, many individuals find ways to create spaces of liberation. Regardless of whether one is examining the general functioning of religion or a specific religious tradition, using a critical gendered lens enables you to understand more about how gender influences religious identity and how religion influences the construction of gender. Especially given the energy religion expends on delimiting acceptable forms of sexuality, the study of religion is central to understanding the construction of and intersections among sex, gender, and sexuality.

We end with a discussion of media, a communication institution that also functions as an amplifier for other institutions. We approach media as an institution to make clear that to focus on a particular broadcast or single medium is inadequate. Media share conventions regarding construction of content and construction of audience. Additionally, media are one of the primary mechanisms that reiterate gender while also providing locations in which resistance can occur.

These chapters illustrate the power macro- and mesolevel communication can have on individuals' and groups' daily lives. Much of the power comes from the ways in which social institutions interlock to influence each other. We argue the key to bringing about social justice is through the critical analysis and change of these social institutions. This is not to dismiss the important roles such institutions play in reducing the uncertainty of social life, creating a sense of belonging, offering shelter, providing order, and organizing mass initiatives. Rather, the ultimate goal is to recognize these important needs and see how all people could be better served. As you delve into the specific dynamics of each social institution, we suggest you look for key institutional characteristics described in this chapter to see them at work in constructing, maintaining, and changing gender identities and dynamics. In what ways do the unique institutional norms liberate and/or restrict gender identity constructions?

KEY CONCEPTS

cultural ideology 133

hegemony 133

institutionalized
discrimination 131

institutionalized violence 134

macropolitics 130

mesopolitics 130

micropolitics 130

social institutions 129

systemic inequalities 131

DISCUSSION QUESTIONS

1. What are the characteristics of a social institution? Can you identify other characteristics? What roles do they play in the institution?

2. How do institutions wield power? What are cultural ideology and cultural hegemony?

3. Why is an institutional approach to gender in communication important?

4. What is institutionalized gendered/sexed violence? Why does it exist?

CHAPTER 7

Families

Photographer Crystal Kells's son, 5-year-old Cian, loves Iron Man, Paw Patrol, playing cars and superhero, and wearing his hair short. He also loves to wear dresses (Bologna, 2017). In a post on Bored Panda that went viral, Kells (2017) described attempting to raise a child without gender stereotypes, explaining, "His gender does not dictate what he should wear or what he should play with." Kells went on to say, "We've never actually taught it to him 'This is for girls and this is for boys' and we never will. Why should we? What difference does it ACTUALLY make?" Kells concluded the essay by declaring that Cian's health and happiness are the main priority and offered nine photos of Cian in dresses, skirts, a tutu, and a suit with suspenders showing how "he loves to look just like his Daddy sometimes too." For the full story and photographs, see http://www.boredpanda .com/my-son-cian-yes-my-son-who-wears-dresses/.

Kells's essay received 36,000 views within a week and generated passionate responses both criticizing and supporting their parenting decisions. Some commenters criticized Kells for using images of Cian to promote Kells's photography business. Others felt that Kells was putting Cian in a precarious position by publicly sharing photos of him wearing a dress. One commenter wrote, "I keep on feeling uncomfortable with parents sharing children's pics on social medias [sic], [e]specially if these children might be in a delicate situation. I wouldn't call this 'good parenting'" (giovanna commenting on Kells, 2017). Another person wrote, "While the ultimate goal of your social experiment may be noble, using your own son as a guinea pig, knowing full well the abuse he will endure, before he's capable of giving his fully considered, independent consent, is not just 'unconventional', it's unconscionable" (Len Clements commenting on Kells, 2017).

Others wrote to thank Kells and shared their own experiences of trying to raise children without gender stereotypes. One wrote, "You are doing great, as long as he feels he is being loved and respected nothing else matters" (Eframit Orozco commenting on Kells, 2017). Another wrote, "When I was a kid if I had worn dresses, I would have been beaten up at school and spanked at home. . . . It's not perfect now, but looking at how it was 20 years ago compared to how it is now, we're headed in the right direction. There will always be judgmental people. But we're getting there. You should be proud of him. He looks so happy" (Robert Burford commenting on Kells, 2017).

The volume and intensity of responses to Kells's essay demonstrate that people have strong opinions on how others should raise children and a strong resistance to efforts to embrace more fluid gender in families. What do the responses reveal about the relationship between gender/sex and family communication? Why is parenting without gender stereotypes receiving so much feedback? How do you react to the photos of Cian?

This example illustrates a number of themes in this chapter. Families are an important location where people are gendered. Even though people think of families as composed of personal choices, public communication about families and pressures from people outside of a specific family seek to influence how people construct, and act in, families. Cultural norms (like about how children should be clothed) become visible as institutional social constructions when people challenge those norms. And, although many argue gender norms are natural, people invest intensive energy into reinforcing those norms.

In this chapter, we explore how gendered expectations about parenting tend to constrain families. To understand how gender is constructed through families and how families are organized around gender, we unpack ideologies associated with the institution of families. Historical information on families shows how the concept of the nuclear family relies on the ideology of dating, romance, and heteronormativity. Next, we discuss the state of families and challenge the idea that the family is in crisis. Researchers noted that U.S. people tend to value family life as much as ever, the structure of families and roles of members are more diverse, and fluid gender identities are the solution for maintaining families as a vital aspect of culture (Gerson, 2010; Walsh, 2012). We next focus on the cultural messages about how women should mother. We continue with a discussion of communication in families, specifically parent-child communication and couple communication, to show how gender norms are established and challenged through familial communication practices. We conclude with a discussion of doing, and undoing, family.

Defining Family and Gender/Sex Roles

The concept of *family* is difficult to define because no set structure, purpose, or communicative meaning-making process defines family (Segrin & Flora, 2011). Instead, multiple family structures exist (e.g., single parent, extended, stepfamilies, childfree couples, LBGTQ couples, nonbiological families of choice) and the structures shift across time and cultures. The functions families perform as well as the meanings created are diverse (Karraker & Grochowski, 2012). You may have noticed we avoid using the term *the family*. Instead we refer to *family* (as an institution) or *families*. *The* family suggests only one model of family exists. The highly respected academic journal previously named *Journal of Marriage and the Family* changed its name in 2001 to *Journal of Marriage and Family* to better recognize the diversity of actual families.

Because *family* is not a fixed concept, it requires a fluid description (Hoover, Clark, & Alters, 2004). How researchers define *family* influences what types of families are studied and legitimized. Thus, we adopt a definition of **family** that takes into account two conceptions that inform definitions of families:

> (1) a task or function conception that defines a family based on the enactment of key functions commonly associated with a family (e.g., nurturing and socializing children), and (2) an interactional or transactional conception that defines family based on a shared identity, anticipated future together, and presence of an affective bond. (Suter, Baxter, Seurer, & Thomas, 2014, p. 62)

We appreciate that this definition focuses on affective bond rather than sex or biogenetics. However, despite being expansive, it still privileges childrearing, an issue we discuss later in this chapter.

The institution of family is gendered and genders. Quite simply, "families and gender are so intertwined that it is impossible to understand one without reference to the other. Families are not merely influenced by gender; rather, families are *organized* by gender" (Haddock, Zimmerman, & Lyness, 2003, p. 304). This organization is apparent in the prescribed gender/sex roles played in many families: mother, father, daughter, son, sister, brother, grandmother, grandfather, aunt, uncle. **Gender/sex roles** refer to binary gender social expectations based on a person's sex (Ryle, 2012). These roles are gender/sex marked and designate responsibilities, expectations, and power.

You may think, "Strict gender/sex roles aren't followed today . . . at least not in my family." Although stereotypical gender/sex roles do not define families completely, your awareness of noncompliance means the stereotypical expectations persist. Most people think of themselves as the exception to the norm. If you like to cook, being the primary food preparer does not seem like a gender/sex role demand (or burden). However, this leaves unanswered the questions: Why are more women than men socialized to like cooking and expected to be skilled at it? Why are more men than women socialized to like working on cars and expected to be skilled at it? Even when people do not want, or are unable, to live up to gender/sex roles, why are they still judged against the norms?

By focusing on family as an institution, we make clear how families' practices contribute to systemic gender/sex discrimination. Micropractices (who cleans the toilet) are maintained by individual socialization (who is typically assigned the chore of cleaning the toilet) as well as mesopractices (families' expectations for cleanliness) and macrostructures of discourse (toilet bowl cleaner is not advertised during the Super Bowl but is during weekday television soap operas).

The Nuclear Family

Where did family gender/sex roles come from? During the Industrial Revolution of the 1800s, stereotypical notions of masculinity and femininity emerged along with the concept of the nuclear family. The **nuclear family** presumes a self-supporting, independent unit composed of two legally married heterosexual parents performing separate masculine and feminine family roles. For nuclear families, the male is the primary wage earner and the female is the primary homemaker. The nuclear family has been promoted as the ideal, healthy family and the foundation of society (Ruane & Cerulo, 2008; Walsh, 2012). In reality, the nuclear family has never been the most common family structure, and any family structure is susceptible to being unhealthy.

Sociologists describe the nuclear family as the elusive traditional family because historians cannot point to one specific time when this family structure actually was the most common (Coontz, 1997, 2006, 2016). Most scholars found "the form of the 'typical' American family has changed quite frequently throughout our nation's history. Indeed, historically speaking, the nuclear family is a fairly recent as well as a relatively rare phenomenon" (Ruane & Cerulo, 2008, p. 208). Even during the Industrial Revolution, it was an ideal, a status symbol, achieved by some on the backs of others—racial and ethnic minority women who were domestic help in other people's homes (Coontz, 1992).

In preindustrial, pre–mass production times before the 1700s, more often families were work units, and all members (including children, boarders, and hired hands) worked to contribute to a family's economic livelihood. Work was shared across sexes and age groups, extended family lived under one roof, and single-parent households were common due to early mortality. As the Industrial Revolution progressed, manliness was demonstrated by a man's ability to support his family with his income alone. The sphere of business was thought to be exclusively for men, even though not all families could afford to live on the man's wages alone, nor did all families have men. Only middle- and upper-class White Western women were able to focus exclusively on the family's social activities and household needs. Although not all women could afford to stay at home, domesticity became the norm for judging women's worth. True womanhood was defined as pure, pious, domestic, and submissive (Welter, 1976).

In spite of the influence of the Industrial Revolution, the nuclear family and its rigid gender/sex roles did not become firmly planted into U.S. ideology until the 1950s. Rapid economic growth enabled, and popular media representations normalized, the male wage earner. Situation comedies such as *Father Knows Best* (1954–1960), *Ozzie & Harriet* (1952–1966), and *Leave It to Beaver* (1957–1963) modeled White, middle-class nuclear families. Interestingly, during this time an additional two million White, middle-class women began working outside the home. However, most poor White, African American, Asian American, and Hispanic American women never left the workforce; they have always had to juggle work and family demands (Ruane & Cerulo, 2008).

The assumption that heterosexual romantic love should be the basis of marriage and family is a prominent U.S. value, but it is not universally shared and was never the basis of all marriages. Into the 1800s, marriage was based on financial need, control of reproduction, political concerns, and family arrangements, not love (Cancian, 1989). These factors still play a role in many marriages, particularly outside the United States. Passionate love is only one form of love between sexual partners, and it does not tend to be the most enduring (Guerrero, Andersen, & Afifi, 2018).

Why has the myth of the nuclear family and its accompanying gender/sex roles persisted in the face of diverse and rapidly changing families? A major contributor to maintaining this myth is heteronormativity. **Heteronormativity** encompasses legal, cultural, organizational, and interpersonal practices that reinforce unquestioned assumptions about gender/sex. These include

> the presumptions that there are only two sexes; that it is "normal" or "natural" for people of different sexes to be attracted to one another; that these attractions may be publicly displayed and celebrated; that social institutions such as marriage and the family are appropriately organized around different-sex pairings; that same-sex couples are (if not "deviant") a "variation on" or an "alternative to" the heterosexual couple. (Kitzinger, 2005, p. 478)

The "socially approved economic and sexual union" represented by heteronormative romance and heterosexual marriage is the cornerstone of the traditional nuclear family (Ruane & Cerulo, 2008, p. 215).

Although people often think of family as a safe haven, it also is a location of abuse. According to the Centers for Disease Control and Prevention (CDC, 2017a), "one in 4 children have experienced abuse or neglect at some point in their lives." Four-firths (80.3%) of those children are abused by a family member (CDC, 2014). In addition, one in three women and one in four men will experience violence at the hands of an intimate partner at some point during their lifetime, accounting for 15% of violent crime (NCADV, 2015). The problem is compounded by the valorization of the nuclear family. After researching domestic violence for over 2 years, public health scholar Sara Shoener (2014) came to a startling conclusion: "One of the most common barriers to women's safety was something I had never considered before: the high value our culture places on two-parent families." Shoener found that because women "had internalized a public narrative that equated marriage with success" they were reluctant to leave abusers. When they did, "mental health professionals, law enforcement officials, judges and members of the clergy often showed greater concern for the maintenance of a two-parent family than for the safety of the mother and her children."

To be clear, we are not criticizing individual families who fit the nuclear family model, nor are we suggesting this structure of family is innately harmful. We are criticizing prominent ideologies that insist there is only one type of normal or healthy family. Whether in a nuclear family or not, the narrow definition of family directly or indirectly affects everyone. Even in non-U.S. cultures, the ideal of the nuclear family is increasingly becoming the standard by which one judges their own and others' families (Ingoldsby & Smith, 2006).

The State of Families

In 2016, Alan Robertson, of *Duck Dynasty* fame, spoke to the annual Values Voter Summit and worried, "We are in a perilous time, where from positions of power, I don't know that if in my lifetime I have ever seen more of an attack on traditional values, traditional family and really, religious liberty" (as cited in Smith, 2016). This view has been around since the early 1990s when U.S. politicians and clergy repeatedly used the slogan "family values," in which *family* meant nuclear family (Cloud,

1998). They used the slogan to refer to a heterosexual married couple and multiple children living together in a home guided by conservative Christian principles and blamed increasing diversity of family structures for the decline of the family.

We argue the institution of the family is in *transition* rather than in crisis or under attack. Most U.S. people want to marry, including same-sex couples seeking legal recognition of their marriages. But according to the U.S. Census Bureau, as of 2016 almost one third of all adults (32%) have never been married, up from about one quarter (23%) in 1950. Around 10% of people (LGBTQ and heterosexual) cohabitate instead of marrying. Others cohabitate before marriage, marry later in life (age 26 for women, 28 for men), do not marry because of pregnancy (Gibson-Davis, 2011), or stay single (Traister, 2016).

Although the divorce rate is higher than it was before no-fault divorce laws were enacted in the 1970s, divorce rates have been decreasing. In 2014, 3.2 divorces occurred per 1,000 total population, compared to 4.0 in 2000 (see Figure 7.1). The 2 to 1 U.S. divorce ratio commonly cited is misinterpreted. It means in a given year, for every two new marriages, one will fail. The ratio does not include previously existing marriages. Furthermore, the ratio for first-time marriages decreased a bit (Centers for Disease Control and Prevention, 2005; "Fifty Percent," 2012).

Some may not perceive families as healthy today because families are adapting to increased economic demands, changed standards of living, and more flexible gender/sex expectations. Yet these very transitions enable families to thrive. In *Unfinished Revolution: How a New Generation Is Reshaping Family, Work, and Gender in America*, sociologist Kathleen Gerson (2010) interviewed a random sample of 120 people ages 18 to 32 living in New York, who grew up in different parts of the United States, with diverse race, ethnicity, social class, sexual orientation, and family backgrounds. She found, across a wide variety of family-of-origin experiences, participants wanted parents to provide emotional and economic support. The structure of the family was basically irrelevant. Regarding the expectations for their future family life, the young adults expressed hope and concern. The concerns were largely tied to gender expectations, because they wanted long-lasting egalitarian relationships but worried about balancing work and family demands. For example, most of the women wanted to be autonomous and self-reliant and saw employment as essential for their well-being. Many of the men were concerned about how sharing parenting and domestic tasks might negatively affect their careers. Gerson argued for a focus on family as a process, not a structure. The process that seemed to work best for participants was one in which their parents were able to demonstrate gender flexibility and adjust to families' changing challenges. Gerson recommended gender flexibility as a way for families to prepare for and adapt to 21st century uncertainties:

> Most young women and men do not see the sexes as opposites who possess different capacities and occupy different planets. They reject a forced choice between personal autonomy and lasting commitment, preferring a relationship and a vision of the self that honors both. (p. 190)

More rigid parental behaviors may leave families ill prepared to cope with unexpected contingencies.

Figure 7.1 Provisional Number of Divorces and Annulments and Rate:
United States, 2000–2014

Year	Divorces and Annulments	Population	Rate per 1,000 Total Population
2014[1]	813,862	256,483,624	3.2
2013[1]	832,157	254,408,815	3.3
2012[2]	851,000	248,041,986	3.4
2011[2]	877,000	246,273,366	3.6
2010[2]	872,000	244,122,529	3.6
2009[2]	840,000	242,610,561	3.5
2008[2]	844,000	240,545,163	3.5
2007[2]	856,000	238,352,850	3.6
2006[2]	872,000	236,094,277	3.7
2005[2]	847,000	233,495,163	3.6
2004[3]	879,000	236,402,656	3.7
2003[4]	927,000	243,902,090	3.8
2002[5]	955,000	243,108,303	3.9
2001[6]	940,000	236,416,762	4.0
2000[6]	944,000	233,550,143	4.0

Source: National Center for Health Statistics (2015).

1. Excludes data for California, Georgia, Hawaii, Indiana, and Minnesota.

2. Excludes data for California, Georgia, Hawaii, Indiana, Louisiana, and Minnesota.

3. Excludes data for California, Georgia, Hawaii, Indiana, and Louisiana.

4. Excludes data for California, Hawaii, Indiana, and Oklahoma.

5. Excludes data for California, Indiana, and Oklahoma.

6. Excludes data for California, Indiana, Louisiana, and Oklahoma.

Note: Rates for 2001–2009 have been revised and are based on intercensal population estimates
from the 2000 and 2010 censuses. Populations for 2010 rates are based on the 2010 census.

Doing and Undoing Motherhood

While first lady of the United States, Michelle Obama was a symbol of U.S. womanhood. As the first African American woman to step into this role, Obama's performance of womanhood highlighted the intersections of gender, race, and class,
especially when it came to her performance of motherhood. At the 2012 Democratic

National Convention, Obama (2012) stated, "You see, at the end of the day, my most important title is still 'mom-in-chief.'" This statement received varied responses. Many White feminists lamented Obama's prioritization of her maternity, viewing her performance of motherhood as a reaffirmation of the ideology of intensive motherhood, which defines women solely in relation to their children. Black women, on the other hand, praised Obama and saw potential in her maternal role. Scholar Sara Hayden (2017) studied Obama's speeches and people's reactions to them and concluded that while traditions of White mothering were invoked, "the denigration of Black motherhood in mainstream, White culture, and the African American tradition of othermothering" were also invoked (p. 12). In the following section, we discuss various ways the picture of the ideal mother is painted in U.S. culture. We explore intensive mothering and its consequences, as well as alternative approaches to motherhood, such as othermothering.

In *Of Woman Born: Motherhood as Experience and Institution,* Adrienne Rich (1976) distinguished between the institution of motherhood and the experience of mothering. Institutional motherhood is premised on the hegemonic ideology of "good mothering," also referred to as intensive mothering (Hays, 1996). **Intensive mothering** ideology paints a picture of ideal mothering wherein children are at the center of their mother's lives, and mothers always place children's needs above their own. It requires mothers to spend excessive amounts of time, energy, and money on their children. Although mothers are expected to be naturally fulfilled by motherhood, they are not expected to be fully adept at the role and are encouraged to seek out expert advice to guide their parenting (Hays, 1996).

The expectations of intensive mothering begin with pregnancy. Prior to childbirth, mothers must make myriad decisions that are considered indicative of their identity as a mother. Will you learn your child's sex? Will you use a midwife, doula, or OB-GYN? Are you preparing for a nonmedicated birth or planning to get an epidural? Home birth? Hospital birth? Water birth? Are you going to encapsulate your placenta? Cloth diaper? Babywear? Breastfeed? For how long? Co-sleep? Crib? Make your own baby food? Buy organic? Are you going to use attachment parenting? Slow parenting? French parenting? Will you let your child "cry it out"? If you are exhausted by this list of questions, imagine how an expectant mother feels. Others judge mothers based on what these questions reveal about how far mothers will go for their children. The pressure to answer all these questions, and to back up one's answers with expert advice, is exhausting and divisive.

Described in various media as "mommy wars," intensive parenting pits those with differing parenting philosophies against each other and establishes unrealistic ideals, leaving parents, especially mothers, feeling inadequate. Sociologists Angie Henderson, Sandra Harmon, and Harmony Newman (2016) surveyed 283 mothers and found that "even women who do not subscribe to these ideologies are at-risk for experiencing increased stress and anxiety, and decreased self-efficacy in the face of the pressure to be perfect and guilt for not living up to high mothering expectations" (p. 512). The pressure to be a perfect mother is detrimental to mothers whether or not they subscribe to intensive motherhood ideologies. Noticeable in these descriptions of intensive mothering is the absence of public discussion of and pressure for intensive fathering.

Intensive motherhood is not adopted by all women and is not possible for most. An intersectional approach reveals how intensive motherhood assumes a very particular type of woman. Communication scholar D. Lynn O'Brien Hallstein (2017) explained how

> this "good mothering" ideology assumes and promotes privileged motherhood, primarily by reinforcing White, at least middle-class, cisgender, heterosexual privilege, and an even more intensive ideology of good mothering, and any mother who "fails" to meet the standards of intensive mothering is policed and labeled a "bad mother." (p. 3)

Fortunately, other models of motherhood exist.

Many African American women develop communities of "*othermothers* and *fictive kin* to help each other with balancing work and family" (Parker, 2003, p. 268). Here, the assumption is that a lone woman cannot do it all. Instead, **othermothers**, biological and nonbiological people who are important sources of guidance and support, participate in childrearing. Feminist scholar Patricia Hill Collins (1994) described an alternative form of motherhood evident among those who must prepare children to face discrimination: **militant motherhood**. Although many (mostly upper-class Whites) think of mothers as gentle souls who provide unconditional love and protective nurturing, others (many working-class people and African Americans) think of mothers as the people who gave them the strength and ability to handle life's hard knocks. Many Latinx immigrants redefine *mother* to mean "wage earner" as they leave their own children in order to earn money caring for others' children (Hondagneu-Sotelo & Avila, 1997). Women of diverse races and economic backgrounds reimagine motherhood and create more room for various approaches to parenting to be recognized as healthy, productive practices.

Communicating in Families

In this section, we explore how traditional gender/sex roles are expressed and challenged in families, focusing on two types of interactions: parent-child communication and couple communication.

Parent-Child Communication

Even before children are born, parents are concerned about their gender identity. When sociologist Emily Kane (2009) interviewed 42 women and men, most knew what sex they wanted their child to be and why:

> African American, working-class, heterosexual father: I always wanted a son, someone that would respect me the most, and that would be a male, since I am a male. . . . I wanted to teach my son to play basketball. I wanted to teach my son to play baseball, and so forth.

White upper/middle-class, lesbian mother: I envisioned that a daughter would be sweet, a great companion in old age.... We would do things together, a lot of girl time.... A girl would never forget your birthday, would be much more emotionally connected. (p. 372)

Most participants preferred boys, and the parents' comments suggested the sex of their child would influence how they interacted with their child and the type of relationships they would seek to build. Before the child was even born, they were "rehearsing for potential interactions," and gender/sex was central to those interactions (Kane, 2009, p. 378).

Although most research suggested parents teach gender norms through nonconscious, routine forms of interaction, such as dads roughhousing and moms baking, parents also consciously work to gender/sex their child. In Kane's (2006) study, parents, regardless of race, ethnicity, sexual orientation, or whether they were single or dual parenting, preferred to encourage their children toward activities culturally seen as masculine. They reported "enjoying dressing their daughters in sports themed clothing, as well as buying them toy cars, trucks, trains, and building toys. Some described their efforts to encourage . . . what they considered traditionally male activities such as t-ball, football, fishing, and learning to use tools" (pp. 156–157). Fathers especially wanted their daughters to be athletic. An African American, working-class, heterosexual father said, "I don't want her just to color and play with dolls, I want her to be athletic" (p. 157).

Although 21 of the 42 parents praised their son's abilities in domestic chores and being nurturing and empathic, most did so with a counterbalance to ensure that he was not too soft, such as reprimanding sons who cried frequently. Boys' desire to own or play with Barbie was particularly troublesome to most, especially heterosexual fathers. Even parents who said they personally were more open to such behaviors expressed concern that their sons would be teased and labeled homosexual. One White, heterosexual, middle-class mother whose son wanted a Barbie explained, "I would ask him, 'What do you want for your birthday' . . . and he always kept saying Barbie. . . . So we compromised, we got him a NASCAR Barbie" (Kane, 2006, p. 161). Lesbian/gay parents expressed similar concerns but for different reasons—fear of mistreatment of their child by others. Parents tend to give children gender/sex-specific toys, and children tend to choose gender/sex-specific toys once they learn their prescribed gender identity and which toys are gender/sex appropriate (Eliot, 2009b).

These parents believed their choices would help steer their children in gendered and sexually oriented ways and that gender is not simply a matter of allowing some natural identity to emerge. One also can infer the parents realized that girls who adopt traditional masculine behaviors will improve their social status, but boys who adopt feminine behaviors risk losing social status. The parents were not maintaining binary gender differences as one might expect. Instead, they devalued activities and characteristics associated with girls, whether they had girl or boy children. A White, middle-class, heterosexual father said of his son,

If [he] were to be gay, it would not make me happy at all. I would probably see that as a failure as a dad . . . because I'm raising him to be a boy, a man I don't want him to be a little "quiffy" thing, you know. . . . It's probably my own insecurities more than anything. I guess it won't ruin his life. (Kane, 2006, p. 163)

This comment demonstrated that parent-child communication affects parents' gender identity, too.

Parenting seems to encourage some adults to become more restrictive in their own gender performance. Once they realize they are role models and need to set an example that will help their children fit in socially, some seem to become less flexible in their own gender performance: For example, fathers became careful not to cry in front of their children, mothers became conscious of what color clothing they buy their children (lavender and pink for girls, blue and green for boys; Kane, 2012). However, the way parents model gender is neither static nor universal. Communication scholars Mark Morman and Kory Floyd (2006a, 2006b) reported that fathers today are generally more affectionate with sons than fathers in previous generations and that both value physical affection in the relationship, at least until adolescence.

Regardless of ethnicity, class, or sexual orientation, from a young age children are socialized to want marriage. Related rituals reinforce the desire. The debutante ball from African American culture and quinceañera from Latin American culture are coming-out parties families throw for their daughters when they turn 15 or 16. Girls wear fancy white gowns, and the family invites everyone they know to a dinner dance. The events mark a girl's transition into womanhood. Purity balls are a more recent trend (1998 was the first) among some conservative Christian groups where fathers are the daughters' date for a formal evening culminating in the girls promising their fathers chastity until marriage and their fathers promising to protect and guide their daughters' lifestyle (Frank, 2014). Held about the time of a girl's onset of menstruation, they mark her entry to womanhood, but it is a particular type of womanhood—a virginal, upper-class, largely White heterosexual one. You might notice there seems to be no parallel public event for young men. A possible exception is the Jewish coming-of-age celebrations, Bar Mitzvah for 13-year-old boys and Bat Mitzvah for 12-year-old girls. While clearly gendered/sexed events, these are not tied to marital availability. Ingraham (2008) believed that the romanticized white wedding (and we would add the debutante ball, quinceañera, and purity ball) is a primary cultural tool for institutionalizing heterosexuality as the norm, the standard by which all relationships are judged.

Children can resist parents' normative cisgender expectations. Psychologist Diane Ehrensaft (2011), director of the Bay Area Youth Gender Acceptance Project in California, wrote,

In the feedback loop between parent and child [interaction and influence], the transgender or gender non-conforming child may be shaping the parent far more than the parent is shaping the child. The shaping begins with a child who is presenting the original kernel of the true gender self that existed at birth, whether as a result of genetics, biochemistry, prenatal environment, or some yet to be explained phenomenon. (p. 536)

Ehrensaft suggested some parents transform because loving and supporting their child requires it. They do this through time and work: recognizing their own gender and recognizing their child has a separate identity. Parents who do not do this may adhere to rigid gendered expectations for themselves as parents and for their child, enabling bullying and sexual harassment toward the child inside and outside the home.

Couple Communication

Given the powerful ideology of romantic relationships, heterosexual marriage is the most studied type of interpersonal relationship (Chevrette, 2013). Interpersonal communication textbooks' tradition of focusing on how "heterosexual couples initiate, develop, and maintain relationships" ignores "society's influence on these relationships" and erases the existence of LGBTQ people (Chevrette, 2013, p. 178). With these limits in mind, we explore two prominent topics in the literature on heterosexual couple communication: domestic labor and family leave.

Domestic Labor

Domestic labor refers to housework, support work, status production, and childcare duties within the home (Kemp, 1994). Some families hire others to do this work, hence the distinction between *paid* and *unpaid* domestic labor. The way people talk about unpaid domestic labor makes it invisible. *Working mothers* are those women with young children who *also* work outside the home for a wage. Of course, if you were to ask a mother who does not have a wage-paying job that requires her to leave the home, "Do you work?" the answer ought to be a resounding, "Yes!" Domestic labor is *labor*, but because it is not paid, people do not think of it as work (Daniels, 1987).

Domestic labor not only produces household goods and services but also has historically produced gender (Coltrane, 1989; Hochschild, 2003). Men's traditional gender/sex role has been financial provider for the family. The assumption that all fathers work outside the home for wages explains why *working fathers* is not a common phrase. As more women entered the paid labor force in the 1950s, who would do the necessary, unpaid, and often unrecognized duties at home fell into question. Until very recently, the overwhelming answer for heterosexual homes has been women.

Imbalanced housework distribution between men and women has been one of the clearest indicators of the continuing influence of the nuclear family norm and its inequitable gender roles. Now, in most families both parents are wage earners. Only one-fourth of families have the father as the sole earner; in almost two-thirds of families, both parents work (Parker & Livingston, 2016). However, even as more families have dual earners, household duties and childcare still fall more heavily on women.

As Figure 7.2 indicates, even though the distribution is the most even in the history of the United States, men still spend more time than women at paid work and leisure, while women spend more time than men doing childcare and housework. In 2014, full-time working mothers spent 21.9 hours a week doing childcare and housework and men spent 15.1. Looking more closely at Figure 7.2, some interesting gender/sex differences still exist with men getting 4 more hours of leisure. Women spend 6.8 more hours in childcare and housework while men spend 6 more hours working in paid employment.

If you ask the partners who does more work around the home, the answer depends on whom you ask. As Figure 7.3 indicates, when dads are asked about the distribution of work related to handling children's activities, caring for sick children, and doing chores, most suggest it is about equal. But when moms are asked, they are twice as likely to say they do more of the work. It is important to note, though, that 59% of moms and dads feel the work is equally shared (Horowitz, 2015).

Both charts show that men are more involved in their children's lives than in previous generations and are sharing more of the cooking, cleaning, and other domestic tasks, but it is still not equal.

Figure 7.2 How Full-Time Working Moms and Dads Spend Their Time

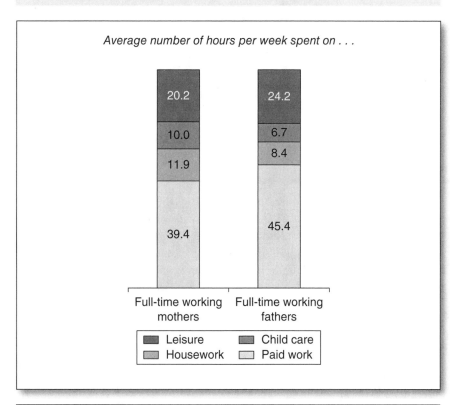

Source: Pew Research Center analysis of American Time Use Survey, 2014 data. "Who Does More at Home When Both Parents Work? Depends on Which One You Ask," Pew Research Center, Washington, DC (November 5, 2015), http://www.pewresearch.org/fact-tank/2015/11/05/who-does-more-at-home-when-both-parents-work-depends-on-which-one-you-ask/ft_15-11-05_divlabor_time.

Figure 7.3 Perceptions of Domestic Labor

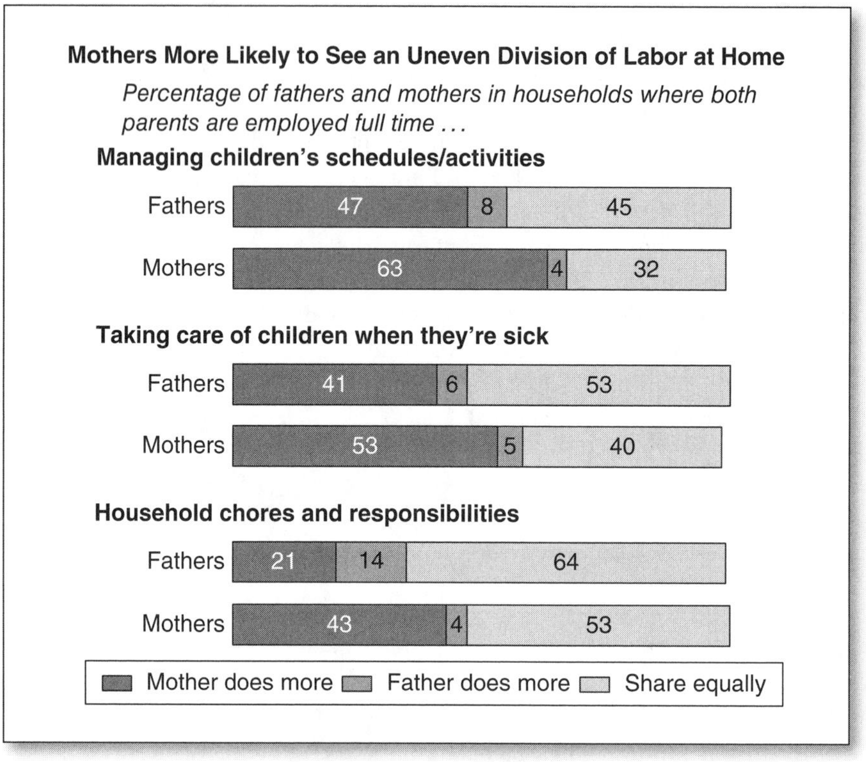

Mothers More Likely to See an Uneven Division of Labor at Home

Percentage of fathers and mothers in households where both parents are employed full time ...

Managing children's schedules/activities

	Mother does more	Father does more	Share equally
Fathers	47	8	45
Mothers	63	4	32

Taking care of children when they're sick

	Mother does more	Father does more	Share equally
Fathers	41	6	53
Mothers	53	5	40

Household chores and responsibilities

	Mother does more	Father does more	Share equally
Fathers	21	14	64
Mothers	43	4	53

■ Mother does more ■ Father does more ☐ Share equally

Source: Pew Research Center survey of parents with children under 18, Sept. 15–Oct.13, 2015. "Who Does More at Home When Both Parents Work? Depends on Which One You Ask," Pew Research Center, Washington, DC (November 5, 2015), http://www.pewresearch.org/fact-tank/2015/11/05/who-does-more-at-home-when-both-parents-work-depends-on-which-one-you-ask.

Norms about who should do unpaid domestic labor and paid wage labor are not determined by sex alone. While women who work outside the home face criticism for placing their children in day care, poor women who have had to rely on welfare if they remain home to care for young children are considered bad mothers because they do not work: "The only women for whom wage work is an unambivalently assigned social responsibility are welfare mothers" (Mink, 1995, pp. 180–181). Only women who seek assistance through government programs are encouraged to work; for mothers who have other sources of economic stability, work is often perceived as a temporary indulgence or, at worst, selfishness.

Additionally, the expectation that women can more easily give up work for their family is particularly dismissive of African American women's lives. With a history of being single parents, earning more than their husbands, and needing to help support extended family, "for generations black women have viewed work as a means for elevating not only their own status as women, but also as a crucial force in elevating their family, extended family and their entire race" (Clemetson, 2006, p. G1).

Thus, when thinking about gender and sex in the institution of family, it is good to heed Martin's (2003) point that "multiple masculinities and femininities exist, and people practice, and are held accountable to specific kinds depending on their bodies (health, attractiveness), class, race/ethnicity, religion, sexual orientation, age, nation, and other social statuses" (p. 355).

Not as much research analyzes same-sex couples and household labor, but existing research indicates a more egalitarian distribution between the partners. A systematic review of 28 studies from 2000 to 2015 of lesbian couples showed the couples tend to engage in a more equal distribution of household labor than heterosexual couples, and they assign tasks based on nontraditional gendered divisions of labor. However, this research is not highly generalizable across race, class, or geographic location (Brewster, 2016).

Family Leave

In 2012, Marissa Mayer was hired by Yahoo for its CEO post and then publicly announced her pregnancy, explaining, "My maternity leave will be a few weeks long and I'll work throughout it" (quoted in Sellers, 2012, para. 10). Reaction was swift and ranged from scoffing dismissals of her plans to questions about whether she could do her job as the parent of a newborn. While Mayer's story was front-page news, it is telling that a similar situation was not. Two months after Larry Page became CEO at Google in 2011, it was announced he was expecting his second child. In his case, "there were no follow-up headlines, no social media debates, no loud conversations about how he could lead an Internet giant and still be a father" (Petrecca, 2012, p. A1). These stories demonstrate the persistent challenge of work-life balance, a challenge faced by all people but that seems to fall disproportionately on women.

In 2016, Mayer again gave birth, this time to twins. Stories again debated whether Mayer should be praised or berated for working right up to the day before their birth and then calling Yahoo's chairperson from the hospital bed after their birth (Grantham, 2016; Kim, 2016). In contrast, Facebook founder and chief executive Mark Zuckerberg announced they would take 2 months leave after the birth of their child. This move was roundly praised.

The reactions to these cases illustrate how family leave issues affect mothers and fathers in distinct ways. The institutions of work and family present conflicting demands (be a good wage worker willing to put in overtime to get the job done and earn more money vs. spend more time at home with family), causing many people to feel they must choose one over the other. In the case of new parents, this issue of whether work or family comes first causes many to feel as though their work life and family life are out of balance.

Work-life balance could be recalibrated. Work and home *could* be structured to mutually support each other. For example, in Nordic countries, work pay continues even during parental leave; benefits provided at the birth of a child are reduced if both parents do *not* take time off work; and parental leave is nontransferable, thus prompting both parents to take time off. Lawmakers in Nordic countries have structured work benefits to challenge the pattern whereby women carry disproportionate responsibility in child rearing (Moss & Deven, 1999). Unfortunately, U.S. family leave is not structured this way, meaning the tensions between work and family persist.

U.S. laws seek to address potential discrimination tied to childbirth and family care, for example, the Pregnancy Discrimination Act of 1978 and the Family Medical Leave Act of 1993 (the latter allowing people up to 12 weeks of unpaid leave for pregnancy, personal, or family reasons). These U.S. laws are meant to create conditions whereby people affected by pregnancy and caregiving are not penalized and are able to return to their jobs after a leave. Although both laws are necessary and significant, they demonstrate that legal change alone is not sufficient to create equality; a change in the communication about an issue also is necessary. A law can be enacted in hopes of creating more gender/sex equality, but until communication surrounding the issue changes, the law's effect is incomplete.

In the case of family leave, a vocabulary that recognizes the complex ways in which women experience parenthood has not yet been developed. Lori Peterson and Terrance Albrecht (1999) found that in discussions of work and women's childbearing processes, maternity leave was interpreted as a *benefit* (something that would be a bonus or a business's choice and not a guaranteed right), and pregnancy was interpreted as a *disability*. Even with family leave policies in place, work's male-centered structure continues to present challenges to women about to be parents. A study done by organizational communication scholars Patrice M. Buzzanell and Meina Liu (2005) confirmed that the work-family culture and supervisory relationships played key roles in determining the degree to which women were satisfied with a company's leave policy and, hence, were able and willing to return to work after childbirth. The law alone did not make the difference in their work lives; it was the specific supervisor's approach to the law that made the difference.

Regarding men's reaction to supportive work-family policies (e.g., paid family leave, flexible scheduling, subsidized childcare), sociologists Sarah Thébaud and David Pedulla (2016) found that policies alone were not enough to make men more likely to equitably share childcare and housework. Men's responses to these policies were "highly dependent upon their beliefs about what their male peers actually want, rather than on their beliefs about what others should want" (p. 1). This meant that "men's perceptions of masculinity norms play an important role in shaping how they respond to work-family policies" (p. 22). If men thought their peers preferred equitable relationships between men and women, then they were "more likely to recognize supportive policies as a mechanism that better enables them to contribute at home" (p. 22). What supportive work-family policies communicated *and* what men communicated to each other about family leave affected their willingness to use the policy

In explaining why "progress toward gender equality has stalled in both the workplace and the home," Thébaud and Pedulla (2016) argued that a "leading explanation" is that "work and family institutions remain based on outdated notions of workers and families, which impose constraints on an individual's ability to equally share earning and caregiving with a spouse or partner" (p. 2). A critical gendered lens examines work-family dilemmas not as individual problems or private choices but as "social arrangements over which individual women and men have only limited control" and thus redirects researchers away from blaming individuals and toward "understanding the larger social contexts in which personal choices and strategies are crafted" (Gerson, 2004, p. 164). Those larger social contexts include both family leave policies enacted by workplaces and government *and* the perceptions people have about family gender/sex roles.

(Un)Doing Family

Families are one important place where tolerance of diversity can be taught and lived. More flexible gender/sex roles and acceptance of gender/sex diversity can help families be more adaptable to cultural *and* individual needs. In a review of research on gender in families, Froma Walsh (2012) argued the new norm is pluralistic family structures. We conclude by offering examples of diverse family structures thriving today. We are not attempting to replace one ideology (nuclear family) with another suggesting one alternate family structure is perfect. Instead, we offer these examples to illustrate the variety of ways in which gender/sex is being constructed and changed within diverse families and how more flexible gendered communication is actually at the center of helping families, in all their forms, thrive.

Singles and Childfree People

Contrary to popular assumptions, a large number of childfree singles and single parents (widowed, divorced, or never married) live in the United States. The ideology of the nuclear family declares them inadequate, as lacking, due to the romantic expectation for adults to be coupled and have children. Given the increasingly delayed age of first marriage, people now spend more years of their adult lives unmarried than married (DePaulo & Trimberger, 2008). Although it continues to be more acceptable for men to delay commitment or remain single, single people experience gender discipline when they are labeled unwanted, abnormal, selfish, homosexual, or socially inept (DePaulo, 2006). In interviews with 43 single, middle-class women, sociologist Kay Trimberger (2005) found that across ethnicity and sexual orientation, most of the women struggled with the cultural expectation that they must marry and have children, even if they were satisfied in their single lives.

According to the Pew Research Center (2015), "While the likelihood of remaining childless has been on the decline recently among women at the end of their childbearing years, childlessness has been consistently rising among younger women since the 1970s." In the United States, women are having fewer children overall and many choose to forgo childbearing altogether. As the language used by the Pew Research Center indicated, people without children are commonly called child*less* rather than child*free*, as if not having children signals a lack (Morrell, 1994). Based on an analysis of childfree LiveJournal Communities, communication scholar Julia Moore (2014) defined **childfree** as "a contested identity that refers to individuals who have made the choice never to have children and identify as such" (p. 176). Much like single people, childfree individuals or couples have been stigmatized as selfish, materialistic, or are assumed to dislike children. Gender sociologists Amy Blackstone and Mahala Dyer Stewart (2012) debunked these assumptions and found that childfree people think carefully about their decision to be childfree, are deeply concerned about the world and want to contribute, and are satisfied and happy with their choice to not have children.

Singles are not only stigmatized for not being partnered, when singles do have children, critics worry the children will miss out on important social learning the other parent might provide. They fear boys raised by women may become effeminate and girls raised by men may become tomboys. This concern is overstated for three reasons. First, sometimes being raised by a single parent is better than being raised in an abusive or neglectful structure. Second, single parents, like co-parents, usually have a network of family and friends to help. Third, all men do not father in the same way, and all women do not mother in the same way.

In a review of research on singles, Bella DePaulo (2012) stressed the need to reframe the way society thinks about singles. Most are not without family, and people need to recognize the variety of ways single adults are contributing members of families. They may have families of choice in the form of friendships, and biological or adoptive parents, siblings, cousins, children, nieces, and nephews. Most have important, long-term relationships. Given being a single adult male is still considered normative, but being a single adult female is not, single females offer more flexibly gendered identities. Author Rebecca Traister (2016) stated,

> To be clear, the vast increase in the number of single women is to be celebrated not because singleness is in and of itself a better or more desirable state than coupledom. The revolution is in the expansion of options, the lifting of the imperative that for centuries hustled nearly all (non-enslaved) women, regardless of their individual desires, ambitions, circumstances, or the quality of available matches down a single highway toward early heterosexual marriage and motherhood. There are now an infinite number of alternative routes open; they wind around combinations of love, sex, partnership, parenthood, work, and friendship, at different speeds. Single female life is not prescription, but its opposite: liberation. (p. 9)

Single adult women are less likely to settle for a relationship that is not healthy, and they have the skills of being autonomous and connected.

Creative Undoing of Family

The dissolution of a relationship, particularly in the context of a divorce, can be stressful, embarrassing, and adversarial. But what if those involved in ending a relationship were committed to supporting one another through the breakup, continued to refer to their ex-partners as family, and were dedicated to fairness? This is precisely what Jen Bacon (2012) found when collecting "divorce" stories from 25 lesbians, who, though not legally married (that was not an option for the couples at the time the data were collected), were in serious, long-term, committed relationships. Bacon found their stories radically reframed divorce in a way that might prove useful to all divorcing couples.

First, the lesbian couples in the study offered a creative undoing of family by viewing the breakup not as an end to the relationship, but as a revision. Bacon (2012) explained, "the couples did not, in fact, make a mistake in pledging their lives to each other. Instead, their only mistake was in assuming that their pledge would necessarily continue to be a romantic one" (p. 165). Because the relationship was not over, but was just different, the couples continued to be committed to supporting each other. Bacon described the level of support the couples offered each other:

> In one case, my informants exchanged "parting gifts" with each other during their breakup even as they were cosigning a lease on a joint business venture. In another case, an informant described their planned yearly "dates" on the anniversary of their breakup. Others described their work to negotiate alimony payment (without any legal requirement that they do so) or child-support payments. (p. 165)

The couples avoided using the adversarial language typically used in breakups and instead worked toward continual support to "maintain the integrity of both individuals involved" (p. 166).

One way they maintained integrity was by viewing their ex-partner as a family member, although as a sibling rather than a spouse. One participant in the study reported, "Sandra [the ex] is now like a sister to me—one of those absolutes in my life. She really annoys me. She talks too much; she interrupts people. I just adore her" (as cited in Bacon, 2012, p. 169). Many of the couples continued to attend familial events and do jobs typically done by family members, such as taking care of each other's pets.

Finally, without the framework of legal marriage and divorce, the couples had to negotiate the details of their breakup on their own. The couples communicated a desire for mutual support and pledged to make decisions that would benefit everyone involved. One participant wrote, "We calmly sat down together and figured out what each of us was going to need to split everything up and made an agreement, and we stuck to it" (as cited in Bacon, 2012, p. 171). The couples' intentions toward fairness created the groundwork for their relationship going forward.

Although Bacon (2012) did not offer a gendered analysis of the stories collected, the researcher speculated the lesbian couples approached breakups as they did, at least in part, because "women are socialized to build friendship" and because of "the tendency for lesbian romantic relationships to begin as friendships" (p. 159). The "divorce" stories collected by Bacon offer an alternative model for relationship dissolution wherein the parties involved are committed to an ethic of fairness. This "kinder, gentler" divorce allows the relationship to evolve from a romantic familial one to a nonromantic familial one (p. 170). This study offers a model for creative and healthy ways to undo, and redo, family.

Engaged Fatherhood

Most fathering research, like the research on mothers, has focused on White, middle-class fathers who are primarily secondary caretakers and playmates for their children. Research on noncustodial divorced fathers, regardless of ethnic background, has shown an even more limited nurturing role. Compounding negative portrayals of fathers of color is the stereotype of Black fathers as irresponsible (which ignores the economic and educational disadvantages faced by many who are trying to provide for families) and the macho, dictatorial image of Asian and Hispanic men (which makes it difficult for them to be seen as nurturing in the home).

Law professor Nancy Dowd (2000) argued that when researchers examine the roles fathers play, they must do so from an intersectional perspective:

> Men's identities as fathers do not exist in isolation from their identities as men. Indeed, that broader masculine identity arguably poses the most difficult challenge to a redefined and differently lived fatherhood.... As long as masculinity is defined in opposition to femininity, and requires devaluing and stigmatizing things labeled feminine, men will be blocked from or conflicted by learning from female role models. The learning and valuing of nurtur[ing] is blocked by misogyny and homophobia.... It is also challenged by the embrace of violence as a part of masculinity, a value or trait antithetical to nurture and care. (pp. 181–182)

Thus, noninvolvement of fathers may be tied to social class. Poor men, regardless of race, ethnicity, or sexual orientation, have a more difficult time being involved in parenting. As long as men are expected to be the primary wage earners, their ability to share parenting will be limited. Thus, if people want to seriously reconsider fatherhood, they also must reconsider motherhood and work (Dowd, 2000).

For example, Swedish parental insurance guarantees parents 480 days to take care of an infant, 390 of which are fully paid. Most dual-parent homes choose to split this time in some way. In interviews and observations with 20 gay and heterosexual, middle- and working-class fathers, one researcher suggested they are constructing new ideals of fathering. The Swedish fathers are sharing not just the more rewarding tasks (e.g., rocking or playing with a child) but the jobs of changing diapers, cleaning bottles, and caring for the child. They were not comfortable talking about their role as "fathering," instead preferring "parenting." This does not mean they denied their masculinity but rather were redefining their masculine identities, placing more priority on their family life and seeking a balance between work and family. However, this arrangement is easier for middle-class and older fathers (Johansson, 2011).

If the norm has been for fathers to play more emotionally distant, wage-earning roles, then an alternative is for fathers to play more interpersonally active, emotionally engaged roles in the day-to-day caretaking of their children and other family members. Researchers continue to find more evidence of fathers playing central roles in child rearing (Cabrera & Tamis-LeMonda, 2013; Dienhart, 1998), but the myth of the distant, wage-earning father persists. The reality is that many men *are* primary caregivers. A 2016 U.S. Census Bureau report shows nearly 2.5 million men report being single fathers, up from 393,000 in 1970. In cases where men co-parent, emerging research points to a far more engaged form of parenting.

A growing body of research documents men's increased efforts at engaged parenting. The benefits of engaged fathers are many, not only for children and mothers but also for fathers. In a review of research, communication scholars William Doherty and John Beaton (2004) found a positive relationship between involved parenting and a father's psychological well-being, confidence, and self-esteem. Interestingly, engaged fathering does not call for the collapse of a man's identity into their parent role alone, like intensive mothering does. Instead, engaged fathering calls for them to be engaged in their children's lives in a capacity beyond that of provider.

Same-Sex Parents

Most of the research on nonheterosexual couples focuses on gay and lesbian families. Same-sex couples are gaining social acceptance due to legalization of same-sex marriage, the increased number of couples who are public, and the increased number of children being raised by gay and lesbian couples (Pew Research Center, 2010; Walsh, 2012). A substantial amount of research has examined whether having gay or lesbian parents negatively affects children's gender identity development. In a review of this research, Letitia Peplau and Kristin Beals (2004) reported the following:

> There is no evidence that the children of gay and lesbian parents differ systematically from children of heterosexual parents. . . . No significant differences have been found in psychological well-being, self-esteem, behavioral problems, intelligence, cognitive abilities, or peer relations. . . . There is no evidence that the children of gay or lesbian parents are confused or uncertain about their gender identity. (p. 242)

Walsh (2012) concurred: "A large body of research over two decades has clearly documented that children raised by lesbian and gay parents fare as well as those reared by heterosexual parents in relationship-quality, psychological well-being, and social adjustment" (p. 14; see also Wainright & Patterson, 2008). In a quantitative study, researchers found children of same-sex couples fared equally well in quality of life (van Gelderen, Bos, Gartress, Hermanns, & Perrin, 2012).

One of the common criticisms of same-sex couples is that they will raise their children to be homosexual, which suggests that sexual orientation is a teachable choice. Existing research shows that the majority of children from lesbian and gay parents grow up to identify as heterosexual, just like most children from heterosexual parents (Patterson, 2000).

Raising Transgender Children

Kristen Norwood (2012) and Melissa MacNish and Marissa Gold-Peifer (2011) studied how families adjust to gender nonconformity in their children. Both studies showed parents navigate complex tensions between accepting and loving their child and protecting their child from external social rejection. Ari Lev and Jean Malpas (2011) shared their experiences as family therapists facilitating support groups for such families. In one case, a mother clarified how the gender disciplining of her child also gender disciplined her:

> The hardest part is not my relationship with my daughter and her fluidity, but it is having everyone, my family, the outside world, school, everyone scrutinizes my parenting. I feel watched and always on the fault line. I feel bullied as a parent who loves my child for who she is. But I know she is going to grow up and I will be in her life. She will want to be with us because we have believed in her. (p. 5)

Society's disciplining of parenting, whether for letting a son wear a dress or loving a gender non-conforming child, needs to stop.

Many parents struggle to comprehend transgender identity, especially when it is a part of their family, but love can induce adaptation. For example, a father described as "a gruff man with an 8th grade education" agreed to attend a clinical support group. Here is what happened:

> "How do I raise a son without a penis?" he whimpered. He readily came into therapy and shared an experience he'd had at a construction site with "a woman . . . a person . . . a girl who looked like a guy." He watched his friends make jokes about her, and he said with anger in his voice, "That could be my child they are making fun of. Until this happened to us, I never would've understood. I would've laughed too . . . but now I understand when I see people on the street, who are, you know, queer in some way, I am the first person to defend them. . . . This has changed me." (p. 7)

Empathy, seeing others as fully human, may be the most important lesson this father learned.

The key for these families was becoming more flexible by accepting diverse gender identities, using more flexible interaction styles, employing more sensitive communication to respect the child's identity (e.g., proper pronoun usage), and providing a sense of stability for the child and the whole family through the communication of love and support.

Conclusion

The father just quoted summarized this chapter's lesson: "Talking about gender and sexuality will not only help families like us, families with a gay or gender-variant child. It will free everyone from having to think in such narrow ways. It will free us all from fear" (Lev & Malpas, 2011, p. 6). The importance of gender flexibility is a key research finding across studies and is important because "families who move beyond the limits of traditional gender are more able to respond to contemporary life challenges. . . . Children benefit developmentally when gender stereotypes are challenged and more possibilities are open to fit their needs and preferences" (Knudson-Martin, 2012, p. 340). Instead of forcing boys to shoot Nerf guns and girls to coddle baby dolls, parents can encourage more fluid gender roles and challenge stereotypes in their home by allowing children's imagination to run wild. We conclude by offering some suggestions for adults who want to encourage a full range of children's potential.

Subtle Way Adults Can Encourage Gender Flexibility

Model flexible gender/sex behaviors—parents should take turns cooking or fixing the car.

Be aware of what you model—in criticizing their own bodies, parents may be modeling unhealthy behaviors.

Provide diverse gendered/sexed experiences—encourage a child to play sports *and* participate in theater; encourage a variety of playmates rather than only same-sex playmates.

Buy gender-inclusive toys to develop skills and creativity.

Monitor your interruptions.

Stop behaviors of bullying and other dominance patterns.

Promote gender/sex equality through values, rules, and norms.

Teach thoughtfulness—avoid talk that perpetuates "boys will be boys" or "girls should be doormats."

Compliment a range of attributes—recognize all of a child's strengths, not just those that are gender specific. Instead, compliment children for being inquisitive, fearless, caring, and creative.

(Adapted from Forbeswoman, 2012; Knudson-Martin, 2012)

In this chapter, we traced how family as a social institution, through the cultural ideology of the traditional nuclear family, constructs and maintains gendered/sexed identities of difference and inequality. The importance of the family becomes especially vivid when examining the prevalence of gendered/sexed violence and norms that contribute to it. As research better documents the diverse ways individuals construct families across cultures, families may be better able to create the good homes they are expected to provide.

KEY CONCEPTS

childfree 155

domestic labor 150

family 141

gender/sex roles 141

heteronormativity 143

intensive mothering 146

militant motherhood 147

nuclear family 141

othermothers 147

DISCUSSION QUESTIONS

1. What evidences do the authors give to illustrate Haddock et al.'s (2003) claim that "families and gender are so intertwined that it is impossible to understand one without reference to the other. Families are not merely influenced by gender; rather families are *organized* by gender" (p. 304).

2. Does studying family as a social institution affect the way you understand your own family experience? If so, how?

3. How does family construct and constrain gender?

4. How do you see people resisting the nuclear family stereotype?

CHAPTER 8

Education

Most North American schools have codes of conduct that include a dress code that typically "describes unacceptable dress, frequently citing short skirts, revealing tops, ripped or torn clothing, heavy chains, and so forth" (Raby, 2010, p. 333). In many cases, the codes specify what is acceptable for boys and what is acceptable for girls. In the past few years, these codes have been enforced in the following ways: A New Jersey middle school banned strapless dresses at a school dance; an Ohio high school barred two girls from attending prom because of their dresses; a California high school sent 40 girls home from a winter dance; schools in California, Minnesota, Iowa, and Illinois banned girls from wearing tight pants (like leggings and yoga pants); a Georgia kindergarten student was forced to change out of a skirt deemed too short; and a Virginia school announced a surprise spot check on short lengths for girls' skirts (Harbach, 2016; Miller, 2015; Strasser & Culp-Ressler, 2013).

In all these cases, girls were the students targeted for dress code enforcement; the rationale was that the girls were a "distraction" to boys. Writing about the lesson taught by these codes, Marinda Valenti (2013) noted: "When you deem a girl's dress 'inappropriate,' you're also telling her, 'Because your body may distract boys, your body is inappropriate. Cover it up.' You recontextualize her body; she now exists through the male gaze." Not only are students barred from cocurricular events, but in the process of enforcing dress codes, students often are removed from classes and end up missing learning opportunities.

In 2015, four middle school girls in Portland decided to testify to their school board about changing the dress code. They noted that 100% of the students sent home were girls and that the message this sent to each girl sent home was that "boys are more entitled to their education than she is. And I don't think that's acceptable" (as cited in Porter, 2016). School dress codes illustrate a variety of ways in which education, as an institution, genders people.

First, dress codes illustrate how schools teach implicit lessons, not just explicit subject content (like reading, writing, and arithmetic). Scott Richardson (2015), an educator and researcher, studied how U.S. schools "institutionalize gender" by teaching children "the rules and expectations of performing masculinity and femininity." Dress codes are an example of teaching rules about masculinity and femininity.

Second, dress codes often reinforce a binary understanding of gender/sex. Many codes have rules specifically for boys and specifically for girls. This approach, however, is not necessary. In an assessment of best practices, law professor Meredith Harbach (2016) argued that sex-differentiated standards should be avoided to comply with constitutional guarantees of equal protection and legal requirements of Title IX (a law we explain in more detail later). This move is a precursor to Richardson's (2015) prediction: "Generations from now, people will wonder why society, and schools in particular, were so hell-bent on perpetuating an overly simplistic gender binary that was deeply limiting and discriminatory to students" (p. 182).

Third, dress codes, and students' reaction to them, demonstrate not only how teachers educate students, but also how students educate each other in their daily interactions. In a qualitative study of secondary school girls, Raby (2010) found they had a nuanced understanding of the rules as they negotiated girlhood and the "fine line between attractive and provocative" (p. 334). Raby found that the girls' reactions were "embedded within educational structures" and illustrated how "young women actively, and sometimes critically, construct gender" (p. 334). The girls, in some cases, disciplined each other's clothing choices as they reproduced "wider structures" in their commentary about others' clothing (p. 344).

Finally, resistance to dress codes shows that students can be advocates for their own education. Student resistance to dress codes in Portland (Porter, 2016) and Virginia (Harbach, 2016) have led to changes in the codes so that they do not disproportionately affect one sex and so that they do not gender girls in a way that sexualizes them.

Thinking about the gendered lessons taught in the institution of education is necessary. From first grade on, during your most formative psychological, physical, moral, and intellectual developmental period, most of you spent an average of 7 hours a day, 5 days a week (approximately 3,780 hours a year) in a formal education institution. A good education can contribute to higher income, career options, health, and quality of life. However, education is not only about imparting information and developing skills; it is a major socializing agent. It may be that school is socializing students in a way that is limiting. In a qualitative study of K–12 classrooms in suburban schools in Pennsylvania, Richardson (2015) identified two reasons why the gendered classroom is harmful: It limits children and it prevents equality and equity.

Studying the way communication in educational settings and about education genders is necessary. Education influences identity formation, self-esteem, aspirations, determination, and gender. To make visible the multiple ways education is gendered, we first explore the politics of knowledge—the hidden history of education and biases about what gets included in its curricula. Second, we identify gendered expectations and interpersonal communication within school systems, such as teacher stereotypes, microaggressions, peer pressure, bullying, and gendered violence. Third, we explore the emancipatory potential of education through micro-, meso-, and macrolevels of systemic change made possible by school- and teacher-led initiatives in instructional change, curricular innovation, and the implementation of laws such as Title IX.

The Politics of Knowledge

Education has never been about just imparting neutral information; implicit in what you learn are the values and biases of the predominant culture (Ballantine & Hammack, 2015). The institution of education is a creator and keeper of socially sanctioned knowledge. This is perhaps the most pervasive influence of education: It legitimizes what is recognized as knowledge, who gets to create it, and who is given access to that knowledge.

The History of Education: Gendered/Sexed, Raced, and Classed

Although education is an institution with the potential to be a great equalizer and a promoter of individual growth, much of its history has been about being a great divider (Freire, 1972; Sadker & Zittleman, 2009). For the majority if its history, education has been a bastion of White male privilege. The history of U.S. education goes back to the early 1800s, to British public schools that taught wealthy boys how to be ruling-class men, preparing them for leadership in the armed services and business. U.S. public education originally was intended exclusively for White, upper-class boys. During the Victorian era, opponents of women's education believed female bodies could not withstand the rigors of education. Scientists who studied blood circulation believed that if women used their brains too much, it would divert blood from their wombs. Additionally, the stress of study might cause them to stop menstruating and become barren and unfit for marriage (Minnich, 1998). Only White women from wealthy families could obtain higher education before the 1900s, and they were discouraged from taking courses in what were considered the masculine domains of business, science, and mathematics. Colleges for women were usually finishing schools, focused on domestic skills to make a woman a good wife for a successful husband. Educators also worried that coeducation would emasculate college curricula by presenting it at a slower pace and simplifying it for women; they feared working side by side with girls would feminize boys. Critics not only worried boys would become effeminate; they worried boys would become gay (Kimmel, 2012a; Minnich, 1998).

As more women sought higher education in the early 1900s, women's colleges formed, following the highly successful model of Black colleges of the South. However, the majors and career options for women remained tied to rigid gender/sex roles. Faculty, parents, future employers, and students themselves believed the appropriate career options for women were secretary, teacher, and nurse (not all of which required college degrees). Furthermore, a woman's marital status determined if she could work outside the home at all. Until the 1950s, in many states, women who were grade school teachers were forcibly "retired" when they married.

The assumption was that they had a male provider (and should let someone else have the paying job) and that visible pregnancy would encourage promiscuity among students. Men were largely barred from these professions, and the lower pay discouraged men from pursuing nontraditional gender/sex careers. These norms still linger, although more men are now teaching in grade school (National Center for Education Statistics, 2014).

Race and ethnicity also have played a significant role in the history of education. The migration of European immigrants into the United States in the early 1900s finally propelled the establishment of coeducational public schools from kindergarten to 12th grade. The government created public schools to assimilate immigrants into the English language and U.S. values (Andersen, 2015). However, despite the push for assimilation of immigrants, schools in the South remained racially segregated until forced to integrate in 1954, when the Supreme Court ruled in *Brown v. Board of Education* that separate schools are never equal.

Hidden Curriculum: Sexist, Racist, Classist, and Heterosexist

Curriculum refers to what is taught in schools—the content. If you were to name the key subjects you studied before college, you would probably include language arts, math, and science. These are the explicit core subjects of educational curriculum. The **hidden curriculum** refers to the implicit, and often unintentional, lessons, cultural norms, and values students learn in school (Alsubaie, 2015). Hidden curriculum is the byproduct of the institution of education that society often fails to question.

For example, history tends to be told as a series of battles where men play all the roles. Students are taught who the founding fathers are, but were there no founding mothers? Where in history lessons are the contributions and struggles of Native Americans, African Americans, Hispanics, Asians, people with disabilities, and people who are LGBTQ? When people in marginalized groups are noted, they tend to be presented as an exceptional member of their group or this part of their identity is not disclosed. For example, only recently has evidence surfaced to suggest President Abraham Lincoln had homosexual relations prior to his presidency (Morris, 2009). As a quick thought exercise, see if you can identify the following people and their contributions to the topic listed.

Topic	White Men	Women and People of Color
Abolition of slavery	Abraham Lincoln	Frederick Douglass, Maria Miller Stewart, Harriet Tubman, Sojourner Truth
U.S. revolution	George Washington, John Adams	Abigail Adams, Deborah Sampson Ganet, Margaret Corbin
Civil rights	John F. Kennedy, Lyndon Baynes Johnson	Rev. Martin Luther King, Jr., Fannie Lou Hamer, Thurgood Marshall, Ella Baker, Septima Poinsette Clark

Curricula are gendered in terms of what is taught and to whom. Home economics traditionally is seen as feminine, whereas shop/auto mechanics is seen as masculine. Literature and language arts classes are associated with expressiveness, emotion, and relationships—in short, femininity. Social sciences linked to the humanities are called "soft" sciences. In contrast, math, technology, and science traditionally have been described as rigorous and objective—"hard" sciences. If these descriptions make you think of sexuality and female and male anatomy, the similarity is not an accident (Alcoff & Potter, 1993).

The hidden curriculum makes clear that a critical gender analysis must go further than simply comparing individual women and men for possible differences in educational experiences. A critical gender analysis of education reveals that what gets taught to students as truth and knowledge reflects predominant cultural values.

A salient example of an overt attempt to construct knowledge took place in 2010, when the Texas Board of Education voted to approve new guidelines for social studies curriculum in elementary, middle, and high schools. The board dictated to publishers what would and would not be included in the textbooks the state chose to endorse. As you read some of what was passed in 2010, consider the underlying values and beliefs embedded in them.

- Eliminating the history of the Ku Klux Klan in Texas
- Excluding names of the Tejanos who died defending the Alamo
- Reinterpreting Thomas Jefferson's intent regarding the separation of church and state
- Making light of the need for the human rights movements in the 1960s
- Not including women and people of color (e.g., in a list of Congressional Medal of Honor recipients, the lone female recipient—Mary Edwards Walker—is not included)
- Including conservative, antifeminist author Phyllis Schlafly as a key contributor to society but excluding names of women who advocated for the right to vote in 1920 or Title IX in 1972
- Ignoring Dorothea Dix, Clara Barton, the Grimke sisters, and other abolitionists in general, even though their work helped raise consciousness to end slavery
- Naming many White women who contributed to Texas history but not African American or Mexican/Hispanic women
- Claiming slavery was not a cause of the Civil War and that slaves benefited from slavery
- Denying human responsibility in climate change (Jervis, 2014; Rockmore, 2015; "Texas Board," 2010)

These dictates reached five million public school students in Texas and beyond. As the second largest state in the textbook market (California is first), the books Texas adopts influence the remaining 48 states' textbook options. The mandates were to remain as law until 2020. However, many of the board members have since been voted out of office and the Texas Freedom Network, a nonprofit group, recruited 43 academics around the country to review the books and demand corrections from publishers. Three publishers agreed to do so, but not all the corrections have been made.

This rewriting of the curriculum is an example of abuse of institutional power. Then U.S. education secretary Arne Duncan said at one of the board meetings, "We do a disservice to children when we shield them from the truth, just because some people think it is painful or doesn't fit with their particular views" (as cited in "Texas Board," 2010). Clearly, much of what has been given the status of knowledge in the United States is the product of White, Western, capitalist, masculine viewpoints.

Even the sciences, which are considered objective, are influenced by gender biases. In a classic study, feminist scholar Inge K. Broverman and colleagues (1970) asked 79 therapists to define the psychological characteristics of three people: a healthy adult person, a healthy adult man, and a healthy adult woman. They described the healthy man and healthy adult almost identically: active, independent, adventurous, and logical. The healthy woman, by contrast, was described as dependent, emotional, subjective, passive, and illogical, characteristics ascribed to an "unhealthy" adult. The findings suggest women are in a double-bind; an active, logical, and independent woman would be unwomanly under the definitions and a dependent, emotional, and passive woman would be womanly, but psychologically unhealthy. Until this study, mental health was defined according to stereotypical masculine qualities. These sexist assumptions were then reinforced in college courses, medical schools, and clinicians' assessments of patients.

Hidden curriculum not only produces different educational outcomes based on a student's gender, race, and class, but it also limits all students' awareness of the contributions of marginalized groups, thus maintaining inequalities. Furthermore, a hidden curriculum creates a context in which biased expectations for student performance seem to persist and sexism, racism, classism, homophobia, and violence are enabled.

Gendered Expectations and Interpersonal Communication

You may have heard claims of a "gender gap in education," that girls or boys are being left behind in rates of achievement. The gender gap has been hotly debated for nearly 30 years. Although research substantiates girls and women have historically been left behind in science and math in the United States, it was not because of ability. We know this because when the U.S. government developed science, technology, engineering and math (STEM) programs, exclusions of and discrimination toward girls and women were revealed and targeted for redress. Female students are responding positively, excelling in sciences, and yet women are still a minority in STEM administrative positions. Some research also indicated that boys are being left behind in education. The reasons are complex: Lessons may not be geared toward active learning styles; some are poor readers, act out and get in trouble, underperform, or are disengaged from school for a variety of reasons; or teachers may expect minority boys to be problems (e.g., Sax, 2016; Schwabe, McElvany, & Trendtel, 2015).

While the debate over which sex is being left behind continues, the current education gap affects students with more than one minority barrier, such as social class, race, and sex (e.g., MacPhee, Farro, & Canetto, 2013). Simply put, parents who have more resources are better able to help their children learn and excel. Indeed, the groups who seem to be falling most behind in the United States are African American and Hispanic boys and men, particularly those from low-income families, poor neighborhoods, and single mothers. While African American and Hispanic girls and women also face challenges due to the double oppressions of race/ethnicity and sex, they are more likely than their male counterparts to finish high school and college (National Center for Education, 2015).

Sadly, students can internalize racist and sexist social expectations that then affect their performance; stereotype threat affects educational achievement. Additionally, being smart is not seen as masculine for boys from many poor backgrounds. Researcher Edward Morris (2012) found in studying two low-income schools, one Black majority and one White, there is a "hidden cost of the power associated with masculinity" (p. 1). Regardless of race, the boys and teachers together created a culture in which it was acceptable for low-income boys to be more carefree and less engaged in their studies. Similarly, Michael Kimmel (2012a) argued that many boys do poorly in school because it is not okay for boys to like reading and do well. In fact, he reported that homophobia often is used to discipline boys who excel, especially in reading and language. The ability to excel is described by students as "That's so gay" (p. 212).

Similarly, in a longitudinal study of 13 girls as they advanced from fourth- to seventh-grade science, girls who initially performed as "good" students increasingly struggled, not with the work, but with the contradiction they felt between being good at science and being able to perform as a "girly girl" (Carlone, Johnson, & Scott, 2015, p. 474). They were afraid of being seen as too smart. The imposed societal expectations about what kind of girl they wanted to be restricted their individual ability to excel in science.

These observations point out that gendering students fails them all, and for those in socially marginalized groups the oppression is greater. The desire to be hypermasculine or feminine works against excelling in school.

Classroom Interactions

Classroom interactions are a central place where gender is done in educational institutions. Sociologist Margaret Andersen (2015) explained, "Schools are the stage where society's roles—roles defined by gender, class, race, sexuality, and age—are played out" (p. 303). Consequently, educators have a tremendous amount of power to influence children. Traditionally, students have been cast in binary and unequally valued gender/sex roles, making the reproduction of masculine/feminine identities a central part of children's education (Richardson, 2015). Practices such as dividing students by sex for activities, unconsciously judging them based on how well they conform to stereotypical gendered behaviors, advising students toward sex-segregated jobs or careers, assuming children have preferences for same-sex friends, and organizing competitions as girls against boys all contribute to this problem. These practices are not based on sound pedagogical learning practices. Such practices encourage girls and boys to see each other not only as different but as unequally valued opponents (Andersen, 2015; Sadker & Zittleman, 2009).

The vast majority of teachers and guidance counselors do not set out to treat boys and girls differently, just as they do not set out to treat children differently because of ethnicity, but like us all, teachers' worldviews are influenced by the dominant culture. For example, two teachers recently wrote this in an online discussion about how to keep students engaged:

> I will have a classroom of very few girls (6/20) so [I try to] make sure that whatever project we begin with it will hold the interest of those young ladies. (preK/K teacher, 20 years)

> I will also only have 2 boys this year in my room so trying to get them engaged in a topic that is not of interest to them may be a challenge as well. (Toddler teacher, 2 years)

As their supervisor noted, "The teachers are not observing individual children's interests. . . . My hunch is [they] are thinking according to gender lines for projects (a project on babies for girls and balls or trucks for boys)" (Mary Donegan-Ritter, personal communication, August 19, 2016).

Although most teacher-education programs now include some form of diversity awareness, gender/sex is still not systematically addressed in most curricula (Sadker & Silber, 2007; Victoria Robinson, personal communication, July 22, 2016). Educators have to take the initiative to learn about gender/sex on their own and mentor others. Dr. Victoria Robinson, a university vice president for educator preparation and former principal and teacher with 45 years of classroom experience, explained the dilemma this way:

> I remember when I was a student teacher coordinator (late 1990s) hearing student teachers say, "Now boys and girls . . ." and I always addressed that and coached the student teachers to refer to them as students or something that all would identify with when speaking to the group. I always smiled to myself because that phrase "boys and girls" was exactly what my teachers in the '50s said. Long held habits and "teacher speak" is a hard nut to crack. When I started teaching in 1971, even though I might have learned one thing in my educator prep, I often deferred to applying what I saw my own PK–12 teachers do . . . so in a funny way we not only teach the way we learned, [but] we often teach the way we were taught. Over the past three generations, there have been gains in a more gender fair and neutral approach with pockets of "old" school still influencing instruction. There still seems to be a pattern suggesting many teachers' behaviors and stereotypical gendered/sexed expectations toward children do exist. (personal correspondence, July 22, 2016)

In a statistical meta-analysis of 32 studies from 1970 to 2000 (when most of this research was done in the United States), Susanne Jones and Kathryn Dindia (2004) found teachers initiated interactions with those identified as male students more than with female students, but these interactions were more negative than positive, such as correcting perceived misbehaviors. The sex difference was small to moderate, suggesting something other than the sex of the students influenced behaviors, such as the gender/sex of the teacher, the topic, class level, and race. In a qualitative research review, Beaman, Wheldall, and Kemp (2006) found teachers did not differ in the *amount* of attention they gave to boys or girls, but the *type* of attention varied. Boys received attention for misbehaving, girls for complying.

In a 2015 study at a New England urban elementary school with 244 students, researchers found no differences for race or sex regarding the total number of positive behaviors recognized by staff (including self-responsibility, understanding, and fairness) over the course of a school year, but girls were recognized most for respectful actions. Further, White students received more positive behavior recognition for safe behaviors, and boys and Black students received the most negative recognition for bad behaviors. Black boys received 15 or more bad conduct identifications, even though this was a school that had trained its staff about race and gender/sex bias in behavioral expectations and implemented a program to reduce it. The researchers concluded the staff may have been less likely to notice ways in which girls misbehave or the ways Black students were respectful and demonstrated safe behaviors (Silva, Langhout, Kohfeldt, & Gurrola, 2015).

A relatively new label helps researchers identify types of daily mistreatments that contribute to such inequalities: **microaggressions**—commonplace, brief, often subtle verbal, behavioral, or environmental acts that (intentional or not) can injure targeted groups based on gender/sex, sexual orientation, race, ethnicity, or religion. Microaggressions can be committed by teachers, administrators, and students. While the individual act may seem insignificant, patterns of such behaviors can create an oppressive environment for learning, sending the message that the targeted group does not belong (Sue, 2010). Below are some common classroom examples.

Teacher Microaggressions

- Naming—referring to the class as "boys and girls" (where does the transgender child stand?)
- Resisting—continuing to use an obsolete name or pronoun to refer to transgender students, instead of their chosen name and pronouns
- Referencing—knowing and using names of children from dominant groups more than others
- Attention—calling on students from dominant groups more than others
- Negative reinforcement—noticing when some groups of children do things wrong but not right
- Grouping by cultural identities—placing "girls against boys"
- Expecting—assuming boys do not like to read, girls struggle with math, Asian students are smart, African American boys are unruly

(Continued)

(Continued)

- Unequal rules—allowing children from some groups to shout out answers but rewarding others for taking their turn
- Complimenting—praising for gender stereotypic behaviors, like girls being quiet and polite and boys being assertive or aggressive
- Calling out—asking a minority student to speak for all people of color, LGBTQ people, disabled people

Microaggressions are important to recognize because, even when they are unintentional, they invalidate individuals. They can create daily stress, depression, exhaustion, and other physical health problems, and they can lower productivity, confidence, and performance (for a full review see Sue, 2010). Microaggressions can work as a self-fulfilling prophecy; if a student is subject to continued lack of positive affirmation, the student may come to act and believe in the negative inferences about them. Microaggressions reinforce stereotype threat.

Many educators are creating more inclusive classrooms that provide an encouraging climate for all students to reach their potential. Here are a few simple strategies to correct microaggressions:

Ways Teachers Challenge Binary and Unequal Treatment

- Avoid generalizing, as in "you boys," "you girls," or "you people"
- See students' intersectional, holistic identities
- Listen for students' needs
- Give time, the most valued commodity a teacher has to offer, equitable one-on-one time
- Offer diverse examples that reflect multiple students' identities
- Look for and address covert oppressions
- Learn to pronounce students' names correctly and call each by their preferred name
- Have a peer observe for unconscious biases, such as inclusiveness in calling on all students
- Be creative in grouping students to avoid self-selections that leave out minority students
- Engage in self-reflexivity by examining one's own stereotypical assumptions, expectations, and values (Adams, 2016; Richardson, 2015; Sadker & Zittleman, 2009; Sue, 2010)

As you know from your own experiences, classroom dynamics affect if and how you engage the learning opportunity. Learning does not happen in a vacuum. It is a relational experience. Teachers will continue to play a key role in the socialization of children, but they have the opportunity to do so in ways that do not negatively limit opportunities or the development of individual identities.

Bullying, Harassment, and Sexual Assault

The institution of education is expected to protect students against anything that would impede their learning and general well-being; unfortunately, violence is pervasive within educational institutions. People do not notice because it often occurs in subtle, nonphysical ways, such as through microaggressions and bullying among peers. In a longitudinal study of 979 U.S. students, researchers found perpetrators of bullying and homophobic teasing in early middle school were likely to escalate to bullying and sexual harassment of others in later middle school (Espelage, Basile, De La Rue, & Hamburger, 2015).

The Department of Education has defined **bullying** as "any unwanted aggressive behavior(s) by another youth or group of youths who are not siblings or current dating partners that involves an observed or perceived power imbalance and is repeated multiple times or is highly likely to be repeated" (Gladden, Vivolo-Kantor, Hamburger, & Lumpkin, 2014, p. 7). Bullying includes nonverbal (e.g., hitting, kicking, pushing, shoving), verbal (e.g., name-calling, teasing), and/or social (e.g., spreading rumors, social exclusion) aggression to inflict physical, psychological, social, or educational harm.

Bullying can be done face-to-face or through phones or computers. The use of social media to engage in bullying is called **cyberbullying**. Cyberbullying includes insults or nasty rumors spread through cell phone texts, e-mail, or social media; tricking someone into sharing embarrassing information via social media; or forwarding private messages to hurt or embarrass someone (Office of Women's Health, 2014). No federal law against bullying existed as of 2016, but every state in the United States has a law or policy regarding it (Espelage, 2016).

Harassment is distinct from bullying because the victim is targeted based on their race, national origin, color, sex, age, disability, or religion. Thus, harassment is legally a form of discrimination. For the victim, however, bullying and harassment may be experienced in similar ways. In schools, older children tend to bully or harass younger or physically smaller children, boys bully or harass girls and effeminate boys, girls bully or harass girls, and heterosexuals bully or harass LGBTQ and gender non-conforming students, who tend to receive the most violent abuse (Kosciw, Greytak, Palmer, & Boesen, 2014; Mitchell, Ybarra, & Korchmaros, 2014; Office of Women's Health, 2014). A national survey of nearly 8,000 LGBT youth showed 71.4% had been referred to as "gay" in a derogatory way, 64.5% heard homophobic remarks, and 55.5% of the students reported hearing negative remarks about their gender expression from teachers or other school staff. Bullying and harassment can have short- and long-term negative impacts on the victim's education, mental and physical health, and safety (Kosciw et al., 2014). In the LGBT survey, 55.5% felt unsafe at school "because of their sexual orientation" and 37.8%

because of their "gender expression"; 30.3% missed at least a day of school in the last month because they felt "unsafe or uncomfortable," and over a tenth (10.6%) missed 4 or more days; and over a third avoided sex-segregated areas in school because they felt "unsafe or uncomfortable" (bathrooms: 35.4%, locker rooms: 35.3%; Kosciw et al., 2014, p. xvi).

Although bullying is not legally defined as gender discrimination, bullying often has gendered motivations and messages. Through bullying, students pressure each other to comply with heteronormative social rules and attempt to protect their own presumed gender and heterosexual status. Boys who conform too much to school expectations instead of expectations of masculinity may get labeled a *wimp*, *sissy*, *girly girl*, *gay*, or *fag*. Students in grade school through high school report the words

Figure 8.1   Bullying at School and Cyberbullying Anywhere: Students Ages 12 to 18

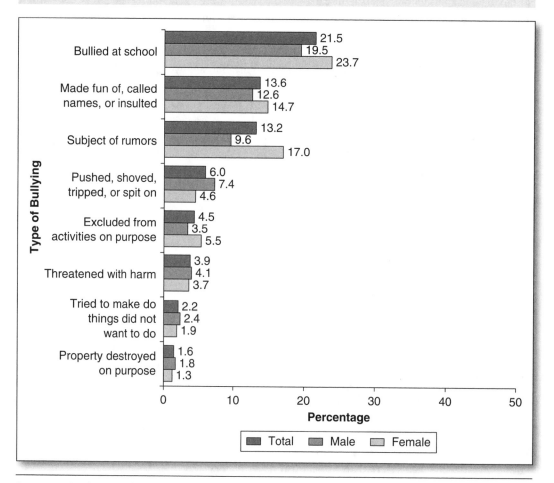

Source: National Center for Education Statistics. (2013). *School Crime Supplement (SCS) to the National Crime Victimization Survey.* U.S. Department of Justice, Bureau of Justice Statistics. As cited in https://nces.ed.gov/pubs2016/2016079.pdf

Note: Students who reported experiencing more than one type of bullying at school were counted only once in the total for students bullied at school.

gay and *fag* are commonly used to bully others, particularly among boys (Pascoe, 2011). The derogatory comments are intended to humiliate boys and men in particular, presumably for acting in feminine ways. Homosexuality and effeminate behaviors are seen as a threat to masculinity, and so the person using the term against others is actually attempting to distance themselves from such labels (Swain, 2005). Boys get the message that they should perform masculinity at all costs. Transgender and gender non-conforming students are treated as if they are a threat to others who do not understand or disagree with their gender identity (Gattis & McKinnon, 2015).

Researchers found girls use similar forms of abuse as boys, but tend to be less physical, relying more on mean-spirited words and actions of exclusion. These can be just as harmful, contributing to victims' underachievement, depression, eating disorders, and suicide. Girls tend to use cyberbullying more than boys. Like boys, girls' bullying also tends to be gendered and heterosexist. Girls often patrol whether other girls conform to heterosexual expectations and yet, when they do, they may be bullied because they compete with each other for boys' attention. Thus, girls who do not conform to social expectations of femininity by wearing baggy clothing, having short hair, or expressing little romantic interest in boys may be bullied, and girls considered too pretty or sexy may be bullied. Calling other girls a *lesbian* or *slut* may seem like contradictions, but both serve to monitor gender and sexual orientation.

At the college level, sexual assault remains one of the barriers to gender equality in education. The U.S. Department of Justice (n.d.) defined **sexual assault** as

> any type of sexual contact or behavior that occurs without the explicit consent of the recipient. Falling under the definition of sexual assault are sexual activities [such] as forced sexual intercourse, forcible sodomy, child molestation, incest, fondling, and attempted rape.

Rape was redefined in 2012 to include all sexes as the perpetrator *or* victim. Rape is "the penetration, no matter how slight, of the vagina or anus with any body part or object, or oral penetration by a sex organ of another person, without the consent of the victim" (U.S. Department of Justice, 2012). Domestic violence, dating violence, and stalking are also serious gendered problems on college and university campuses.

Whether they are in school or not, women ages 18 to 24 reportedly experience the highest rate of rape and sexual assault, more than all other age groups combined, and 80% knew their attacker (Sinozich & Langton, 2014). In one of the largest student surveys on sexual assault, which included 27 campuses and 150,000 students, about 1 in 10 females reported a male sexually assaulted them involving penetration. Transgender students experience even higher rates of sexual assault and rape (Association of American Universities, 2015; Krebs et al., 2016). In a 2016 study by the Bureau of Justice Statistics, the researchers pointed out sexual assault and rape can negatively affect the victim's mental and physical health and their academic performance. The college campus creates a unique barrier for the victim because the close proximity makes anonymity in reporting difficult (Krebs et al., 2016).

The culture of casual sex and abuse of alcohol and drugs are contributing factors to sexual violence in college contexts (Anderson & Clement, 2015). Together these factors reduce inhibitions, but consent is still necessary. When alcohol is involved, it is more difficult to distinguish hookups from sexual assault because inebriation interferes with the ability to give consent. Leading researchers on alcohol and sexual assault report that in over three quarters of college rapes, the offender, the victim, or both were drinking (Sampson, 2011; Zinzlow & Thompson, 2011). This is partially why universities across the country are adopting an affirmative consent standard for student conduct.

Affirmative consent requires the person initiating sexual relations to explicitly ask permission and receive it throughout the duration of the sexual acts, and, if the partner is incapacitated for any reason, consent cannot be obtained. In attempting to determine responsibility for assault, the correct question to ask is "Did the initiator solicit and receive clear affirmative consent?" Not "Did the other person say 'no'?" Harry Brod, a gender violence prevention activist and scholar, likened sexual consent to the right-of-way rule when driving a vehicle. Brod's driver's education teacher taught:

> "The right of way is not something you have. The right of way is something the other driver gives you, and if the other driver doesn't give it to you, you don't have it, no matter what you think the rules of the road are supposed to be or what you think you're entitled to. And if people really understood that, there would be far fewer tragic collisions on our roads." Consent is like that. Consent is not something you have. Consent is something the other person has to give you, and if the other person doesn't give it to you, you don't have it, no matter what you think the rules are supposed to be or what you think you're entitled to. (as cited in Jhally, 2010)

Jackson Katz (2010), a gender violence prevention educator who works with college campuses and U.S. military groups, argued that the predominant U.S. culture's definition of masculinity as aggressive, virile, dominant, and heterosexual perpetuates violence against women, LGBTQ persons, *and* other men. In his view, educating students and faculty to recognize and support alternative and diverse forms of masculinity is at the heart of preventing violence.

Emancipatory Education

Mix It Up at Lunch Day is a national campaign launched by Teaching Tolerance. October 26, 2016, marked its 15th year, with over 4,000 schools encouraging students to create a more inclusive school climate by identifying, questioning, and crossing social boundaries. The program includes blogs and online curriculum to help teachers "mix it up."

Teaching Tolerance (n.d.) explained their focus on the cafeteria, rather than the classroom:

> Students have identified the cafeteria as the place where divisions are most clearly drawn. So for just a day, we ask students to move out of their comfort zones and connect with someone new over lunch. It's a simple act with profound implications. Studies have shown that interactions across group lines

can help reduce prejudice. When students interact with those who are different from them, biases and misperceptions can fall away.

Emancipatory education is possible. It requires you to think about what is taught in the classroom by teachers and textbooks, and across the school by peers, staff, and administrators.

Education more than any other institution has the potential to level the playing field of social injustices and to help each student advance but, as this chapter documents, the institution is a long way from accomplishing this goal. Educator Scott Richardson (2015) called for the deinstitutionalization of gender in education. In other words, Richardson argued one way to ensure that school is an empowering experience for all students is to stop framing education through a narrow, binary gendered/sexed lens. Students and teachers would no longer be assessed according to compliance to stereotypical gendered/sexed expectations, and hopefully the bullying, sexual harassment, and assault in the current school system would be reduced. And maybe a person's sex and race would not determine who they sat with at lunch.

We are not naïve, however. We realize deinstitutionalizing gender in education will take time and require micro-, meso-, and macrolevel changes in curricula, hidden curriculum, classroom interactions, school policies, and peer interactions (Bell, 2016). For education to be a truly egalitarian institution, we must embrace what Brazilian educator Paulo Freire (1972) named **emancipatory education**: educational practices, policies, and laws that seek to challenge accepted stereotypes, unexamined norms, and repressive practices. Below we offer examples of strategies used to promote such change related specifically to gender/sex.

Curricula

The content of what is taught matters. Educators on diversity inclusion and social justice have called for an examination of underlying cultural privileges and omissions in course content, as well as the need to teach students to be critical readers.

One might think that teaching children to critically assess course content is not possible until they are older, but educators such as Vivian Vasquez, a Canadian professor, have observed classrooms using a critical literacy approach as early as ages 3 to 5. Not only is critical literacy effective for young children, but it is essential at this age given this is when students are first forming their conceptions of themselves and others. While the questioning strategies need to be more simplistic in the early grades, Vasquez (2014) offered a set of questions students and teachers at all levels should ask when selecting teaching materials:

- What is this text trying to do to me?
- Whose interests are marginalized or privileged by this text?
- Whose account of a particular topic is missing? Said differently, whose voices are silenced?
- Whose voices are dominant?
- What are the positions from which I am reading this text?
- What experiences am I drawing from to make meaning from the text? (p. 4)

Another Canadian scholar, Kate Paterson (2014), offered an interesting example of helping young students play with and examine stereotypical gender identities. She led reading groups with students ages 6 to 7, using traditional fairytales with a twist. She asked them discussion questions after reading a tale. Here are her questions and their responses for *Goldilocks and The Three Bears*:

KP: Is this a bear family?

Chorus: Yes!

KP: What makes you think this is a family?

Jessica: Because there's a big bear, middle bear, and little bear so that's the dad, mom, and baby.

Josh: The big bear is the father because he's bigger than the mom, tough, strong, and he's playing with the little bear. [Nods of agreement from classmates]

Liam: I do that with my dad! [In the picture the big bear is flipping his cub in the air]

Rachel: The middle[-sized] bear is the mom because she's wearing a headband.

Chris: She's wearing an apron and moms wear aprons.

This exchange demonstrated the children already knew stereotypical gender assignments and readily added descriptions such as: If the big bear is a male, he must also be tough and strong. But look what Paterson asked next:

KP: But have you ever seen a mom who's bigger than a dad in real life? [Children paused to consider then nodded yes]

Chloe: My grandma is bigger than my grandpa.

Amy: My mom is taller than my dad.

Although the children had strongly gendered expectations, the questions encouraged them to challenge these and think about real-life gender diversity.

Laws

One important way to propel change toward emancipatory education is to make people and institutions accountable. In the United States, Title IX was instituted to do just that. Under **Title IX** of the Education Amendments Act of 1972, it is illegal for any federally funded educational program to discriminate on the basis of sex. The law declared, "No person in the United States shall, on the basis of sex, be excluded from participation in, be denied the benefits of, or be subjected to discrimination under any education program or activity receiving Federal financial assistance" (20 U.S.C. § 1681). The Office for Civil Rights (OCR) in the U.S. Department of Education monitors compliance with the law. All schools and universities from kindergarten up that receive federal funds are expected to comply or risk losing essential funds.

Most people associate Title IX with sex equity in school sports, but the original intent was to achieve equity in education. Since sports have traditionally been a realm of masculinity, those who felt men's sports would be in jeopardy resisted the law (Ware, 2015). Although Title IX has been in effect for nearly 50 years, full sports equity has not been achieved. The goal is that qualified athletes receive comparable scholarship awards (not necessarily the same awards) at a given institution and have comparable equipment, schedules, tutoring, and coaches, based on proportional female and male student enrollment. Some variance is accepted, but based on 2009 data from the Department of Education, for Division I (largest schools) in the National Collegiate Athletic Association (NCAA), the average university gap in athlete number and resources was 13.3% in favor of men athletes (Yanus & O'Connor, 2016), whereas the largest gap considered acceptable by most courts has been 5% (Stafford, 2004). This means that, unless legally contested, most schools get by with a margin of over 13% more support in favor of men's sports.

The institution of education has a way to go to attain full compliance, but the law is inducing schools to be more inclusive of sex, as well as race, ethnicity, class, and sexual orientation (Hanson, Guilfoy, & Pillai, 2009). Advocates for transgender and gender non-conforming students' are also using Title IX as support for their rights to a safe learning environment. Researchers report the law has changed sports, other extracurricular opportunities, and student conduct and that these changes have social justice implications far beyond the institution of education (Hanson et al., 2009). The most visible evidence of long-term improvement may be found in the Olympics.

Women in the Olympics

1900: Women first participate in the Olympics

1972: Title IX became law; women represented 21% of the U.S. Olympic team (84 of 400)

2012: For the first time in history, women represented 50.7% of the U.S. Olympic team (269 of 530).*

2016: U.S. women athletes outnumbered men (53% to 47%) and were the most women ever from a single nation to compete in an Olympic event. For the first time in history, U.S. women took home more medals than men (53% to 47%, 291 for women and 263 for men).* Eleven openly gay male Olympians competed, but none were from the United States.

*Analysts believe the rise in women's participation is a direct result of Title IX. Although the tipping over of the 50% mark in 2012 may be partially attributable to the men's soccer team not qualifying. In 2016, there were also more sports and more U.S. athletes than ever before (Buzinski, 2016; Myre, 2016; Team USA RIO 2016, 2016; Whiteside, 2012).

In 2011, the OCR sent what is known as a "Dear Colleagues letter" to all levels of educational institutions to remind them Title IX applies to sex and gender discrimination beyond the playing field (Ali, 2011). The letter spelled out that sexual harassment, sexual assault, bullying, stalking, and any other gendered violence are forms of discrimination that prevent equal opportunities in educational experiences. For the first time, the OCR stipulated specific ways schools could demonstrate compliance, including the following:

- Ensure that everyone is educated on the school's policies related to Title IX
- Develop clear procedures for reporting, investigating, and punishing cases that are fair to both parties involved
- Provide adequate training for administrative staff
- Report all cases to the OCR
- Implement violence prevention programs (Ali, 2011)

While this reporting process demands more paperwork from individual school administrators, more victims are likely to report because they now know how. Reporting of cases to the OCR provides a clearer picture of the size of the problem across the country and the hope is that, in time, the predominant culture of gendered violence in schools will no longer be a social norm.

Globally

Emancipatory education must also occur at the global level. Sex inequity in education persists globally. In October 2015, the United Nations Educational, Scientific and Cultural Organization (UNESCO) reported:

There are still 31 million girls of primary school age out of school. Of these, 17 million are expected to never enter school. There are 4 million fewer boys than girls out of school.

Three countries have over a million girls not in school: In Nigeria there are almost five and a half million, Pakistan, over three million, and in Ethiopia, over one million girls out of school.

The reasons for the inequity are complex and culturally specific, but in general where there are economic limitations and patriarchal traditions, girls are usually the last to be placed in schools and the first to be removed. For example, in South Asia the barriers to education for girls tend to include cultural biases such as preferences for sons, gender role restrictions that keep girls working at home, early marriage practices, lack of gender/sex–sensitive infrastructure (such as latrines), unfriendly school environments, lack of community involvement to ensure girls' safety at school, lack of positive role models for girls who aspire to be educated, weak legal frameworks that do not implement free primary education or enforce child labor legislation, and labor market discrimination (Subrahmanian, 2005).

Yet education for women can break a cycle of poverty in just one generation. Women with an education tend to marry later, have fewer children, earn higher pay, and support healthier families with a better quality of life (UNESCO, 2013). Consequently, the United Nations targeted girls' and women's education for improvement. The number of girls attending school is increasing due to individual programs, but equality in numbers enrolled alone is not enough.

This recognition of the unique oppressions of girls and women in education worldwide provides a fuller picture of the challenges regarding gender/sex in education. It also provides an educational model that attends to intersecting, systemic influences of gender/sex oppressions across social institutions, a model the U.S. education system may find useful.

Conclusion

Ultimately, each person must demand an education. Philosopher Adrienne Rich (1977/2005), in a lecture at Douglass College, explained,

> You . . . cannot afford to think of being here to receive an education; you will do much better to think of yourselves as being here to claim one. . . . You do not need to rely on teachers or peers to receive an emancipatory education. You can demand to be taken seriously so that you can also go on taking yourself seriously. This means seeking out criticism, recognizing that the most affirming thing anyone can do for you is demand that you push yourself further, show you the range of what you *can* do. . . . It means assuming your share of responsibility for what happens in the classroom. (pp. 608, 611)

Education is composed of communicative practices—lectures, books, activities—that teach students to perform gender. Detailed analysis of educational practices demonstrates the gendered/sexed elements of education include who is educating whom, about what, in what way, and for what purpose. Educators and those being educated have an opportunity and responsibility to think about how the classroom can be a microcosm for multiple social inequalities *and* for social change.

KEY CONCEPTS

affirmative consent 176

bullying 173

cyberbullying 173

emancipatory education 177

harassment 173

hidden curriculum 166

microaggression 171

rape 175

sexual assault 175

Title IX 178

DISCUSSION QUESTIONS

1. Did anything surprise you about the history of education and the hidden curriculum discussion? If so what was it and why did it draw your interest?

2. What are some ways in which the institution of education has constructed and constrained gender/sex? Can you offer examples of any of these from your own educational experiences?

3. How have microaggressions, bullying, and sexual harassment affected your educational experience or that of others you know?

4. Brainstorm about the notion of deinstitutionalizing gender as the central framework for education. What would it look like?

CHAPTER 9

Work

The summer of 2016 was typical for Kansas teenagers Jensen Walcott and Jake Reed; they got summer jobs at a pizzeria. But when the two discovered Jake was being paid 25 cents per hour more, Jensen asked the manager why. Instead of correcting the pay disparity, the manager fired Jensen. Then, the manager fired Jake. Why? Because they had violated the company prohibition against discussing salaries. (Note that some state laws and federal rules prohibit companies from enacting pay secrecy rules because such rules "serve to perpetuate [pay] disparity" [Women's Bureau, 2014, p. 1].) *Seventeen* magazine, *New York* magazine, and the New York *Daily News* reported the story, presidential candidate Hillary Clinton tweeted about it, and the two friends spoke at the Democratic National Convention (Gutierrez, 2016).

Although 25 cents may seem insignificant, and the parent company indicated it was not a case of sex-based wage disparity, the case is still illustrative. Why would two teens, hired at the same time, be paid differently? And when that difference was noted, why were the workers punished instead of the discrepancy fixed? Because work is gendered and sexed. Gender and sex influence how much people are paid, which jobs people are steered toward, and people's experiences at work.

To illustrate how central sex and gender are to workplace treatment, consider the experience of workers who transition while working. In a study of their work experiences, sociologist Catherine Connell (2010) found that "transgender workers who transitioned on the job described changes in their employers' assumptions about their abilities" (p. 47). The person is the same person; the only thing that changed is their gender/sex designation. Yet that alone was enough to trigger different treatment from their employers.

The patterns of treatment are telling. Sociologist Kristen Schilt (2011) found "transwomen are more likely to face workplace barriers than transmen" (p. 133). Transwomen reported resistance to their transition while transmen reported support. This also translated into different judgments of work products. Transmen experienced "an increase in allocation of resources such as respect, authority, and in some cases, financial resources," influenced by "race, height, perceived sexuality, and masculine embodiment" (Tesene, 2012, p. 677). In contrast, transwomen experienced superiors questioning their abilities after their transition. The conclusion: "The workplace is not a gender-neutral location that equitably rewards workers based on their individual merits . . . but rather 'a central site for the creation and reproduction of gender differences and gender inequality' (C.L. Williams 1995, 15)" (Schilt, 2011, p. 132).

Not only does gender/sex influence one's treatment in the workplace, but work affects how you understand your own gender/sex identity. In the United States, work is considered a characteristic of what makes Americans American. "What do you do?" is one of the first questions many people ask when getting to know each other. What they usually mean is "What is your job?" The prominence of the question is indicative of how U.S. people tend to define identity by the wage-earning work they do.

The way a culture's economy is structured exposes much about what is valued in that culture. **Capitalism**, an economic system in which individuals and corporations (rather than the state) own and control the means of production and distribution of goods and services and the exchange of wealth, depends on creating and maintaining a culture where people value materialism and purchasing power. Work is how people gain purchasing power and the status that comes with it. The very definition of work contains cultural ideologies.

In the United States, the predominant ideology is that hard work pays. The belief is that people who work hard will be rewarded with job security, financial independence, and a better quality of life. This cultural ideology persists even in the face of economic downturns individual workers cannot control, increased work hours, and people living in poverty regardless of how hard they work in the midst of a country that considers itself economically advanced. Minimum wage jobs held by poor women and men of color drive the capitalist economy by providing processed foods, clothing, and other consumer products, but they do not provide enough for workers to do more than minimally survive (Ehrenreich, 2001; Mawdsley, 2007). Given the centrality of work in the United States, one cannot study gender without studying the institution of work because "the workplace is a crucial site for the reproduction of gender inequality" (C. Connell, 2010, p. 32).

Scholars have noted that workplaces are never just about doing work because they are populated with people doing gender (Carlson & Crawford, 2011, p. 360). Dennis Mumby (2001), a critical organizational theorist, has definitively declared, "It is impossible to study and theorize adequately about organizational power without addressing its gendered character" (p. 609). But studying organizational structure is not enough. Studying communication is essential because "communication produces, not merely expresses, the realities of organization" (Ashcraft & Mumby, 2004, p. xviii). **Critical organizational communication** scholars study work organizations by analyzing communication and power and exploring how work and communication are co-constitutive, meaning they create, maintain, and alter each other. Work organizations are not neutral sites, but are places where control and resistance are exercised. Such scholars (e.g., Ashcraft, 2009; Ashcraft & Mumby, 2004; Buzzanell, 2000; Calás & Smircich, 2001; Trethewey, 2001) examine communication on a range of levels, from an individual's "engrained personal communication habits" and daily interactions, to the form of an organization, to social narratives about work (Ashcraft & Mumby, 2004, p. 28).

This chapter explores gender in work at the micro-, meso-, and macrolevels of communication (Ashcraft, 2014). At the microlevel, interpersonal communication between people in workplace settings involves the performance and construction of gender. At the mesolevel, organizational discourses and structures enable and constrain gender. At the macrolevel, the way society communicates about work constructs gender.

To explore these three levels of gendered work communication, we offer two examples: pay equity/job segregation and workplace sex discrimination/sexual harassment. In each case, we explore how micro-, meso-, and macrocommunication constructs, maintains, and challenges gender. We discuss all three levels because workplace gender problems cannot be solved exclusively by personal change; if work as an institution is gendered, telling people who are disadvantaged by their sex/gender to change is an incomplete and problematic solution. Because gender issues always operate at the interpersonal *and* institutional levels, "meaningful change requires more than creative individuals and interactions; it also necessitates new institutional forms to support such innovation" (Ashcraft, 2009, p. 312).

Pay Equity and Job Segregation

Wage disparity, or different groups of people being paid different wages for doing the same job, is not a new problem. Recognition of the problem emerged when women entered the workforce in higher numbers during World War II. In 1942, the National War Labor Board urged employers to voluntarily pay women comparable wages to what they had paid men. Employers did not comply and, when men returned from war, women were forced out of their jobs. During the war, women were encouraged to work as an act of patriotism; then, they were told they needed to give their jobs to returning veterans, also to be patriotic (Yesil, 2004).

Throughout the 1950s and into the 1960s, separating jobs on the basis of sex was the norm. For example, newspapers separated job listings for men and women. Some job listings declared "no women need apply" (Walsh, 1977). The different jobs also meant different pay scales. During this era, women tended to earn only 59 cents to every dollar a man earned. Intensifying this disparity was job segregation on the basis of the socially constructed category of race. Until the 1964 Civil Rights Act, it was legal to discriminate against potential employees on the basis of race.

On June 10, 1963, the U.S. Congress passed the Equal Pay Act, which requires that people who work at jobs of "equal skill, effort, and responsibility, and which are performed under similar working conditions" at the same workplace should be paid the same wage. The law explicitly prohibits sex as a basis for differential pay (section 206.d.1). Despite this law, wage disparity persisted and additional legislation sought to address it: Title VII of the 1964 Civil Rights Act, which prohibited employment discrimination on the basis of race, color, religion, sex, or national origin; the Age Discrimination in Employment Act of 1967, which prohibited employment discrimination on the basis of age; Title I of the Americans with

Disabilities Act of 1990, which prohibited discrimination against those with disabilities; and the Lilly Ledbetter Fair Pay Act of 2009, which extended the statute of limitations for bringing a wage discrimination claim. Fifty years after the passage of the Equal Pay Act, and despite the other legal remedies, wage disparities persist between the sexes. When generally comparing the wages men as a group make to the wages women as a group make, U.S. Labor Department statistics indicate women make about 78 cents to every dollar a man makes.

The U.S. Bureau of Labor Statistics (2016b) indicated that in 2014 (the most recent data available), "women who worked full time in wage and salary jobs had median usual weekly earnings of $719, which was 83 percent of men's median weekly earnings ($871)." In construction, food service, and office and administrative support work, women made 90% as much as men, while in legal work, sales, and protective services, women earned 70% or less. The degree of disparity differs between professions, but in almost all professions, men's pay is higher than women's.

Many professions are sex segregated (e.g., firefighters tend to be men, nurses tend to be women). Predominantly male occupations possess more social value, as indicated by more pay, prestige, authority, and opportunities for advancement. Numerous studies demonstrated that if an occupation is female dominated, it tends to carry less prestige, authority, and autonomy. Even in part-time work, people (usually young men) who mow and care for lawns tend to be paid more than people (usually young women) who babysit children.

Pay inequality is not unique to the United States. Based on data from the World Bank, UN Women (2015) estimated that "globally, women are paid less than men. Women in most countries earn on average only 60 to 75 per cent of men's wages." Contributing to this imbalance is the fact that women tend to bear responsibility for unpaid household work, and often women are restricted to home-based employment, further limiting their earnings (Chen, Vanek, Lund, & Heintz, 2005). Although the global wage gap is shrinking, at its current rate of reduction, the World Economic Forum (2015) reported it would take another 118 years before the gap is closed.

Those who do not believe sexism explains the pay disparity offer a range of explanations, including "differences in occupations, positions, education, job tenure or hours worked per week" (Hoff Sommers, 2014). However, a number of studies have controlled for these variables. Even the most conservative analysis recognized at least a 5% pay gap in the United States across all jobs (Kolesnikova & Liu, 2011). In a meta-analysis of studies on pay and performance appraisal from the last 30 years, the researchers found

> sex differences in rewards . . . (including salary, bonuses, and promotions) were 14 times larger than sex differences in performance evaluations . . . , and that differences in performance evaluations did not explain reward differences between men and women. (Joshi, Son, & Roh, 2015, p. 1516)

One factor tended to lessen the pay differential: higher percentages of women in executive positions in the industry studied.

Table 9.1 Gender/Sex Work Segregation and Wage Disparities

Occupation	Total Population Employed in This Occupation	Percentage of Female Employees	Median Weekly Earning, Female	Median Weekly Earning, Male
Registered nurses	2,382,000	88.3	$1,098	$1,222
Janitors and building cleaners	1,536,000	28.7	$429	$547
Maids and housekeeping cleaners	876,000	84.7	$407	$475
Elementary and middle school teachers	2,806,000	80.6	$957	$1,077
Secondary school teachers	1,048,000	58.2	$1,006	$1,149
Physicians and surgeons	740,000	38.2	$1,553	$1,915
Police and sheriff's patrol officers	655,000	13.1	$1,009	$1,001
Construction laborers	1,181,000	2.1	No data available	$642

Source: Data extracted from Bureau of Labor Statistics, U.S. Department of Labor (2016a).

Note: Women represent 44.3% of the labor force.

When specific professions are analyzed, the differences become quite large. A report by the U.S. Government Accountability Office (2010) found that "female managers earned 81 cents for every dollar earned by male managers in 2007" (p. 3). The report even adjusted for other characteristics such as age, hours worked, race, location, education level, and whether there were dependent children. In other words, sex was the only difference.

Another study examined people who were employed full time 1 year after graduation from college and had similar education, age, and family responsibilities.

Figure 9.1 Women and Men's Earnings 1 Year After College Graduation

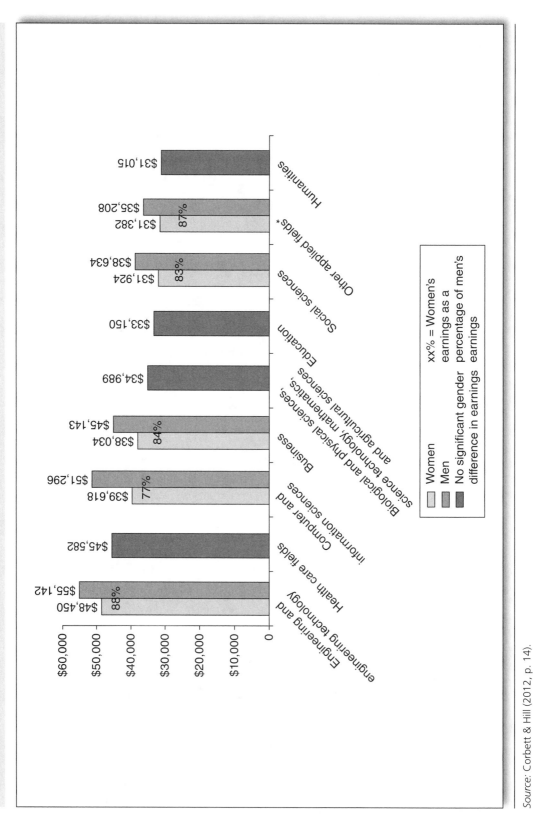

Source: Corbett & Hill (2012, p. 14).

The result: women earned only 82% of what men earned. After controlling for "hours, occupation, college major, employment sector, and other factors associated with pay, the pay gap shrinks but does not disappear" (Corbett & Hill, 2012, p. 1). Approximately a 7% difference remained (Corbett & Hill, 2012, p. 20).

What might explain these differences? The aggregate difference between men and women in general can be explained by the majors and professions men and women tend to choose. Men tend to go into engineering or technical jobs, which pay more than professions like teaching and clerical work. But that leads us to another question: Why is there sex segregation between jobs? Here is a where a macrolevel analysis is helpful. What social messages urge women into some professions and men into others?

The wage gap also needs an intersectional analysis. Pay gaps are influenced not only by sex, but also by race, with the gap being intensified in many cases. Job segregation occurs not only across sex lines but also across the social category of race within sex. Within ethnic categories, men tend to make more than women. Whites and Asian Americans make more than African Americans, Latinx, and Native peoples.

An intersectional approach enables you to see how systemic inequalities manifest themselves. As a paradigmatic example:

> Black women's initial overrepresentation in domestic service reflects the intersections of race, gender, and class—the idea that Blacks are best suited for servitude, that women belong in the private sphere of the home, and that work done in the home does not deserve significant economic reward. (Harvey, 2005, p. 791)

With the globalization of the economy, this dynamic has been extended to cover not only Black women but also Filipina women in Canada (Welsh, Carr, MacQuarrie, & Huntley, 2006) and Latina immigrants in the United States (Hondagneu-Sotelo & Avila, 1997).

Sociologist Mignon Duffy (2005) analyzed how paid care work is segregated along race, class, and sex lines. We would add age, with young and old women being valued less, paid less, and more often hired as care workers. Duffy analyzed jobs such as domestic service, health care, childcare, teaching, food preparation, and cleaning and building services. Her analysis was situated within broader research that establishes the U.S. labor market as "stratified, segmented into various sectors that provide workers with grossly unequal wage levels and access to opportunities for advancement" (p. 71). This stratification is neither race nor sex neutral, because "interlocking systems of gender and racial oppression act to concentrate women and people of color in those occupations that are lower paying and lower status" (p. 71). Even within care labor, stratification can be found in which White women assume the public face of care work, populating those jobs that call for the most interaction with others, are most professionalized, and pay more. In contrast, "women of color are disproportionately represented in the 'dirty, back-room' jobs such as maids and kitchen workers" (p. 72).

A 2016 study by the Economic Policy Institute noted that the wage gap between Blacks and Whites is larger than it was in 1979. Although the size of the gap has fluctuated over the years,

> as of 2015, relative to the average hourly wages of white men with the same education, experience, metro status, and region of residence, black men make 22.0 percent less, and black women make 34.2 percent less. Black women earn 11.7 percent less than their white female counterparts. The widening gap has not affected everyone equally. Young black women (those with 0 to 10 years of experience) have been hardest hit since 2000. (Wilson & Rodgers, 2016, p. 1)

The study found that level of education does not explain the wage gaps given that completing a college degree does not appear to lessen the gap.

Figure 9.2   Gender/Sex Pay Gap

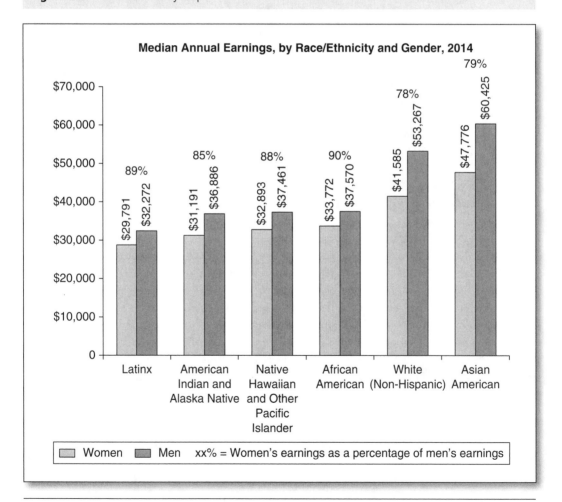

Source: AAUW (2016, p. 10).

Just as the general gap between men and women cannot be explained away by differences in education, position, age, seniority, and so on, neither can the Black-White gap. Researchers attribute the Black-White wage disparity to discrimination (Wilson & Rodgers, 2016, p. 1). How might that discrimination manifest? Patricia S. Parker (2003) provided an exhaustive review of the literature on African American women and how they experience control (and exercise resistance and create empowerment) in raced, gendered, and classed work contexts. Parker highlighted the way in which race, gender/sex, and class "structure communicative practices in everyday organizational life—such as hiring and recruitment rituals, interaction patterns, and symbolic processes—that contribute to African American women's continued subordination and oppression in the U.S. labor market" (p. 258). What is important to note is that African American women face this subordination not just from White men but also from White women (Parker, 2003, p. 271; for research on Hispanic women, see Calás, 1992; for research on working-class women, see Gregg, 1993).

Work practices that maintain and create subordination are not always overt, but can be subtle, located in "ordinary, daily procedures and decisions" (Parker, 2003, p. 264), such as who is asked to do which type of tasks. Racism and sexism are not located in individuals' prejudices but in institutional practices that inform "everyday social practices," or microlevel communication, that individual "organizational members enact to make, maintain, and modify meanings of constructions of difference" that benefit some people, but not others (Parker, 2014, p. 626). Studies of African American women make clear that their experiences of subordination begin in school, when counselors and teachers tend to steer them away from particular work aspirations (Parker, 2003). The problems African American women face are intensified at the time of job entry and then exacerbated with job advancement (or the lack thereof). Summarizing the research, Parker (2003) concluded that "research on African American women's work experiences reveals the persistent structuring of organizational divisions along race, gender[/sex], and class lines that occurs through power-based communicative practices" (p. 268). How African American women are talked to and talked about influences the types of work they and others consider suitable for African American women. Daily practices, which often appear insignificant when viewed as isolated instances, accumulate to create sexist and racist work organizations and accumulate to result in wage disparity. At the meso- and macrolevels, "historical, cultural, social, and discursive patterns" then hold those "organizational divisions, inequities, traditions, and practices" in place (Parker, 2014, p. 628).

Looking at the pay gap from the level of microcommunication, namely how different people might negotiate for pay, one might conclude that differences in pay are the result of differences in negotiating styles. Some research ties one possible explanation for some of the wage gap to people's communication practices. Linda Babcock and Sara Laschever (2007) found that women's reluctance to initiate and directly negotiate their initial salary offer directly contributed to the salary gap between women and men. As the title of their book pointed out, "women don't ask"—for salary, for work opportunities, for perks. In fact, communication may influence whether one receives a job offer given "assertive women are more likely to be hired" (Basow, 2008, p. 22). However, simply attributing the pay gap to interpersonal differences in negotiating styles is an incomplete explanation and places too much of the onus on individual workers and ignores the way organizations are gendered and how institutional norms may penalize people for violating gendered expectations. What happens when women do negotiate illustrates this.

In a follow-up study, Bowles, Babcock, and Lai (2007) found that evaluators "penalized female candidates more than male candidates for initiating negotiations" regarding pay (pp. 84, 99). They also explored why women and men might be more or less willing to negotiate for pay. They found that "gender differences in the propensity to initiate negotiations may be motivated by social incentives as opposed to individual differences" (p. 85). Basically, women recognized they face greater social costs for negotiating than men. Thus, they choose not to negotiate for fear of being penalized, not because they were personally unwilling or unable to negotiate. In fact, in the experiment, the negative judgment of evaluators was "5.5 times greater" for women regardless of whether their request was simple or assertive (p. 91). These studies make clear that individual changes alone are insufficient. The solution is not that individual women should negotiate. Instead, an institutional correction is needed: The social environment of work needs to change.

For example, actors on *The Big Bang Theory* called attention to pay inequity. Female costars Mayim Bialik and Melissa Rauch earned $200,000 per episode while Jim Parsons, Johnny Galecki, Kaley Cuoco, Kunal Nayyar, and Simon Helberg made $1 million per episode (Amoroso, 2017). In an attempt to remedy the pay gap, the three highest paid actors on the show took a pay cut to fund raises for their female costars. While the gesture was a thoughtful and creative way to minimize the pay gap, should costars or Warner Brothers shoulder the responsibility for pay inequity?

At the mesolevel, communication from the organization creates conditions that widen pay gaps. Sociology professor Janice F. Madden (2012) analyzed the pay gap in brokerage firms, one of the jobs where the pay gap is largest, with women earning only about two thirds as much as men. Because pay in such a position is commission-based, many argue that the pay gap merely reflects performance. However, this is not what Madden found. Instead, "performance-support bias" accounted for wage disparity: "Differences in management's discretionary assignments of sales opportunities, and not in sales capacities, account for the gender pay gap among stockbrokers in these two firms" (p. 4). A wage gap also persists among physician researchers. Even after a study took into account "differences in specialty, institutional characteristics, academic productivity, academic rank, work hours, and other factors," the researchers still found that men earned over $12,000 a year more than women (which would accumulate to over $350,000 over a lifetime; Jagsi et al., 2012).

This illustrates how "organizational structure is not gender neutral" (Acker, 1990, p. 139) and tends to benefit some to the detriment of others. Sociologist Joan Acker (1990) explained:

> To say that an organization . . . is gendered means that advantage and disadvantage, exploitation and coercion, action and emotion, meaning and identity, are patterned through and in terms of a distinction between male and

female, masculine and feminine. Gender is not an addition to ongoing processes, conceived as gender neutral. Rather, it is an integral part of those
processes, which cannot be properly understood without an analysis of
gender. (p. 146)

Acker's work made clear "gender is a constitutive feature of organizations and organizing" (McDonald, 2015, p. 311).

Despite all the statistical evidence about pay gaps, differential opportunity for
advancement, sexual harassment, and job segregation, college students still tend to
believe they will face no discrimination once they enter the workplace. In a study
of 1,373 college students taking business courses at a public southeastern university,
the researchers reported:

College students fail to perceive that gender discrimination might affect their
own careers or the careers of women in business. . . . Almost 90% of all student respondents reported that their opportunities for advancement, networking, mentoring, and pay would not be affected by their gender[/sex].
Similarly, 90% of students perceived that women would not have fewer
opportunities for networking and mentoring because of their gender[/sex].
Moreover, 75% believed that women would not face pay disparity, and 60%
believed that gender[/sex] would present no obstacle to women in the workplace. (Sipe, Johnson, & Fisher, 2009, p. 344)

These findings are particularly troubling because awareness of and knowledge
about the way work is gendered, sexed, raced, heteronormative, and cisnormative
are necessary to minimize the effects of workplace discrimination. If one does not
expect to find work gendered/sexed and then experiences discrimination, the
effects on self-esteem tend to be greater and the ability to seek ways to productively
counter these effects is lessened. It is extremely difficult to resist unequal treatment
if one is unwilling to recognize it exists.

Sex Discrimination in the Workplace

Organizational communication scholar Patrice Buzzanell (2000) urged people to
be aware of how "organization members 'do gender' . . . in the course of their mundane, everyday organization practices" (p. 4). When we reference *doing gender*, we
refer to how a person talks or acts *and* to how each person interprets others' talk
and actions. Research makes clear that "gender differences in actual communication and leadership behaviors are slight, although expectations of gender differences are strong" (Basow, 2008, p. 27). Women and men do not communicate
differently in the workplace, but they are assessed differently because people
impose gendered expectations on them, and these expectations benefit some and
disadvantage others.

An example of different expectations and perceptions occurs when "the same
actions can be evaluated very differently depending on whether they are enacted by

a man or woman manager" (Mullany, 2007, p. 47). For the most part, the expression of emotions at work is considered inappropriate. Men (and women) are expected not to cry or show fear, sadness, or joy; it is considered appropriate, however, for men to show anger. Ultimately, though, it is impossible to compare and contrast women's and men's emotions because emotions considered organizationally appropriate when expressed by a man tend to be perceived as inappropriate when expressed by a woman (Hearn, 1993; Martin, 2006).

If one studies activities rather than emotional expression, it appears that men engage in practices that are stereotypically attributed to women more than to men, such as

wasting time talking to coworkers, pretending to like people they dislike, making decisions based on affect rather than "objective" evidence, and ignoring rules in favor of particularistic sentiments. . . . When women coworkers socialize, they waste time; when men coworkers socialize, they advance their careers. (Martin, 2003, p. 358)

The one distinction is that men tend to do some communicative behaviors differently from women. "Peacocking" and other self-promoting behaviors, in particular, were directed only at other men: "The audience(s) to whom/that men hold themselves accountable at work relative to gender is . . . primarily other men" (p. 358). In other words, the differences claimed by some do not exist, and the differences that do exist tend not to be recognized as distinctive masculine behavior because the work institution is gendered masculine, and so the behavior appears neutral.

These subtle practices highlight how mechanisms of exclusion and discrimination are not always readily apparent, even if they are demonstrably present. As Martin (2003) explained:

Men need not invent schemes for excluding women from daily work processes in order for women to experience exclusion. As men engage in gendering practices consistent with institutionalized norms and stereotypes of masculinity, they nonetheless create social closure and oppression. (p. 360)

For this reason, the insights offered by communication studies become important. The following is an example from Martin's (2006) research.

Maria [Systems Analyst, Latina, age 35]: I would talk to my boss about a problem, just to think it through. . . . I found out my boss was taking my problem to his boss and they were solving it for me. I did not like this. This was not what I had asked my boss to do. I felt he meant well. . . . But this was not what I meant or wanted to happen. I wanted to have his ear and thoughts in working through the problem myself. So I told my boss, "Don't do this to me. When I come to you to discuss something, that's [all] I want. Don't solve the problem for me, OK?" If he solves my problems, this will make me look like I can't solve my problems. (p. 263)

Maria's boss was perhaps unconsciously performing his own gendered masculinity to fix the problem and imposing unfair assumptions about his employee's technical abilities as a woman. Close analysis of microlevel communication dynamics can enable one to trace, and challenge, the gendered norms of interaction at work (Martin, 2006).

Subtle forms of discrimination and exclusion are not the only things that affect the sexes differently. Researchers found that "workplace aggression and violence . . . does not affect men and women equally" (Magley, Gallus, & Bunk, 2010, p. 423). In a meta-analysis of 57 empirical studies, M. Sandy Hershcovis and colleagues (2007) found men tended to be more aggressive at work than women. Men were more likely to engage in physical and psychological aggression, view aggression as acceptable behavior, and seek revenge (Magley et al., 2010, p. 431).

In the workplace, the normalization of violence takes the form of **sexual harassment**, or repeated, unwanted verbal or nonverbal communication of a sexual nature. Prior to the 1970s, *sexual harassment* as a term did not exist, even though workplace sexual violence did (Cortina & Berdahl, 2008). When women experienced hostile, abusive, and violent workplaces, it was explained as having a "bad boss" or as further proof that women did not belong in the rough world of paid employment. In the 1970s, women's movements developed language to name the problem. The Women's Center at Cornell University held the first speak-out in 1975, where women around the country came together to name these experiences *sexual harassment* and articulate the harm as discrimination. In 1980, the Equal Employment Opportunity Commission (EEOC) issued guidelines recognizing sexual harassment to be a violation of Title VII of the Civil Rights Act of 1964. According to the U.S. Code of Federal Regulations, which the EEOC (2012) enforces,

> (a) Harassment on the basis of sex is a violation of section 703 of title VII. Unwelcome sexual advances, requests for sexual favors, and other verbal or physical conduct of a sexual nature constitute sexual harassment when (1) submission to such conduct is made either explicitly or implicitly a term or condition of an individual's employment, (2) submission to or rejection of such conduct by an individual is used as the basis for employment decisions affecting such individual, or (3) such conduct has the purpose or effect of unreasonably interfering with an individual's work performance or creating an intimidating, hostile, or offensive working environment. (29 C.F.R. § 1604.11)

In 1986, in *Meritor Savings Bank v. Vinson* (477 U.S. 57), the Supreme Court held that creating a hostile work environment is actionable under Title VII, explaining that the prohibition against employment discrimination "is not limited to 'economic' or 'tangible' discrimination" like losing a job (p. 64). The courts also recognized that acquiescing to sexual demands was not necessary to prove an injury. One person did not need to touch another to harm another. Instead, what people said, words alone, could create an environment in which it was impossible to work. According to the Eleventh Circuit Court of Appeals, language could be used to subordinate another on the basis of sex (*Henson v. City of Dundee,* 682 F.2d at 902, 1982).

The naming of sexual harassment and the creation of legal redress for those who experienced it have helped counter gendered/sexed violence in the workplace. The law recognizes two types of sexual harassment: **Quid pro quo**, translated as *this for that*, refers to pressures to provide sexual favors in exchange for job security, and **hostile work environment** refers to behaviors that create a negative culture where work becomes impossible.

The EEOC (n.d.) reported that in fiscal year 2015, women filed 82.9% of the 6,822 charges of sexual harassment (charges can also be filed with the Fair Employment Practice Agency, state EEOCs, or internally with a company). In the United States, 13% to 31% of men and 40% to 75% of women have been sexually harassed by others in the workplace (McDonald, 2012). Although some examples exist of women harassing men, men harassing men, and women harassing women, by far the most predominant form of harassment is men harassing women (McDonald, 2012).

However, even with law in place, many do not feel comfortable reporting that a coworker has harassed them. An analysis of 10 years of research found that only about a third of those who experience harassment report it to an official, and only between 2% and 20% actually file a formal complaint (Cortina & Berdahl, 2008). The reason: The harassed person fears retaliation. In explaining this research, a *New York Times* article pointed out that "organizations that are very hierarchical or masculine can breed more harassment, and less reporting of it, because gendered power dynamics are a big driver" (Miller, 2017).

In the wake of reports that Fox News had paid out $13 million in damages to women who accused host Bill O'Reilly of sexual harassment, the corporation defended itself by saying no employees had used the company's hotline to report concerns. This led to discussions about why someone might not report harassment. A *New York Times* story provided some insight:

> A male colleague grabbing her leg. Another one suggestively rubbing her back. Others at work dinners discussing who they'd want to sleep with.

> Jane Park talked about experiencing all of this behavior in her career in business consulting and strategy. Never has she reported any of it to human resources or management.

> "It's made into such a big deal that you have to make a decision: Do you want to ruin your career? Do you want this to be everything that you end up being about?" said Ms. Park, who is now chief executive of Julep, a beauty company she founded. "What you really want to happen is that it doesn't happen again." (Miller, 2017)

Even though national and corporate policies exist on the macrolevel, mesolevel communication may interfere with their implementation. Even though corporations think they have clear policies that define specific behaviors as illegal, mesolevel communication about the policy can hinder its effectiveness by focusing on perceptions of the behaviors rather than the behaviors themselves (Dougherty & Hode, 2016). In addition, workplace culture can work against legal norms against harassment. Consensus concerning which behaviors constitute sexual harassment is lacking. Women tend to define more acts as harassment and are more likely to perceive coercion, whereas masculine men are more likely to blame the person being harassed (Quinn, 2002).

Sociologist Beth A. Quinn (2002) studied "**girl watching**," a practice where men as a group comment on and observe women coworkers' physical appeal. The women being watched may not be aware; comments are not made to the women, but to other men about the women. A famous example of this is the audio, released in 2016, of a 2005 conversation between Donald Trump and *Access Hollywood* reporter Billy Bush. The two men were in a workplace setting (a bus taking them to a taping) and were about to meet a coworker, Arianne Zucker. In the audio, Trump commented about how he "moved on" Bush's coanchor and then the two men begin commenting on Zucker's appearance, at which point Trump commented, "I've got to use some Tic Tacs, just in case I start kissing her. You know I'm automatically attracted to beautiful—I just start kissing them. It's like a magnet. Just kiss. I don't even wait.... And when you're a star, they let you do it. You can do anything.... Grab them by the pussy. You can do anything" (as cited in Fahrenthold, 2016). This exchange illustrates how this practice objectifies women in the workplace and Trump's comments are an example of how power dynamics in a workplace make it difficult for those who are harassed to object.

Girl watching is a form of harassment that tends to be labeled as play by men who engage in it. Because the woman being watched is unaware, the target of the action may not be the particular woman being watched but other men and, indirectly, other women in the organization. Quinn (2002) found girl watching functioned as a form of gendered play among the men that bolstered masculinity by being premised on "a studied lack of empathy with the feminine other" (p. 391). Watching targets the woman as a game piece, an object rather than another player. The other players are men. Quinn found that sexual joking and girl watching is "a common way for heterosexual men to establish intimacy among themselves" (p. 394). This begs the question: Why do some men base their bonding on the sexual objectification of women?

In a culture of hegemonic masculinity, men become men by performing their virility in front of other men. When asked what "being a man" entailed, the men Quinn (2002) interviewed indicated that it involved "notions of strength (if not in muscle, then in character and job performance), dominance, and a marked sexuality, overflowing and uncontrollable to some degree and natural to the male 'species'" (p. 394). Men could perform uncontrollable sexuality through girl watching where, "through the gaze, the targeted woman is reduced to a sexual object," which "exclude[s] recognition of her competence, rationality, trustworthiness, and even humanity. In contrast, the overt recognition of a man's heterosexuality is normally compatible with other aspects of his identity" (p. 392).

When pushed to look at girl watching from a woman's perspective, the men who claimed not to see the act as constituting a hostile work environment *did* understand the harm. Thus, Quinn (2002) concluded that differences between men and women "in interpreting sexual harassment stem not so much from men's not getting it . . . but from a . . . lack of motivation to identify with women's experiences" (p. 397). Men who have learned to perform hegemonic masculinity *correctly* must not demonstrate empathy. Sexual harassment is an example not only of one man exerting power over one woman but of how masculinity itself is premised on a relation of dominance of men over women.

This has important implications for training programs. It is not enough to inform people which actions constitute sexual harassment. It also is necessary to challenge prevailing notions of hegemonic masculinity that discourage empathy in men. The solution to harassment is not just at the microlevel. When people respond to reports of harassment by saying the person harassed could have put a stop to it, they ignore the power dynamics involved. Addressing harassment requires changes at the micro-, meso-, and macrolevels.

Absent from the general statistics about harassment is how race intersects with sex. Communication researchers Brian K. Richardson and Juandalynn Taylor (2009) explained that "women of color experience sexual harassment at the intersection of race and gender" (p. 249). African American women reported they "faced sexual harassment that was often based upon racial stereotypes or was carried out by powerful cultures (White males) at the expense of marginalized cultures" (p. 265). Not only did race inflect the harassment, but it also limited the women's responses to it. African American women often chose not to report the harassment because "speaking out was made difficult by concerns over fulfilling stereotypes of being 'overly emotional' or 'angry' minority women. In fact, at least one participant quit her job rather than fulfill the stereotype of the angry Black woman" (pp. 265–266).

In a study of Canadian women, researchers sought to determine how diverse women understood harassment (Welsh et al., 2006). They conducted focus group research with Black women; Filipinas working as part of the Live-In Caregiver Program; White women in unionized, male-dominated manufacturing settings; and mixed-race women employed by the federal government. They found that race and citizenship played a significant role in how women defined harassment. White women's definitions were most similar to the legal definition. In contrast, the Black women and Filipinas tended to not label harassing behaviors *sexual* harassment, in part because the behaviors could not be distinguished from harassment tied to race and/or citizenship status.

Finally, it is important to turn a gendered lens on sexual harassment laws themselves. Given sexual harassment laws tend to presume heteronormativity, they tend only to envision men harassing women (or occasionally women harassing men). This makes the law blind to cases of same-sex gender harassment, wherein people are harassed because their gender does not match the expectations attached to their sex. In other words, sexual harassment is not something men do to women because they are women but something that people do to other people to maintain strict gender/sex binary normativities and inequalities.

Conceiving of sexual harassment as an attempt to maintain gender norms enables one to recognize the harassment of masculine women and feminine men. Law professor Francisco Valdes (1995) argued the belief that gender discrimination is a woman's issue only makes the law blind to the fact that women could harass men for being feminine. Similarly, because gender and sexual orientation are conflated, many assume that feminine men are gay and harass them on the basis of a falsely attributed sexuality. This makes it difficult for straight, feminine men to receive redress, because their harassers will say they harassed not because of sex but because of sexual orientation—and limited protections exist for harassment based on orientation. The complexity of the issue of sexual harassment makes clear why it is important to apply a critical gender analysis. It also provides a fascinating example to explore how the macrodiscourse of law structures social understandings of sex, gender, and orientation.

Work as Liberation and Locations of Empowerment

In 2016, as President Barack Obama's administration neared its end, and the nation faced the possibility of its first woman president, some interesting stories about sex dynamics in the White House workplace surfaced (e.g., Eilperin, 2016). When he took office, two thirds of Obama's aides were men and many had worked for his campaign. Women working in the administration had to elbow their way into important meetings and, even when included, they often were ignored. Recognizing this dynamic from other workplaces, the women developed a strategy: *amplification*. When a woman made an interesting or important point, other women would repeat it and give credit to the person who initially made the point (Eilperin, 2016). This meant the men in the meeting could not appropriate the idea. The staffers who reported using this technique also reported that Obama noticed, and started including women in more meetings and listening to them when they spoke. The point of this story is twofold. First, it demonstrates that forms of sex-based discrimination can be quite subtle. Second, it demonstrates that a range of creative tactics can be used to respond to oppressive gendered/sexed dynamics at work.

Institutions are locations of subordination *and* resistance. In the case of work, resistance is more than a one-time effort and requires individual and collaborative agency (Allen, 1996, also see 1995, 1998). Resistance is more than a strategy; it is a way of rethinking, renaming, and remaking the world. Organizational scholar Patrice Buzzanell (2000) urged people to "focus more on the ways that people incorporate resistant thinking and behaving into their identities and interactions. Resistance takes many forms" (p. 260).

Empowerment at the microlevel occurs as people makes choices about work. For women pursuing work outside the home, the reality is that even as work can constrain, it also "provides women with the same rewards that it has historically offered men, including a degree of economic independence and enhanced self-esteem" (Gerson, 2004, p. 166). Knowing your options can both protect your own self-esteem and also create potential solutions. When one confronts an instance where work has been gendered/sexed, as when a man is discouraged from pursuing a profession that traditionally has been populated by women, understanding that such job segregation can be challenged may enable that person to pursue career dreams.

For another example, to balance work-life demands, many African American women develop communities of "*othermothers* and *fictive kin* to help each other with balancing work and family" (Parker, 2003, p. 268). Parker (2003) identified five forms of resistance and empowerment that individuals, in this case African American women, used: "a) developing and using voice, b) being self-defined, c) being self-determined, d) connecting to and building community, and e) seeking spirituality and regeneration" through spiritual growth and church support (p. 280). Many Latina immigrants redefine *mother* to mean "wage earner" because they leave their own children to earn money caring for others' children (Hondagneu-Sotelo & Avila, 1997). Even as power dynamics in the institution of work constrain people's options, microlevel resistance is possible.

Empowerment at the mesolevel occurs when business schools reflect on their own practices. Walter and Artiz (2015) revealed that even when women displayed leadership behaviors, they were not recognized as leaders. The researchers reflected:

> To put this more bluntly, teaching women to enact masculine leadership behaviors will likely not aid in improving their numbers in management. Instead, business schools need to focus on the value of changing organizational cultures to become more supportive and inclusive and to understand the value of talk in creating those realities. (p. 474)

Walker and Artiz provided ideas for how business schools can educate people on ways to promote more equitable work environments. These changes at the mesolevel are necessary for empowerment.

Changes at the macrolevel also are possible. A society's understandings of gender/sex, race, and class are not static. Norms can be altered—sometimes quite subtly or even unintentionally and sometimes quite overtly and very intentionally. How gender is institutionalized makes clear that this practice finds its persistence and stability in its institutionalization. However, gender also is "dynamic, emergent, local, variable, and shifting" (Martin, 2003, p. 351).

Conclusion

Work is something virtually every person does, whether it is paid or unpaid. Work can be extremely rewarding, and people can consider their jobs a core part of their identities. However, work also can be extremely dehumanizing, something done because you must earn money to pay for the necessities of life.

Work as an institution both genders and is gendered. The jobs people do, people's interactions with others at work, law, and discourse all influence the performance of gender/sex. In turn, gender/sex influences how people understand work and its relation to family, identity, and culture. The tensions and intersections between work and family, work and leisure, and work and law can be improved only if one overtly considers gender as part of that mix.

When thinking through gender in work, it is important to remember that gender occurs on the micro-, meso-, and macrolevels. Gender is constructed, maintained, and challenged in interpersonal interactions, through institutional forms and workplace communication, and through broad social conversations about, and laws governing, work. When individuals face challenges because of the way work is gendered (unequal pay, work-life imbalance, discrimination, and harassment), the solution never rests with just the individual. Instead, it also requires institutional and social change.

KEY CONCEPTS

capitalism 184

critical organizational communication 184

girl watching 197

hostile work environment 196

quid pro quo 196

sexual harassment 195

wage disparity 185

DISCUSSION QUESTIONS

1. Think about places you have worked or about the school you attend. How is gender or race communicated at the micro-, meso-, and macrolevels?

2. People may know the definitions of sexual harassment and the two types, but they often have difficulty identifying specific behaviors as potentially illegal. Brainstorm possible examples of behavior that is an example of hostile work environment and quid pro quo harassment.

3. When you think about your own career goals, have gender expectations had an effect on your plans? If so, in what ways? If not, how do you think you were able to avoid gendered expectations?

CHAPTER 10

Religion

In the summer of 2012, gender, sex, and religion entered the public consciousness from a rather surprising source: Catholic nuns. The Leadership Conference of Women Religious (LCWR), the organization that represents about 80% of U.S. nuns, found itself under scrutiny by the Vatican, then headed by Pope Benedict XVI, a pontiff known for his doctrinal rigidity. Because the Vatican believed U.S. nuns had strayed from Catholic doctrinal teachings, it scheduled an apostolic visit. After 3 years of visiting 400 religious institutes in the United States, in 2012, Mother Mary Clare Millea reported that the "enduring reality" of U.S. women religious was "one of fidelity, joy, and hope" (as cited in Apostolic Visitation, 2012, p. 1). However, when she submitted her report to the Congregation of the Doctrine of the Faith, it responded that U.S. nuns were pushing "radical feminist themes incompatible with the Catholic faith" because the LCWR mission focused on social justice rather than taking an overt public stand against abortion, euthanasia, homosexuality, same-sex marriage, and the ordination of women (Congregatio Pro Doctrina Fidei, 2012, p. 3). The Vatican called for a complete reform of the group.

Sister Beth Rindler highlighted the role of gender/sex in the Vatican's view of U.S. nuns: "The church in Rome believes in the patrimony of God. But we believe that God created men and women equally. That's where we clash" (as cited in Nadeau, 2012, para. 6). Despite the LCWR's claim that the Vatican's accusations were unsubstantiated, the Vatican decided that "for the next five years, the LCWR will effectively be under Vatican receivership," meaning the men in the hierarchy determined how women religious practiced the gospel (Winfield, 2012, para. 14).

Although internal disputes within the Catholic Church might typically pass under the radar of public attention, this did not. During July 2012, Network (a national Catholic social justice lobby) sponsored a nine-state "Nuns on the Bus" tour, during which nuns met with Republican legislators who supported deep spending cuts in social programs proposed by Representative Paul Ryan's (R-WI) budget, a budget the nuns believed "harms people who are already suffering" (Nuns on the Bus, 2012, para. 1). As Sister Simone Campbell (2012) explained,

We remain committed to Gospel values: healing the sick, feeding the hungry, welcoming the immigrant.

Some might prefer that we sit down and keep quiet. Instead, we just finished a nine-state bus tour to highlight the critical work Catholic sisters do in leading anti-poverty initiatives and calling attention to a Republican budget that the U.S. Conference of Catholic Bishops has criticized as failing a moral test. (paras. 1–2)

Between the tour and media coverage of the Vatican response to the LCWR, the issue rose to public consciousness. Stories appeared in the *New York Times*, *Washington Post*, and *Philadelphia Enquirer* and on CNN, MSNBC, CBS, and NPR. *The Colbert Report* covered the controversy with a segment on "Radical Feminist Nuns" and interviews with Sister Simone aired on June 11 and December 13, 2012.

In April 2015, the Vatican oversight ended 2 years early with a final agreement that allowed the LCWR to continue the work in "social justice and theological inquiry that it was doing before" (Gibson, 2015). Two things contributed to the early resolution: Pope Benedict was succeeded by Pope Francis in March 2013, and the president of the LCWR, Sister Sharon Holland, had worked for 20 years in the Vatican as a canon lawyer (Gibson, 2015). Basically, the change in leadership of the Catholic Church influenced how rigidly religious doctrine would be enforced, and one of the key players representing the LCWR had the training to communicate within a complex system. Reflecting on why the conflict arose, Holland explained that the nuns might have been disciplined for "asking questions and thinking

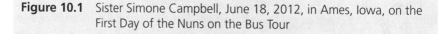

Figure 10.1 Sister Simone Campbell, June 18, 2012, in Ames, Iowa, on the First Day of the Nuns on the Bus Tour

Source: AP Photo/Charlie Neibergall.

critically," things that are acceptable for U.S. women, but "might easily be perceived as disrespectful in another setting" (as cited in Stockman, 2017).

As this example illustrates, religious institutions participate in the construction of sex, gender, and sexuality. Using a critical gendered lens enables one to understand how gender/sex intersects with religious identity and how religion influences the construction of gender/sex. Religion constructs, constrains, and liberates gender.

First, the messages of religious institutions influence people's gender/sex roles. Second, religious institutions' messages about gender delimit acceptable forms of sexuality; thus, the study of religion is central to understanding the construction of and intersections among sex, gender, and sexuality. Third, religious institutions can empower as much as they constrain. But before delving into an analysis of religion, we first want to offer a few thoughts about why it is important to talk about religion.

Why Study Religion, Gender, and Communication?

Institutionalized religion refers to the institutions that mediate people's relations with a higher power or divinity, not a person's personal relationship with that power, which is typically referred to as **spirituality** (Klassen, 2003). Clearly, spirituality and religion are intertwined insofar as religion influences a person's spirituality. However, one can be spiritual without participating in institutionalized religion.

This distinction between spirituality and religion is a Western artifact and makes little sense when discussing South and East Asian religious practices. In many Asian cultures, one is not religious because one belongs to a particular church, temple, or shrine but because one lives in the culture. In China, Confucianism influences understandings of morality; in Japan, people practice ancestor worship (Dorman, 2006); and in Taiwan, the prevailing religion does not have a specific name but is composed of "beliefs, rituals and organizations that deeply permeate the secular life of the individual and society" (Yang, Thornton, & Fricke, 2000, p. 121). Spirituality is infused throughout the culture in every daily practice and is not split off into a formal religion (Narayanan, 2003).

Thus, when we describe religion as an institution, we are speaking from a Western perspective. Our examples presume that religion can be distinguished from the broader culture, even as we recognize that religion influences the broader culture. This is not to discredit our insights into how religion functions but to point out why a more extensive discussion of the religious practices of South and East Asia is missing from this text and to make clear that many of our points would not explain those practices.

Because a person's religion is based on faith, a belief in a higher, infallible power, analyzing religion as an institution might cause discomfort. However, religion can be analyzed as one of many institutions of cultural influence, and religions' messages inform how people are sexed and gendered. Influential postcolonial theorist Gayatri Spivak (2004) explained, "Religion in this sense is the ritual markers of how we worship and how we inscribe ourselves in sexual difference" (p. 104). Religion informs not only people's personal relationships with their god(s) but also people's relationships with their gender/sex.

Religion and Gender/Sex Roles

Religious institutions communicate a number of messages about gender and sex. Religions invite people to participate in different ways depending on their sex, provide guidance on how the sexes should relate, and define what it means to be a good man, good woman, or good person. Religion clearly is an important source of information on how to do gender/sex.

Gender, Sex, and Religiosity

Many people operate under the fallacious assumption that women and men experience religion differently. In fact, most studies of religion that assume women are "more religious" than men (Preston, 2003) link religious activity to sex and not to gender identity. Like most assumptions about difference, this one does not survive close scrutiny. While numerically more women than men participate in religion, one's gender orientation is the variable that most determines one's level of religiosity, not one's sex. Women who tend toward more masculine gender orientations tend to be less religious, and men who are more feminine in their orientations tend to be more religious. Obviously, because of social pressures for women to be feminine, it makes sense that a correlation between sex and religiosity might appear, but one must remember that the intervening variable of gender, not sex, is *the* influential factor.

Research bears this out. Leslie J. Francis (2005), a psychology of religion expert, studied almost 500 English women and men in their 60s and 70s. She had all participants complete the Bem Sex Role Inventory and the Francis Scale of Attitude toward Christianity. Francis found "the data demonstrated that psychological femininity is key to individual differences in religiosity . . . within the sexes and that, after taking gender role orientation into account, biological sex conveyed no additional predictive power in respect of individual differences in religiosity" (p. 179). This study is a vivid example of why researchers need to carefully think about sex and gender as distinct and not conflate them when researching. Here gender (not sex) influenced religiosity, a relationship many other studies miss because they look at sex as the only variable.

Sex and Institutional Religious Power

Although there is no compelling evidence that one sex is more religious than another, sex does affect the role you can play in religious institutions. Many religious institutions are gendered/sexed insofar as they assign relatively rigid roles according to your sex. Who is allowed to communicate for (and sometimes to) a religious deity is sometimes determined by sex. In Roman Catholic and Eastern Orthodox churches, women cannot be ordained as priests, and the Southern Baptist Convention in 2000 announced that only men could serve as pastors. In Islam, women are not allowed to serve as imams except for women-only congregations. Even in the Christian churches in which women can be ordained, they tend to serve as assistant or associate pastors, not senior pastors. When a woman does ascend to a position of power, it can spark controversy, as demonstrated by the 2006 election of Bishop Katharine Jefferts Schori to lead the U.S. church in the Anglican Communion ("Presiding Bishop," 2012). Although there was widespread support by most U.S. Episcopal churches of the ordination of women, conservative dioceses, such as the Diocese of Fort Worth, asked for an alternative Primatial oversight to not be under Schori's leadership (Episcopal Diocese of Fort Worth, 2007).

How institutionalized forms of religion have delimited gender/sex roles is illustrated by two of the dominant religions, Christianity and Islam. The history of antipathy between these two religions (as embodied in the Roman Catholic Crusades to capture the Holy Land from Muslims from the 11th through the 13th centuries) might make one think they have little in common. However, religious scholars have noted the ways in which these two religions share much when it comes to defining women's and men's roles.

Religion scholar Elina Vuola (2002) analyzed how much Christian and Islamic fundamentalisms share given the rise of both forms has been "accompanied by a vigorous promotion and enforcement of gender roles whose explicit intent entails the subordination of women" (p. 175). In particular, Vuola noted how Western Christianity (as represented by the Vatican) and Islam (as represented by some Muslim states) cooperated on a wide range of issues concerning women's political and social rights, reproductive freedoms, and roles in their religious traditions. Vuola found that "Judaism, Christianity and Islam have more in common in their image of women (and sexuality) than they have differences" (p. 183). Thus, the Vatican and Islamic states have worked together against changes on the international and national levels that would have protected women's human rights. At the international level, the Vatican aligned with Muslim nations to attempt to block progressive language on reproductive and sexual rights in the Beijing Platform for Action on Women's Rights (Petchesky, 1997).

However, for Vuola (2002), this is not an argument for forsaking religion. Instead, it is an argument for understanding how religion constructs gender and for people to more consciously think through religion and how it influences their understandings of themselves. Religion informs many people's identities. Thus, "women are not going to—nor do they have to—give up their cultural, political and religious traditions simply because they are used against them" (p. 191).

Complementarians and Egalitarians

The religious struggles over sex and gender are about the relationship between men and women. Are they equal in God's eyes, or are they meant to be complementary to one another with God giving men authority over women? In her work on gender and religion, Carolyn James (2011) described **complementarians** and **egalitarians**:

Complementarians believe the Bible establishes male authority over women, making male leadership the biblical standard. According to this view, God calls women to submit to male leadership and take up supportive roles to their husbands and to male leaders in the church. The complementarian jury is split over whether this includes the public sphere. *Egalitarians* believe that leadership is not determined by gender but by the gifting and calling of the Holy Spirit, and that God calls all believers to submit to one another. At the heart of the debate is whether or not God has placed limits on what women can or cannot do in the home and in the church, although the discussion inevitably bleeds into other spheres of life. (pp. 154–155, emphasis in original)

Consider the Roman Catholic Church's "Letter to the Bishops of the Catholic Church on the Collaboration of Men and Women in the Church and in the World" (Ratzinger, 2004; for a full text of the letter, see www.wf-f.org/CDF-collaboration-men-and-women-church). The letter was written by then cardinal Joseph Ratzinger, who served as Pope Benedict XVI from April 19, 2005, to February 28, 2013. The letter offered the definitive statement of men's and women's roles in the Church and the world. The introduction explained that the letter was written because the "Church is called today to address certain currents of thought which are often at variance with the authentic advancements of women" (sec. 1), ways of thinking that tend to emphasize "conditions of subordination in order to give rise to antagonism" and to deny natural differences between the sexes (sec. 2).

Sister Joan Chittister, O.S.B., (2004) noted how the letter both empowered and constrained. The letter was progressive in its call for the institution of work to be altered given the demands working mothers face and in its celebration of values traditionally associated with women, values that embrace an orientation toward others. The letter recognized those values can be found in women as well as men.

The letter also constrained. First, it embraced a binary understanding of sex and gender. Second, the letter posited feminism as an adversary of the Church and treated feminism and its theories as a monolithic whole, which the diversity of theories in this text ought to make clear is not accurate. Third, the letter conflated sex and gender to the extent that it saw women as the sole repository of feminine values, even as it recognized that men might be able to participate in those values. Fourth, women's role was consigned to two sexual locations: A woman is either a mother or a virgin. Finally, even though the letter encouraged a form of active collaboration between women and men and sought to move away from a metaphor of battle as descriptive of the relationship between the sexes, the letter almost exclusively focused on what women should do and spent little to no time on what men should do. Theology professor Edward Collins Vacek (2005) explained that the letter is "not really about collaboration," for it "scarcely mentions the myriad ways men and women collaborate" (p. 159).

Muscular Christianity

In the last few years, a number of stories have assessed the relationship between Christianity and masculinity. In the wake of arrests of people who were plotting to join the Islamic state in 2015, *Fox News* televised a panel discussion that included reality TV star Rachel Campos-Duffy. The diagnosis was *not* that social isolation and frustration might induce some to join jihadist groups. Instead, Campos-Duffy focused on the idea that Christianity was too "feminized," declaring: "Christianity needs to offer a more robust, manly, not feminized version of Christianity" (as cited in Blumberg, 2015). Campos-Duffy was not the only one concerned about the feminization of Christianity. Cardinal Raymond Burke worried about the Catholic Church because, "apart from the priest, the sanctuary has become full of women. . . . The activities in the parish and even the liturgy have been influenced by women and have become so feminine in many places that men do not want to get involved" (as cited in Blumberg, 2015).

While some think Christianity has become too feminine, other Christian writers believe that men have become too feminine and that Christianity is the solution. John Eldredge (2011), in *Wild at Heart*, declared a Christian man's "masculine heart" was defined by the image of a passionate god. One journalist for *Religion News* noted:

> Christian tomes grace bookstore shelves with not-so-subtle titles like *The Dude's Guide to Manliness* and *Act Like Men. The Manual to Manhood*, the No. 1 book for Christian teens on Amazon, includes essays that instruct boys on how to fulfill godly, manly duties like grilling steaks, changing tires, impressing girls, and wearing the right cologne. Church men's ministries are awash with military-inspired, chest-thumping curricula that liken life to war and equate strength with valor. (Merritt, 2016)

The intersection between religion and gender in these discussions argues that to be a good Christian, one needs to be manly, and to be manly, one should enact a particular form of Christianity.

This concern with masculinity and religion is not new. Buck (2017) noted that during the Victorian era, when the image of Jesus as "a gentle man who hugged children and forgave more sinners than he smote" became the dominant image,

> Western scholars—white men, all—felt the church and its Son of God had become "too feminine," and it was trickling down to the congregation. . . . So, English thought-leaders teamed up with the church to launch a new campaign. Muscular Christianity was born. The movement would correct the progressive fluffery that was poisoning the nation. Rugged physical education and aggressive faith would inspire a new era of controlled nationalism, a prescription which conveniently left out women, minorities, non-Christians, and more.

The point of these examples is to illustrate that gender and religion intersect with one another. And the concerns that arose at the turn of the 19th into the 20th century are recurring at the turn of the 20th into the 21st century.

Researchers who studied the intersection of religion and gender found that specific religious traditions called forth specific forms of masculinity (Bradstock, Gill, Hogan, & Morgan, 2000). Researchers identified one particular way in which religion has gendered some men: muscular Christianity. **Muscular Christianity** was "defined simply as a Christian commitment to health and manliness" (Putney, 2001, p. 11) premised on the belief that an association existed between "physical strength, religious certainty, and the ability to shape and control the world around oneself" (Hall, 1994, p. 7). Protestant men were encouraged to embrace a form of Christianity that connected bodily strength and religion. Healthy bodies were linked to healthy faith. This idea supported the creation of Boy Scouts and YMCA and influenced leaders like Teddy Roosevelt. Muscular Christianity linked bodily practice to religious ideas and defined how men should behave in society to be *good* men. Now, many Christians take for granted that there is a link between bodily and religious strength, but this is a link that was intentionally formed.

Muscular Christianity did not emerge as a dominant theme until the 1850s, when it appeared as a term describing a popular novel of the day, Charles Kingsley's (1857) *Two Years Ago*. The concept emerged in England and quickly traveled to the United States.

The muscular Christianity movement sought to make Protestant Christianity masculine but faced resistance from evangelical Protestant churches that at that point were particularly enamored of feminine iconography such that by the 1850s, they were "channeling much of their energy into praising such stereotypically 'female' traits as nurturance, refinement, and sensitivity" (Putney, 2001, p. 24). The feminization of Protestant religions could be found in "an altered rhetorical style for preaching, popular depictions of the divine, and the increased presence and influence of women in Christian sects" (Maddux, 2012, p. 44). In response, muscular Christians glorified such "stereotypically 'male' traits as strength, courage, and endurance" (Putney, 2001, p. 24) as they sought to "masculinize the rhetorical style of preaching, popular images of Jesus, and the leadership and membership of the churches" (Maddux, 2012, p. 44).

Muscular Christianity also faced resistance from the Puritan tradition that viewed sport as a "sinful diversion" because "exercising one's muscles for no particular end except health struck many Protestants in the mid-nineteenth century as an immoral waste of time" (Putney, 2001, pp. 20, 24). Puritans believed people found salvation through work, and sport was viewed as play. Thus, for U.S. Protestants during the antebellum period, organized sports were an abomination. In fact, in his book exploring the rise of muscular Christianity in the United States, Clifford Putney (2001) cited Washington Gladden (Congregational church pastor, leader of the Social Gospel movement, and Progressive movement member), who grew up in the 1840s thinking, "If I became a Christian it would be wrong for me to play ball" (p. 20).

The push for more muscular forms of religion emerged in the late 1800s in the United States as a response to the insecurities and fears many men faced during an age in which change overwhelmed them. The United States had just survived the Civil War, women in increasing numbers were working, and the nation was industrializing. As Donald E. Hall (1994) explained in his book on muscular Christianity, "The broad strokes in the discourse of the muscular Christians were reactions to threats posed by a world growing ever more confusing and fragmented. . . . Muscular Christianity was an attempt to assert control over a world that had seemingly gone mad" (p. 9). Muscular Christianity not only gendered White, Protestant, native, male U.S. citizens, but it also functioned as a location to discipline, through caricature, the bodies of lower-class, Irish, and non-European men. The struggle was not only over how particular male bodies would act in the world but also over "social, national, and religious bodies," for which the male body functioned as a metaphor (p. 8). The male body was a site for struggle, because it served "as a paradigm and metaphor for male-dominated culture and society" (p. 6).

During the 1880s and through the 1920s in the United States, a number of factors influenced the willingness to accept muscular Christianity. First, Protestant church leaders as well as secular reformers were worried about the church becoming feminized because women came to outnumber men in church attendance and also began to assume more leadership positions. Communication scholar Kristy Maddux (2012) argued that "the movement for muscular Christianity was aimed at least in part to winning men back to the churches" (p. 49). Second, depopulation of the rural areas and the increasingly urbanized population meant that men could not be assured of physical activity doing farm work. Legitimizing physical activity for nonwork-related tasks helped some men maintain their physical masculinity and their religious identity. The two were no longer in conflict. Third, the influx of Catholic immigrants began to threaten the dominance of Protestantism. The U.S. Protestant establishment "entertained fears of well-bred but overeducated weaklings succumbing before muscular immigrant hordes" (Putney, 2001, p. 31). And fourth, the emergence of the modern woman (meaning working woman) worried male church leaders. From 1900 to 1920, the number of women working in white-collar jobs increased threefold (Putney, 2001).

For an example of feminine and muscular Christianity in conflict, see Kristy Maddux's (2012) analysis of Aimee Semple McPherson:

McPherson attracted controversy because she persisted with a feminized preaching style long after that style had proved threatening to Christianity and after it had suffered rebuke from the proponents of masculine, or muscular, Christianity. Unlike her contemporaries Billy Sunday and Paul Rader, whose sermons boasted of their athletic exploits, McPherson performed the feminized style of evangelical preaching, drawing upon its emotional and embodied conventions, and she innovated feminized personae, including the servant and the bride. Her critics, in turn, derided her for being a deceptive temptress who preyed upon her listeners' emotional vulnerabilities. (p. 60)

Figure 10.2   Aimee Semple McPherson Delivering a Sermon at the Spreckels Organ Pavilion During the 1935 Exposition, San Diego

Figure 10.3   Billy Sunday, 1917

Source: San Diego History Center.

Source: Library of Congress.

Figure 10.4   Paul Rader, 1922

Source: Library of Congress.

Given this history, it becomes clear that the centrality of sports to U.S. hegemonic masculinity is tied to religion. Muscular Christianity and its secular counterpart of the strenuous life (as advocated by Theodore Roosevelt) would dominate social life at the turn of the 19th century and into the 20th. Even though its prominence waned in the years after World War I (1914–1918) because many thought muscular Christianity had fanned the flames of war, its effects persisted. Although the movement lost some of its intellectual influence, "paeans to health and manliness continued to emanate both from the mainline churches and from best-selling authors" (Putney, 2001, p. 200). The recent resurgence of muscular Christianity among the Promise Keepers and the Fellowship of Christian Athletes indicates that the connection between religion and masculine identity is not a thing of the past.

Religion and Sexuality

Institutionalized religions make overt pronouncements about gender/sex and offer teachings about sexuality. Some people's condemnation of homosexuality is informed by religious beliefs. Despite many religious traditions' rejection of homosexuality, people of faith struggle to find ways to reconcile their faith and their sexuality. DignityUSA works toward respect and justice for all gay, lesbian, bisexual, and transgender persons in the Catholic Church (www.dignityusa.org). Queer Jihad (www.well.com/user/queerjhd) provides a location for lesbian, gay, and queer Muslims to work through issues of homosexuality in Islam. The documentary *Trembling Before G-d* (DuBowski, 2003) portrayed the stories of lesbian and gay Hasidic and Orthodox Jews who seek to reconcile their love of faith with their homosexuality.

Of course, the religious teachings on sexuality do not affect only those who participate in a particular religion. As the recent U.S. debates over same-sex marriage and access to birth control demonstrate, religion enters into the secular world, informing which unions receive civil recognition and which health services are supported as part of preventative care. In other words, if one wants to understand how gender, sex, and sexuality are political issues, one must attend to the role religion plays in defining gender/sex/sexuality and the role that sexuality plays in drawing the lines between what is a religious issue and what is a secular public issue.

Religion as Liberation and Locations of Empowerment

Religion is one location in which people find validation of their intrinsic worth as human beings. Most religions declare **spiritual equality** before their supreme deity. For example, Christians cite Paul: "There is neither Jew nor Greek, there is neither slave nor free person, there is not male and female; for you are all one in Christ Jesus" (Galatians 3:28, New American Standard Version). Islam believes that both women and men are capable of knowledge and "seeking knowledge is an obligation for every Muslim man and woman" ("Understanding Islam," n.d., question 11). The Qur'an describes men and women's requirements and responsibilities as equal and parallel. These examples raise the question of how spiritual equality before God's eyes intersects with social equality. How do people reconcile the spiritual equality of all people with the institutional and social inequality of some people?

Even when religious institutions dictate rigid sexualities and gender/sex roles, individuals still find empowerment and fulfillment in their religious traditions. We take seriously the fact that people, particularly people of color in the United States, see religion as a safe haven and site of resistance to broader social injustices. As religion structures people's understanding of who they are and where they fit in the universe, it also highlights how "institutions are constituted and reconstituted by embodied agents" (Martin, 2004, p. 1257). Religion is as much about people's daily practices of religion as it is about scripture and belief systems.

To explore diverse expressions of religion, one can study the communication about and of religion in the form of "religious experiences, texts, transcriptions of interviews, personal accounts, rituals, or religious communities," as well as images of divinity and the documents declared definitive by church leaders (Thie, 1994, p. 232). When you study expansive forms of religious communication, it becomes clear that "religions and divinities are more than a source of violence; . . . religions are also a source of resistance, hope, and struggle" (p. 232). So we now turn to three distinct instances where people have negotiated gender, sex, religion, and empowerment.

African Americans and Religion

Although religious appeals have been used to outline strict gender roles, and scriptural grounds have been used to justify women's and minorities' social inequality (see Gaffney, 1990), religion also has long played a significant role in people's liberation. Maria Miller Stewart (1803–1879), the African American woman who was the first woman to speak to a mixed-sex audience, declared she had been called by God to speak against the evil of slavery. Even though she knew she would face extreme opposition to speaking in public—and she did—she cited her faith in God and her belief that she was doing God's work as authorization for her entry into the public sphere (Sells, 1993).

Spirituality and religion play a central role in much African American women's rhetoric (Pennington, 2003). Sojourner Truth (circa 1797–1883), Harriet Tubman (1820–1913), and Fannie Lou Hamer (1917–1977) provide archetypal examples. They all cited their spirituality as enabling and motivating them to take incredible risks as an abolitionist, a conductor on the Underground Railroad, and a voting rights activist. For them, their church provided a location for the development of a powerful spirituality that is "not merely a system of religious beliefs similar to logical systems of ideas" but rather "comprises articles of faith that provide a conceptual framework for living everyday life" (Collins, 1998, p. 245). Religion is a powerful motivating force for individuals.

Religion also creates a sense of group worth and community. In the antebellum United States, slaves' singing of spirituals constituted an act of resistance insofar as the songs "constituted themselves as members of a valued community, as fully human in their desire and ability to create, as chosen for special notice by God, and as capable of acting on their own behalf" (Sanger, 1995, p. 190). During the civil rights movement (1955–1965), the Christian churches attended by African

Americans played a vital role in their struggle for employment and voting rights, not only organizationally but also philosophically (Chappell, 2004).

Even as religion motivated those who struggled for civil rights, gender/sex continued to define the roles played by women and men, consigning women to serve invisible (though essential) leadership roles in the movement at the grassroots level (such as directing the choirs or organizing community meals), placing them as a vital bridge between the movement and potential constituents (McNair Barnett, 1993; Robnett, 1996). Those who have studied the role of religion in the civil rights movement have concluded "one cannot understand Black women's ability to cope, or their activity to ensure liberation and empowerment, without addressing their religious and spiritual heritages, beliefs, and practices" (Klassen, 2003, para. 11).

Religion also played a role for Whites. White women became involved in the civil rights movement not as a result of direct experiences of oppression (such as those inflicted on African Americans) but because of feelings of empathy informed by their religious beliefs (Irons, 1998).

Veiling Practices

Veiling practices have both religious and secular significance, are used by men and women as well as by Christians and Muslims, and have been misread by the West. Veiling practices provide an excellent example of how religion is a site of resistance and emancipation, but also can be used as a justification for subordination.

Fadwa El Guindi (1999), an anthropologist who revolutionized the study of covering practices, explained how **veiling practices** are "a language that communicates social and cultural messages" (p. xii). A critical gendered lens, attentive to issues of intersectionality and colonialism, embraces the role of the world traveler (rather than the arrogant perceiver) and can avoid the error of many Western critics who view the veil as "a sign of women's backwardness, subordination, and oppression" (p. 3). World travelers recognize the complexity of cultural practices, the way in which their own cultures veil (or impose a dress code), and that many Islamic women wear the veil as a form of empowerment.

A world traveler should note how the term *veil* is problematic. It is the lone word English-speaking peoples use to describe a vast range of clothing options. El Guindi (1999) explained that Arabic has no single linguistic referent for the veil. Because the practice differs among groups, cultures, and times, multiple words exist: "*burqu', abayah, tarhah, burnus, jilbab, jellabah, hayik, milayah, gallabiyyah, dishdasha, gargush, gina', mungub, lithma, yashmik, habarah, izer*" (p. 7). Each type can be differentiated by whether it is a face cover, a head cover, or a body cover. This linguistic subtlety contrasts to the "indiscriminate, monolithic, and ambiguous" Western term *veil* (p. 7). El Guindi reminded analysts that each form of covering reveals, conceals, and communicates differently. This is why we use the phrase *veiling practices*.

Within Arabic, multiple terms distinguish among subtle differences, whereas in English the single term obscures the complexity of body-covering practices. In Afghanistan, women (were forced to under the Taliban but now might choose to) cover their bodies and faces with the *burqu'*; in Iran women (choose to but are sometimes forced to) wear the *chador*, which covers the body but leaves the face free; and women from Indonesia choose to wear the *hijab* (which covers the hair and neck but leaves the face revealed) even when living in the United States because it is part of their identities. Despite this complexity, those in the West obsessively critique the harem (another misunderstood concept), polygamy, and the veil, all of which have been held to be "synonymous with female weakness and oppression" (El Guindi, 1999, p. 10).

What might explain the West's misreading of veiling practices? The veil has a longer history in Christian traditions (where it is associated with living secluded from worldly life and sex) than in Islam. Most images of the Virgin Mary show her wearing a headscarf much like a hijab, and Catholic women were required to wear head coverings to church until the 1960s. The narrow interpretation of Islamic covering practices may be more informed by Christianity's interpretation of the practice than by the meaning of the Islamic practice.

Veiling practices' religious connections are not unique to Islam (many Christian women veil their faces during wedding ceremonies), and not all practices have religious foundations. At the time of Islam's rise in the 7th century, veiling was already practiced by many cultures in the Eastern Mediterranean and the Middle East (Cichocki, 2004). Even though the *burqu'*, due to media coverage of the Taliban in Afghanistan, is perceived to be an expression of Islam, it actually is part of a secular tradition (El Guindi, 2005a, p. 262). It was imposed not as part of religious expression, but as part of a culture in a particular country at a particular time.

Additionally, body covering practices are embraced by women *and* men. The contemporary dress code for Muslim men and women is to "wear full-length gallabiyyas (jilbab in standard Arabic), loose fitting to conceal body contours, in solid austere colors made of opaque fabric. They lower their gaze in cross-sex public interaction and refrain from body or dress decoration or colors that draw attention to their bodies" (El Guindi, 2005b, p. 59). Researchers who examine only women's clothing practices fail to notice that the standards of dress expected of women *and* men call for a de-emphasis of the body. It would be unfair to read dress standards calling for head and body coverings as evidence of women's oppression. This becomes even more evident when women's political uses of the veil are recognized.

Veiling did not take on its overt political dimensions until the 19th century, "when European powers justified the colonial project by claiming to rescue Muslim women from the oppression of savage faith, most readily visible in the practices of veiling and seclusion" (Cichocki, 2004, p. 51). At the same time that colonial powers were seeking to save Muslim women from Muslim men, no one was calling for the rescue of Catholic nuns who also wore veils (in the form of the habit) and lived in the seclusion of their convents. As colonized nations began to fight against colonial powers, veils became a form of resistance. Women donned the veil to protest Westernization and modernization's pressure on women to adopt revealing clothing.

In 1936, Iran's Shah Reza Pahlavi's embrace of Westernization included banning women from wearing the chador. The Shah's impetus for this move was a belief that women served best as decorative accessories to men. In response, even women who considered themselves modern began wearing the chador to protest the Shah's regime. When the Shah's son was eventually overthrown in 1979, the Ayatollah Khomeini then required women to wear the chador, causing many women who had worn it as a form of resistance now to protest against it. The garment was not the problem; the mandate to wear it or not to wear it was.

Egypt presents a similar pattern. In mid-1970s Cairo, young, urban, female college students began veiling themselves from head to toe in contrast to the more Western forms of dress favored by their parents. The "Islamizing of life politics and resistance" as represented by young women's wearing of veils "is directly related to the colonial/imperial assault on Arabs and Muslims" (El Guindi, 2005b, p. 55). Women veiled as a way to renew traditional cultural beliefs of reserve and restraint and as a response to pressures from Western materialism, consumerism, and commercialism. Even though the Egyptian government tried to resist women's move to veil (universities banned veils), courts eventually threw out the prohibitions.

We provide so much detail on veiling practices to make clear how people in the West misread non-Western cultural practices. El Guindi (2005b) highlighted the missteps those interested in gender, sex, and religion should avoid. When Christian people filter their understanding of a non-Christian culture through their own religious tradition, "efforts to understand the Middle East have resulted in distorted perspectives about Islamic constructions of gender, space, and sexuality" (El Guindi, 2005b, p. 69). Western European society's understanding of the relationship between the domestic (private) and the public is distinct from Arab and Islamic society's understanding. The West's understanding of piety as separate from worldliness and sexuality results in a focus on seclusion and virginity, missing the nuances of Islamic conceptions of space and privacy as they pertain to veiling.

It also is important to recognize the specific meanings of the veil for women living in the United States. In an ethnographic study of 13 Muslim women living in the United States who used veiling practices, Rachel Droogsma (2007) found they saw six major functions for the veil: "defining Muslim identity, functioning as a behavior check, resisting sexual objectification, affording more respect, preserving intimate relationships, and providing a source of freedom" (p. 301). The women reported that wearing the hijab was important because it enabled them to bond with other Muslims, please God, and take control of their bodies. In many ways, the women saw Western dress practices as far more oppressive than the hijab, which gave them a measure of agency; they could control who saw their bodies. Participants also pointed out how some very revered women of the Christian faith (nuns and the Virgin Mary) covered their bodies in a similar way (p. 307; see also Piela, 2013).

Western misinterpretations of non-Western traditions have real effects. Communication studies scholars Kevin Ayotte and Mary Husain (2005) analyzed how the *burqu'* was used in portrayals of Afghan women to present them as slaves in need of rescue by the West. They track how "the image of the Afghan woman shrouded in the burqa has played a leading role in various public arguments seeking to justify U.S. military intervention in Afghanistan following the 9/11 attacks" (p. 113). Prior to September 11, President Bush never commented on the repressive conditions under which Afghan women lived. However, after September 11, the administration "launched a new initiative to publicize the brutal treatment of Afghan women and girls by the Taliban regime. Events include meetings with women leaders, a Saturday radio address by First Lady Laura Bush (2001), and release of a U.S. State Department report on gender apartheid by Secretary of State Colin Powell" ("Bush Administration," 2001).

Administration comments and media coverage provided a justification for military intervention in Afghanistan. Ayotte and Husain (2005) explained that "collapsing differences among Muslim women through the use of the burqa as a generalized symbol of female oppression performs a colonizing function" and hence justified a military engagement in Afghanistan (p. 118). Unfortunately, such a justification may have resulted in an engagement that did more harm to those it was meant to help. First, demonization of the *burqu'* diverted attention from the fact that the garment was mandated. The issue is not the *burqu'* but the lack of freedom of choice. Second, the demonization of the *burqu'* denied the possibility that women might choose to wear it. The result is that many U.S. citizens now believe that because Afghan women are unveiled, they are free. This ignores how Afghan women continue to face enormous structural and physical violence.

Rereading the History of Women Religious

One of the ways people have attempted to reappropriate religion is to reread its history. In most religions, men have held institutionalized power and hence have been the ones with the authority to interpret key religious texts. However, women have long sought to make clear the central role played by women in religion. Religious communication scholar Helen Sterk (1989) examined the ways women are represented in the Bible. She argued that most (male) religious authorities typically focus on women's limited roles as wives, slaves, or mothers of important men. However, this particular understanding of women's role in the Christian tradition is not an accurate representation of what is in the Bible. In part, translations have created artificial limits for women's roles. For example, *anthropos* was long translated as *man* rather than as *humanity*, which is more accurate. Additionally, numerous stories in which women play important roles, such as the stories of Rahab, Jael, Deborah, Esther, Mary Magdalene, Martha, Joanna, and Susanna, could be highlighted. However, these more expansive readings of women's roles have been constrained in Christian religious traditions. In turn, these religious traditions then inform the secular roles allowed to women and men.

Sterk's (1989) point was not that the Bible is sexist but that society's sexism has led to interpretations of the Bible that ignore women's presence. Sterk argued that women's centrality to the Christian tradition is easy to find in Scripture. It also is easy to find in practice.

Within Catholicism, women played a significant role, writing on issues of morality and doctrine. In medieval times, a life in service to the Church was the only option for women who wanted to live a life of the mind. Hildegard of Bingen (1098–1179), a 12th century German nun, spoke to the life of women in *Scivias*, her major religious work (1151/1152/1990). In the 13th century, Hadewijch, a Flemish mystic, joined the Beguines, a group of devout women who lived "a life of apostolic poverty and contemplation without taking vows as nuns" (Hart in Hadewijch, 1980, p. 3). Catherine of Sienna (1347–1380), an Italian nun of the Dominican order, was one of two women to be granted the title of Doctor of the Roman Catholic Church. Julian of Norwich (1342–1423), an English nun, wrote about the spiritual problems encountered between the soul and God (1393/1978).

Later, Sor Juana Inés de la Cruz (1651–1695), a Mexican nun, was a poet and theological writer. Following the distribution of one of her essays (de la Cruz, 1701/1987a), a bishop chastised her. Her response, *La Respuesta* (de la Cruz, 1701/1987b), defended women's rights to education and culture, presaging the demands of the U.S. first-wave women's movement by almost a century. The writings of these women all demonstrate that despite constraints, women were drawn to religious traditions and found locations of resistance within them.

Conclusion

Religious institutions construct the gender of their own members through doctrinal declarations, historical narratives, and intersections with other dominant institutions. Religion informs how people understand *man* and *woman*, delimits acceptable sexual practices, and is inextricably linked with race and nationality. Religion also informs people's understandings of the gender of those of other faiths through misreadings of verbal and nonverbal practices such as veiling. A gendered lens attentive to issues of intersectionality and informed by a world traveler ethic can offer a nuanced understanding of religious communication.

Even as religion constructs, and in the process constrains expression of, people's sex, gender, and sexuality, it also provides a location from which people can engage in resistance. Religion is not solely an institution of constraint; it empowers. In religion's celebration of grace and the inherent worth of humanity, it reassures those whose humanity has been denied by others that they are blessed. The complexity of religion makes clear why continued scholarship on the intersections of religion, sex, gender, sexuality, race, and nationality is warranted.

Sterk (2010) outlined seven areas for future research in the area of gender and religion in communication:

First, where do gender constructions intersect with particular faith communities? . . .

Second, what gendered communication principles, practices, and structures do various religious groups bring to life? . . .

Third, how do various uses of language either empower or constrain people's full humanity within religious traditions? . . .

Fourth, what sorts of constructions of masculinity and masculine communication practices are enhanced by various religious traditions? . . .

Fifth, how do race, gender, and faith come together? . . .

Sixth, how do faith, sexual identity, and communication come together? . . .

And seventh, how do race, sexual identity and faith come together? (pp. 212–213)

We hope that this chapter encourages you to keep asking these questions and provides you some foundational ideas to begin formulating answers to them. As Sterk (2010) explained, asking and answering these questions

matters because if we care about human beings and their flourishing and God's presence and love as shown in the whole panoply of religions, we will care about how individuals flourish spiritually due to the communication they create and experience. (p. 213)

KEY CONCEPTS

complementarians 207

egalitarians 207

institutionalized religion 205

muscular Christianity 210

spiritual equality 213

spirituality 205

veiling practices 215

DISCUSSION QUESTIONS

1. Why is it necessary to understand relationships between spiritual equality and social equality?

2. What "gendered communication principles, practices, and structures" of religion construct and constrain gender?

3. What are some ways in which religion has liberated and/or empowered persons or groups?

CHAPTER 11

Media

The commercial entertainment media you watch (and play) are not real. The Rebel Alliance does not steal the plans for the Death Star, Master Chief John-117 is not fighting the Covenant, Barb is not dragged away by and Eleven does not escape the Demogorgon in the Upside Down, and Juan does not befriend Chiron. Even reality television is not real: Producers artificially construct scenarios, manipulate footage, show events out of sequence, and use creative editing to increase drama. Yet viewers often forget that everything they see on television, in magazines, and on their computer screens has been manipulated.

A few recent controversies illustrate the prevalence of digital manipulation. In 2014, Target was criticized for photoshopping a "thigh gap" onto already thin youth swimsuit models (ABC News, 2014; Sidell, 2014). In 2015, Zendaya criticized *Modeliste* on Instagram, declaring she "was shocked when I found my 19 year old hips and torso quite manipulated" (as cited in CNN Staff, 2015). In 2016, Meghan Trainor talked back after her waist was altered in the music video for "Me Too" (France, 2016).

Particularly frustrating is that all this occurred *after* warnings about the negative effect of photoshopping. In 2011, the American Medical Association (AMA) released a policy statement denouncing the use of alterations of models' images:

> Such alterations can contribute to unrealistic expectations of appropriate body image—especially among impressionable children and adolescents. A large body of literature links exposure to media-propagated images of unrealistic body image to eating disorders and other child and adolescent health problems. (para. 5)

A spokesperson likely referred to a 2009 Ralph Lauren ad that photoshopped supermodel Filippa Hamilton when saying,

> In one image, a model's waist was slimmed so severely, her head appeared to be wider than her waist. We must stop exposing impressionable children and teenagers to advertisements portraying models with body types attainable only with the help of photo editing software. (AMA, 2011, para. 6)

Although media images are not real, they have real effects on how people perceive sex and gender.

Female beauty is just one example of media power over gender. Beauty norms change, and a driving force in that change is media, from Renaissance paintings (see Figure 11.1), to computer-generated images of the perfect thigh in Christian Dior's advertisements for cellulite control (Bordo, 1997; see Figure 11.2), to computer-generated images of the perfect woman in the digitally idealized form of Lara Croft (see Figure 11.3).

Because people often think of media products as merely entertainment or artistic expression, they forget that media play an ideological role, too. As social learning theory explains, human beings learn by watching others, and this includes watching characters on television or in the movies. Communication scholar Bonnie Dow's (1996) insight about television is true of all media forms; they are "simultaneously, a commodity, an art form, and an important ideological forum for public discourse about social issues and social change" (p. xi).

Our goal is to encourage you to develop critical consciousness about media even as you take pleasure from them and to use that critical consciousness as the basis for political action. Philosophy professor Susan Bordo (1997) pointed out, "Cultural criticism clears a space in which we can stand back and survey a scene that we are normally engaged in living in, not thinking about" (p. 14). Media criticism is not about dismissing people's personal choices and pleasures; it is about "preserving consciousness of the larger context in which our personal choices occur, so that we will be better informed about their potential consequences, for ourselves as well as for others" (p. 16). Without the ability to see the external influences on what you think of as your personal choices, you lose the ability to analyze, challenge, and change institutionalized power.

We first examine what media are and how they work. Second, we explore the gaze people use to watch media. Third, we note that whom media show, and who use which forms of media, is sexed and gendered, as well as raced and aged. Fourth, we explore two examples of how media sex and gender people. Broad trends in media include the sexualization of women (and increasingly of younger girls) and the resecuring of men's masculinity.

Defining Media and How They Function

Media are ubiquitous in contemporary U.S. society: prints, paintings, television, streaming content, movies, radio, newspapers, comics, comix, novels, zines, magazines, CDs, MP3s, podcasts, video games, blogs, videos, and tweets, to name just a few. A variety of forms and content exists, as well as different economic types, including mass for-profit communication and specialized communication that may be noncommercial or subsidized (Budd, Entman, & Steinman, 1990). Note that we talk about plural *media* and avoid the phrase *the media*. Media are not a monolith; no such thing as "the media" operates as a single, unified, controlling entity. Instead, media compose a complex set of production and consumption practices. Thus, the gender representations found in one medium can respond to gender representations in another.

Figure 11.1 Tintoretto's *Susanna and the Elders*, c. 1555–1556

Source: DeAgostini/Getty Images.

Figure 11.2 Christian Dior Advertisement, 1994

Figure 11.3 The character figure of computer game heroine Lara Croft stands on display in the Tomb Raider exhibition at the computer game museum in Berlin, Germany, February 26, 2013.

Source: Christian Dior ad from 1994, reprinted from reproduction of ad in Bordo, Susan. *Twilight zones: The hidden life of cultural images from Plato to O.J.* (University of California Press, 1997), page 4.

Source: Jörg Carstensen/picture-alliance/dpa/AP Images.

For example, the Guerrilla Girls' zap actions used the pop-art medium of posters to criticize the absence of women from the high-culture medium of major New York art museums and galleries (Demo, 2000). Like other institutions, even as media reiterate norms concerning gender, media also enable people to work the weaknesses in the norms and challenge common assumptions. English professor Sherrie A. Inness (2004) noted that "action chick" characters—such as Lara Croft of *Lara Croft, Tomb Raider*; Buffy of *Buffy the Vampire Slayer*; Xena of *Xena: Warrior Princess*; Aeryn Sun of *Farscape*; and (we would add) Zoe Washburne of *Firefly*, Katniss Everdeen of *The Hunger Games*, and Diana Prince of *Wonder Woman*—"can be rooted in stereotyped female roles but can simultaneously challenge such images" (p. 6). Despite these contradictions within and across media forms, dominant messages from culture industries support hegemonic constructions of gender.

It is useful to recognize the existence of **culture industries** to draw attention to the way popular culture mirrors industrial factory processes, creating standardized goods for consumption (Horkheimer & Adorno, 1972). Media function as culture industries when they convey messages that generate demand for specific products; media influence how people dress, what they eat, what they look like, the games they play, the music they listen to, and the entertainment they watch. Media convey these messages in two ways: first, in the message content of the shows, articles, songs, and movies and, second, in the advertising that surrounds these messages.

Advertisements would not dominate commercial media unless they worked: creating demand within consumers for products. To give a sense of how much is spent on advertising, consider the statistics from 2014 (in Table 11.1).

Mitchell Stephens (1998), in *The Rise of the Image, the Fall of the Word*, argued that the most recent shift in communication, particularly in more economically privileged countries, is from the word to the image, such that "most of the world's inhabitants

Table 11.1   Selected Examples of Amount Spent on Advertising in 2014

Corporation	Amount Spent on Advertising
Proctor & Gamble	4.6 billion
AT&T	3.3 billion
General Motors	3.1 billion
Comcast	3.0 billion
Verizon	2.5 billion
Ford	2.5 billion
American Express	2.4 billion

Source: Data from Johnson (2015).

are now devoting about half their leisure time to an activity that did not exist two generations ago"—watching television (p. 7). In the United States, most people spend at least 2.8 hours a day watching TV (Bureau of Labor Statistics, 2017). The ubiquity of mediated images from television, streaming content, movies, and music videos "are perhaps the most powerful familiarizing influences shaping our contemporary society" (Westerfelhaus & Brookey, 2004, p. 305). Media scholars believe that just as religion, and then science, outlined how people should behave, "mass entertainment now performs a similar normative role in our media-saturated society" by providing myths, or recurrent story structures, through which human beings understand who they are and where they fit in a social order (Westerfelhaus & Brookey, 2004, p. 305). Given the explosion of visual media, this chapter focuses on them.

Part of the video revolution is the digital revolution. As of January 2017, 78% of U.S. adults own a computer and 51% own a tablet (Pew Research Center, 2017). For a small taste of how quickly the digital revolution has impacted media, consider the following time line: In the late 1980s, e-mail became privatized and commercially available. In the 1990s, cell phones became widely used when they became small enough to fit in a pocket, the Internet emerged when the U.S. government allowed the commercialization of the networking technologies, and Google and Dreamweaver were launched. In the 2000s, blogs became popular due to software making them easy to create; Wikipeida, Facebook, YouTube, Twitter, and Tumblr were founded; and the release of the Apple iPhone effectively put computers and cameras in the pockets of everyday people. In the 2010s, Instagram, Pinterest, Snapchat, and Vine were launched and Facebook achieved one billion monthly users. Things that 20-somethings take for granted as a normal part of the media landscape are relatively recent phenomena.

The Internet differs from other media forms because its users have access to interactive technology that enables them to be media producers as well as consumers. Users can create their own mediated forms (YouTube videos, blogs, Twitter feeds, webpages) in a context with its own unique and constantly evolving norms for communication (Manago, Graham, Greenfield, & Salimkhan, 2008). This new context offers increased opportunities for users to seek inclusion, construct and promote their desired identities, make social comparisons to others, network beyond geographic boundaries, organize group actions, create expression, and create and play group games (Manago et al., 2008; Zhao, Grasmuck, & Martin, 2008). Feminist media scholar Carrie A. Rentschler (2014) studied how young feminists used blogs, digital video, and digital photography as a form of "do-it-yourself activity media-making" to respond to rape culture. They digitally recorded and transcribed "personal stories based in their experiences of sexual violence and harassment, and in their roles as witnesses to others' harassment and experience of sexual violence," posted these stories, and then "re-distribute[d] them on feminist blogs, YouTube, Instagram, Facebook, and Tumblr sites" to respond to events like the Steubenville rape case (p. 66). Rentschler found that "feminist bloggers utilize social media in order to respond to rape culture, and hold accountable those responsible for its practices when mainstream news media, police and school authorities do not" (p. 67).

Unfortunately, the noncentralized nature of the Internet also provides opportunities for rallying hate groups, consumer targeting, and new forms of gendered violence such as sexting and violently misogynistic games. Research about online harassment indicated that men and women tend to experience different forms of harassment:

> In broad trends, the data show that men are more likely to experience name-calling and embarrassment, while young women are particularly vulnerable to sexual harassment and stalking. Social media is the most common scene of both types of harassment, although men highlight online gaming and comments sections as other spaces they typically encounter harassment. Those who exclusively experience less severe forms of harassment report fewer emotional or personal impacts, while those with more severe harassment experiences often report more serious emotional tolls. (Duggan, 2014, p. 3)

However, sex is not the only variable that affects harassment. Age affects the type and severity of harassment, with young women being exposed at much higher rates to the most extreme forms of harassment (see Figure 11.4).

Figure 11.4 Online Harassment

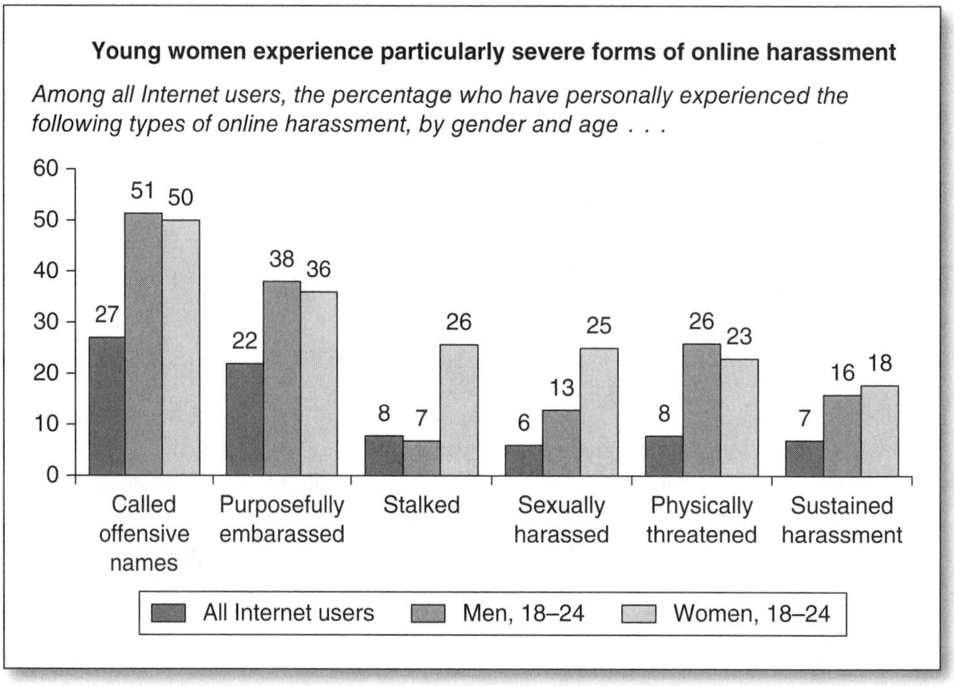

Young women experience particularly severe forms of online harassment

Among all Internet users, the percentage who have personally experienced the following types of online harassment, by gender and age . . .

Legend: All Internet users | Men, 18–24 | Women, 18–24

Called offensive names: 27, 51, 50
Purposefully embarrassed: 22, 38, 36
Stalked: 8, 7, 26
Sexually harassed: 6, 13, 25
Physically threatened: 8, 26, 23
Sustained harassment: 7, 16, 18

Source: Duggan (2014).

The Guardian newspaper analyzed the 70 million comments left on its digital news site since 2006 and found: "Of the 10 most abused writers eight are women, and the two men are black" (Gardiner et al., 2016). The 10 writers who received the least abuse were men. The research provided "the first quantitative evidence for what female journalists have long suspected: that articles written by women attract more abuse and dismissive trolling than those written by men, regardless of what the article is about" (Gardiner et al., 2016).

At the macro-level, social media policies gender and sex people in problematic ways. The policies regarding what are, and are not, acceptable images lead to some interesting patterns of representation. Feminist writer and media critic Jessica Valenti (2015) pointed out an interesting contrast:

> There's a predictable social media formula for what women's pictures online should look like. Breasts in barely-there bikinis are good (thumbs-up emoji, even), but breasts with babies attached them are questionable. Women wearing next to nothing is commonplace, but if you're over a size 10 your account may be banned. Close-up shots of women's asses and hardly-covered vaginas are fine, so long as said body parts are hairless.

Social media sites' Terms of Service Agreements have led to Instagram removing an artist's self-portrait because it showed menstrual blood on the bedsheet, although the image was later restored and Instagram said it was an "accidental removal" (Brodsky, 2015). Facebook's nudity standards used to ban images of post-mastectomy scars and of women breastfeeding until public outcry induced them to change their policies (Narula, 2015). Valenti's point was to get people thinking about whom these standards and rules serve. What does it tell people that "SeXXXy images are appropriate, but images of women's bodies doing normal women body things are not"? Valenti's (2015) answer:

> It's difficult to imagine women being offended by pictures of breastfeeding, unkempt bikini lines or period blood—that's a standard Monday for a lot of us. It's men that social media giants are "protecting"—men who have grown up on sanitized and sexualized images of female bodies. Men who have been taught to believe by pop culture, advertising and beyond that women's bodies are there for them. And if they have to see a woman that is anything other than thin, hairless and ready for sex—well, bring out the smelling salts.

But Valenti sees how social media actually provide a way to challenge these norms: "When we have the power to create our own images *en masse*, we have the power to create a new narrative—one that flies in the face of what the mainstream would like us to look and act like." Thus, even as interactive communication enabled by digital media enable forms of oppression, they also offer ways to resist.

Media Hegemony or Polysemy

The concept of **hegemony** is particularly useful when discussing media. The predominant social group can make its beliefs appear to be common sense through media representations that shape the cognitive structures through which people perceive and evaluate social reality (Dow, 1996). However, this hegemonic system is not all-powerful. It must be maintained, repeated, reinforced, and modified to respond to and overcome the forms that challenge it. Thus, "hegemony, rather than assuming an all powerful, closed text, presumes the possibility of resistance and opposition" (Dow, 1996, p. 14). Media maintain hegemonic understandings of gender even as they create gaps and fissures in representations of gender.

Most of the debate about media is about the precise scope of their power. One side, represented by the work of Theodor Adorno (1991) and the Frankfurt School, argued that mass media have considerable power (or a hegemonic hold) over people because they "churn out products which keep the audience blandly entertained, but passive, helping to maintain the status quo by encouraging conformity and diminishing the scope of resistance" (Gauntlett, 2002, p. 41). Media create false consciousness, making people believe they exert control over what they view (and what they think about what they view) when in reality they have little or no control. The other side, represented by the work of John Fiske (1987) and cultural studies, argued that people do not consume media offerings mindlessly but, instead, actively and creatively engage with them, "using 'guerilla' tactics to reinterpret media texts to suit their own purposes" (Gauntlett, 2002, p. 41). These varied purposes are possible because, Fiske believed, media message are **polysemous**, or open to a range of different interpretations at different times. Meaning is not determined by the media providers but created individually by each person.

The best explanation of media power is somewhere between these two. Clearly, pervasive media messages have an effect, particularly in U.S. consumer culture. However, it also is clear that people can resist media influence if they are critical media consumers. Thus, it would be counterproductive for us to side exclusively with the media hegemony side of the debate if we want to enable you to be creative and productive contributors to the public discourse in which media participate. Like British media scholar David Gauntlett (2002), we believe that "it seems preferable to assume that people are thoughtful and creative beings, in control of their own lives—not least of all because that is how most people surely see themselves" (p. 111). However, it also is true that people's level of thoughtfulness and creativity is influenced by their education (formal and otherwise).

Media Polyvalence

Fiske may be correct that textual polysemy exists, but the range and richness of the possible meanings depend on the ability of audiences to produce them. Additionally, media texts cannot be all things to all people, because media foreground some interpretations as preferred. Celeste Condit (1989) argued that instead of the concept of polysemy (having a multitude of meanings), researchers should use **polyvalence** (having a multitude of valuations): "Polyvalence occurs when audience members share understandings of the denotations of a text but disagree about the valuation of these denotations to such a degree that they produce notably different interpretations" (p. 106). For example, when looking at an advertisement aired during Super Bowl halftime, viewers may agree that it links the consumption of beer to the performance of masculinity but disagree on whether the performance of that masculinity should be encouraged.

Oppositional interpretations of mainstream media texts are influenced by the social context; some contexts provide more opportunities and training for resistant readings. Peer groups influence the reception of messages. In a study of girls at two middle schools, one predominantly White and the other predominantly Mexican American and African American, journalism professor Meenakshi Gigi Durham (1999) found that "girls *on their own* may be somewhat more able to critically examine and deconstruct media messages than in the peer group context" (p. 210, italics in original). Oppositional readings of texts are constrained by the social structures reproduced in peer groups: "The peer group was shown to be a training ground where girls learned to use the mass media to acquire the skills of ideal femininity," although sometimes rejections of these norms could be voiced (p. 212). Thus, when cultural studies researchers claim that mediated messages are polysemous, they may be ignoring the fact that media consumption and interpretation often are a group activity, not an individual one.

Different people at any given time also have different resources available for resistance and must expend more or less effort to construct resistant readings. It is easy to "acquire the codes necessary for preferred readings"; however, "the acquisition of codes for negotiated or oppositional readings is more difficult and less common" (Dow, 1996, p. 13), and transforming those readings into political action is the most difficult and least common of all. Because the acquisition of such codes requires work, one consequence is "the tendency of such burdens to silence viewers" (Condit, 1989, p. 109).

Think about how you look at magazines. What can you say about the images in them? If the language (or code) you have only enables you to compare the relative attractiveness of the models, it is a very limited code that operates within hegemonic understandings. It measures people's worth only regarding their appearance. But you can develop a more nuanced code.

The Gaze(s)

Two parallel lines of research emerged in the 1970s to explain how visual media gender the practice of watching, create a legitimating gender ideology, and influence gender identity. The first theory focuses on the way media position audiences. The second theory uses psychoanalysis to explain how cinema's form speaks exclusively to a male spectator.

Ways of Seeing

In the 1970s, the British Broadcasting Company aired a television series titled *Ways of Seeing*. A book by the same name soon followed. John Berger's (1972) *Ways of Seeing* argued that in European art, from the Renaissance onward, men were the presumed viewers because they were the presumed purchasers (p. 64). In one of the book's most quoted passages, Berger described how artistic representations construct an image of men and women:

> *Men act* and *women appear*. Men look at women. Women watch themselves being looked at. This determines not only most relations between men and women but also the relation of women to themselves. The surveyor of woman in herself is male: the surveyed female. Thus she turns herself into an object—and most particularly an object of vision: a sight. (p. 47)

The presumed sex of the viewer is male, and even when the viewer is female she views herself through men's eyes. Berger's observation is quite similar to the point made by objectification theory: Women are seen as objects—things to be looked at rather than people who can act.

In case you do not believe that men long were presumed the "'ideal' spectator," try this experiment: Examine the two images of a traditional nude in Figures 11.5 and 11.6, and imagine replacing the image of a woman with the image of a man. How do you perceive the female form? Did you even notice the form was female? Now, imagine how you would perceive a male form posed in the same way. Would a male nude positioned in a similar way be remarkable?

Figure 11.5 *Reclining Bacchante*, Trutat, 1844

Source: Catalogue officiel illustré de l'Exposition centennale de l'art français de 1800 à 1889. (1900). http://www.archive.org/stream/catalogueofficiel00expo#page/66/mode/2up.

Now, try this experiment with contemporary images. Look at a women's fashion magazine and imagine men's bodies posed in the same way.

The oddity of men's bodies posed in the same way as women's was highlighted by artist Kevin Bolk, who challenged the different ways the bodies of male and female comic book superheroes are presented. Bolk parodied the poster for the superhero movie *The Avengers* by placing the male superheroes in the same sexualized pose that female superhero Black Widow adopted in the original movie poster (see Figure 11.7). Berger's point was that the way the body is positioned, whether in paintings or in advertisements, employs a series of codes that audiences can read.

Communication professor Sut Jhally (2009), in the video *Codes of Gender*, referred to Berger's work when analyzing contemporary advertising. Jhally explained how mass mediated images construct an understanding of gender in which feminine women are physically passive and ineffective and masculine men are physically active and capable. Using the writings of sociologist Erving Goffman (1979), Jhally sought to "make visible what seems to be invisible" (p. 4), enabling people to read the codes of gender as they are performed by bodies (see Table 11.2).

Figure 11.6 *Vanity*, Hans Memling, 1485

Source: Musée des Beaux-Arts, Strasbourg, http://www.kfki.hu.

Figure 11.7 Kevin Bolk's Reimagining of the Poster for *The Avengers*

Source: © kevinbolk.com.

Table 11.2 How People Read Codes of Gender

	Male	Female
Whole-body posture	More often shown standing and moving	More often shown lying down
Head	Straight and positioned directly at the camera	Tilted at an angle or looking away from the camera
Eyes	Focused and watching the world around them	Not paying attention, spaced out
Hands	Controlling and assertive; hands use the objects to do something; men touch others	Passive and controlled by environment; objects rest in them; women touch themselves
Legs	Legs are straight, in motion, or solidly planted	Knees are bent so that the body is tilted and off-center; legs are crossed or women hold one of their feet
Performance of age	Mature and manly	Infantile, shown snuggling into men; women presented as looking like girls, and girls presented looking like women

As an exercise, find a copy of a recent magazine (e.g., *Elle, Mademoiselle, Vogue, Maxim, GQ*). Look at the images and see if you read them differently now that you have a new way to decode them.

Berger's insights also can help explain images people post of themselves on social media. In studies about presentation of self on social media, researchers found that people perform gender in distinct ways. College-age men's portrayals followed "stereotypical norms of masculinity in which playboys embody strength and power and . . . women portray themselves as attractive and affiliative" (Manago et al., 2008, p. 453). In an international sample of Facebook users, men's profile pictures "accentuated status and risk taking" while women's "accentuated familial relations and emotional expression" (Tifferet & Vilnai-Yavetz, 2014, p. 388). Researchers who summarized studies on social media use by teens found that the photos girls posted focused on appearance and sexual attractiveness (Herring & Kapidzic, 2015). People engage in practices of gazing, and those practices, in turn, influence how they present themselves. According to Berger, women have internalized a male gaze and engage in self-objectification while men believe they should always be the gazers and to be gazed upon threatens their heterosexuality. More recent research supports this finding (e.g., Krasnova, Veltri, Eling, & Buxmann, 2017).

Even female athletes, bodies that *do* and not just *appear*, present versions of themselves on social media that apologize for their doing. In a study of the personal websites of female athletes, the researcher found that at the same time "women promote their brawn, beauty, and brands," they make clear they "have not abandoned traditional feminine roles of sex object, mother, or caretaker" (Barnett, 2017, p. 97). The athletes made sure to present images of themselves as objects of desire or as maternal figures. For the athletes, their skill, their ability to act, was not enough; they also have to appear "pretty" (Barnett, 2017, p. 116).

Berger's insights are useful insofar as they encourage those studying media to think about the ways audiences look. However, his work has limits. First, it explained ways of looking unique to Western art traditions. In a cross-cultural study of advertising, Frith, Shaw, and Chang (2005) argued that one reason why Western women's bodies are sexually objectified but Asian women's bodies are not is the Western art tradition. In contrast to Western art, "displaying the female body has not been the tradition in Chinese art" (p. 65). Thus, "traditions of 'gaze' may very well have developed differently in the East and the West" (p. 65).

Second, Berger's book predated important changes in the way advertising presents men's bodies. From Robert Mapplethorpe's art photography to Abercrombie & Fitch's advertising, men's bodies are increasingly on display. Susan Bordo (1999) explored how recent advertising images of men create gender tensions, stating that "men are not supposed to enjoy being surveyed *period*. It's feminine to be on display" (p. 173, italics in original). However, images of men that have appeared since the 1990s, particularly in Calvin Klein underwear advertisements, present men as on display. Consistent with Berger, Bordo argued that "to be so passively dependent on the gaze of another person for one's sense of self-worth is incompatible with being a real man"; thus, "men and women are socially sanctioned to deal with the gaze of the Other in different ways" (pp. 172–173). Yet, as Jhally's analysis pointed out, it is still mostly women's bodies presented as ineffective, inactive, and to be surveyed.

Third, "Berger's opposition of 'acting' and 'appearing,' . . . is something of a false duality—and always has been" because women's appearance involves immense action: "It takes time, energy, creativity, dedication. It can *hurt*" (Bordo, 1999, pp. 220–221). However, the fiction that appearance is act-free persists. Few stars admit their bodies have been surgically sculpted, and most magazine readers gleefully engage in the willing suspension of disbelief, accepting pictures as perfect reflections of the models even as most should be aware that virtually every image appearing in fashion magazines has been digitally altered.

The Gaze

At the same time Berger's series and book appeared, media theorist Laura Mulvey (1975) published what would become one of the most frequently cited essays in media studies. Using psychoanalytic theory, Mulvey posited that cinema operates with a **gaze** that not only highlights woman's to-be-looked-at-ness but actually builds the way woman is to be looked at into the film itself. The way the camera, the audience, and the male character (with whom all spectators—male and female—identify) look at women reinforces the male as active and the female as passive. For Mulvey, the cinematic gaze is male. Mulvey's criticism applied to all mainstream cinema, and she believed the only way to avoid the dominance of the male gaze is through avant-garde film that undermines the system of representation.

Evidence of the effect of the male gaze can be found in how two movies were rated differently by the Motion Picture Association of America (MPAA). In late 2010, the films *Blue Valentine* and *Black Swan* were released. Both received Academy Award nominations for the female lead, were widely critically acclaimed, and contained scenes depicting a woman receiving oral sex. However, the MPAA rated the movies differently, assigning *Black Swan* an R and *Blue Valentine* the more restrictive NC-17 (unless it removed the oral sex scene). Intrigued by this different treatment of similar films, communication scholars Katie L. Gibson and Melanie Wolske (2011) analyzed the films to determine what might explain the ratings. Confirming other scholars' findings that "explicit and/or graphic films are more likely to receive a lenient MPAA rating if they show heterosexual and male-centered sex," they found because *Black Swan* participated in sensationalized rather than realistic depictions of sex, it received the more lenient rating (p. 92). *Blue Valentine* resisted the male gaze while *Black Swan* played to the male gaze. It was not the sex scene that determined the rating; it was the way one movie challenged the male gaze, and the way the other movie did not, that triggered the different ratings.

Mulvey's theory is criticized because it identified a single, universal gaze. Mulvey assumed that there was only one White male gaze and that no possibility for a female or a non-White gaze existed. Others challenged this, arguing that female (Gamman & Marshment, 1989; Kaplan, 1983) and transgender (Halberstam, 2005) gazes are possible, that people can read against the grain of the male gaze (de Lauretis, 1984; Walters, 1995), and that the focus of psychoanalysis on sexual difference as the fundamental organizing principle of human subjectivity was misplaced in light of the centrality of race to identity (DiPiero, 2002). The most trenchant criticism of Mulvey is provided by bell hooks (1992):

> Feminist film theory rooted in an ahistorical psychoanalytic framework that privileges sexual difference actively suppresses recognition of race, reenacting and mirroring the erasure of black womanhood that occurs in films, silencing any discussion of racial difference—of racialized sexual difference. (p. 123)

Mulvey also assumed a lone media text directly and unilaterally affected the spectator at the moment of consumption, ignoring that multiple factors simultaneously influence the spectator, such as socialization, education, other texts, and peer pressure.

Not only can multiple gazes exist, but Brenda Cooper (2000) argued that you can find a rejection of the dominant male gaze even in mainstream Hollywood films. Cooper argued that *Thelma & Louise* (1991) encouraged viewers to identify not with the males on the screen but with the female figures who actively mock and challenge patriarchal conventions. Cooper's analysis was bolstered by an earlier study (Cooper, 1999) of spectator responses, which found that men and women saw the film differently. Men tended to see the film as an example of unjustified male bashing (perhaps because they identified with the men in the film, few of whom were sympathetic), and women tended to see it as a commentary on women's marginalized social position (because they identified with the women in the film). Cooper's study illustrated Condit's point about polyvalence; male and female audiences' readings were polyvalent. The "resistant female gaze" that Cooper found in *Thelma & Louise* is also present in *The Hunger Games*, which scholars argued "advances a female gaze that summons its audience to look at gender, agency, and power through a resistant feminist consciousness and to question the logics of patriarchy that routinely shape the scripts of heroism in our culture" (Keller & Gibson, 2014, p. 29).

Despite the criticisms of Mulvey, the recognition of the gendered pleasures of the gaze continues to spark research and creativity. *Signs*, the premiere journal of feminist scholarship, devoted an entire special issue to feminist theories of visual culture. Every essay made clear the importance of intersectionality to understanding how the gaze operates. To answer the question "How do I look?" you must think about "gender . . . as inextricably entwined (embodied, experienced, thought, and imagined) with other aspects of identity, including race and ethnicity, nationality, sexual orientation, and class" (Doyle & Jones, 2006, p. 608). In particular, Eve Oishi (2006) offered a theory of *perverse spectatorship*, which calls for attention to "the infinitely oblique and circuitous routes through which identification passes" (p. 649). In 2016, a group of 20 female artists created an exhibit, "In The Raw: The Female Gaze on the Nude." They wanted to "creat[e] a cultural discourse of women on women, a female intervention, so to speak, on patriarchal culture" and the male gaze. The exhibit sought to release female nudes from simply being an object of male desire to "brave and honest" images whether they are "beautiful or shocking, gross or glorious" ("In the Raw," 2016; see also Frank, 2016).

Reflection opportunity: After having "grown up and being socialized as a man," Jennifer came out as trans in her early 40s, and reflected on how interactions with men changed:

"After all these years, I was suddenly on the receiving end of the male gaze. I had enjoyed—in a facile, superficial way—the validation this gave me, at least at first. But pretty soon, validation had turned to irritation. All at once, it seemed, I had arrived in a world in which men were incapable of leaving me alone.

I had been a feminist before transition, so the many ways in which women are both vulnerable and unsafe in this world didn't arrive as shocking news to me. But it's different when it's you."

Jennifer Finley Boylan (2017)

Of course, being able to read, watch, and create against the grain (to be perverse) requires being able to identify the grain, and that requires you to be able to identify the hegemonic preferred readings and offer an oppositional interpretation of them.

An Oppositional Gaze

To be an active participant in media discourse about gender, instead of a passive recipient of it, you need a vocabulary. You cannot engage in creative readings of media unless you know such readings are necessary and possible. bell hooks labeled this an **oppositional gaze**.

Although hooks's (1992) *Black Looks* focused mostly on race, the arguments apply to gender, sex, and sexual orientation as well. hooks argued that discussions of race need to expand beyond debates about good and bad representations and instead ask: "From what political perspective do we dream, look, create, and take action?" (p. 4). Media's positioning of the audience is not determinative as long as audiences are conscious of media's attempt to position them. Audience members can reposition themselves. African Americans can refuse to look through White eyes. Women can refuse to look through men's eyes. LGBTQ people can refuse to look through heterosexual eyes. All people can learn to look through each other's eyes. A number of elements compose an oppositional gaze.

First, you must "consider the perspective from which we look, vigilantly asking ourselves who do we identify with, whose image do we love" (hooks, 1992, p. 6). This is a call to all people. hooks challenged Blacks to unlearn their cherishing of hateful images of themselves. hooks challenged Whites to "interrogate their perspective"; otherwise, "they may simply recreate the imperial gaze—the look that seeks to dominate, subjugate, and colonize" (p. 7). You should ask to whom and for whom a media representation speaks. When you enjoy mediated depictions of gendered/sexed violence, with whom are you identifying—the perpetrator or the victim?

Second, you must recognize the degree to which you participate in culture. People are not merely passive audiences for media messages and images. Bordo (1997) explained, "Unless one recognizes one's own enmeshment in culture, one is in no position to theorize about that culture or its effects on others" (p. 13). Recognizing the way in which people are "culture makers as well as culture consumers" enables each person to transform the culture (p. 15). Remember, we chose not to write about *the* all-powerful *media*. Instead, we chose to write about *media* and the ways each person participates in the institution as both recipient and creator. However, we also chose to speak of media as an institution to highlight the way in which it is social and economic and creates hegemonic messages that require work to read from an oppositional perspective. Personal choices about gender are not sufficient to change the gendered institution of media, nor do personal cultural choices necessarily translate into political action in the public sphere.

Our point in highlighting individual agency in relation to media representations is not to imply that each person individually controls the effect of media. An institutional focus makes clear that even those choices considered the most personal are influenced by larger social forces. Do you wear makeup or not? Do you seek to develop muscles or not? Do you wear jeans or not? Like Bordo (1997), our call for critical consciousness is meant to celebrate "those choices that are undertaken in full consciousness that they are not only about 'creating' our own individual lives but constructing the landscape of our culture" (p. 16). Bordo explained,

> Each of us shapes the culture we live in every moment of our lives, not only in our more public activities but also in our most intimate gestures and personal relationships, for example, in the way we model attitudes toward beauty, aging, perfection, and so on for our children, friends, students, lovers, colleagues. (p. 16)

A person's embrace of cosmetic and fashion industry beauty ideals influences not only that person's body but others' bodies as well.

Third, an oppositional gaze necessarily moves from social critique to political action. You should examine popular culture not just to critique the image but to transform the image, to create alternatives, to find images that subvert, and to pose critical alternatives that move people beyond thinking merely about good or bad images. Cultural criticism becomes just another pastime if not linked to institutional change.

Fourth, an oppositional gaze is conscious of the way in which contemporary media engage in **commodification**—the selling of cultural, sexual, or gender difference in a way that supports institutionalized discrimination. People must recognize when presentations of ethnicity are not signs of inclusiveness but the production of "colorful ethnicity for the white consumer appetite that makes it possible for blackness to be commodified in unprecedented ways, and for whites to appropriate black culture without interrogating whiteness or showing concern for the displeasure of blacks" (hooks, 1992, p. 154). Some rap music videos demonstrate how particular representations of Black masculinity and femininity are sold to White youth, often by White corporations for the benefit of White shareholders (Yousman, 2003). White youth obsession with Black culture is not a sign of progressive social change but rather a form of consuming the other because "the particular nature of the images that White youth are consuming—images of Black youth who are violent or hostile, often unemployed and/or involved in criminal practices—may in fact reinforce, rather than challenge, the tendency of White youth" to support institutionalized racism (Yousman, 2003, p. 387).

hooks's oppositional gaze both celebrated *and* critiqued Beyonce's 2016 visual album, *Lemonade*. Although many argue the album "was created solely or primarily for black female audiences," hooks noted that it still was a commodity, "made, produced, and marketed to entice any and all consumers." Even though the album placed "black female bodies . . . at the center, making them the norm," it still treated them as a commodity, which undercut the album's radical or revolutionary potential. hooks celebrated how the "visual landscape" of the album was distinctive because it constructed a

> powerfully symbolic black female sisterhood that resists invisibility, that refuses to be silent. This in and of itself is no small feat—it shifts the gaze of white mainstream culture. It challenges us all to look anew, to radically revision how we see the black female body. (para. 5)

However, for hooks, this was not enough to "truly overshadow or change conventional sexist constructions of black female identity." In addition, the visual album's celebration of "violence does not create positive change" (hooks, 2016). To be clear, assuming an oppositional gaze does not mean that you have to reject everything in a media text. Instead, it means you need to recognize both the liberatory *and* hegemonic elements of the text.

An oppositional gaze enables you to see not everyone is equally represented in media; in commercial television and news, White men tend to predominate while people of color and women are underrepresented. An oppositional gaze also enables recognition of the way people are represented. Media representations not only are a reflection of social reality but also actively construct it.

Who Is Represented in Media

Women are underrepresented in U.S. media, regardless of the form, both in front of and behind the camera. Representations of male characters far outnumber women in news, television shows, film, and video games. Whites also outnumber people of color in media representations and production positions. Even in the realm of social media, which people produce as well as consume, representational differences emerge.

News

The Women's Media Center's (WMC) 2017 report found women are underrepresented in news media. Although women are more than 50% of the population, during evening news broadcasts, women are on camera only 25% of the time. In print, television, Internet, and wire news, men are credited with 62% of the bylines (p. 9). The percentage of women in newsrooms has remained at 37 since 1999.

This disparity is exacerbated by ethnicity. According to the U.S. Census Bureau (n.d.), as of July 2015, 61.6% of the U.S. population identified as non-Hispanic White. Yet 92.5% of TV news general managers are White. The number of "minority general managers—a group whose ranks had declined 5 percent between 2013 and 2014—saw a 1.3 percent decline in 2015" (WMC, 2017, p. 46).

Disparities arise not just regarding who reports the news, but also who is shown as an expert. On Sunday morning news shows during 2015, 73% of the guests were men and only 27% were women (WMC, 2017, p. 53).

Film

Women and people of color are underrepresented in film, both in front of and behind the camera. Regarding leading roles in the top 100 grossing films, the percentage of women in speaking roles hovers around 28.7, and only 18% of films have a balanced cast (WMC, 2017, p. 92). The statistics behind the camera are even worse. The Center for the Study of Women in Television and Film offered a yearly assessment of "the celluloid ceiling" by analyzing the 250 top-grossing films each year in the United States. Its findings for 2016: "Women comprised 17% of all directors, writers, producers, executive producers, editors, and cinematographers.... This represents a decline of 2 percentage points from last year and is even with the percentage achieved in 1998. Women accounted for 7% of directors, down 2 percentage points from 9% in 2015 and 1998. Last year, 92% of films had no female directors" (Lauzen, 2017, p. 1). The Oscars play out the result of the lack of women behind the camera (see Figure 11.8).

Figure 11.8 Oscar Nominations by Sex

Source: Women's Media Center (2017, p. 113).

Regarding ethnicity, the Annenberg School for Communication and Journalism analyzed the top 100 grossing fictional films each year from 2007 to 2016. Across the 1,000 films, directed by 1,114 directors, only 5.1% were directed by Black or African American directors and only 3% were directed by Asian or Asian American directors (Smith, Pieper, & Choueiti, 2017). The researchers identified a range of solutions, including that "audience members have a powerful and persuasive tool at their disposal—their wallets. . . . Buying a ticket and increasing films' box-office receipts provides a director with evidence that their work is marketable and financially lucrative" (Smith, Pieper, & Choueiti, 2017, p. 20).

This lack of representation became painfully visible in 2016 with the "Oscars so white" protest. When, for a second straight year, all 20 nominees for the major acting categories were White, a number of artists of color drew attention to the "whitewash" (J.T., 2016). The statistics make clear that Whites, in comparison to their percentage of the population, are overrepresented as Oscar nominees and winners. Although Blacks win Oscars in proportion to their representation in the population, Latinx and Asian people are extremely underrepresented (see Figure 11.9).

According to a June 2014 study from Columbia University's Center for the Study of Ethnicity and Race, even though the Latinx population quintupled between 1950 and 2013, rising from less than 3% to 17% of the U.S. population, the percentage of Latinx people appearing in the top 10 grossing films "dropped from 2.8% in the 2000s to 1.4% in the 2010s" and Latinx people in leading roles in the top 10 scripted television shows dropped from 3.9% in the 1950s to 0% in the 2010s (Negrón-Muntaner, 2014, pp. 6, 9–10).

Figure 11.9 Oscar Nominations by Race

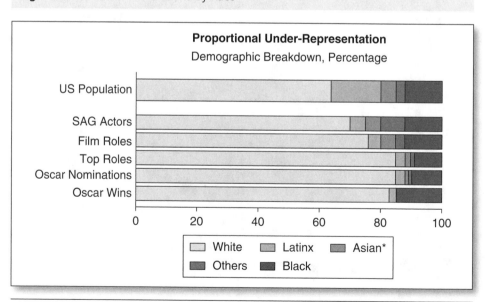

Source: J.T. (2016, January 21). How racially skewed are the Oscars? *The Economist.* Retrieved from http://www.economist.com/blogs/prospero/2016/01/film-and-race.

Television and Scripted Programming

Women are underrepresented in television. In 2015 to 2016, women were only 38% of all major characters and 39% of all speaking characters on broadcast, cable, and streaming shows (Lauzen, 2016, p. 2). In broadcast programs, these statistics have remained relatively steady, or declined, for the last decade. For precise statistics, researchers studied a 1-week period of prime-time programming by ABC, AMC, CBS, CW, FOX, NBC, USA, TBS, and TNT during the fall of 2013. This sample yielded 89 programs and 1,254 characters. The results: 60.4% of the characters were male and 39.6% were female, virtually the same proportion between women and men that was found in the late 1990s, meaning "no meaningful improvements have emerged in the rate of representation in at least 15 years" (Sink & Mastro, 2016, p. 16).

Women's numbers are not much better in media boardrooms; only around 20% of corporate boards, CEOs, and executive management team members are women (Smith, Choueiti, & Pieper, 2016, p. 6), statistics that have not improved over the last decade (Lauzen, 2016, p. 3). Why might this matter? The cancellation of Amazon's *Good Girls Revolt* is an illustration.

The scripted series is based on the events surrounding the 1970 landmark sex discrimination suit filed by 46 women against *Newsweek*. The show received a 4.5 star rating and was named "one of the best shows released in 2016" (Ziv et al., 2016). But just 5 weeks after it premiered, and soon after Hillary Clinton's loss in the 2016 presidential election, Amazon video canceled the show because it was not meeting its viewership expectations (Cooper, 2016). Reports indicated no women were on the leadership team that made this decision. However, this is a leadership team that in the past had said it is important not to think only about numbers, but also about where interest might increase.

In analyzing this decision, sociologist Marianne Cooper (2016) explained:

> Just as important [as viewership numbers] is the ability to read the cultural tea leaves to be able to foresee which shows will map on to the national zeitgeist. And that's where the homogeneity of the decision-makers becomes relevant, as a room full of men is going to read the culture differently than a group that looks more like all of America. As the cancellation of *Good Girls Revolt* shows, men-only decision-making committees can misread the cultural moment in spectacular fashion. . . . One has to wonder if Amazon video's decision about *Good Girls Revolt* may have been different if even one woman was in the room.

Even though women are half of media consumers, fewer than 20% are in the executive positions that make decisions about what media content to circulate.

Blacks, too, are underrepresented in television. Analysis of eight week-long periods of prime-time television shown from 2000 to 2008 found the appearance of Black characters had actually declined toward the end of the time period (Signorielli, 2009). This decline in the representation of African Americans is startling given that their representation actually reflected their proportion of the population in the 1970s and 1980s. The troubling conclusion is that prime-time programming "was less diverse at the end of the first decade of the 21st century than it was earlier in the decade"; and, even when parity was approached mid-decade, "it was a representation of segregation and isolation, particularly for Black women" because when Black characters did appear, it often was in all-Black situation comedies, with 60% of Black women characters appearing in that type of show (Signorielli, 2009, p. 334).

Video Games

The gaming industry estimates that, as of 2016, 63% "of U.S. households are home to at least one person who plays video games regularly (3 hours or more per week)" (Entertainment Software Association, 2016, p. 2), making attention to video games important. Video games underrepresent women and minorities. One study analyzed 150 games from across nine platforms. The researchers found "a systematic over-representation of males, white[s] and adults and a systematic under-representation of females, Hispanics, Native Americans, children and the elderly" (Williams, Martins, Consalvo, & Ivory, 2009, p. 815). The most popular games tended to be the least representative. Even when underrepresented groups were present, they were usually only in secondary roles. Such underrepresentation is a problem because it "makes those groups seem less visible, while social identity theory additionally suggests that they will be seen as less important" (p. 829).

Even though these are only games, they are communication media that influence how people see the world. Ian Bogost (2008), in a study of the rhetoric of video games, explained:

> Video games are not just stages that facilitate cultural, social, or political practices; they are also media where cultural values themselves can be represented—for critique, satire, education, or commentary. When understood in this way, we can learn to read games as deliberate expressions of particular perspectives. In other words, video games make claims about the world, which players can understand, evaluate, and deliberate. (p. 119)

When video games make claims about the world, they make claims about gender.

How People Are Represented

A nearly infinite range of themes can be explored relating to media and gender. We focus on two that cross a variety of media forms, including magazines, television shows, advertisements, movies, and video games: the hypersexualization of women and girls and the trope that masculinity needs to be resecured.

Sexualization of Women

In 2007, the American Psychological Association (APA) commissioned a task force to report on the sexualization of girls. Contrasting it to healthy sexuality, the task force defined **sexualization** as occurring when

- a person's value comes only from his or her sexual appeal or behavior, to the exclusion of other characteristics;
- a person is held to a standard that equates physical attractiveness (narrowly defined) with being sexy;
- a person is sexually objectified—that is, made into a thing for others' sexual use, rather than seen as a person with the capacity for independent action and decision making; and/or
- sexuality is inappropriately imposed upon a person. (p. 1)

Examples include "dolls wearing black leather miniskirts, feather boas, and thigh-high boots," thongs for 7- to 10-year-olds, and child beauty pageants (p. 1). Textiles and apparel scholar Annette Lynch (2012) added to the list: "midriff marketing," sexy Halloween costumes, T-shirts sold for teens at Walmart in 2007 saying "Some call it stalking—I call it love," and T-shirts sold at Next for 5- to 6-year-olds saying "So many boys, so little time" (p. 62).

Depictions of sexuality dominate television. After reviewing 1,154 programs, researchers found that from 1998 to 2005, 77% of prime-time shows had sexual content (Kunkel, Eyal, Finnerty, Biely, & Donnerstein, 2005). However, men's and women's bodies are not sexualized in the same way or to the same extent.

The male gaze persists, where women are treated as objects of desire, rather than as agents of action. The Comprehensive Annenberg Report on Diversity (CARD) provided the most recent assessment of sexualization. Researchers analyzed 109 films released during 2014 and 305 TV shows and digital series aired during 2014 to 2015. The result: Women characters were at least three times more likely than male characters to be sexualized (Smith et al., 2016, p. 3; see Figure 11.10).

Figure 11.10 Character Sexualization by Gender

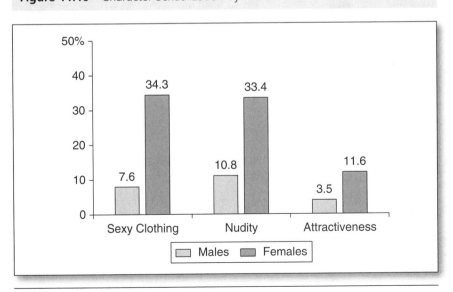

Source: Smith, Choueiti, & Pieper (2016).

Table 11.3   Female Character Sexualization by Race/Ethnicity

Sexualization Measures	White	Latina	Black	Asian	Other
In sexualized attire	34.8%	39.5%	29.5%	28.9%	41.6%
With some nudity	34.2%	35.5%	28.6%	27.7%	39.7%
Referenced attractive	12.6%	11.4%	7.9%	7.7%	15.3%

Source: Smith, Choueiti, & Pieper (2016).

Unsurprisingly, race influenced the extent to which and how a female character was sexualized (Smith et al., 2016, p. 9; see Table 11.3).

Although the APA has criticized the hypersexualization of women and girls since 2007, the problem has not improved. In fact, it appears to be worsening, as Figure 11.11 shows.

Figure 11.11   Hypersexualization of Female Characters

Hypersexualization of female character on screen, 2007–2013

Hypersexuality	2007	2008	2009	2010	2012	2013
Sexualized attire	27%	25.7%	25.8%	33.8%	31.6%	30.2%
With some exposed skin	21.8%	23.7%	23.6%	30.8%	31%	29.5%
Referenced attractive	18.5%	15.1%	10.9%	14.7%	not measured	13.2%

Source: USC Annenberg School for Communication and Journalism Media.

Female sexualization by age in top grossing films, 2013

Percentage	13–20 year olds	21–39 year olds	40–64 year olds
In sexy attire	39.4	40.5	18.8
Partially/fully naked	37.4	39.6	18.5
Referenced attractive	14.8	16.1	7.3

Source: USC Annenberg School for Communication and Journalism Media.

Source: Smith, Choueiti, & Pieper (2014).

The sexualization of women affects how women see themselves. Researchers studied whether exposure to sexually explicit images affected young women's acceptance of the male gaze. The findings: "Women exposed to more explicit centerfolds [where breasts and genitalia were exposed] expressed stronger acceptance of the male gaze than women exposed to less explicit centerfolds [where models were scantily clad but did not expose breasts or genitalia]" (Wright, Arroyo, & Bae, 2015, p. 8). The more often women are exposed to more explicitly sexualized images of women, "the stronger the message . . . that women are sights to be observed by others" (p. 8). Images that present women as objects reinforce the male gaze, objectify women and, in turn, women self-objectify and internalize the idea that "their worth is inherent in their appearance and that men's sexualization of their bodies is appropriate and inevitable" (p. 8). This sexualization is neither necessary nor inevitable. Researchers have found that when people become aware that the female body has been constructed as "*a gazed-upon body*," they can begin to resist (Ponterotto, 2016, p. 133).

The sexualization of women also has effects on men. In a study of magazines targeted at young men in Great Britain, called "lads' mags," researchers found they were "normalizing extreme sexist views by presenting those views in a mainstream context" (Horvath, Hegarty, Tyler, & Mansfield, 2012, p. 454). The researchers came to this conclusion after performing two different studies. In one, they gave 90 young men "derogatory quotes about women drawn from recent lads' mags, and from interviews with convicted rapists"; the young men identified more with the quotes when they were attributed to the magazines, even when they actually came from rapists. In the second study, the researchers asked 40 young women and men to identify the source of derogatory quotes about women; they "could not reliably judge the source." Even though the people studied generally indicated they saw lads' mags' statements as "normal" and rapists' comments as "extreme," they could not tell the difference between the two (p. 454).

Peter Hegerty explained these studies

tell us that there is an overlap in the content of the legitimations that rapists use to legitimate their violence against women and the kinds of things that are said about women in lads' mags. . . . And at the same time, they show us that when those things are attributed to lads' mags that they're easier for young men to identify with. ("Are Sex," 2011, video)

Miranda Horvath warned,

These magazines support the legitimisation of sexist attitudes and behaviours and need to be more responsible about their portrayal of women, both in words and images. They give the appearance that sexism is acceptable and normal—when really it should be rejected and challenged. ("Are Sex," 2011, para. 9)

These studies make clear exactly how problematic sexual objectification is. How men's magazines talk about women is not all that different from how rapists talk about their victims.

Sexualization occurs not just to women's bodies, but increasingly affects younger girls. Girls as young as 6 years old have started to judge themselves in relation to their sexual attractiveness. In one study, which used sexualized and nonsexualized dolls as prompts, "girls overwhelmingly chose the sexualized doll over the non-sexualized doll for their ideal self and as popular" (Starr & Ferguson, 2012, p. 463). The conclusion? "Young girls overwhelmingly demonstrate a sexualized view of their desired selves and equate sexiness with popularity" (p. 473).

Researchers studied adolescent girls to see what relationship existed between watching "sexually objectifying music television, primetime television programs, fashion magazines, and social networking sites" to determine whether there was a relationship between that viewing and "the internalization of beauty ideals, self-objectification, and body surveillance" (Vandenbosch & Eggermont, 2012, p. 870). The researchers found a relationship: "Our results suggested that exposure to sexually objectifying media is related to the internalization of beauty ideals, self-objectification, and body surveillance for a younger sample as well" (p. 884). This worried the researchers because "even 'small' increases in self-objectification can cause fundamental changes in an individual's self-image. . . . Girls with higher levels of internalization, self-objectification, and body surveillance may construct a more objectified self image," and over years those small increases from repeated exposure to media accrue (p. 884).

Changes in self-image lead to changes in behavior. Researchers from the University of Texas and the New York City Department of Health conducted a series of experiments to explore the effect of internalizing sexualization on girls age 10 to 15. They found that girls who had internalized sexualization differed from girls who did not in three ways. First, they scored lower on standardized tests and earned lower grades. Second, when preparing to deliver a mock newscast, they spent more time on their makeup and less time on practicing their script (McKenney & Bigler, 2016a). Third, they tended to wear more sexualized clothing and engage in more body surveillance and body shame (McKenney & Bigler, 2016b). Internalized sexualization has psychological and behavioral consequences. Even though many commentators focus on media representations of femininity as the primary place in which women are socialized to body image ideals, "the degree to which this message is internalized varies depending on factors such as race, nationality, and sexual orientation" (Harvey, 2005, p. 796).

The prevalence of the sexual objectification of women has so dominated media, it should be unsurprising that people self-objectify when they become producers of mediated messages. Sexting, "the sending or receiving of sexually-explicit or sexually-suggestive images or video via a cell phone" (Hinduja & Patchin, 2010, p. 1), is one example of the practice of self-objectification. A 2008 study by the National Campaign to Prevent Teen and Unplanned Pregnancy and CosmoGirl.com found 20% of teens ages 13 to 19 and 30% of young adults ages 20 to 26 had posted or sent nude or seminude pictures of themselves. Communication researcher Hugh Curnutt (2012) believed teens, and especially girls, sext "as a kind of remediation in which the libidinal focus of the media industry is internalized and reproduced by its consumers" (p. 355). In other words, the sexualization initially presented in media outlets (television, film, music videos) is internalized by teens who then seek to outwardly re-present it in their images of themselves. If the primary image one sees of women is sexualized, then the most likely way to self-represent is through a sexualized image.

Video games also sexualize women. Although women now represent 41% of the game playing market (Entertainment Software Association, 2016, p. 3), an international survey found only 22% of the people working in the game industry identify as women, 1.2% are trans, 1% are other, and a handful are nonbinary (Weststar & Legault, 2015, p. 11). In 2012, in response to the underrepresentation, misrepresentation, and harassment of women, game blogger Anita Sarkeesian launched a Kickstarter campaign to fund a web series that would explore the sexist themes in games. Male gamers responded to this call with death and rape threats (Chess & Shaw, 2015).

"Masculinity in Crisis"

During the 2010 Super Bowl, a series of advertisements aired that shared a common theme: Men's masculinity was under attack and needed to be reasserted (Green & Van Oort, 2013). Dodge advertised its Charger by showing close-ups of beleaguered men's faces as a voiceover intoned a series of men's complaints against a "generalized capitalist superior" and a "generalized female intimate other" (Duerringer, 2015, p. 144–145). These last complaints included the following: "I will be civil to your mother. I will put the seat down. . . . I will carry your lip balm. I will watch your vampire TV shows with you . . . and because I do this, [vroom] I will drive the car I want to drive. Charger: Man's last stand." In a Dockers ad, a motley group of pantless men in styleless shirts and tighty whities marched across a field singing, "I wear no pants." The end of the ad provided a solution: "Calling all men. It is time to wear the pants." In an advertisement for FloTV, Jason was shown standing forlornly in the lingerie department holding shopping bags with a red lace bra over his shoulder while his girlfriend browses. The narrator explained that we have an "injury report": Jason's "girlfriend has removed his spine, rendering him incapable of watching the game." The solution: "Get yourself a FloTV personal television . . . so that now live sports goes where you go. Change out of that skirt, Jason." These ads all told a similar story: Men's masculinity was under attack and consuming the right product would resecure it. (The ads can all be seen on YouTube by searching for Dodge Charger Super Bowl 2010, Dockers 2010 SuperBowl, and flo-tv-spineless.)

For an interesting example of how new digital media enable people to critically respond to media messages, see "Woman's Last Stand: Dodge Charger Commercial Spoof" (www.youtube.com/watch?v=ou5Ens-qNRc). Filmmaker MacKenzie Fegan parodied the original advertisement, offering a political intervention into consumer culture.

The concern about a crisis in masculinity is not new, nor has it dissipated since 2010. In August 2016, *National Review* writer David French worried that people are living in a "post-masculine reality" because college-age men's grip strength declined between 1985 and 2016 and because men are no longer learning how to be a man—"a protector, builder, fixer." French (2016) worried: "Men were meant to be strong. Yet we excuse and enable their weakness. It's but one marker of cultural decay, to be sure, but it's a telling marker indeed." For French, masculinity is in crisis and needs to be reasserted.

Why might masculinity need to be resecured? Communication scholar Casey Kelly (2016), in an assessment of the "masculinity crisis thesis" noted how there are "cycles of de-stabilization/re-stabilization" during which masculinity appears to be under assault and needs to be reaffirmed (p. 97). What causes destabilization? Communication scholar Christopher Duerringer (2015) noted how, at the end of the 20th century, computer technology and production dominated by automation and robotics led to the loss of nearly 6 million manufacturing jobs

> and the loss of status for many blue- and white-collar American men. To the extent that hegemonic masculinity articulates manhood with employment in the skilled, productive, physical work that male bodies perform, these events represented significant injuries to hegemonic masculinity. (p. 139)

This echoes French's argument: Men are masculine when their bodies do tasks that require physical labor.

However, economic shifts alone do not explain why masculinity appears to be in crisis. Instead, Kelly (2016) observed that masculinity claims to be in crisis during those moments when "women, queer communities, and racial minorities" advance (p. 97). As proof that the crisis was not just about economics, Michelle Rodino-Colocino (2014) noted how a range of press stories decried the "hecession" or "mancession" of 2008 because men's unemployment appeared to have surpassed women's, but failed to recognize that structural poverty continues to disproportionately impact people of color and women. For these reasons, Kelly (2016) concluded that the "crisis . . . is less a sign of real material disadvantage than a strategic performance of victimhood" (p. 97).

Reassertions of traditional masculinity appear across media as a response to a perceived fear of its erosion. But just because masculinity may be in flux does not mean dominant forms of masculinity have lost their normative force. Media representations are one location where hegemonic masculinity is identifiable, particularly in relation to sports coverage. In his analysis of baseball star Nolan Ryan, Nick Trujillo (1991) identified five defining characteristics of **U.S. hegemonic masculinity**:

1. power means physical force and control
2. occupational achievement
3. familial patriarchy, in which the man is the breadwinner
4. symbolized by the frontiersman and the outdoorsman
5. heterosexual

Media representations of ideal men present an image to which other men can aspire and by which all men are judged. Media scholar Robert Hanke (1998) explained that "hegemonic masculinity is won not only through coercion but through consent, even though there is never complete consensus" (p. 190). People *want* to participate in the socially sanctioned and idealized notions of masculinity. A discussion of a media-created "crisis in masculinity" adds to the conversation by recognizing that additional pressures have been placed on men to be manly by overperforming a very particular type of masculinity.

In their review of discussions of masculinity across media forms, communication scholars Greg Dickinson and Karrin Vasby Anderson (2004) argued that when masculinity "figures itself as in crisis and figures white men as vulnerable to attack," it can "justify the constant securing of its borders" (p. 290). Just as muscular Christianity was a response to the perceived effeminization of men at the end the 19th century, popular culture at the turn of the 21st century is a response to the perceived effeminization of men caused by the "over-civilized and emasculat[ing] obligations to work and women" (Ashcraft & Flores, 2003, p. 2). Movies turned to what Karen Ashcraft and Lisa Flores labeled a "'civilized/primitive' masculinity, embodied by the hardened white man who finds healing in wounds" (p. 2). Men employ physical and psychological violence (their primitive side) to maintain or recapture their masculinity even in the world of business (their civilized side). This theme is continued in reality television shows like *Doomsday Preppers* (Nat Geo, 2011–present), *Doomsday Castle* (Nat Geo, 2013), *Apocalypse Preppers* (Discovery, 2013), and *Meet the Preppers* (2012). Kelly (2016) argued these shows resecure a hegemonic masculinity that is described as in crisis. The recent upsurge in doomsday reality TV represents an attempt to resecure "hegemonic masculinity by restaging the plausible real world conditions under which the performance of manly labor appears instrumental to collective survival" (p. 96). The narrative told by these shows is that masculinity is necessary to survive a doomsday scenario and that manhood might only be reclaimed with the "inevitable demise of civilization" (p. 110).

The centering of White hegemonic masculinity occurs in reality television because "performances of white male identity are often constructed as more authentic than racial minorities because whiteness itself operates with seemling [*sic*] naturalness" (Kelly, 2016, p. 99). Ashcraft and Flores (2003) argued people should pay particular attention to the way in which masculinity "is inevitably raced and classed" (p. 3). They noted that hegemonic masculinity refers to hegemonic *White* masculinity, even though race is not overtly mentioned. This is part of the power of hegemonic White masculinity: It "co-opts discourses of race, class, and sexuality without deposing its white, heterosexual, and middle-class footing" (p. 4).

Primitive masculinity expressed through violence is a staple in video games as well. The video game culture predominantly portrays a hypermasculinity (Kimmel, 2012a). One can understand video games as an example of an attempt to secure masculinity by overperforming it. In a comprehensive review of video games, media scholars Richard Campbell, Chris Martin, and Bettina Fabos (2013) concluded that gaming is dominated by White men as the creators, producers, actors, and players, and the adventures created in the games are those of violence, power, domination, and misogyny. Some of the hypermasculinized characteristics in the most violent ("mature audience") genre of games are the following:

Combat with guns and every other type of weapon imaginable is featured.

The action is intentionally violent.

The storyline is a dark fantasy or horror.

Players take on villainous roles (e.g., serial killers, gun-wielding assassins, underworld criminals out for revenge).

Players earn points by killing or hurting as many others as possible.

Human characters are predominantly White men and (rarely) women.

Women do not exist in most games.

The women portrayed tend to be scantily dressed even if they enact aggression; others are the target of abuse, rape, and murder. (Campbell, Martin, & Fabos, 2013)

Unfortunately, virtual violence seeps into the material world. While it would be too simplistic to say there is a direct relationship between video game use and violent behavior, or that gaming alone influences behavior, media representations of violence are *one* of the ways gendered violence is normalized in U.S. culture. Reviews of the research on gaming indicate it leads to aggression and violence in children and adults (e.g., American Psychological Association, 2015; Kierkegaard, 2008). Being manly in a game may be one way to assert masculinity when it is perceived to be under threat.

Conclusion

The artistry involved in media creations open spaces for creative performances of gender—within limits. Even though the politics of much media are regressive, most people take pleasure in going to movies, reading novels, perusing magazines, playing video games, and surfing the web. The danger is not that people do these things but that they often do them uncritically. Audiences act as though they are passive recipients of media, not active participants in culture. The more you realize that you can *talk back* to the screen, the page, or the picture, the more you are not merely buying a commodity. The more you become an engaged member of the cultural conversation, the more you learn to employ an oppositional gaze. Condit (1989) explained that audience's complex relationship to media "is a consequence of the fact that humans, in their inherent character as audiences, are inevitably situated in a communication *system*, of which they are a part, and hence have some influence within, but by which they are also influenced" (p. 120). This chapter should make clear the ways in which people can engage in the active and dynamic practice of resistant readings of media. People can use "media texts to serve their own interests in unpredictable ways" (Dow & Condit, 2005, p. 457).

Although creative uses of media are important, an institutional approach to media also makes clear they may be insufficient. First, media are ephemeral, making them a "fragile basis for lasting social change" (Dow, 2001, p. 137). Second, changes in representation do not necessarily translate into changes in policy (Budd et al., 1990). Although we believe that images, texts, and messages matter, we also want to clarify the limits of personalized politics; institutional-level change is required, and heightened consciousness of media images of women and men, masculinity and femininity, Whiteness and otherness does little if it is not translated into political action.

KEY CONCEPTS

commodification 237

culture industries 224

the gaze 233

hegemony 228

oppositional gaze 236

polysemous 228

polyvalence 229

sexualization 242

U.S. hegemonic masculinity 248

ways of seeing 230

DISCUSSION QUESTIONS

1. The next time you watch a television show or movie, keep a record of the following:

   • the characters with whom you identify

   • the characters you want to emulate or be

   • the characters you find attractive

   What does this tell you about your gaze? Through whose eyes are you watching? Using an oppositional gaze, what might you see differently?

2. The next time you use media, count the number of times characters are sexualized. How many times are women and men presented in a way that makes sexuality their primary attribute? Are there examples of women characters whose sexuality is completely irrelevant to their identity? Are there examples of men? Are gender non-conforming people presented as sexually desirable?

3. What messages do the media you read and watch give you about masculinity? Is masculinity secure and certain? Is it something natural? Is it something that can be maintained only through action? If so, what actions must be taken?

CHAPTER 12

One Last Look Through a Critical Gendered Lens

I n 2015, a 12-year-old took on the video game industry. One of Maddie Messer's favorite games was *Temple Run*. The problem: to play as a female character you had to pay, even though male characters were free. Maddie decided to research how common this was. After downloading the 50 most popular "endless running games" in the iTunes store for iPhones, Maddie found 37 offered free male characters while only five offered free female characters (Henn & Jiang, 2015). The average cost of a female character was $7.53, and in one Disney game it cost $30. Maddie's op-ed that *The Washington Post* published argued:

> These biases affect young girls like me. The lack of girl characters implies that girls are not equal to boys and they don't deserve characters that look like them. I am a girl; I prefer being a girl in these games. I do not want to pay to be a girl. (Messer, 2015)

One of the creators of *Temple Run*, Natalia Luckyanova, read the editorial, which made them realize "the white male is always the default, and anything else, it's like, you have to work for it" (as cited in Henn & Jiang, 2015). The issue did not end with just this personal realization. The *Temple Run* creators, on the day the editorial came out, wrote to Maddie and promised a free female character, then Disney changed its pricing so there is no longer a $30 female character, and then another game maker created a new character . . . named Maddie (Henn & Jiang, 2015).

This example illustrates a number of themes in this book. *The male and masculine persists as the default*, and it takes work to develop a gendered lens that can bring this into focus. *Attention to patterns of systemic bias is important*. If Maddie had criticized just a single game, no change might have resulted. Because Maddie did the work (reviewing 50 games), the systemic bias became clear. *Binary gender/ sex differences are reinforced through communication*. Even though free female characters are now available, when will characters not trapped in the sex binary become available? *Seemingly innocent practices* (like game characters) *affect children's perceptions of themselves and others.* But the good news is that people talk back against these restrictive norms. A 12-year-old girl, using only communication (a newspaper editorial), asked for change. Maddie challenged the pink tax and succeeded. So if a 12-year-old could find a way to see beyond, engage in research about patterns of discrimination, and make a place in the world where they would feel equal, what can you do?

Using your critical gendered lens, you can

- recognize the drawbacks of the gender differences approach;
- embrace an oppositional gaze that enables you to see when people of a particular sex, gender, sexuality, ethnicity, class, and/or religion are left out, missing, or unrecognized; and
- make interventions in the world—intrapersonally, interpersonally, and publicly—that make the world work (and play) for everyone.

The long-dominant differences approach to gender in communication reinforces the gender/sex binary. It assumes there are only two sexes (male and female), which are opposites. It also assumes there are only two genders (masculine and feminine) and men are masculine and women are feminine, and the more you are of one, the less you are of the other. Embedded within this gender/sex binary is heteronormativity. Everyone is presumed heterosexual, and if one violates this presumption, then intense questions are raised about one's gender, and if one violates presumptions about one's gender, then questions are raised about one's sexual orientation.

Many problems plague a differences approach. A focus on differences between women and men

- ignores the vast array of similarities among people;
- ignores the existence of intersex and transgender people;
- assumes that sex determines gender; and
- ignores the differences among women and among men and thus fails to accurately account for the importance of issues such as ethnicity, class, religion, and nationality.

Perhaps most important, a differences approach tends to ignore the issue of power and its offspring, violence. If you simply assume men and women are different, then you can too easily explain away power inequalities as the natural outcome of differences. We hope you realize that understanding gender in communication is nowhere near as simple as identifying differences. In fact, accepting a heteronormative and cisnormative gender/sex binary is more likely to induce you to commit errors when you assess communicative exchanges. Accordingly, we have not offered a list of differences between women's and men's communication.

It would simply be wrong, a categorical error, to talk about gender in communication by talking about differences between women's and men's communication patterns. The most up-to-date research demonstrates that looking for gender differences in communication by studying women as one group and men as another yields no meaningful results. Even though many tend to believe that men (as men) and women (as women) communicate differently, "the literature shows unstable, context-specific, relatively small, and variable effects" (Dow & Condit, 2005, p. 453). According to meta-analyses of research on gender in communication, biological sex accounts for "a miniscule 1% of the variance in communication behaviors" (p. 453). *One percent.* Biological sex is not the determining element; rather, gender role characteristics and expectations are. It would be a waste of time to devote an entire book to explaining only 1% of communicative actions.

Further complicating one's understanding of gender/sex in communication is the fact that gender is not an isolable component of a person's identity. Identity is intersectional. Your performance of gender is inextricably influenced by your race, ethnicity, class, sex, sexual orientation, physical ability, nationality, religion, education, work status, family, citizenship status, and every other identity ingredient that makes up who you are. A book about gender in communication is necessarily about much more than gender.

Gender communication scholar John Sloop (2005) wrote in a review of research on sex, race, class, and gender,

> a gender/sexuality project that avoids questions of, say, class and race, not only reinforces the larger material and economic ways in which class and racial borders are reinforced and delimited, but also provides a critique of gender/sexuality issues that has limited explanatory power. (p. 326)

Our goal is to make clear that you cannot understand gender unless you also understand the complexity of each person's identity, the influences of institutions on gender, and how questions of power are woven throughout. If you examine gender diversity using a critical gendered lens, many more subtleties and complexities emerge.

Despite the complexities and fluidities of identity, many institutions are still structured around identity categories as if each were permanently fixed, unproblematically identifiable, and easily distinguished. For this reason, even though gender is highly interdependent with other identity ingredients, it still is useful as a category of analysis when trying to understand the dynamics of communication.

By attending to violence throughout this book, we make clear that differences are rarely innocent cultural constructions. Instead, these constructions (e.g., man, woman, Black, White, rich, poor, citizen, noncitizen, physically able, disabled) have consequences. These consequences become clearest when one tracks issues such as rape, domestic violence, poverty, and genocide. Our point is not that men and masculinity are the cause of all society's ills. Instead, hegemonic masculinity and the normalization of violence as a solution to problems contribute to those ills.

We realize that our approach to understanding gender in communication is complex. We also realize that accounting for complexity is not easy. However, we do not consider this a drawback. We would rather be overly complex to get you thinking about gender diversity than overly simple and risk ignoring important variables that influence human communication. Human beings are wonderfully complex, and so it makes sense that the identity ingredient of gender would be, too. Gender communication scholars Bonnie Dow and Celeste Condit (2005) made this clear: "Sex and gender are not simply variables deserving incorporation in equations, but are complex factors that require careful, sustained attention to their formation and to the nonsimple ways in which they play out in human communication" (p. 454).

We have tried to highlight moments of emancipation and liberation, as well as moments of oppression and subordination. Although institutional structures and social power create inequalities, those inequalities do not persist unchallenged. Despite grinding poverty, people live full lives. Despite oppression and subordination, people find ways to creatively express themselves. Despite constant threats of violence, people resist. In many cases, acts of resistance use the very gender structures meant to subordinate. These acts of resistance are not without consequence, but for many the risk of backlash is not enough to deter them from finding ways to have livable lives. Of course, for many, accommodation is the selected path by which they find ways to live with the demands social institutions place on them.

Although many gender scholars are criticized (if not condemned) for denying that differences exist, we believe this criticism is based on a misunderstanding of our (and others') argument. In recognizing gender diversity, we are not denying differences between women and men. Instead, we highlight the diversity that exists between women, between men, and between all people. There are not two genders that neatly correspond to two sexes. Instead, a multiplicity of genders exists, genders that intersect with, influence, and are influenced by the vast array of other identity ingredients. Gender is constructed through institutional, interpersonal, and public discourse, and these constructions demand and maintain expectations of gender differentiation. Thus, we do not reject difference but account for far more differences, and far more similarities, than people usually think about. Our goal is not to deny the existence of gender/sex; rather, it is to open up possibilities for more genders and sexes. We simply reject the notions that the differences can be understood solely as differences between women and men and that differences exist solely within individual women and individual men.

Because we operate from a perspective of gender diversity, we also want to make clear that all people have at their disposal a range of communication strategies, even though those strategies may not always neatly fit within the gender identity a person typically performs. Adaptability and flexibility are the marks of a good communicator. The same is true when you consider gender in communication: Gender flexibility is good. Different contexts, different interpersonal relationships, and different times in a person's life will call for different gendered styles of communication.

As important as personal choices about gender performance are, and as much as we want to empower people to exercise agency in their communication choices about gender, we also want to make clear that those choices exist in larger social and institutional structures. Choice is never totally free of external constraints. Some choices are more valued and more validated than others, such as choosing to have children in a traditional, heterosexual marriage. Some choices are easier to make because people recognize their possibility, such as men's choices to be firefighters and women's to be nurses. Some choices are not seen as choices, because they participate in hegemonic patterns and practices, such as women's wearing of skirts and men's wearing of pants. Some choices are devalued or condemned, such as the choice of a woman to be childfree or a man's choice to be the primary caregiver to young children. Some choices seem impossible, such as the choice of women in the 1800s to speak publicly. Some choices are highlighted as choices, as people flaunting something, such as the choice of men to dress in skirts or the choice of same-sex couples to kiss in public. For these reasons, one cannot discuss personal choices about gender in communication without also discussing the public politics of sex and gender.

A critical gendered lens is necessary to study public communication about gender and to study institutions that construct and maintain gender/sex. Attention to how media messages reinforce gender/sex is necessary. Understanding how communication patterns about work gender particular groups is essential. Exploring how public statements about religion define what it means to be (only) a man or a woman is important. Analysis of what gets to be considered a family helps one understand who gets to be considered fully human. Analysis of public discourse about education enables one to track the ways stereotypes about gender/sex are maintained.

Personal gender/sex politics, although essential and important, are not the whole story. Personal choices matter. But political choices matter, too, and one should not lose sight of them. Gender in communication is not just about interpersonal relationships but also about larger social structures and the way they interact with the realities of people's personal lives. It *does* matter who does the dishes, cleans the toilet, takes out the trash, and changes diapers. It also matters what the minimum wage is—or what an economically privileged person pays another to perform this labor.

We hope we have provided you with the skills to ask the complicated questions, to ask whether a pattern exists along gender or sex lines, to ask why people do things the way they do, to ask whether something can be changed, to ask for something to change, to ask whether gender alone really explains it all. Sex privilege exists, and race privilege exists, but class privilege can complicate both. More than sex difference, power seems to be one of the most important analytical categories. Research on gender in communication must take into account ethnicity, class, citizenship, sexuality, and religion as well as the specific context if it is to say anything meaningful about the human condition.

Gender/sex is about real lives. Everyone faces real consequences if people do not recognize and resist the intensification of hegemonic masculinity and hyperfemininity. We hope you can help create a future in which the people around you—friends, family, acquaintances, coworkers, children—will be freer to be themselves without fear of harm. It will take everyone—women and men and intersex people, queer and straight, cisgender and transgender, young and old, Whites and people of color—working (and playing) together.

DISCUSSION QUESTIONS

1. Review the book and select four theories, concepts, images, or findings that are most helpful in creating your critical gendered lens. Be able to explain your choices.

2. What does it mean to recognize gender diversity and not focus on gender differences in the study of gender in communication?

3. Consider Maddie Messer's critique of video games. Can you identify a simple act of social justice you could do relating to gender/sex, race, ethnicity, class, physical ability, body size, age, or sexual orientation in communication? What would it take for you to implement this action?

References

We have taken some liberties with APA reference style. To better enable readers to see the contributions of women and men to our subject, we have included first names of authors where known. Although we recognize the artificiality of sex distinctions and the complexity of identity, we also realize that no matter how artificial, identity categories matter. M. Jacqui Alexander and Chandra Talpade Mohanty (1997) note that even as postmodernist theories attempt to pluralize and dissolve

> the stability and analytic utility of the categories race, class, gender, and sexuality . . . the relations of domination and subordination that are named and articulated through the processes of racism and racialization still exist, and they still require analytic and political specification and engagement. (p. xvii)

AAUW. (2016, Spring). The simple truth about the gender pay gap. Retrieved from http://www.aauw.org/files/2016/02/SimpleTruth_Spring2016.pdf

Abbasi, Jennifer. (2012, July 17). Why 6-year-old girls want to be sexy (study). *Huff Post Parents*. Retrieved from http://www.huffingtonpost.com/2012/07/17/6-year-old-girls-sexy_n_ 1679088.html

ABC News. (2014, March 12). Target apologizes for "thigh gap" Photoshop fail. *Good Morning America*. Retrieved from http://abcnews.go.com/blogs/lifestyle/2014/03/target-apologizes-for-thigh-gap-photoshop-fail/

Abdul-Jabbar, Kareem. (2015, July 20). Body shaming black female athletes is not just about race. *Time*. Retrieved from http://time.com/3964758/body-shaming-black-female-athletes/

Abeydeera, Shantell Yasmine. (2016). Jaden smith, is all the man I need. *Huffington Post*. Retrieved from http://www.huffingtonpost.com/shantell-yasmine-abeydeera/jaden-smith-is-all-the-ma_b_8953062.html

Ablow, Keith. (2011, April 11). J. Crew plants the seeds for gender identity. *FoxNews.com*. Retrieved from http://www.foxnews.com/health/2011/04/11/j-crew-plants-seeds-gender-identity

Abrams, Rachel. (2016, January 28). Barbie adds curvy and tall to body shapes. *New York Times*. Retrieved from https://www.nytimes.com/2016/01/29/business/barbie-now-in-more-shapes.html?_r=0

Acker, Joan. (1990, June). Hierarchies, jobs, bodies: A theory of gendered organizations. *Gender & Society, 4*(2), 139–158.

Adams, Maurianne. (2016). Pedagogical foundations for social justice education. In Maurianne Adams & Lee Ann Bell with Diane J. Goodman & Khyati Y. Joshi (Eds.), *Teaching for diversity and social justice* (pp. 27–54). New York, NY: Routledge.

Addis, Michael E., Mansfield, Abigail K., & Syzdek, Matthew R. (2010). Is "masculinity" a problem? Framing the effects of gendered social learning in men. *Psychology of Men & Masculinity, 11*(2), 77–90.

Adorno, Theodor W. (1991). *The culture industry: Selected essays on mass culture.* London, England: Routledge.

Agbese, Aje-Ori. (2003, Spring). Maintaining power in the face of political, economic and social discrimination: The tale of Nigerian women. *Women and Language, 26*(1), 18–26.

Alcoff, Linda. (1995). The problem of speaking for others. In Judith Roof & Robyn Weigman (Eds.), *Who can speak? Authority and critical identity* (pp. 97–119). Urbana: University of Illinois Press.

Alcoff, Linda, & Potter, Elizabeth. (Eds.). (1993). *Feminist epistemologies.* New York, NY: Routledge.

aleclair. (2006, February 21). You guys. Retrieved from http://www.urbandictionary.com/define.php?term=you guys

Alexander, M. Jacqui, & Mohanty, Chandra Talpade. (1997). Introduction: Genealogies, legacies, movements. In M. Jacqui Alexander & Chandra Talpade Mohanty (Eds.), *Feminist genealogies, colonial legacies, democratic futures* (pp. xiii–xlii). New York, NY: Routledge.

Ali, Russlynn. (2011, April 4). Dear colleagues letter: Sexual violence, background, summary, and facts. Washington, DC: Department for Civil Rights, U.S. Department of Education. Retrieved from http://www2.ed.gov/print/about/offices/list/ocr/letters/colleague-201104.html

Allen, Brenda J. (1995). "Diversity" and organizational communication. *Journal of Applied Communication Research, 23*, 143–155.

Allen, Brenda J. (1996). Feminist standpoint theory: A Black woman's (re)view of organizational socialization. *Communication Studies, 47*(4), 257–271.

Allen, Brenda J. (1998). Black womanhood and feminist standpoints. *Management Communication Quarterly, 11*, 575–586.

Aloia, Lindsey Susan, & Solomon, Denise Haunani. (2017). Sex differences in perceived appropriateness of receiving verbal aggression. *Communication Research Reports, 34*(1), 1–10.

Alsubaie, Merfat Ayeshi. (2015). Hidden curriculum as one of current issue of curriculum. *Journal of Education and Practice, 6*(33), 125–128.

American Dialect Society. (2016, January 8). 2015 Word of the Year is singular "they." Retrieved from http://www.americandialect.org/2015-word-of-the-year-is-singular-they

American Dialect Society. (n.d.). About the American Dialect Society. Retrieved from http://www.americandialect.org/

American Medical Association. (2011, June 21). AMA adopts new policies at annual meeting. Retrieved from http://www.ama-assn.org/ama/pub/news/news/a11-new-policies.page

American Psychiatric Association. (2000). *Diagnostic and statistical manual of mental disorders* (4th ed., text rev.). Washington, DC: Author.

American Psychiatric Association. (2012). *Diagnostic and statistical manual of mental disorders. DSM-5 Development.* Retrieved from http://www.dsm5.org/Pages/Default.aspx

American Psychiatric Association. (2013). *Diagnostic and statistical manual of mental disorders* (5th ed.). Arlington, VA: American Psychiatric Publishing.

American Psychological Association. (2007). *Report of the APA task force on the sexualization of girls.* Washington, DC: Author. Retrieved from http://www.apa.org/pi/women/programs/girls/report-full.pdf

American Psychological Association. (2015, August 13). APA review confirms link between playing violent video games and aggression. Retrieved from http://www.apa.org/news/press/releases/2015/08/violent-video-games.aspx

Amoroso, Michelle. (2017, March 03). "The Big Bang Theory," the gender pay gap and implications for employers. Retrieved from http://www.buzzbinpadillaco.com/big-bang-theory-gender-pay-gap-implications-employers/

An open letter from Black women to the SlutWalk. (2011, September 23). *Huffington Post.* Retrieved from http://www.huffingtonpost.com/susan-brison/slutwalk-black-women_b_980215.html

Andersen, Margaret L. (2015). *Thinking about women: Sociological perspectives on sex and gender* (10th ed.). Boston, MA: Pearson.

Anderson, Kristin J., & Leaper, Campbell. (1998, August). Meta-analyses of gender effects on conversational interruption: Why, what, when, where, and how. *Sex Roles, 39*(3–4), 225–252.

Anderson, Nick, & Clement, Scott. (2015, June 12). College sexual assault: 1 in 5 women say they were violated. *Washington Post.* Retrieved from http://www.washingtonpost.com/sf/local/2015/06/12/1-in-5-women-say-they-were-violated/?tid=a_inl

Anderson, Rindy C., Klofstad, Casey A., Mayew, William J., & Venkatachalam, Mohan. (2014). Vocal fry may undermine the success of young women in the labor market. *PLOS One, 9*(5). Retrieved from http://journals.plos.org/plosone/article?id=10.1371/journal.pone.0097506

Angier, Natalie. (1999). *Woman: An intimate geography.* New York, NY: Anchor Books.

Ankney, Davison C. (1992). Sex differences in relative brain size: The mismeasure of woman, too? *Intelligence, 16*(3/4), 329–336.

Ansolabehere, Joseph, & Germain, Paul. (Writers). (2002, October 24). Neither boy nor girl [Television episode]. *Lloyd in space.* Disney.

Anzaldúa, Gloria. (1987). *Borderlands/La Frontera: The new Mestiza.* San Francisco, CA: Aunt Lute Books.

Anzaldúa, Gloria. (1990). Bridge, drawbridge, sandbar or island: Lesbians-of-Color *hacienda alianzas.* In Lisa Albrecht & Rose M. Brewer (Eds.), *Bridges of power: Women's multicultural alliances* (pp. 216–231). Philadelphia, PA: New Society.

Apostolic Visitation of Institutes of Women Religious in the United States. (2012, January 9). *Apostolic visitation closes with final report submission* [Press release].

Archer, John. (2006). Testosterone and human aggression: An evaluation of the challenge hypothesis. *Neuroscience and Biobehavioral Reviews, 30*(3), 319–345. doi:10.1016/j.neubiorev.2004.12.007

Are sex offenders and lads' mags using the same language? (2011, December 6). University of Surrey. Retrieved from http://www.surrey.ac.uk/mediacentre/press/2011/69535_are_sex_offenders_and_lads_mags_using_the_same_language.htm

Aries, Elizabeth. (2006). Sex differences in interaction: A reexamination. In Kathryn Dindia & Daniel J. Canary (Eds.), *Sex differences and similarities in communication* (2nd ed., pp. 21–36). Mahwah, NJ: Erlbaum.

Armstrong, Jeannette. (1990). Words. In The Telling It Book Collective (Ed.), *Telling it: Women and language across cultures* (pp. 23–30). Vancouver, British Columbia, Canada: Press Gang.

As G.I. Joe bulks up, concern for the 98-pound weakling. (1999, May 30). *New York Times,* p. 2.

Ashcraft, Karen Lee. (2009). Gender and diversity: Other ways to make a difference. In Mats Alvesson, Todd Bridgeman, & High Willmott (Eds.), *The Oxford handbook of critical management studies* (pp. 304–327). Oxford, UK: Oxford University Press.

Ashcraft, Karen. (2014). Feminist theory. In Linda L. Putnam and Dennis K. Mumby (Eds.), *The Sage handbook of organizational communication* (pp. 127–150). Thousand Oaks, CA: Sage.

Ashcraft, Karen. (2016, February). Lean in to the evidence: Breaking the "glass slipper" of technical professions. *Proceedings of the 47th ACM Technical Professions Symposium on*

Computing Science Education. New York, NY: ACM Digital Library. Retrieved from http://dl.acm.org/citation.cfm?id=2846011&CFID=769371699&CFTOKEN=86214183

Ashcraft, Karen Lee, & Flores, Lisa A. (2003, January). "Slaves with white collars": Persistent performances of masculinity in crisis. *Text and Performance Quarterly, 23*(1), 1–29.

Ashcraft, Karen Lee, & Mumby, Dennis K. (2004). *Reworking gender: A feminist communicology of organization*. Thousand Oaks, CA: Sage.

Association of American Universities. (2015, September 5). AAU climate survey on sexual assault and sexual misconduct. Retrieved from https://www.aau.edu/key-issues/aau-climate-survey-sexual-assault-and-sexual-misconduct-2015

Ayotte, Kevin, & Husain, Mary E. (2005). Securing Afghan women: Neocolonialism, epistemic violence, and the rhetoric of the veil. *NWSA Journal, 17*(3), 112–133.

Babcock, Linda, & Laschever, Sara. (2007). *Women don't ask: The high cost of avoiding negotiation—and positive strategies for change*. New York, NY: Bantam Dell.

Bacon, Jen. (2012). Until death do us part: Lesbian rhetorics of relational divorce. *Women's Studies in Communication, 35*(2), 158–177. doi.10.1080/07491409.212.724523

Bacon, Margaret Hope. (1989). "One great bundle of humanity": Frances Ellen Watkins Harper, 1825–1911. *Pennsylvania Magazine of History & Biography, 113*(1), 21–43.

Ballantine, Jeanne H., & Hammack, Floyd M. (2015). Sociology of education: A unique perspective for understanding schools. In Jeanne H. Ballantine & Joan Spade (Eds.), *Schools and society: A sociological approach to education* (5th ed., pp. 13–17). Thousand Oaks, CA: Sage.

Bandura, Albert. (2002). Social cognitive theory of mass communication. In Jennings Bryant & Dolf Zillman (Eds.), *Media effects: Advances in theory and research* (2nd ed., pp. 121–153). Mahwah, NJ: Erlbaum.

Bandura, Albert, & Walters, Richard H. (1963). *Social learning and personality development*. New York, NY: Holt, Rinehart & Winston.

Barnett, Barbara. (2017). Girls gone web: Self-depictions of female athletes on personal websites. *Journal of Communication Inquiry, 41*(2), 97–123.

Barnett, Rosalind, & Rivers, Caryl. (2004). *Same difference: How gender myths are hurting our relationships, our children, and our jobs*. New York, NY: Basic Books.

Barreca, Regina. (1991). *They used to call me Snow White . . . but I drifted: Women's strategic use of humor*. New York, NY: Penguin.

Basow, Susan A. (2008). Speaking in a "man's world": Gender differences in communication styles. In Michele A. Paludi (Ed.), *The psychology of women at work: Challenges and solutions for our female workforce* (pp. 15–30). Westport, CN: Praeger.

Bate, Barbara. (1988). *Communication and the sexes*. Prospect Heights, IL: Waveland.

Baucom, Donald H., Snyder, Douglas K., & Gordon, Kristina Coop. (2009). *Helping couples get past the affair: A clinician's guide*. New York, NY: Guilford Press.

Baxter, Leslie A. (2011). *Voicing relationships: A dialogic perspective*. Thousand Oaks, CA: Sage.

BBC. (2009, March 6). What would a real life Barbie look like? *BBC News Magazine*. Retrieved from http://news.bbc.co.uk/2/hi/uknews/magazine/7920962.stm

Beaman, Robyn, Wheldall, Kevin, & Kemp, Coral. (2006). Differential teacher attention to boys and girls in the classroom. *Educational Review, 58*(3), 339–366.

Beech, Eric. (2016, June 2). Obama says transgender directive based on law. *Reuters*. Retrieved from http://www.reuters.com/article/us-obama-lgbt-idUSKCN0YO03Y

Begley, Sharon, & Murr, Andrew. (1995, March 27). Gray matters. *Newsweek*, pp. 48–54.

Bell, Lee Ann. (2016). Theoretical foundations for social justice education. In Maurianne Adams & Lee Ann Bell, with Diane J. Goodman & Khyati Y. Joshi (Eds.), *Teaching for diversity and social justice* (pp. 1–26). New York, NY: Routledge.

Bell, Leslie C. (2004). Psychoanalytic theories of gender. In Alice H. Eagly, Anne E. Beall, & Robert J. Sternberg (Eds.), *The psychology of gender* (2nd ed., pp. 145–168). New York, NY: Guilford Press.

Bem, Sandra. (1974). The measurement of psychological androgyny. *Journal of Counseling and Clinical Psychology, 42*, 155–162.

Bennett, Jeffrey. (2008). Passing, protesting, and the arts of resistance: Infiltrating the ritual space of blood donation. *Quarterly Journal of Speech, 94*, 23–43. doi:10.1080/003 35630701790818

Berendzen, Gerri. (2017, March 24). AP style for first time allows use of they as singular pronoun. *American Copy Editors Society*. Retrieved from http://www.copydesk.org/ blog/2017/03/24/ap-style-for-first-time-allows-use-of-they-as-singular-pronoun/

Berger, John. (1972). *Ways of seeing*. London, England: Penguin Books.

Berger, Peter L., & Luckmann, Thomas. (1966). *The social construction of reality: A treatise in the sociology of knowledge*. New York, NY: Doubleday.

Berlant, Lauren, & Warner, Michael. (1995, May). What does queer theory teach us about X? *PMLA, 110*(3), 343–349.

Berlatsky, Noah. (2014, June 6). How boys teach each other to be boys. *The Atlantic*. Retrieved from http://www.theatlantic.com/health/archive/2014/06/how-boys-teach-each-other-to-be-boys/372246/

Blackless, Melanie, Charuvastra, Anthony, Derryck, Amanda, Fausto-Sterling, Anne, Lauzanne, Karl, & Lee, Ellen. (2000). How sexually dimorphic are we? Review and synthesis. *American Journal of Human Biology, 12*, 151–166.

Blackstone, Amy, & Stewart, Mahala Dyer. (2012). Choosing to be childfree: Research on the decision not to parent. *Sociology Compass, 6*, 718–727. doi:10.1111/j.1751-9020 .2012.00496.x

Blakey, M. L. (1999). Scientific racism and the biological concept of race. *Literature and Psychology, 45*, 29–43.

Blatch, Harriot Stanton, & Lutz, Alma. (1940). *Challenging years: The memoirs of Harriot Stanton Blatch*. New York, NY: G.P. Putnam's Sons.

Blay, Zeba. (2015, October 5). Reclaiming the word "slut" is an entirely different beast for black women. *Huffington Post*. Retrieved from http://www.huffingtonpost.com/entry/ reclaiming-the-word-slut-is-an-entirely-different-beast-for-black-women_us_ 56128706e4b0af3706e14d49

Blum, Haley. (2016, February). Totally fried: What is vocal fry? *ASHA Leader, 21*(2), 50–57.

Blumberg, Antonia. (2015, April 22). Former "Real World" star thinks Christianity has become too "feminized." *Huffington Post*. Retrieved from http://www.huffingtonpost .com/2015/04/22/rachel-campos-duffy-manly-church_n_7119492.html

Boddice, Rob. (2011). The manly mind? Revisiting the Victorian "sex in brain" debates. *Gender & History, 23*(2), 321–340.

Bode, Leticia. (2017). Closing the gap: Gender parity in political engagement on social media. *Information, Communication & Society, 20*(4), 587–603.

Bogaert, Anthony F. (2015). Asexuality: What is it and why it matters. *Journal of Sex Research, 52*(4), 362–379.

Bogost, Ian. (2008). The rhetoric of video games. In Katie Salen (Ed.), *The ecology of games: Connecting youth, games, and learning* (pp. 117–140). Cambridge, MA: MIT Press.

Bologna, Caroline. (2017, June 1). Mom takes joy-filled photos of son who likes to wear dresses. *Huffington Post*. Retrieved from http://www.huffingtonpost.com/entry/mom-takes-joy-filled-photos-of-son-who-likes-to-wear-dresses_us_59302626e4b0e09 b11ee15b1

Bordo, Susan. (1997). *Twilight zones: The hidden life of cultural images from Plato to O.J.* Berkeley: University of California Press.

Bordo, Susan. (1999). *The male body: A new look at men in public and private.* New York, NY: Farrar, Straus & Giroux.

Bordo, Susan. (2003). *Unbearable weight: Feminism, western culture, and the body* (10th ann. ed.). Berkeley: University of California Press.

Bowles, Hannah Riley, Babcock, Linda, & Lai, Lei. (2007). Social incentives for gender differences in the propensity to initiate negotiations: Sometimes it does hurt to ask. *Organizational Behavior and Human Decision Processes, 103,* 84–103.

Boylan, Jennifer Finney. (2017, April 7). From best man to puzzled woman. *New York Times.* Retrieved from https://www.nytimes.com/2017/04/07/style/modern-love-jennifer-finney-boylan.html?mc=aud_dev&mcid=keywee&mccr=domdesk&kwp_0=382716&kwp_4=1417773&kwp_1=623989&_r=0

Bradstock, Andrew, Gill, Sean, Hogan, Anne, & Morgan, Sue. (Eds.). (2000). *Masculinity and spirituality in Victorian culture.* New York, NY: St. Martin's Press.

Brannon, Linda. (2011). *Gender: Psychological perspectives* (6th ed.). Boston, MA: Pearson Education.

Brief for San Francisco Dykes on Bikes Women's Motorcycle Club, Inc. as Amicus Curiae Supporting Respondent, Michelle K. Lee v. Simon Shiao Tam. (2016). (no. 15-1293). Retrieved from http://www.scotusblog.com/wp-content/uploads/2016/12/15-1293-amicus-respondent-SAN-FRANCISCO-DYKES-ON-BIKES-WOMEN%E2%80%99S-MOTORCYCLE-CONTINGENT....pdf

Brief for Simon Shiao Tam, Michelle K. Lee v. Simon Shiao Tam. (2016). (no. 15-1293). Retrieved from http://www.scotusblog.com/wp-content/uploads/2016/06/BIO-15-1293-Lee-v-Tam.pdf

Brighe, Mari. (2016, February 23). We updated "The Vagina Monologues" for 2016 to make it more trans-inclusive. *Wikimedia Commons.* Retrieved from https://mic.com/articles/135266/we-updated-the-vagina-monologues-for-2016-to-make-it-more-trans-inclusive%23.GVmbpZfTm

Brod, Harry. (1987). The case for men's studies. In Harry Brod (Ed.), *The making of masculinities: The new men's studies* (pp. 39–62). Boston, MA: Allen & Unwin.

Brodsky, Alexandria. (2015, March 27). Instagram bans photo for showing menstruation. *Feministing.* Retrieved from http://feministing.com/2015/03/27/instagram-bans-photos-for-showing-menstruation/

Brooks, Meredith, & Peiken, Shelly. (1997). Bitch [Music lyrics]. Retrieved from http://www.musicfanclubs.org/meredithbrooks/bitc.html

Broverman, Inge K., Broverman, Donald M., Clarkson, Frank E., Rosenkrantz, Paul S., & Vogel, Susan R. (1970). Sex-role stereotypes and clinical judgments of mental health. *Journal of Counseling and Clinical Psychology, 34*(1), 1–7.

Brown, Erin R. (2011, April 8). *J. Crew pushes transgendered child propaganda.* Culture and Media Institute. Retrieved from http://www.mrc.org/cmi/articles/2011/JCREW_Pushes_Transgendered_Child_Propaganda_.html

Brown, Penelope, & Levinson, Stephen. (1978). Universals in language usage: Politeness phenomenon. In Esther N. Goody (Ed.), *Questions and politeness* (pp. 56–89). Cambridge, UK: Cambridge University Press.

Brown, Penelope, & Levinson, Stephen. (1987). *Politeness: Some universals in language usage.* Cambridge, UK: Cambridge University Press.

Brumbaugh, Claudia C., & Wood, Dustin. (2009, June). Using revealed mate preferences to evaluate market force and differential preference explanations for mate selection. *Journal of Personality & Social Psychology, 96*(6), 1226–1244.

Brummett, Barry. (1976). Some implications of "process" or "intersubjectivity": Postmodern rhetoric. *Philosophy & Rhetoric, 9*(1), 21–51.

Buchbinder, David. (2013). *Studying men and masculinities.* London, England: Routledge.

Buck, Stephanie. (2017, January 19). When Jesus got "too feminine," white dudes invented muscular Christianity. Retrieved from https://timeline.com/muscular-christianity-20d7c88839b9#.3me4tp8z3

Budd, Mike, Entman, Robert M., & Steinman, Clay. (1990, June). The affirmative character of U.S. cultural studies. *Critical Studies in Mass Communication, 7*(2), 169–184.

Burchette, Jordan. (2017, April 10). "Manspreading" on public transport—New name for age-old issue. *CNN.* Retrieved from http://www.cnn.com/2016/06/22/travel/manspreading-public-transport/index.html

Bureau of Labor Statistics, U.S. Department of Labor. (2016a, February 10). Labor force statistics from the current population survey. Retrieved from http://www.bls.gov/cps/cpsaat39.htm

Bureau of Labor Statistics, U.S. Department of Labor. (2016b, January 15). Women's earnings 83 percent of men's, but vary by occupation. Retrieved from http://www.bls.gov/opub/ted/2016/womens-earnings-83-percent-of-mens-but-vary-by-occupation.htm

Bureau of Labor Statistics. (2017, June 24). American time use survey summary. USDL-16-1250. Retrieved from https://www.bls.gov/news.release/atus.nr0.htm

Burke, Kenneth. (1966). *Language as symbolic action: Essays on life, literature, and method.* Berkeley: University of California Press.

Burke, Kenneth. (1969). *A rhetoric of motives.* Berkeley: University of California Press.

Burleson, Brant R., & Kunkel, Adrianne. (2006). Revisiting the different cultures thesis: An assessment of sex differences and similarities in supportive communication. In Kathryn Dindia & Dan J. Canary (Eds.), *Sex differences and similarities in communication* (2nd ed., pp. 137–160). Mahwah, NJ: Erlbaum.

Burleson, Brent R., & MacGeorge, Erina, L. (2002). Supportive communication. In Mark L. Knapp & John A. Daly (Eds.), *Handbook of interpersonal communication* (3rd ed., pp. 374–424). Thousand Oaks, CA: Sage.

Bush administration publicizes plight of Afghan women. (2001, November 16). *Feminist Daily News Wire.* Retrieved from http://www.feminist.org/news/newsbyte/uswirestory.asp?id=5948

Bush, Laura. (2001, November 17). *Radio address by Laura Bush to the nation.* Retrieved from http://www.whitehouse.gov/news/releases/2001/11/20011117.html

Busse, Meghan, R., Israeli, Ayelet, & Zettlemeyer, Florian. (2017). Repairing the damage: The effect of gender and price knowledge on auto-repair price quotes. *Journal of Marketing Research, 54*(1), 75–95.

Butler, Judith. (1990). *Gender trouble: Feminism and the subversion of identity.* New York, NY: Routledge.

Butler, Judith. (1991). Imitation and gender insubordination. In Diana Fuss (Ed.), *Inside/out: Lesbian theories, gay theories* (pp. 13–31). New York, NY: Routledge.

Butler, Judith. (1992). Contingent foundations: Feminism and the question of "postmodernism." In Judith Butler & Joan W. Scott (Eds.), *Feminists theorize the political* (pp. 3–21). New York, NY: Routledge.

Butler, Judith. (1993). *Bodies that matter: On the discursive limits of "sex."* New York, NY: Routledge.

Butler, Judith. (1997). *Excitable speech: A politics of the performative.* New York, NY: Routledge.

Butler, Judith. (2004). *Undoing gender.* New York, NY: Routledge.

Buzinski, Jim. (2016, August 1). There are a record 11 openly gay male Olympians in Rio. None is an American. *SB Nation.* Retrieved from http://www.outsports.com/2016/8/1/12209162/american-male-gay-athletes-rio-olympics

Buzzanell, Patrice M. (Ed.). (2000). *Rethinking organizational and managerial communication from feminist perspectives*. Thousand Oaks, CA: Sage.

Buzzanell, Patrice M., & Liu, Meina. (2005, February). Struggling with maternity leave policies and practices: A poststructuralist feminist analysis of gendered organizing. *Journal of Applied Communication Research, 33*(1), 1–25.

Buzzanell, Patrice M., Sterk, Helen, & Turner, Lynn H. (Eds.). (2004). *Gender in applied communication contexts*. Thousand Oaks, CA: Sage.

Byne, William M. (2005). Why we cannot conclude sexual orientation is a biological phenomenon. In J. Kenneth Davidson & Nelwyn B. Moore (Eds.), *Speaking of sexuality* (2nd ed., pp. 245–248). Los Angeles, CA: Roxbury.

Cabrera, Natasha J., & Tamis-LeMonda, Catherine S. (2013). *Handbook of father involvement: Multidisciplinary perspectives* (2nd ed.). New York, NY: Taylor & Francis.

Cahill, Larry. (2005, May). His brain, her brain. *Scientific American, 292*(5), 40–47.

Caiazza, Amy. (2005). Don't bowl at night: Gender, safety, and civic participation. *Signs, 30*(2), 1607–1631.

Calafell, Bernadette Marie. (2014). The future of feminist scholarship: Beyond the politics of inclusion. *Women's Studies in Communication, 37*, 266–270. doi:10.1080/07491409.2014.955436

Calás, Marta B. (1992). An/other silent voice? Representing "Hispanic woman" in organizational texts. In Albert J. Mills & Peta Tancred (Eds.), *Gendering organizational analysis* (pp. 201–221). Newbury Park, CA: Sage.

Calás, Marta B., & Smircich, Linda. (2001). From "the woman's" point of view: Feminist approaches to organization studies. In Stewart R. Clegg, Cynthia Hardy, & Walter N. Nord (Eds.), *Handbook of organization studies* (pp. 218–257). Thousand Oaks, CA: Sage.

Calogero, Rachel, M., Boroughs, Michael, & Thompson, J. Kevin. (2007). The impact of Western beauty ideals on the lives of women: A sociological perspective. In Viren Sami & Adrian Furnham (Eds.), *The body beautiful: Evolutionary and sociocultural perspectives* (pp. 259–298). London, England: Palgrave Macmillan.

Cameron, Deborah. (1997). Performing gender identity: Young men's talk and the construction of heterosexual masculinity. In Sally Johnson & Ulrike Hanna Meinhof (Eds.), *Language and masculinity* (pp. 47–64). Oxford, UK: Basil Blackwell.

Cameron, Deborah. (1998). Lost in translation: Non-sexist language. In Deborah Cameron (Ed.), *The feminist critique of language* (2nd ed., pp. 155–163). New York, NY: Routledge.

Campbell, Anne. (1993). *Men, women and aggression*. New York, NY: Basic Books.

Campbell, Karlyn Kohrs. (1973, February). The rhetoric of women's liberation: An oxymoron. *Quarterly Journal of Speech, 59*, 74–86.

Campbell, Karlyn Kohrs. (1989). *Man cannot speak for her* (Vols. 1 and 2). Westport, CT: Praeger.

Campbell, Karlyn Kohrs. (2005). Agency: Promiscuous and protean. *Communication and Critical/Cultural Studies, 2*(1), 1–19.

Campbell, Richard, Martin, Christopher R., & Fabos, Bettina. (2013). *Media and culture: An introduction to mass communication* (8th ed.). Boston, MA: Bedford/St. Martin's.

Campbell, Richard, Martin, Christopher, & Fabos, Bettina. (2015). *Media and culture: Mass communication in a digital age* (10th ed.). Boston, MA: Bedford/St. Martin's.

Campbell, Sister Simone. (2012, July 2). Nuns on the Bus sister: Women religions respond to real-world struggles. *National Catholic Reporter*. Retrieved from http://ncronline.org/news/women-religious/nuns-bus-sister-women-religious-respond-real-world-struggles

Canary, Daniel J., & Hause, Kimberley S. (1993, Spring). Is there any reason to research sex differences in communication? *Communication Quarterly, 41*(2), 129–144.

Cancian, Francesca M. (1989). Love and the rise of capitalism. In Barbara J. Risman & Pepper Schwartz (Eds.), *Gender in intimate relationships* (pp. 12–25). Belmont, CA: Wadsworth.

Carbaugh, Dan. (2002). "I can't do that!" But I "can actually see around corners": American Indian students and the study of public "communication." In Judith N. Martin, Thomas K. Nakayama, & Lisa N. Flores (Eds.), *Readings in intercultural communication: Experiences and contexts* (pp. 138–149). Boston, MA: McGraw-Hill.

Carlone, Heidi B., Johnson, Angela, & Scott, Catherine M. (2015). Agency amidst formidable structures: How girls perform gender in science class. *Journal of Research in Science teaching, 52*(4), 474–488.

Carlson, Jessica H., & Crawford, Mary. (2011, July). Perceptions of relational practices in the workplace. *Gender, Work and Organization, 18*(4), 359–376.

Carney, Dana R., Cuddy, Amy J. C., & Yap, Andy J. (2010). Power posing: Brief nonverbal displays affect neuroendocrine levels and risk tolerance. *Psychological Science, 21*, 1363–1368.

Carney, Dana. R., Hall, J., & Smith LeBeau, L. (2005). Beliefs about the nonverbal expression of social power. *Journal of Nonverbal Behavior, 29*, 105–123.

Caroland. (2014, December 18). Voice training for trans women vol. 1–3—Our trans journey. Retrieved from https://www.youtube.com/watch?v=Ch5gBKsvSwo

Carr, Joetta L. (2013). The SlutWalk movement: A study in transnational feminist activism. *Journal of Feminist Scholarship, 4.* Retrieved from http://www.jfsonline.org/issue4/articles/carr/

Carroll, Janell L. (2005). *Sexuality now.* Belmont, CA: Wadsworth.

Catalano, Shannan. (2012, November). *Special report: Intimate partner violence, 1993–2010.* U. S. Department of Justice, Office of Justice Programs. Retrieved from http://www.bjs.gov/index.cfm?ty=pbdetail&iid=4536

Caughlin, John P., & Ramey, Mary E. (2005). The demand/withdraw pattern of communication in parent-adolescent dyads. *Personal Relationships, 12*, 337–355.

Centers for Disease Control and Prevention. (2005, May 3). Births, marriages, divorces, and deaths: Provisional data for November 2004. *National Vital Statistics Reports, 53*(19).

Centers for Disease Control and Prevention. (2014). Child maltreatment. Retrieved from https://www.cdc.gov/violenceprevention/pdf/childmaltreatment-facts-at-a-glance.pdf

Centers for Disease Control and Prevention. (2017a, April 17). Child abuse prevention. Retrieved from https://www.cdc.gov/features/healthychildren/index.html

Centers for Disease Control and Prevention. (2017b, March 20). Disability and functioning. Retrieved from https://www.cdc.gov/nchs/fastats/disability.htm

Chait, Jonathan. (2016, December 5). Mike Pence strongly believes Donald Trump's shoulder width guarantees his foreign-policy acumen. *New York Magazine.* Retrieved from http://nymag.com/daily/intelligencer/2016/12/12-times-mike-pence-praised-donald-trumps-shoulders.html

Chappell, David. (2004). *A stone of hope: Prophetic religion and the death of Jim Crow.* Chapel Hill: University of North Carolina Press.

Charteris-Black, Jonathan, & Seale, Clive. (2009). Men and emotion talk: Evidence from the experience of illness. *Gender and Language, 3*(1), 81–113.

Chávez, Karma R., & Griffin, Cindy L. (2014, September). Women's studies in communication still matters. *Women's Studies in Communication, 37*(3), 262–265. doi:10.1080/07491409.2014.955434

Chemaly, Soraya. (2016, May 27). DC metro rape highlights why women are always aware of rape. *Huffington Post.* Retrieved from http://www.huffingtonpost.com/soraya-chemaly/for-women-rape-isnt-a-mom_b_9997350.html

Chen, Martha, Vanek, Joann, Lund, Francie, & Heintz, James. (2005). *Progress of the world's women 2005: Women, work and poverty*. New York, NY: United Nations Development Fund for Women.

Chess, Shira, & Shaw, Adrienne. (2015). A conspiracy of fishes, or, how we learned to stop worrying about #GamerGate and embrace hegemonic masculinity. *Journal of Broadcasting & Electronic Media*, 59(1), 208–220. doi:10.1080/08838151.2014.999917

Chevrette, Roberta. (2013). Outing heteronormativity in interpersonal and family communication: Feminist applications of queer theory "beyond the sexy streets." *Communication Theory*, 23, 170–190.

Chicago Manual. (2017, April 3). Chicago Style for the singular *they*. Retrieved from http://cmosshoptalk.com/2017/04/03/chicago-style-for-the-singular-they/

Chittister, Joan Sr., O.S.B. (2004, August 13). To the "experts in humanity": Since when did women become the problem? [Electronic version]. *National Catholic Reporter*, 40(36), 7.

Chodorow, Nancy. (1978). *The reproduction of mothering: Psychoanalysis and the sociology of gender*. Berkeley: University of California Press.

Christensen, Andrew, Eldridge, Kathleen, Catta-Preta, Adrianna Bokal, Lim, Veronica, & Santagata, Rossella. (2006). Cross-cultural consistency of the demand-withdraw interaction pattern in couples. *Journal of Marriage and Family*, 68, 1029–1044.

Chu, Judy Y., & Gilligan, Carol. (2014). *When boys become boys: Development, relationships, and masculinity*. New York, NY: New York University Press.

Chun, Jennifer Jihye, Lipsitz, George, & Shin, Young. (2013). Intersectionality as a social movement strategy: Asian Immigrant Women Advocates. *Signs*, 38(4), 917–940.

Cichocki, Nina. (2004, November). Veils, poems, guns, and martyrs: Four themes of Muslim women's experiences in Shirin Neshat's photographic work. *Thirdspace*, 4(1). Retrieved from http://www.iiav.nl/ezines/web/Thirdspace/2004/N01/thirdspace/4_1_Cichocki.htm

Clark, Rep. (1918, January 23). 56 Cong. Rec. H762-811.

Clemetson, Lynette. (2006, February 9). Work vs. family, complicated by race. *New York Times*, p. G1.

Cloud, Dana L. (1998, Fall). The rhetoric of "family values": Scapegoating, utopia, and the privatization of social responsibility. *Western Journal of Communication*, 62(4), 387–419.

Cloud, Dana L. (2004). "To veil the threat of terror": Afghan women and the "clash of civilizations" in the imagery of the U.S. war on terrorism. *Quarterly Journal of Speech*, 90(3), 285–306.

CNN Staff. (2015, October 2015). Model-actress Zendaya "shocked" to find herself Photoshopped. *CNN*. Retrieved from http://www.cnn.com/2015/10/22/living/zendaya-modeliste-photoshop-feat/index.html

Coates, Jennifer. (1996). *Women talk: Conversations between women friends*. Oxford, UK: Basil Blackwell.

Coates, Jennifer. (1997). One-at-a-time: The organization of men's talk. In Sally Johnson & Ulrike Hanna Meinhof (Eds.), *Language and masculinity* (pp. 107–129). Oxford, UK: Basil Blackwell.

Coates, Jennifer. (2003). *Men talk: Stories in the making of masculinities*. Malden, MA: Basil Blackwell.

Coates, Jennifer. (2004). *Women, men, and language: A sociolinguistic account of gender differences in language*. London, England: Pearson Education.

Coates, Jennifer. (2013). *Women, men and everyday talk*. New York, NY: Palgrave MacMillan.

Coates, Jennifer. (2014). Gender and humor in everyday conversation. In Delia Chiaro & Raffaella Baccolini (Eds.), *Gender and humor: Interdisciplinary and international perspectives* (pp. 147–164). New York, NY: Routledge.

Colbert, Stephen (Anchor), & Silverman, Allison (Executive Producer). (2012, June 11). *The Colbert report* [Television broadcast]. Retrieved from http://www.colbertnation.com/the-colbert-report-videos/415111/june-11-2012/radical-feminist-nuns

Collins, Patricia Hill. (1994). Shifting the center: Race, class, and feminist theorizing about motherhood. In Donna Bassin, Margaret Honey, & Maryle Mahrer Kaplan (Eds.), *Representations of motherhood* (pp. 56–74). New Haven, CT: Yale University Press.

Collins, Patricia Hill. (1995). Symposium: On West and Fenstermaker's "Doing difference." *Gender & Society, 9*(4), 491–494.

Collins, Patricia Hill. (1998). *Fighting words: Black women and the search for justice.* Minneapolis: University of Minnesota Press.

Collins, Patricia Hill, & Bilge, Sirma. (2016). *Intersectionality.* Malden, MA: Polity.

Coltrane, Scott. (1989). Household labor and the routine production of gender. *Social Problems, 36,* 473–490.

Combahee River Collective. (1974). Statement. Retrieved from http://www.sfu.ca/iirp/documents/Combahee%201979.pdf

The compact edition of the Oxford English dictionary. (1971). Glasgow, Scotland: Oxford University Press.

Condit, Celeste Michelle. (1989, June). The rhetorical limits of polysemy. *Critical Studies in Mass Communication, 6*(2), 103–122.

Condit, Celeste Michelle. (1998). Gender diversity: A theory of communication for the postmodern era. In Judith S. Trent (Ed.), *Communication: Views from the helm for the 21st century* (pp. 177–183). Boston, MA: Allyn & Bacon.

Congregatio Pro Doctrina Fidei. (2012). Doctrinal assessment of the Leadership Conference of Women Religious. Retrieved from http://www.usccb.org/about/doctrine/doctrinal-assessment-for-lcwr.cfm

Connell, Catherine. (2010). Doing gender, or redoing gender? Learning from the workplace experiences of transpeople. *Gender & Society, 24*(1), 31–55.

Connell, Raewyn W. (1982). Class, patriarchy, and Sartre's theory of practice. *Theory and Society, 11,* 305–320.

Connell, Raewyn W. (1995). *Masculinities.* Berkeley: University of California Press.

Connell, Raewyn W., & Messerschmidt, James W. (2005, December). Hegemonic masculinity: Rethinking the concept. *Gender & Society, 19,* 829–859.

Coontz, Stephanie. (1992). *The way we never were: American families and the nostalgia trap.* New York, NY: Basic Books.

Coontz, Stephanie. (1997). *The way we really are: Coming to terms with America's changing family.* New York, NY: Basic Books.

Coontz, Stephanie. (2006). *Marriage, a history: From obedience to intimacy, or how love conquered marriage.* New York, NY: Penguin.

Coontz, Stephanie. (2016). *The way we never were: American families and the nostalgia trap* (2nd ed.). New York, NY: Basic Books.

Cooper, Brenda. (1999, March). The relevancy and gender identity in spectators' interpretations of *Thelma & Louise. Critical Studies in Mass Communication, 16*(1), 20–41.

Cooper, Brenda. (2000, Fall). "Chick flicks" as feminist texts: The appropriation of the male gaze in *Thelma & Louise. Women's Studies in Communication, 23*(3), 277–306.

Corbett, Christianne, & Hill, Catherine. (2012). *Graduating to a pay gap: The earnings of women and men one year after college graduation.* AAUW: Washington DC. Retrieved from http://www.aauw.org/resource/graduating-to-a-pay-gap/

Cortina, Lilia M., & Berdahl, Jennifer L. (2008). Sexual harassment in organizations: A decade of research in review. In Cary L. Cooper & Julian Barling (Eds.), *The Sage handbook of organizational behavior* (pp. 469–497). Thousand Oaks, CA: Sage.

Crawford, Mary. (1995). *Talking difference: On gender and language.* London, England: Sage.

Crawford, Mary, & Fox, Annie. (2007). From sex to gender and back again: Co-optation of a feminist language reform. *Feminism & Psychology, 17*, 481–486.

Crenshaw, Kimberlé. (1989). Demarginalizing the intersection of race and sex: A Black feminist critique of antidiscrimination doctrine, feminist theory and antiracist politics. *University of Chicago Legal Forum*, 139–167.

Crockett, Emily. (2017, February 8). GOP senator: Elizabeth Warren shouldn't criticize Sessions, because "think of his wife." *Vox.* Retrieved from http://www.vox.com/identi ties/2017/2/8/14546960/elizabeth-warren-jeff-sessions-orrin-hatch-think-of-his-wife

Crum, Maddie. (2016, July 7). It's time to embrace the singular "they," a humanistic pronoun. *Huffington Post.* Retrieved from http://www.huffingtonpost.com/entry/singular-pronoun-they-humanist_us_577d1b21e4b0416464114fbc

Cuddy, Amy J. C., Wilmuth, Caroline A., Yap, Andy J., & Carney, Dana R. (2015). Preparatory power posing affects nonverbal presence and job interview performance. *Journal of Applied Psychology, 100*, 1286–1295.

Curkin, Charles. (2015, November 25). At Bluestockings, a Manhattan activist center, radical is sensible. *New York Times.* Retrieved from http://www.nytimes.com/2015/11/29/nyregion/at-bluestockings-a-manhattan-bookshop-and-activist-center-radical-is-sensible.html?_r=0

Curnutt, Hugh. (2012). Flashing your phone: Sexting and the remediation of teen sexuality. *Communication Quarterly, 60*(3), 353–369.

Dabbs, James McBride, & Dabbs, Mary Godwin. (2001). *Heroes, rogues, and lovers: Testosterone and behavior.* New York, NY: McGraw-Hill.

Daly, Mary. (1987). *Websters' first new intergalactic wickedary of the English language.* Boston, MA: Beacon Press.

Daniels, Arlene Kaplan. (1987). Invisible work. *Social Problems, 34*(5), 403–415.

Davies, Shelagh, Papp, Viktória G., & Antoni, Christella. (2015). Voice and communication change for gender nonconforming individuals: Giving voice to the person inside. *International Journal of Transgenderism, 16*, 117–159.

Davis, Kathy. (2008). Intersectionality as buzzword: A sociology of science perspective on what makes a feminist theory successful. *Feminist Theory, 9*, 67–84. doi:10.1177/1464700108086364

de Beauvoir, Simone. (2010). Stanford encyclopedia of philosophy. Retrieved from http://plato.stanford.edu/entries/beauvoir/#SecSexWomOth

de Beauvoir, Simone. (2011). *The second sex* (Constance Border & Shelia Malovany-Chevallier, Trans.). New York, NY: Vintage Books. (Original work published 1949)

De Fina, Anna, Schiffrin, Deborah, & Bamberg, Michael. (2006). Introduction. In Anna DeFina, Deborah Schiffrin, & Michael Bamberg (Eds.), *Discourse and identity* (pp. 1–23). Cambridge, UK: Cambridge University Press.

de la Cruz, Sor Juana Inés. (1987a). *A woman of genius* (Margaret Sayers Peden, Trans.). Salisbury, CN: Lime Rick Press. (Original work published 1701)

de la Cruz, Sor Juana Inés. (1987b). *La Respuesta.* In *A woman of genius* (Margaret Sayers Peden, Trans.). Salisbury, CT: Lime Rick Press. (Original work published 1701)

de Lauretis, Teresa. (1984). *Alice doesn't: Feminism, semiotics, cinema.* London, England: MacMillan.

deBlasio, Bill, & Menin, Julie. (2015, December). From cradle to cane: The cost of being a female consumer: A study of gender pricing in New York, New York. Retrieved from https://www1.nyc.gov/assets/dca/downloads/pdf/partners/Study-of-Gender-Pricing-in-NYC.pdf

Demo, Anne Teresa. (2000, Spring). The Guerrilla Girls' comic politics of subversion. *Women's Studies in Communication, 23*(2), 133–156.

DePaulo, Bella. (2006). *Singled out: How singles are stereotyped, stigmatized, and ignored, and still live happily ever after*. New York, NY: St. Martin's Griffin.

DePaulo, Bella. (2012). Singles, no children: Who is your family? In Anita L. Vangelisti (Ed.), *The Routledge handbook of family communication* (2nd ed., pp. 190–204). New York, NY: Routledge.

DePaulo, Bella, & Trimberger, E. Kay. (2008). Single women. *Sociologists for Women in Society Fact Sheet*. Retrieved from http://www.socwomen.org/web/images/stories/resources/fact_sheets/fact_win2008-single.pdf

Desmond-Harris, Jenée. (2016, September 7). Serena Williams is constantly the target of disgusting racist and sexist attacks. *Vox Media*. Retrieved from https://www.vox.com/2015/3/11/8189679/serena-williams-indian-wells-racism

Deutsch, Francine M. (2007). Undoing gender. *Gender & Society, 21*(1), 106–127.

Dickinson, Greg, & Anderson, Karrin Vasby. (2004). Fallen: O. J. Simpson, Hillary Rodham Clinton, and the re-centering of white patriarchy. *Communication and Critical/Cultural Studies, 1*(3), 271–296.

Dienhart, Anna. (1998). *Reshaping fatherhood: The social construction of shared parenting*. San Francisco, CA: Sage.

Dindia, Kathryn. (2006). Men are from North Dakota, women are from South Dakota. In Kathryn Dindia & Daniel J. Canary (Eds.), *Sex differences and similarities in communication* (2nd ed., pp. 3–20). Mahwah, NJ: Erlbaum.

Dindia, Kathryn, & Allen, Mike. (1992). Sex differences in self-disclosure: A meta-analysis. *Psychological Bulletin, 112*, 106–124.

Dindia, Kathryn, & Canary, Dan. (2006). *Sex differences and similarities in communication* (2nd ed.). Mahwah, NJ: Erlbaum.

Dines, Gail, & Murphy, Wendy J. (2011, May 8). SlutWalk is not sexual liberation. *The Guardian*. Retrieved from http://www.guardian.co.uk/commentisfree/2011/may/08/slutwalk-not-sexual-liberation

DiPiero, Thomas. (2002). *White men aren't*. Durham, NC: Duke University Press.

Disch, Estelle. (2009). *Reconstructing gender: A multicultural anthology* (5th ed.). Boston, MA: McGraw-Hill.

Doherty, William J., & Beaton, John M. (2004). Mothers and fathers parenting together. In Anita L. Vangelisti (Ed.), *Handbook of family communication* (pp. 269–286). Mahwah, NJ: Erlbaum.

Dorman, Benjamin. (2006, Winter). Tokyo's Dr. Phil. *Religion in the News, 8*(3), 20–21, 26.

Dougherty, Debbie S., & Hode, Marlo Goldenstein. (2016). Binary logics and the discursive interpretation of organizational policy: Making meaning of sexual harassment policy. *Human Relations, 69*(8), 1729–1755.

Dow, Bonnie J. (1996). *Prime-time feminism*. Philadelphia: University of Pennsylvania Press.

Dow, Bonnie J. (2001, June). *Ellen*, television, and the politics of gay and lesbian visibility. *Critical Studies in Media Communication, 18*(2), 123–140.

Dow, Bonnie J. (2003). Feminism, Miss America, and media mythology. *Rhetoric & Public Affairs, 6*, 127–149.

Dow, Bonnie J., & Condit, Celeste. (2005, September). The state of the art in feminist scholarship in communication. *Journal of Communication, 55*(3), 448–478.

Dow, Bonnie J., & Wood, Julia T. (2014, January). Repeating history and learning from it: What can SlutWalks teach us about feminism? *Women's Studies in Communication, 37*(1), 22–43. doi:10.1080/07491409.2013.867918

Dowd, Nancy E. (2000). *Redefining fatherhood*. New York, NY: New York University Press.

Doyle, Jennifer, & Jones, Amelia. (2006). Introduction: New feminist theories of visual culture. *Signs, 31*(3), 607–615.

Droogsma, Rachel Anderson. (2007, August). Redefining hijab: American Muslim women's standpoints on veiling. *Journal of Applied Communication Research, 35*(3), 294–319.

Duberman, Martin. (1993). *Stonewall*. New York, NY: Dutton.

DuBowski, Sandi Simcha. (Director/Producer). (2003). *Trembling before G-d* [Documentary]. Israel: Simcha Leib Productions and Turbulent Arts, presented in Association with Keshet Broadcasting Ltd.

Duck, Steve. (2002). Hyptertext in the key of G: Three types of "history" as influences on conversational structures and flow. *Communication Theory, 12*, 41–62.

Duerringer, Christopher. (2015). Be a man—buy a car! Articulating masculinity with consumerism in Man's Last Stand. *Southern Communication Journal, 80*(2), 137–152. doi:10.1080/1041794X.2015.1017654

Duffy, Mignon. (2005, February). Reproducing labor inequalities: Challenges for feminists conceptualizing care at the intersections of gender, race, and class. *Gender & Society, 19*(1), 66–82.

Duggan, Maeve. (2014). *Online harassment*. Washington, DC: Pew Research Center. Retrieved from http://www.pewinternet.org/files/2014/10/PI_OnlineHarassment_102214_pdf.pdf

Durham, Meenakshi Gigi. (1999, Summer). Girls, media, and the negotiation of sexuality: A study of race, class, and gender in adolescent peer groups. *Journalism and Mass Communication Quarterly, 76*(2), 193–216.

Dworkin, Andrea, & MacKinnon, Catharine A. (1988). *Pornography and civil rights: A new day for women's equality*. Minneapolis, MN: Organizing Against Pornography.

Eagly, Alice H., & Koenig, Anne M. (2006). Social role theory of sex differences and similarities: Implication for prosocial behavior. In Kathryn Dindia & Daniel J. Canary (Eds.), *Sex differences and similarities in communication* (2nd ed., pp. 3–20). Mahwah, NJ: Erlbaum.

Earp, Brian D. (2012, Spring). The extinction of masculine generics. *Journal for Communication and Culture, 2*(1), 4–19.

Eastman, Carolyn. (2009). *A nation of speechifiers: Making an American public after the revolution*. Chicago, IL: University of Chicago Press.

Eckert, Penelope, & McConnell-Ginet, Sally. (1992). Communities of practice: Where language, gender and power all live. In Kira Hall, Mary Bucholtz, & Birch Manwomon (Eds.), *Locating power, proceedings of the 2nd Berkeley Woman and Language Conference* (pp. 89–99). Berkeley, CA: BWLG.

Eckert, Penelope, & McConnell-Ginet, Sally. (2011). Communities of practice: Where language, gender, and power all live. In Jennifer Coates & Pia Pichler (Eds.), *Language and gender: A reader* (2nd ed., pp. 573–582). West Sussex, UK: John Wiley-Blackwell.

Eckert, Penelope, & McConnell-Ginet, Sally. (2013). *Language and gender* (2nd ed.). Cambridge, UK: Cambridge University Press.

Education Amendments of 1972, 20 U.S.C. § 1681–1688. (1972).

Edwards, Renee, & Hamilton, Mark A. (2004, April). You need to understand my gender role: An empirical test of Tannen's model of gender and communication. *Sex Roles: A Journal of Research, 50*(7–8), 491–505.

Eelen, Gino. (2014). *A critique of politeness theory, volume 1*. New York, NY: Routledge.

Ehrenreich, Barbara. (1990). Are you the middle-class? In Margaret L. Andersen & Patricia Hill Collins (Eds.), *Race, class and gender: An anthology* (pp. 100–109). Belmont, CA: Wadsworth.

Ehrenreich, Barbara. (2001). *Nickel and dimed: On (not) getting by in America*. New York, NY: Holt.

Ehrensaft, Diane. (2011). Boys will be girls, girls will be boys: Children affect parents as parents affect children in gender nonconformity. *Psychoanalytic Psychology, 28*(4), 528–548.

Ehrlich, Susan, Meyerhoff, Miriam, & Holmes, Janet. (Eds.). (2014). *The handbook of language, gender and sexuality* (2nd ed.). Malden, MA: John Wiley & Sons.

Eide, Elisabeth. (2010). Strategic essentialism and ethnification. *Nordicom Review, 31*, 63–78.

Eilperin, Juliet. (2016, September 13). White House women want to be in the room where it happens. *Washington Post*. Retrieved from https://www.washingtonpost.com/news/powerpost/wp/2016/09/13/white-house-women-are-now-in-the-room-where-it-happens/?mc_cid=23f41632c6&mc_eid=4cd64fb794&postshare=6251473762897800&tid=ss_tw&wpisrc=nl_daily202&wpmm=1

El Guindi, Fadwa. (1999). *Veil: Modesty, privacy, and resistance*. New York, NY: Berg.

El Guindi, Fadwa. (2005a). Confronting hegemony, resisting occupation. In Faye V. Harrison (Ed.), *Resisting racism and xenophobia: Global perspectives on race, gender and human rights* (pp. 251–268). New York, NY: AltaMira Press.

El Guindi, Fadwa. (2005b, June). Gendered resistance, feminist veiling, Islamic feminism [Electronic version]. *Ahfad Journal, 22*(1), 53–78.

Eldredge, John. (2011). *Wild at heart: Discovering the secret of a man's soul*. Nashville, TN: Thomas Nelson.

Eldridge, Kathleen A., Sevier, Mia, Jones, Janice, Atkins, David C., & Christensen, Andrew. (2007). Demand-withdraw communication in severely distressed, moderately distressed, and nondistressed couples: Rigidity and polarity during relationship and personal problem discussions. *Journal of Family Psychology, 21*, 218–226.

Elgin, Suzette Haden. (2000). *Native tongue*. New York: Feminist Press at City University of New York. (Original work published 1984)

Elgin, Suzette Haden. (2002a). *Earthsong: Native tongue III*. New York: Feminist Press at City University of New York. (Original work published 1993)

Elgin, Suzette Haden. (2002b). *The Judas rose: Native tongue II*. New York: Feminist Press at City University of New York. (Original work published 1987)

Elgin, Suzette Haden. (2004). Retrieved from http://www.sfwa.org/members/elgin

Elias, Marilyn. (1992, August 3). Difference seen in brains of gay men. *USA Today*, p. 8D.

Eliot, Lise. (2009a, September 8). Girl brain, boy brain? *Scientific American*. Retrieved from http://www.scientificamerican.com/article.cfm?id=girl-brain-boy-brain

Eliot, Lise. (2009b). *Pink brain, blue brain: How small differences grow into troublesome gaps and what we can do about it*. Boston, MA: Houghton Mifflin Harcourt.

Elliot, Candice. (2015). The pink tax. *Listen Money Matters*. Retrieved from https://www.listenmoneymatters.com/the-pink-tax/

Emens, Elizabeth F. (2007). Changing name changing: Framing rules and the future of marital names. *University of Chicago Law Review, 74*(3), 761–863.

Emens, Elizabeth. (2014, February). Compulsory sexuality. *Stanford Law Review, 22*(2), 303–386.

Enck-Wanzer, Suzanne Marie. (2009). All's fair in love and sport: Black masculinity and domestic violence in the news. *Communication & Critical/Cultural Studies, 6*, 1–18. doi:10.1080/14791420802632087

Enke, Finn. (2012). Introduction: Transfeminist perspectives and note on terms and concepts. In Anne Enke (Ed.), *Transfeminist perspectives in and beyond transgender and gender studies* (pp. 1–22). Philadelphia, PA: Temple University Press.

Enloe, Cynthia. (1989). *Bananas, beaches, and bases: Making feminist sense of international politics*. Berkley: University of California Press.

Ensler, Eve. (1998). *The vagina monologues*. New York, NY: Villard.

Ensler, Eve. (2000). *The vagina monologues: V-day edition*. New York, NY: Villard.

Entertainment Software Association. (2016). 2016 essential facts about the computer and video game industry. Retrieved from http://www.theesa.com/wp-content/uploads/2016/04/Essential-Facts-2016.pdf

Episcopal Diocese of Fort Worth. (2007, May 16). *Diocese reaffirms pursuit of APO* [Press release]. Fort Worth, TX: Author.

Equal Employment Opportunity Commission. (n.d.). Charges alleging sexual harassment FY 2010-FY 2015.

Espelage, Dorothy L. (2016). Leveraging school-based research to inform bullying prevention and policy. *American Psychologist, 71*(8), 768–775.

Espelage, Dorothy L., Basile, Kathleen C., De La Rue, Lisa, & Hamburger, Merle E. (2015). Longitudinal associations among bullying, homophobic teasing and sexual violence perpetration among middle-school students. *Journal of Interpersonal Violence, 30*(14), 2541–2561.

Etcoff, Nancy, Orbach, Susie, Scott, Jennifer, & D'Agostino, Heidi. (2004). The real truth about beauty: A global report. Findings of the global study on women, beauty and well-being. Retrieved from http://www.clubofamsterdam.com/contentarticles/52%20 Beauty/dove_white_paper_final.pdf

Evaldsson, Anna-Carita. (2002). Boys' gossip telling: Staging identities and indexing (unacceptable) masculine behavior. *Text 22*(2), 199–225.

Fabj, Valeria. (1993). Motherhood as political voice: The rhetoric of the Mothers of Plaza de Mayo. *Communication Studies, 44*, 1–18.

Fägersten, Kristy Beers. (2012). *Who's swearing now? The social aspects of conversational swearing*. New Castle upon Tyne, UK: Cambridge Scholars.

Fahrenthold, David A. (2016, October 8). Trump recorded having extremely lude conversations about women in 2005. *Washington Post*. Retrieved from https://www.washingtonpost .com/politics/trump-recorded-having-extremely-lewd-conversation-about-women-in- 2005/2016/10/07/3b9ce776-8cb4-11e6-bf8a-3d26847eeed4_story.html

Fausto-Sterling, Anne. (1992). *Myths of gender: Biological theories about women and men* (2nd ed.). New York, NY: Basic Books.

Fausto-Sterling, Anne. (2000). *Sexing the body: Gender politics and the construction of sexuality*. New York, NY: Basic Books.

Feinberg, Leslie. (1998). *TransLiberation*. Boston, MA: Beacon Press.

Feldscher, Kyle. (2015, March 24). Michigan laws against cursing in front of women, dyeing animals and walkathons may be repealed. *MLive Michigan*. Retrieved from http://www .mlive.com/lansing-news/index.ssf/2015/03/michigan_laws_against_cursing.html

Felski, Rita. (2006). "Because it is beautiful": New feminist perspectives on beauty. *Feminist Theory, 7*(2), 273–282.

Ferraro, Kathleen J. (2006). *Neither angels nor demons: Women, crime and victimization*. Boston, MA: Northeastern University Press.

Fifty percent of American marriages are ending in divorce—Fiction! (2012). TruthOrFiction. com. Retrieved from http://www.truthorfiction.com/rumors/d/divorce.htm

Fikkan, Janna L., & Rothblum, Esther D. (2012). Is fat a feminist issue? Exploring the gendered nature of weight bias. *Sex Roles, 66*(9–10), 575–592.

Finch, Jenny, with Ann Killio. (2011). *Throw like a girl: How to dream big and believe in yourself*. Chicago, IL: Triumph Books.

Fine, Cordielia. (2010). *Delusions of gender: How our minds, society, and neurosexism create difference*. New York, NY: W. W. Norton.

Fiske, John. (1987). *Television culture*. New York, NY: Methuen.

Flores, Lisa A. (1996, May). Creating discursive space through a rhetoric of difference: Chicana feminists craft a homeland. *Quarterly Journal of Speech, 82*, 142–156.

Foner, Nancy, & Fredrickson, George M. (Eds.). (2005). *Not just black and white: Historical and contemporary perspectives on immigration, race and ethnicity in the United States*. New York, NY: Russell Sage Foundation.

Forbeswoman. (2012, June 28). 7 ways you're hurting your daughter's future. *Forbes.* Retrieved from http://www.forbes.com/sites/learnvest/2012/06/28/7-ways-youre-hurting-your-daughters-future

Forth, Christopher, E. (2008). *Masculinity in the modern west: Gender, civilization and the body.* New York, NY: Palgrave MacMillan.

Francis, Leslie J. (2005). Gender role orientation and attitude toward Christianity: A study among older men and women in the United Kingdom. *Journal of Psychology and Theology, 33*(3), 179–186.

Frank, Priscilla. (2014, May 5). Welcome to the bizarre and beautiful world of purity balls. *Huffington Post.* Retrieved from http://www.huffingtonpost.com/2014/05/05/purity-ball-photos_n_5255904.html

Frank, Priscilla. (2016, May 2). Who's afraid of the female gaze? *Huffington Post.* Retrieved from http://www.huffingtonpost.com/entry/whos-afraid-of-the-female-gaze_us_57238117e4b0b49df6ab19bc

Frassanito, Paolo, & Pettorini, Benedetta. (2008). Pink and blue: The color of gender. *Child's Nervous System, 24*(8), 881–882.

Freeman, Sue J. M., & Bourque, Susan C. (2001). Leadership and power: New conceptions. In Sue J. M. Freeman, Susan C. Bourque, & Christine M. Shelton (Eds.), *Women on power: Leadership redefined* (pp. 3–24). Boston, MA: Northeastern University Press.

Freire, Paulo. (1972). *Pedagogy of the oppressed.* London, England: Penguin.

French, David. (2016, August 16). Men are getting weaker—because we're not raising men. *National Review.* Retrieved from http://www.nationalreview.com/article/439040/male-physical-decline-masculinity-threatened

Freud, Sigmund. (1975). *Three essays on the theory of sexuality.* New York, NY: Basic Books.

Friedan, Betty. (1963). *The feminine mystique.* New York, NY: Dell.

Frisch, Hannah, L. (1977). Sex stereotypes in adult-infant play. *Child Development, 48,* 1671–1675.

Frith, Katherine, Shaw, Ping, & Cheng, Hong. (2005, March). The construction of beauty: A cross-cultural analysis of women's magazine advertising. *Journal of Communication, 55*(1), 56–70.

Fulghum, Robert. (2004). *All I really need to know I learned in kindergarten* (15th ed.). New York, NY: Ballantine Books.

Funk, Michelle E., & Coker, Calvin R. (2016). She's hot, for a politician: The impact of objectifying commentary on perceived credibility of female candidates. *Communication Studies, 67*(4), 455–473.

Gaffney, Edward McGlynn, Jr. (1990). Politics without brackets on religious convictions: Michael Perry and Bruce Ackerman on neutrality. *Tulane Law Review, 64,* 1143–1194.

Galinsky, Adam D., Wang, Synthia S., Whitson, Jennifer A., Anicich, Eric M., Hugenberg, Kurt, & Bodenhausen, Galen V. (2013). The reappropriation of stigmatizing labels: The reciprocal relationship between power and self-labeling. *Psychological Science, 24*(10), 2020–2029.

Gamman, Lorraine, & Marshment, Margaret. (Eds.). (1989). *The female gaze: Women as viewers of popular culture.* Seattle, WA: Real Comet Press.

Garber, Megan. (2017, February 8). "Nevertheless, she persisted" and the age of the weaponized meme. *The Atlantic.* Retrieved from https://www.theatlantic.com/entertainment/archive/2017/02/nevertheless-she-persisted-and-the-age-of-the-weaponized-meme/516012/?utm_source=atlfb

Gardiner, Becky, Mansfield, Mahana, Anderson, Ian, Holder, Josh, Louter, Daan, & Ulmanu, Monica. (2016, April 12). The dark side of Guardian comments. Retrieved from https://www.theguardian.com/technology/2016/apr/12/the-dark-side-of-guardian-comments?CMP=share_btn_link

Gattis, Maurice N., & McKinnon, Sara L. (2015). *School experiences of transgender and gender non-conforming students in Wisconsin.* Madison, WI: GSAFE.

Gauntlett, David. (2002). *Media, gender and identity*. London, England: Routledge.

Gergen, Kenneth J. (1994). *Realities and relationships: Soundings in social construction*. Cambridge, MA: Harvard University Press.

Gerschick, Thomas J., & Miller, Adam Stephen. (2004). Coming to terms: Masculinity and physical disability. In Michael S. Kimmel & Michael A. Messner (Eds.), *Men's lives* (6th ed.). Boston, MA: Allyn & Bacon.

Gerson, Jeannie Suk. (2016, January 25). Who's afraid of gender-neutral bathrooms? *New Yorker*. Retrieved from http://www.newyorker.com/news/news-desk/whos-afraid-of-same-sex-bathrooms

Gerson, Kathleen. (2004, August). Understanding work and family through a gendered lens. *Community, Work and Family, 7*(2), 163–178.

Gerson, Kathleen. (2010). *The unfinished revolution: How a new generation is reshaping family, work and gender in America*. Oxford, UK: Oxford University Press.

Gettler, Lee T., McDade, Thomas W., Feranil, Alan B., & Kuzawa, & Christopher W. (2011). Longitudinal evidence that fatherhood decreases testosterone in human males. *Proceedings of the National Academy of Sciences, 108*(39), 16194–16199. doi:10.1073/pnas.1105403108

Gherovici, Patricia. (2010). *Please select your gender: From the invention of hysteria to the democratizing of transgenderism*. New York, NY: Routledge.

Gibson, David. (2015, May 18). US nuns say Vatican probe cleared up confusion, reinforced their mission. *Huffington Post*. Retrieved from http://www.huffingtonpost.com/2015/05/18/us-nuns-vatican-probe_n_7294678.html

Gibson, Katie L., & Wolske, Melanie. (2011). Disciplining sex in Hollywood: A critical comparison of *Blue Valentine* and *Black Swan*. *Women & Language, 34*(2), 79–96.

Gibson-Davis, Christina M. (2011). Mothers but not wives: The increasing lag between non-marital births and marriage. *Journal of Marriage and Family, 73*, 1–15.

Giffney, Noreen. (2004). Denormatizing queer theory: More than (simply) lesbian and gay studies. *Feminist Theory, 5*(1), 73–78.

Gill, Rosalind. (2017). Rethinking masculinity: Men and their bodies. Retrieved from http://fathom.lse.ac.uk/Seminars/21701720/

Gill, Rosalind, Henwood, Karen, & McLean, Carl. (2005). Body projects and the regulation of normative masculinity. *Body & Society, 11*(1), 37–62.

Gilligan, Carol. (1982). *In a different voice: Psychological theory and women's development*. Cambridge, MA: Harvard University Press.

Gladden, R. M., Vivolo-Kantor, Alana M., Hamburger, Merle E., & Lumpkin, Corey D. (2014). *Bullying surveillance among youths: Uniform definitions for public health and recommended data elements, Version 1.0*. Atlanta, GA: National Center for Injury Prevention and Control, Centers for Disease Control and Prevention, and U.S. Department of Education. Retrieved from https://www.cdc.gov/violenceprevention/pdf/bullying-definitions-final-a.pdf

Glenn, Evelyn Nakano. (2008). Yearning for lightness. *Gender & Society, 22*, 281–302.

Goffman, Erving. (1963). *Behavior in public places: Notes on the social organization of gatherings*. New York, NY: Free Press.

Goffman, Erving. (1979). *Gender advertisements*. New York, NY: Harper & Row.

Goldsmith, Daena, J. (2004). *Communicating social support*. New York, NY: Cambridge University Press.

Goldsmith, Daena J., & Fulfs, Patricia A. (1999). You just don't have the evidence: An analysis of claims and evidence in Deborah Tannen's *You just don't understand*. In Michael E. Roloff (Ed.), *Communication yearbook* (Vol. 22, pp. 1–49). Thousand Oaks, CA: Sage.

Goldstein, Jessica. (2016). Why the star of Louis Vuitton's womenswear campaign is a 17-year-old boy. *Thinkprogress.* Retrieved from https://thinkprogress.org/why-the-star-of-louis-vuittons-womenswear-campaign-is-a-17-year-old-boy-89d70f334487/

Good, Catherine, Aronson, Joshua, & Harder, Jayne Ann. (2008). Problems in the pipeline: Stereotype threat and women's achievement in higher-level math courses. *Journal of Applied Development Psychology, 29,* 17–28.

Goodwin, Marjorie Harness, & Kyratzis, Amy. (2014). Language and gender in peer interactions among children and youth. In Susan Ehrlich, Miriam Meyerhoff, & Janet Holmes (Eds.), *The handbook of language, gender and sexuality* (2nd ed., pp. 509–528). West Sussex, UK: Wiley, Blackwell.

Gottman, John, M. (1994). *What predicts divorce? The relationship between marital processes and marital outcomes.* Hillsdale, NJ: Erlbaum.

Grabe, Shelly, Hyde, Janet Shibley, & Lindberg, Sara M. (2007). Body objectification and depression in adolescents: The role of gender, shame and rumination. *Psychology of Women Quarterly, 31,* 164–175.

Gramsci, Antonio, Rosenthal, Raymond, & Rosengarten, Frank. (1993). *Letters from prison.* New York, NY: Columbia University Press.

Grantham, Anita. (2016, May 5). Give Marissa a f*%*ing break. Retrieved from https://www.linkedin.com/pulse/give-marissa-f-break-anita-grantham?published=u

Green, Kyle, & Van Oort, Madison. (2013). "We wear no pants": Selling the crisis of masculinity in the 2010 Super Bowl commercials. *Signs, 38*(3), 695–719.

Green, Laci. (2015, April 10). Should Rihanna say bitch? [YouTube video]. *Braless.* Retrieved from https://www.youtube.com/watch?v=huP53VG7pLg

Greenberg, Julie A. (1999, Summer). Defining male and female: Intersexuality and the collision between law and biology. *Arizona Law Review, 41,* 265–328.

Greenberg, Julie, A. (2012). *Intersexuality and the law: Why sex matters.* New York, NY: New York University Press.

Gregg, Nina. (1993). Politics of identity/politics of location: Women workers organizing in a postmodern world. *Women's Studies in Communication, 16*(1), 1–33.

Griffiths, Brent. (2016, September 26). Pence denies "broad shoulders" remark is about Trump's masculinity. *Politico.* Retrieved from http://www.politico.com/story/2016/09/trump-broad-shoulders-mike-pence-228703

Grogen, Sarah. (2017). *Body image: Understanding body dissatisfaction in men, women and children* (3rd ed.). Abingdon, UK: Routledge.

Gross, Terry. (2017, May 1). W. Kamau Bell's "awkward thoughts" on racism and Black comedy. *Fresh Air.* Retrieved from http://www.npr.org/2017/05/01/526387278/w-kamau-bells-awkward-thoughts-on-racism-and-black-comedy

Guerrero, Laura K., Andersen, Peter A., & Afifi, Walid A. (2018). *Close encounters: Communication in relationships* (5th ed.). Thousand Oaks, CA: Sage.

Guerrilla Girls. (1995). *Confessions of the Guerrilla Girls.* New York, NY: HarperPerennial.

Gunning, Isabelle R. (1997). Arrogant perception, world traveling, and multicultural feminism: The case of female genital surgeries. In Adrien Katherine Wing (Ed.), *Critical race feminism: A reader* (pp. 352–360). New York, NY: New York University Press.

Guo, Jeff. (2016, January 8). Sorry, grammar nerds. The singular "they" has been declared Word of the Year. *Washington Post.* Retrieved from https://www.washingtonpost.com/news/wonk/wp/2016/01/08/donald-trump-may-win-this-years-word-of-the-year/

Gutierrez, Lisa. (2016, June 27). Teen's wage disparity at KCK pizza shop fired up equal-pay debate—and Hillary Clinton. *Kansas City Star.* Retrieved from http://www.kansascity.com/news/local/article86226237.html

Hackman, Heather. W. (2012). Teaching LBGTQI issues in higher education: An interdependent framework. *Diversity & Democracy: Civic Learning for Shared Futures, 15*(1), 2–4.

Haddock, Shelley A., Zimmerman, Toni Schindler, & Lyness, Kevin P. (2003). Changing gender norms: Transitional dilemmas. In Froma Walsh (Ed.), *Normal family processes: Growing diversity and complexity* (3rd ed., pp. 301–336). New York, NY: Guilford Press.

Hadewijch. (1980). *The complete works* (Mother Columba Hart, O.S.B., Trans.). New York, NY: Paulist Press. (Original work published ca. mid-1200s)

Halberstam, J. (1998). *Female masculinity*. Durham, NC: Duke University Press.

Halberstam, J. (2005). *In a queer time & place*. New York, NY: New York University Press.

Hall, Donald E. (Ed.). (1994). *Muscular Christianity: Embodying the Victorian age.* Cambridge, UK: Cambridge University Press.

Hall, Edward T. (1966). *The hidden dimension*. New York, NY: Doubleday.

Hall, Kira. (2000). Performativity. *Journal of Linguistic Anthropology, 9*(1–2), 184–187.

Hall, Kira. (2009). Boys' talk: Hindi, moustaches and masculinity in New Delhi. In Pia Pichler & Eva Eppler (Eds.), *Gender and spoken interaction* (pp. 139–162). New York, NY: Palgrave Macmillan.

Hall, Stuart. (1993). Encoding, decoding. In Simon During (Ed.), *The cultural studies reader* (pp. 90–103). London, England: Routledge.

Hamilton, Laura, Geist, Claudia, & Powell, Brian. (2011). Marital name change as a window into gender attitudes. *Gender & Society, 25*, 145–175.

Hanke, Robert. (1998, May). Theorizing masculinity with/in the media. *Communication Theory, 8*(2), 183–203.

Hanson, Katherine, Guilfoy, Vivian, & Pillai, Sarita. (2009). *More than Title IX: How equity in education has shaped the nation*. Lanham, MD: Rowman & Littlefield Publishers.

Harbach, Meredith Johnson. (2016, March). Sexualization, sex discrimination, and public school dress codes. *University of Richmond law Review, 50*, 1039–1062.

Harding, Sandra. (1995). Subjectivity, experience, and knowledge: An epistemology from/for Rainbow Coalition politics. In Judith Roof & Robyn Weigman (Eds.), *Who can speak? Authority and critical identity* (pp. 120–136). Urbana: University of Illinois Press.

Harris, Frank, III, Palmer, Robert T., & Struve, Laura E. (2011). "Cool posing on campus": A qualitative study of masculinities and gender expression among Black men at a private research institution. *Journal of Negro Education, 80*(1), 47–62.

Harris, Morgan. (2016). Gender differences in experiences with sexual objectification. *McNair Scholars Research Journal, 12*(1). Retrieved from http://scholarworks.boisestate.edu/mcnair_journal/vol12/iss1/12

Harvey, Adia M. (2005, December). Becoming entrepreneurs: Intersections of race, class, and gender at the Black beauty salon. *Gender & Society, 19*(6), 789–808.

Hayden, Sara. (2017). Michelle Obama, mom-in-chief: The racialized rhetorical contexts of maternity. *Women's Studies in Communication, 40*(1), 11–28. doi:10.1080/07491409.2016.1182095

Hays, Sharon. (1996). *The cultural contradictions of motherhood*. New Haven, CT: Yale University Press.

Hazard, Mrs. B. (1910, June). New York State Association opposed to Woman Suffrage. *The Chautauquan, 88*.

Hearn, Jeff. (1993). Emotive subjects: Organizational men, organizational masculinities and the (de)construction of "emotions." In Stephen Fineman (Ed.), *Emotion in organizations* (pp. 142–166). London, England: Sage.

Heavey, Christopher L., Christensen, Andrew, & Malamuth, Neil M. (1995). The longitudinal impact of demand and withdrawal during marital conflict. *Journal of Consulting and Clinical Psychology, 63*, 797–801.

Hegde, Radha Sarma. (1995). Recipes for change: Weekly help for Indian women. *Women's Studies in Communication, 18*(2), 177–188.

Henley, Nancy. (1977). *Body politics: Power, sex, and nonverbal communication.* Englewood Cliffs, NJ: Prentice Hall.

Henley, Nancy, & Kramarae, Cheris. (1991). Gender, power, and miscommunication. In Nikolas Coupland, Howard Giles, & John M. Wiemann (Eds.), *"Miscommunication" and problematic talk* (pp. 18–43). Newbury Park, CA: Sage.

Henn, Steve, & Jiang, Jess. (2015, April 8). A 12-year-old girl takes on the video game industry. *National Public Radio.* Retrieved from http://www.npr.org/sections/money/2015/04/08/398297737/a-12-year-old-girl-takes-on-the-video-game-industry?utm_source=facebook.com&utm_medium=social&utm_campaign=npr&utm_term=nprnews&utm_content=20150408

Hennessy, Rosemary. (1995). Subjects, knowledges, . . . and all the rest: Speaking for what. In Judith Roof & Robyn Weigman (Eds.), *Who can speak? Authority and critical identity* (pp. 137–150). Urbana: University of Illinois Press.

Henson v. City of Dundee, 682 F.2d at 902 (11th Cir. 1982).

Herman, Jody L. (2013). Gendered restrooms and minority stress: The public regulation of gender and its impact on transgender people's lives. *Journal of Public Management & Social Policy, 19*(1), 65–80.

Hermans, Erno J., Ramsey, Nick F., & van Honk, Jack. (2008). Exogenous testosterone enhances responsiveness to social threat in the neural circuitry of social aggression in humans. *Journal of Biological Psychiatry, 63*, 263–270. doi:10.1016/j.biopsych.2007.05.013

Herring, Susan C., & Kapidzic, Ludwig-Maximilians. (2015). In James D. Wright (Ed.), *International encyclopedia of social and behavioral sciences* (2nd ed.). Oxford, UK: Elsevier.

Hershcovis, M. Sandy, Turner, Nick, Barling, Julian, Arnold, Kara A., Dupré, Kathryne E., Inness, Michelle, LeBlanc, Manon Mireille, & Sivanathan, Niro. (2007). Predicting workplace aggression: A meta-analysis. *Journal of Applied Psychology, 92*(1), 228–238.

Heymsfield, Steven B., Muller, Manfred J., Bosy-Westphal, Anja, Thomas, Diana, & Shen, Wei. (2012). Human brain mass: Similar body composition associations as observed across mammals. *American Journal of Human Biology, 24*, 475–485.

Hildegard of Bingen. (1990). *Scivias* (Mother Columba Hart & Jane Bishop, Trans.). New York, NY: Paulist Press. (Original work published ca. 1151/1152)

Hill, Annie. (2016). SlutWalk as a perifeminist response to rape logic: The politics of reclaiming a name. *Communication & Critical/Cultural Studies, 13*(1), 23–39.

Hinde, Robert A. (2005). A suggested structure for a science of relationships. *Personal Relationships, 2*(1), 1–15.

Hinduja, Sameer, & Patchin, Justin W. (2010). *Sexting: A brief guide for educators and parents.* Cyberbullying Research Center. Retrieved from https://cyberbullying.org/sexting-a-brief-guide-for-educators-and-parents-2

Hines, Caitlin. (1999). Rebaking the pie: The woman as dessert metaphor. In Mary Bucholtz, A. C. Liang, & Laurel A. Sutton (Eds.), *Reinventing identities: The gendered self in discourse* (pp. 145–162). New York, NY: Oxford University Press.

Hitchens, Christopher. (2007, January). Why women aren't funny. *Vanity Fair.* Retrieved from http://www.vanityfair.com/culture/2007/01/hitchens200701

Hochschild, Arlie Russell. (2003). *The second shift* (2nd ed.). New York, NY: Avon Books.

Hodel, Christina. (2014). Performing the ultimate grand supreme: Approval, gender and identity in Toddlers & Tiaras. *Girlhood Studies, 7*(2), · 113–129. doi:10.3167/ghs.2014.070208

Hoerl, Kristen, & Casey, Kelly. (2010). The post-nuclear family and the depoliticization of unplanned pregnancy in *Knocked Up, Juno*, and *Waitress. Communication & Critical/Cultural Studies, 7*, 360–380. doi:10.1080/14791420.2010.523432

Hoff Sommers, Christina. (2016, June 17). 6 feminist myths that will not die. *Time.* Retrieved from http://time.com/3222543/wage-pay-gap-myth-feminism/

Holley, Sarah R., Sturm, Virginia E., & Levinson, Robert W. (2010). Exploring the basis for gender differences in the demand-withdraw pattern. *Journal of Homosexuality, 57*, 666–684.

Holmes, Janet. (1997). Story-telling in New Zealand women's and men's talk. In Ruth Wodak (Ed.), *Gender and discourse* (pp. 263–293). London, England: Sage.

Holmstrom, Amanda J. (2009). Sex and gender similarities and differences in communication values in same-sex and cross-sex friendships. *Communication Quarterly, 57*(2), 224–238.

Hondagneu-Sotelo, Pierette, & Avila, Ernestine. (1997, October). "I'm here but I'm there": The meanings of Latina transitional motherhood [Electronic version]. *Gender & Society, 11*(5), 548–569.

hooks, bell. (1989). *Talking back: Thinking feminist, thinking black.* Boston, MA: South End Press.

hooks, bell. (1992). *Black looks: Race and representation.* Boston, MA: South End Press.

hooks, bell. (2016, May 9). Moving beyond pain. *The bell hooks Institute.* Retrieved from http://www.bellhooksinstitute.com/blog/2016/5/9/moving-beyond-pain

Hoover, Stewart M., Clark, Lynn Schofield, & Alters, Diane F. (2004). *Media, home and family.* New York, NY: Routledge.

Horkheimer, Max, & Adorno, Theodor W. (1972). *Dialectic of enlightenment* (John Cumming, Trans.). New York, NY: Herder and Herder.

Horney, Karen. (1967). The flight from womanhood. In Karen Horney (Ed.), *Feminine psychology* (pp. 54–70). New York, NY: W. W. Norton. (Reprinted from *The International Journal of Psycho-Analysis*, pp. 324–339, by Karen Horney, 1926)

Horvath, Miranda A., Hegarty, Peter, Tyler, Suzannah, & Mansfield, Sophie. (2012, November). "Lights on at the end of the party": Are lads' mags mainstreaming dangerous sexism? *British Journal of Psychology, 103*(4), 454–471.

Horwitz, Linda Diane. (1998). *Transforming appearance into rhetorical argument: Rhetorical criticism of public speeches of Barbara Jordan, Lucy Parsons, and Angela Y. Davis.* Unpublished doctoral dissertation, Northwestern University, Evanston, IL.

Hugenberg, Kurt, & Bodenhausen, Galen V. (2003). Facing prejudice: Implicit prejudice and the perception of facial threat. *Psychological Science, 14*(6), 640–643.

Hunt, Lynn. (Ed.). (1993). *The invention of pornography.* New York, NY: Zone Books.

Hyde, Janet Shibley. (2005). The gender similarities hypothesis. *American Psychologist, 60*(6), 581–592.

Hyde, Janet Shibley. (2007). New directions in the study of gender similarities and differences. *Current Directions in Psychological Science, 16*(5), 259–263.

In the raw: The female gaze on the nude. (2016, May 4–June 4). *Untitled Space.* Retrieved from http://untitled-space.com/in-the-raw-the-female-gaze-on-the-nude/

Ingoldsby, Bron B., & Smith, Suzanna. (Eds.). (2006). *Families in multicultural perspective* (2nd ed.). New York, NY: Guilford Press.

Ingraham, Chrys. (2008). *White weddings: Romancing heterosexuality in popular culture* (2nd ed.). New York, NY: Routledge.

Inness, Sherrie A. (Ed.). (2004). *Action chicks: New images of tough women in popular culture.* New York, NY: Palgrave MacMillan.

Intersex Society of North America. (2008). What is intersex? Retrieved from http://www.isna.org/faq/what_is_intersex

Irons, Jenny. (1998). The shaping of activist recruitment and participation: A study of women in the Mississippi civil rights movement. *Gender & Society, 12*(6), 692–709.

Ivy, Diana. (2011). *GenderSpeak: Personal effectiveness in gender communication* (5th ed.). Boston, MA: Allyn & Bacon.

J.T. (2016, January 21). How racially skewed are the Oscars? *The Economist.* Retrieved from http://www.economist.com/blogs/prospero/2016/01/film-and-race

Jack, Jordynn. (2012). Gender copia: Feminist rhetorical perspectives on an autistic concept of sex/gender. *Women's Studies in Communication, 35*, 1–17.

Jackson, Ronald L., II, & Dangerfield, Celnisha L. (2003). Defining Black masculinity as cultural property: Toward an identity negotiation paradigm. In Larry A. Samovar & Richard E. Porter (Eds.), *Intercultural communication: A reader* (pp. 120–130). Belmont, CA: Wadsworth.

Jagsi, Reshma, Griffith, Kent A., Stewart, Abigail, Sambuco, Dana, DeCastro, Rochelle, & Ubel, Peter A. (2012). Gender differences in the salaries of physician researchers. *Journal of the American Medical Association, 307*(22), 2410–2417.

James, Carolyn Custis. (2011). *Half the church: Recapturing God's global vision for women.* Grand Rapids, MI: Zondervan.

James, Susan Donaldson. (2011, April 13). J. Crew ad with boy's pink toenails creates stir. *ABCNews.com.* Retrieved from http://abcnews.go.com/Health/crew-ad-boy-painting-toenails-pink-stirs-transgender/story?id=13358903

Japp, Phyllis. (1993). Angeline Grimké Weld. In Karlyn Kohrs Campbell (Ed.), *Women public speakers in the United States, 1800–1925* (pp. 206–215). Westport, CN: Greenwood Press.

Jervis, Rick. (2014, November 17). Controversial Texas textbooks headed to classroom. *USA Today.* Retrieved from http://usat.ly/1qPAt83

Jhally, Sut. (Producer/Writer/Editor). (2009). *Codes of gender* [Motion picture]. (Available from Media Education Foundation, 26 Center Street, Northampton, MA 01060)

Jhally, Sut. (Director). (2010). Asking for it: The ethics and erotics of sexual consent, A lecture with Dr. Harry Brod. Retrieved from http://www.mediaed.org/cgibin/commerce.cgi?preadd=action&key=243

Joel, Daphna, Berman, Zohar, Tavor, Ido, Wexler, Nadav, Gaber, Olga, Stein, Yaniv, Shefi, Nisan, Pool, Jared, Urchs, Sebastian, Margullies, Daniel S, Liem, Franziskus, Hänggi, Jürgen, Jäncke, Lutz, & Assaf, Yaniv. (2015). Sex beyond the genitalia: The human brain mosaic. *Proceedings of the National Academy of Sciences, 112*(50), 15468–15473. doi:10.1073/pnas.1509654112

Johansson, Thomas. (2011). Fatherhood in transition: Paternity leave and changing masculinities. *Journal of Family Communication, 11*(3), 165–180.

Johnson, Bradley. (2015, July 5). Big spenders on a budget: What the top 200 U.S. advertisers are doing to spend smarter. *Advertising Age.* Retrieved from http://adage.com/article/advertising/big-spenders-facts-stats-top-200-u-s-advertisers/299270/

Johnson, Fern. (1996). Friendship among women: Closeness in dialogue. In Julia T. Wood (Ed.), *Gendered relationships: A reader* (pp. 79–94). Mountain View, CA: Mayfield.

Johnson, Jessica. (2010, March 2). "Cool pose culture" hurts young black men. *Online Athens Banner-Herald.* Retrieved from http://onlineathens.com/stories/030210/opi_569412104.shtml

Johnson, Michael P. (2006). Gendered communication and intimate partner violence. In Bonnie J. Dow & Julia T. Wood (Eds.), *The Sage handbook of gender and communication* (pp. 71–87). Thousand Oaks, CA: Sage.

Johnson, Michael P. (2011). Gender and types of intimate partner violence: A response to an anti-feminist literature review. *Aggression and Violent Behavior, 16*(4), 289–296.

Jones, Susanne M., & Dindia, Kathryn. (2004, Winter). A meta-analytic perspective on sex equity in the classroom. *Review of Educational Research, 64*(4), 443–471.

Jordan-Zachery, Julia S. (2007). Am I a Black woman or a woman who is Black? A few thoughts on the meaning of intersectionality. *Politics & Gender, 3,* 254–263. doi:10.1017/S1743923X07000074

Joshi, Aparna, Son, Jooyeon, & Roh, Hyuntak. (2015). When can women close the gap? A meta-analytic test of sex differences in performance and rewards. *Academy of Management Journal,* 58, p. 1516–1545.

Journal of Marriage and the Family. (2001). Inside cover. *63*(1).

Julian of Norwich. (1978). *Showings* (Edmund Colledge, O. S. A., & James Walsh, S. J., Trans.). New York, NY: Paulist Press. (Original work published ca. 1393)

Kachru, Braj B. (Ed.). (1982). *The other tongue: English across cultures.* Oxford, UK: Pergamon Press.

Kafer, Alison. (2013). *Feminist, queer, crip.* Bloomington: Indiana University Press.

Kane, Emily W. (2006). "No way my boys are going to be like that!" Parents' responses to children's gender nonconformity. *Gender & Society, 20*(2), 149–176.

Kane, Emily W. (2009). "I wanted a soul mate": Gendered anticipation and frameworks of accountability in parents' preferences for sons and daughters. *Symbolic Interaction, 32*(4), 372–389.

Kane, Emily W. (2012). *The gender trap: Parents and the pitfalls of raising boys and girls.* New York: New York University Press.

Kaplan, E. Ann. (1983). Is the gaze male? In Ann Snitow, Christine Stansell, & Sharon Thompson (Eds.), *Powers of desire: The politics of sexuality* (pp. 309–327). New York, NY: Monthly Review Press.

Kapur, Ratna. (2005). *Erotic justice: Law and the new politics of postcolonialism.* Portland, OR: Cavendish Publishing.

Kapur, Ratna. (2012). Pink chaddis and SlutWalk couture: The postcolonial politics of feminism lite. *Feminist Legal Studies, 20,* 1–20.

Karraker, Meg Wilkes, & Grochowski, Janet R. (2012). *Families with futures: Family studies into the 21st century* (2nd ed.). New York, NY: Routledge.

Katz, Jackson. (2003). *Wrestling with manhood: Boys, bullying and battering* [Videotape]. Northampton, MA: Media Education Foundation.

Katz, Jackson. (2010). It's the masculinity, stupid: A cultural studies analysis of media, the presidency, and pedagogy. In Z. Leonardo (Ed.), *Handbook of cultural politics and education* (pp. 477–507). Rotterdam, The Netherlands: Sense Publishers.

Kaufman, Gloria, & Blakeley, Kay. (1994). *Pulling our own strings: Feminist humor and satire.* Bloomington: Indiana University Press.

Keith, Genevieve Amaris. (2009). *Hailing gender: The rhetorical actions of greeting cards.* Unpublished master's thesis, George Washington University, Washington, DC. Retrieved from http://gradworks.umi.com/14/64/1464059.html

Keller, Alyse, & Gibson, Katie L. (2014). Appropriating the male gaze in *The Hunger Games:* The rhetoric of a resistant female vantage point. *Texas Speech Communication Journal, 38*(1), 21–30.

Kellerman, Kathy. (1992). Communication: Inherently strategic and primarily automatic. *Communication Monographs, 59,* 288–300.

Kelley, Harold H., Berscheid, Ellen, Christensen, Andrew, Harvey, John H., Huston, Ted L., Levinger, George, McClintock, Evie, Peplau, Letitia Anne, & Peterson, Donald R. (1983). *Close relationships.* New York, NY: W. H. Freeman.

Kells, Crystal. (2017, June). My son, Cian. Yes, my son who wears dresses. *Bored Panda*. Retrieved from http://www.boredpanda.com/my-son-cian-yes-my-son-who-wears-dresses/

Kelly, Casey Ryan. (2016). The man-pocalypse: Doomsday preppers and the rituals of apocalyptic manhood. *Text and Performance Quarterly, 36*(2–3), 95–114. doi:10.1080/10462937.2016.1158415

Kelly, Joan B., & Johnson, Michael P. (2008). Differentiation among types of intimate partner violence: Research update and implications for interventions. *Family Court Review, 46*(3), 476–499.

Kemp, Alice Abel. (1994). *Women's work: Degraded and devalued*. Upper Saddle River, NJ: Prentice Hall.

Keren, Roger. (2012, March 15). The language of gender violence. *Middlebury Magazine*. Retrieved from http://sites.middlebury.edu/middmag/2012/03/15/gender-violence/

Khan, Anber Younnus., & Kamal, Anila. (2010). Exploring reactions to invasion of personal space in university students. *Journal of Behavioural Sciences, 20*(2), 80–99.

Kierkegaard, Patrick. (2008). Video games and aggression. *International Journal of Liability and Scientific Enquiry, 1*(4), 411–417.

Kikoski, John F., & Kikoski, Catherine Kano. (1999). *Reflexive communication in the culturally diverse workplace*. Westport, CT: Praeger.

Kilbourne, Jean (Creator), & Jhally, Sut (Director, Editor, Producer). (2010). *Still killing us softly 4* [Motion picture]. (Available from Media Education Foundation, 26 Center Street, Northampton, MA 01060)

Kim, Eugene. (2016, June 20). Yahoo CEO Marissa Mayer worked from her hospital bed shortly after having twins. *Business Insider*. Retrieved from http://www.businessinsider.com/marissa-mayer-worked-in-hospital-after-having-twins-2016-6

Kimmel, Michael S. (2012a). *The gendered society* (5th ed.). New York, NY: Oxford University Press.

Kimmel, Michael S. (2012b). *Manhood in America: A cultural history* (3rd ed.). New York, NY: Oxford Press.

Kingsley, Charles. (1857). *Two years ago*. Cambridge, UK: Macmillan.

Kirtley, Michelle D., & Weaver, James B., III. (Fall, 1999). Exploring the impact of gender role self-perception on communication style. *Women's Studies in Communication, 22*(2), 190–204.

Kissling, Elizabeth Arveda. (1991). Street harassment: The language of sexual terrorism. *Discourse and Society, 2*(4), 451–460.

Kitzinger, Celia. (2005). Heteronormativity in action: Reproducing the heterosexual nuclear family in after-hours medical calls. *Social Problems, 52*(4), 477–498.

Kivel, Paul. (2002). *Uprooting racism: How White people can work for racial justice* (Rev. ed.). Gabriola Island, British Columbia, Canada: New Society.

Klassen, Chris. (2003, November). Confronting the gap: Why religion needs to be given more attention in women's studies. *Thirdspace: A Journal for Emerging Feminist Scholars, 3*(1). Retrieved from http://journals.sfu.ca/thirdspace/index.php/journal/article/viewArticle/klassen/165

Kleinman, S. (2002). Why sexist language matters. *Qualitative Sociology, 25*(2), 299–304.

Knudson-Martin, Carmen. (2012). Changing gender norms in families and society: Toward equality and complexities. In Froma Walsh (Ed.), *Normal family processes: Growing diversity and complexity* (pp. 324–346). New York, NY: Guilford Press.

Kochman, Thomas. (1990). Force fields in Black and White. In Donald Carbaugh (Ed.), *Cultural communication in intercultural contact* (pp. 193–194). Hillsdale, NJ: Erlbaum.

Kohli, Sonali. (2017, February 23). What Trump's policy means for transgender students in California. *Los Angeles Times*. Retrieved from http://www.latimes.com/local/education/la-me-edu-transgender-students-california-20170223-story.html

Kolesnikova, Natalia, & Liu, Yang. (2011, October). Gender wage gap may be much smaller than most think. *The Regional Economist*, 14–15.

Kopelman, Richard J., Shea-Van Fossen, Rita J., Paraskevas, Eletherios, Lawter, Leanna, & Prottas, David J. (2009). The bride is keeping her name: A 35-year retrospective analysis of trends and correlates. *Social Behavior and Personality*, 37(5), 687–700.

Kosciw, Joseph G., Greytak, Emily A., Palmer, Neal A., & Boesen, Madelyn J. (2014). *The 2013 national school climate survey*. New York, NY: Gay, Lesbian & Straight Education Network. Retrieved from https://www.glsen.org/sites/default/files/2013%20 National%20School%20Climate%20Survey%20Full%20Report_0.pdf

Kotthoff, Helga. (2006). Gender and humor: The state of the art. *Journal of Pragmatics*, 38(1), 4–25.

Kovvali, Silpa. (2015, December 5). Let's call everyone "they": Gender-neutral language should be the norm, not the exception. *Salon*. Retrieved from http://www.salon .com/2015/12/05/lets_call_everyone_they_gender_neutral_language_should_be_the_ norm_not_the_exception/?utm_source=Tumblr&utm_medium=Tumblr+ Share&utm_campaign=Tumblr

Kowal, Donna M. (1996). *The public advocacy of Emma Goldman: An anarcho-feminist stance on human rights*. Unpublished doctoral dissertation, University of Pittsburgh, PA.

Kramarae, Cheris. (1992). Harassment and everyday life. In Lana Rakow (Ed.), *Women making meaning: New feminist directions in communication* (pp. 100–120). New York, NY: Routledge.

Kramarae, Cheris, & Treichler, Paula A. (1992). *Amazons, bluestockings and crones: A feminist dictionary* (2nd ed.). London, England: Pandora Press.

Kramer, Laura. (2005). *The sociology of gender: A brief introduction* (2nd ed.). Los Angeles, CA: Roxbury.

Krasnova, Hanna, Veltri, Natasha F., Eling, Nicole, & Buxmann, Peter. (2017). Why men and women continue to use social networking sites: The role of gender differences. *Journal of Strategic Information Systems*. Retrieved from http://dx.doi.org/10.1016/j.jsis.2017.01.004

Krebs, Christopher, Lindquist, Christine, Berzofsky, Marcus, Shook-Sa, Bonnie, Peterson, Kimberly, Planty, Michael, Langon, Lynn, & Stroop, Jessica. (2016). *Campus climate survey validation study: Final technical report*. Washington, DC: U.S. Department of Justice, Bureau of Justice Statistics. Retrieved from https://www.bjs.gov/content/pub/pdf/ccsvsftr.pdf

Krøløkke, Charlotte, & Sørensen, Anne Scott. (2006). *Gender communication theories and analyses: From silence to performance*. Thousand Oaks, CA: Sage.

Kunkel, Dale, Eyal, Keren, Finnerty, Keli, Biely, Erica, & Donnerstein, Edward. (2005, November). *Sex on TV 4*. Menlo Park, CA: Kaiser Family Foundation. Retrieved from http://www.kff.org/entmedia/upload/sex-on-tv-4-full-report.pdf

Kwan, Samantha. (2010). Navigating public spaces: Gender, race, and body privilege in everyday life. *Feminist Formations*, 22(2), 144–166.

Kyratzis, Amy, & Tarim, Seyda D. (2010). Using directives to construct egalitarian or hierarchical relationships: Turkish middle-class preschool girls' socialization about gender, affect and context in peer conversations. *First Language*, 30(3–4), 473–492.

Lacan, Jacques. (1998). *The four fundamental concepts of psychoanalysis. The seminar of Jacques Lacan, Book 11* (1st American ed.). New York, NY: W. W. Norton.

Lakoff, Robin. (1975). *Language and woman's place*. New York, NY: Harper & Row.

Langman, Lauren. (2008). Punk, porn and resistance: Carnivalization and the body in popular culture. *Current Sociology*, 56(4), 657–677.

LaScotte, Darren K. (2106). Singular *they*: An empirical study of generic pronoun use. *American Speech*, 91(1), 62–80.

Lauzen, Martha M. (2016, September). *Boxed in 2015–16: Women on screen and behind the scenes in television.* San Diego, CA: Center for the Study of Women in Television & Film, San Diego State University. Retrieved from http://womenintvfilm.sdsu.edu/files/2015-16-Boxed-In-Report.pdf

Lawrence, Charles R., III. (1993). If he hollers let him go: Regulating racist speech on campus. In Mari J. Matsuda et al. (Eds.), *Words that wound* (pp. 53–88). Boulder. CO: Westview Press.

Leaper, Campbell, & Robnett, Rachael D. (2011). Women are more likely than men to use tentative language, aren't they? A meta-analysis testing for gender differences and moderators. *Psychology of Women Quarterly, 35*(1), 129–142.

Lee, Emily S. (2011). The epistemology of the question of authenticity, in place of strategic essentialism. *Hypatia, 26*(2), 258–279.

Lee, Lin-Lee. (2004). Pure persuasion: A case study of *Nüshu* or "women's script" discourses. *Quarterly Journal of Speech, 90*, 403–421.

Leeds-Hurwitz, Wendy. (2009). Social construction of reality. In Karen A. Foss & Stephen W. Littlejohn (Eds.), *Encyclopedia of communication theory* (pp. 891–894). Thousand Oaks, CA: Sage.

LeMaster, Benny. (2015). Discontents of being and becoming fabulous on *RuPaul's Drag U*: Queer criticism in neoliberal times. *Women's Studies in Communication, 38*, 167–186.

Lennard, Natasha. (2012, December 27). Transgender no longer a medical disorder. *Salon.* Retrieved from http://www.salon.com/2012/12/27/transgender_no_longer_a_medical_disorder

Lev, Arlene Istar, & Malpas, Jean. (2011). Exploring gender and sexuality in couples and families. In Arlene Istar Lev & Jean Malpas (Eds.), *At the edge: Exploring gender and sexuality in couples and families. AFTA Monograph Series, 7* (pp. 2–8). Washington, DC: American Family Therapy Academy.

Levin, Diane E., & Kilbourne, Jean. (2009). *So sexy so soon: The new sexualized childhood and what parents can do to protect their kids.* New York, NY: Ballantine Books.

Levine, Emma E., & Schweitzer, Maurice E. (2015). The affective and interpersonal consequences of obesity. *Organizational Behavior and Human Decision Processes, 127*, 66–84.

Li, Eric P. H., Min, Hyun Jeong, Belk, Russell W., Kimura, Junko, & Bahl, Shalini. (2008). Skin lightening and beauty in four Asian cultures. *Advances in Consumer Research, 35*, 444–449.

Lloyd, Moya. (2007). Radical democratic activism and the politics of resignification. *Constellations, 14*(1), 129–146.

Long, Jeffrey C., & Kittles, Rick A. (2003). Human genetic diversity and the nonexistence of biological races. *Human Biology, 75*(4), 449–471.

Lorber, Judith. (1994). *Paradoxes of gender.* New Haven, CT: Yale University Press.

Lorber, Judith, & Martin, Patricia Yancy. (2011). The socially constructed body: Insights from feminist theory. In Peter Kivisto (Ed.), *Illuminating social life: Classical and contemporary theory revisited* (5th ed., pp. 279–304). Thousand Oaks, CA: Sage.

Lorber, Judith, & Moore, Lisa Jean. (2007). *Gendered bodies: Feminist perspectives.* Los Angeles, CA: Roxbury.

Lorde, Audre. (1984). *Sister outsider.* Trumansberg, NY: Crossing Press.

Love, Heather K. (2011). Queers ____ this. In Janet Halley & Andrew Parker (Eds.), *After sex?: On writing since queer theory* (pp. 180–191). Durham, NC: Duke University Press.

Low, Setha M. (2003). Embodied space(s): Anthropological theories of body, space, and culture. *Space and Culture, 6*(9), 9–18.

Lynch, Annette. (1999). *Dress, gender, and cultural change: Asian American and African American rites of passage.* Oxford, UK: Berg.

Lynch, Annette. (2012). *Porn chic: Exploring the contours of raunch eroticism.* New York, NY: Berg.

Lynch, Annette, & Strauss, Michael. (2007). *Changing fashion: A critical introduction to trend analysis and meaning.* Oxford, UK: Berg.

Lyons, Terry. (2017, April 17). Switzer is "261" and fearless in Boston. *Huffington Post.* Retrieved from http://www.huffingtonpost.com/entry/switzer-is-261-and-fearless-in-boston_us_58f5ec96e4b0156697225276

MacMillan, Craig Dublin, Lynch, Annette, & Bradley, Linda Arthur. (2011). Agonic and hedonic power: The performance of gender by young adults on Halloween. *Paideusis—Journal for Interdisciplinary and Cross-cultural Studies, 5*, E1–E30.

MacNish, Melissa, & Gold-Peifer, Marissa. (2011). Families in transition: Supporting families of transgender youth. In Arlene Istar Lev & Jean Malpas (Eds.), *At the edge: Exploring gender and sexuality in couples and families. AFTA Monograph Series, 7* (pp. 34–42). Washington, DC: American Family Therapy Academy.

MacPhee, David, Farro, Samantha, & Canetto, Silvia Sara. (2013). Academic self-efficacy and performance of underrepresented STEM majors: Gender, ethnic, and social class patterns. *Analysis of Social Issues and Public Policy, 13*(1), 347–389.

Madden, Janice F. (2012). *Performance-support bias and the gender pay gap among stockbrokers* (PSC Working Paper Series, PSC 12–04). Retrieved from repository.upenn.edu/psc_working_papers/35

Maddux, Kristy. (2012). The feminized gospel: Aimee Semple McPherson and the gendered performance of Christianity. *Women's Studies in Communication, 35*, 42–67.

Madill, Cate. (2015, November 4). Keep an eye on vocal fry—it's all about power, status and gender. *The Conversation.* Retrieved from http://theconversation.com/keep-an-eye-on-vocal-fry-its-all-about-power-status-and-gender-45883

Magley, Vivki J., Gallus, Jessica A., & Bunk, Jennifer A. (2010). The gendered nature of workplace mistreatment. In J. C. Chrisler & D. R. McCreary (Eds.), *Handbook of gender research in psychology* (pp. 423–441). New York, NY: Springer.

Majors, Richard. (2001). The cool pose, how Black men present themselves as a spectacle of self-expression and agency, by adopting the cool pose. In Stephen M. Whitehead & Frank J. Barrett (Eds.), *The masculinities reader* (pp. 209–218). Cambridge, UK: Polity Press.

Majors, Richard, & Billson, Janet Mancini. (1992). *Cool pose: The dilemmas of Blackmanhood in America.* New York, NY: Lexington Books.

Maltz, Daniel N., & Borker, Ruth. (1982). A cultural approach to male-female miscommunication. In John J. Gumperz (Ed.), *Language and social identity* (pp. 196–216). Cambridge, UK: Cambridge University Press.

Manago, Adriana M., Graham, Michael B., Greenfield, Patricia M., & Salimkhan, Goldie. (2008). Self-presentation and gender on MySpace. *Journal of Applied Developmental Psychology, 29*, 446–458.

Mansbridge, Jane J. (1986). *Why we lost the ERA.* Chicago, IL: University of Chicago Press.

Mansbridge, Jane. (1998). Feminism and democracy. In Anne Phillips (Ed.), *Feminism and politics* (pp. 142–158). New York, NY: Oxford University Press.

Mapes, Megan. (2016). *Pushing back against gender, fashion and black masculinity: Jaden Smith does fashion and dress.* Unpublished. University of Northern Iowa, Cedar Falls.

Maracle, Lee. (1989, Spring). Moving over. *Trivia: A Journal of Ideas, 14*(Part II), 9–12.

Mare, Lesley Di, & Waldron, Vincent R. (2006). Researching gendered communication in Japan and the United States: Current limitations and alternative approaches. In Kathryn Dindia & Dan J. Canary (Eds.), *Sex differences and similarities in communication* (2nd ed., pp. 195–218). Mahwah, NJ: Erlbaum.

Martin, Patricia Yancey. (2003). "Said and done" versus "saying and doing": Gendering practices, practicing gender at work. *Gender & Society, 17*(3), 342–366.

Martin, Patricia Yancey. (2004, June). Gender as social institution. *Social Forces, 82*(4), 1249–1273.

Martin, Patricia Yancey. (2006). Practising gender at work: Further thoughts on reflexivity. *Gender, Work and Organization, 13*(3), 254–276.

Martin, Rod A. (2014). Humor and gender: An overview of psychological research. In Delia Chiaro & Raffaella Baccolini (Eds.), *Gender and humor: Interdisciplinary and international perspectives* (pp. 123–146). New York, NY: Routledge.

Martyna, Wendy. (1980a). Beyond the "he/man" approach: The case for nonsexist language. *Signs, 5,* 482–493.

Martyna, Wendy. (1980b). The psychology of the generic masculine. In Sally McConnell-Ginet, Ruth Borker, & Nelly Furman (Eds.), *Women and language in literature and society* (pp. 69–78). New York, NY: Praeger.

Martyna, Wendy. (1983). Beyond the he/man approach: The case for nonsexist language. In Barrie Thorne, Cheris Kramarae, & Nancy Henley (Eds.), *Language, gender, and society* (pp. 25–37). Rowley, MA: Newbury House.

Matsuda, Mari. J. (1993). Public response to racist speech: Considering the victim's story. In Mari J. Matsuda, Charles R. Lawrence III, Richard Delgado, & Kimberlè Williams Crenshaw (Eds.), *Words that wound* (pp. 17–51). Boulder, CO: Westview Press.

Matsuda, Mari J., Lawrence, Charles R., III, Delgado, Richard, & Crenshaw, Kimberlè Williams. (Eds.). (1993). *Words that wound.* Boulder, CO: Westview Press.

Matthews, Glenna R. (1992). *The rise of public woman: Woman's power and woman's place in the United States, 1630–1970.* New York, NY: Oxford University Press.

Matthews, Glenna. (1994). *The rise of public woman: Woman's power and woman's place in the United States 1630–1970.* New York, NY: Oxford University Press.

Maurer, Luca. (2017, February 22). Commentary: It's not really about bathrooms. *The Ithacan.* Retrieved from https://theithacan.org/opinion/commentary-its-not-really-about-bathrooms/

Mawdsley, Emma. (2007). The millennium challenge account: Neo-liberalism, poverty and security. *Review of International Economy, 14*(3), 487–509.

Maxwell, Angie, & Shields, Todd. (2017). *The impact of "modern sexism" on the 2016 presidential election.* Diane D. Blair Center of Southern Politics & Society. University of Arkansas. Retrieved from https://blaircenter.uark.edu/the-impact-of-modern-sexism/

May, Vivian M. (2015). *Pursuing intersectionality, unsettling dominant.* New York, NY: Routledge.

Mayer, Tamar. (Ed.). (2000). *Gender ironies of nationalism: Sexing the nation.* London, England: Routledge.

Maza, Carlos, & Brinker, Luke. (2014, March 20). 15 experts debunk right-wing transgender bathroom myth. *Media Matters.* Retrieved from https://mediamatters.org/research/2014/03/20/15-experts-debunk-right-wing-transgender-bathro/198533

McAndrew, Francis T. (2009). The interacting roles of testosterone and challenges to status in human male aggression. *Aggression and Violent Behavior, 14,* 330–335. doi:10.1016/j.avb.2009.04.006

McCall, Leslie. (2005). The complexity of intersectionality. *Signs, 30,* 1771–1800.

McConnell, Allen R., & Fazio, Russell H. (1996). Women as men and people: Effects of gender-marked language. *Personality and Social Psychology Bulletin, 22*(10), 1004–1013.

McConnell, Allen R., & Gavanski, I. (1994, May). *Women as men and people: Occupation title suffixes as primes.* Paper presented at the 66th Annual Meeting of the Midwestern Psychological Association, Chicago, IL.

McCormick, Maggie. (2011, May 12). Origins of boys in blue & girls in pink. *eHow.com.* Retrieved from http://www.ehow.com/info_8406183_origins-boys-blue-girls-pink.html#ixzz 1k9CNhVM5

McDonald, James. (2015). Organizational communication meets Queer Theory: Theorizing relations of "difference" differently. *Communication Theory, 25*, 310–329.

McDonald, Paula. (2012). Workplace sexual harassment 30 years on: A review of the literature. *International Journal of Management Reviews, 14*(1), 1–17.

McGlone, Matthew S., & Pfiester, R. Abigail. (2015). Stereotype threat and the evaluative context of communication. *Journal of Language and Social Psychology, 34*(2), 111–137.

McKee, Stacy (Writer), & Verica, Tom (Director). (2011, October 6). What is it about men [Television series episode]. In Shonda Rhimes (Executive producer), *Grey's Anatomy*. New York, NY: ABC Broadcasting. Retrieved from http://abc.go.com/watch/greys-anatomy/SH559058/VD55146633/what-is-it-about-men

McKenney, Sarah J., & Bigler, Rebecca S. (2016a). High heels, low grades: Internalized sexualization and academic orientation among adolescent girls. *Journal of Research on Adolescence, 26*(1), 30–36.

McKenney, Sarah J., & Bigler, Rebecca S. (2016b). Internalized sexualization and its relation to sexualized appearance, body surveillance, and body shame among early adolescent girls. *Journal of Early Adolescence, 36*(2), 171–197.

McKeown, Eamonn, Nelson, Simon, Anderson, Jane, Low, Nicola, & Elford, Jonathan. (2010). Disclosure, discrimination and desire: Experiences of Black and South Asian gay men in Britain. *Culture, Health & Sexuality: An International Journal for Research, Intervention and Care, 12*(7), 843–856.

McNair Barnett, Bernice. (1993). Invisible Southern Black women leaders in the movement: The triple constraints of gender, race, and class. *Gender & Society, 7*(2), 162–182.

Mendes, Kaitlynn. (2015). *SlutWalk: Feminism, activism and media*. New York, NY: Palgrave Macmillan.

Mendoza-Denton, Norma. (2008). *Homegirls: Language and cultural practice among Latina youth gangs*. Oxford, UK: Blackwell.

Meritor Savings Bank v. Vinson, 477 U.S. 57. (1986).

Merritt, Jonathan. (2016, August 30). How the Christian "masculinity" movement is ruining men. *Religion News Service*. Retrieved from http://religionnews.com/2016/08/30/how-the-christian-masculinity-movement-is-ruining-men/

Messer, Maddie. (2015, March 4). I'm a 12-year-old girl. Why don't the characters in my apps look like me? *Washington Post*. Retrieved from https://www.washingtonpost.com/posteverything/wp/2015/03/04/im-a-12-year-old-girl-why-dont-the-characters-in-my-apps-look-like-me/?utm_term=.2154cb6580cb

Messner, Michael S. (2016). *The gendered society* (6th ed.). New York, NY: Oxford University Press.

Miller, Casey, & Swift, Kate. (1993). Foreword. In Jane Mills, *Womanwords: A dictionary of words about women* (pp. ix–xii). New York, NY: Henry Holt.

Miller, Claire Cain. (2017, April 10). It's not just Fox: Why women don't report sexual harassment. *New York Times*. Retrieved from https://www.nytimes.com/2017/04/10/upshot/its-not-just-fox-why-women-dont-report-sexual-harassment.html?smid=nytcore-ipad-share&smprod=nytcore-ipad

Miller, Dora. (2015, September 22). New dress code controversial. *CBS2Iowa*. Retrieved from http://cbs2iowa.com/news/local/new-dress-code-controversial

Miller, Megan M., & James, Lori E. (2009). Is the generic pronoun *he* still comprehended as excluding women? *American Journal of Psychology, 122*(4), 483–496.

Mills, Jane. (1993). *Womanwords: A dictionary of words about women*. New York, NY: Henry Holt.

Mills, Sara. (2003). *Gender and politeness*. Cambridge, UK: Cambridge University Press.

Mink, Gwendolyn. (1995). *The wages of motherhood: Inequality in the welfare state, 1917–1942.* Ithaca, NY: Cornell University Press.

Minnich, Elizabeth Komarck. (1998). Education. In Wilma Mankiller, Gwendolyn Mink, Marysa Navarrao, Barbara Smith, & Gloria Steinem (Eds.), *The reader's companion to U.S. women's history* (pp. 163–167). New York, NY: Houghton Mifflin.

Minsky, Rosalind. (1998). *Psychoanalysis and culture: Contemporary states of mind.* New Brunswick, NJ: Rutgers University Press.

Mirabello, Doug (Creator). (2009–2013, 2016). *Toddlers and tiaras.* United States: Authentic Entertainment.

Mischel, Walter. (1966). A social learning view of sex differences in behavior. In Eleanor E. Maccoby (Ed.), *The development of sex differences* (pp. 93–106). Stanford, CA: Stanford University Press.

Mission & Vision. (n.d.). Women's March on Washington. Retrieved from https://www .womensmarch.com/mission/

Mitchell, Kimberly, J., Ybarra, Michele, L., & Korchmaros, Josephine D. (2014). Sexual harassment among adolescents of different sexual orientations and gender identities. *Child Abuse & Neglect, 38*(2), 280–295. Retrieved from http://www.sciencedirect.com/ science/article/pii/S0145213413002627

Mizejewski, Linda. (2014). *Pretty funny: Women comedians and body politics.* Austin: University of Texas Press.

Mohanty, Chandra Talpade. (2003). *Feminism without borders.* Durham, NC: Duke University Press.

Moore, Julia. (2014). Reconsidering childfreedom: A feminist exploration of discursive identity construction in childfree LiveJournal communities. *Women's Studies in Communication, 37*(2), 159–180. doi:10.1080/07491409.2014.909375

Moore, Michael. (2017, January 22). Interview with Smerconish. *CNN.* Retrieved from http:// www.cnn.com/videos/tv/2017/01/22/moore-trump-sounds-like-guy-who-lost.cnn

Moradi, Bonnie, & Huang, Yu-Ping. (2008). Objectification theory and psychology of women: A decade of advances and future directions. *Psychology of Women Quarterly, 32*, 377–398.

Morman, Mark T., & Floyd, Kory. (2006a). Good fathering: Father and son perceptions of what it means to be a good father. *Fathering, 4*(2), 113–136.

Morman, Mark T., & Floyd, Kory. (2006b). The good son: Men's perceptions of the characteristics of sonhood. In Kory Floyd & Mark T. Morman (Eds.), *Widening the family circle: New research on family communication* (pp. 37–55). Thousand Oaks, CA: Sage.

Morrell, Carolyn M. (1994). *Unwomanly conduct. The challenges of intentional childlessness.* New York, NY: Routledge.

Morris, Charles E., III (2009). Hard evidence: The vexations of Lincoln's queer corpus. In Barbara Biesecker & John Lucaites (Eds.), *Rhetoric, materiality, and politics* (pp. 185–214). New York, NY: Peter Lang.

Morris, Edward W. (2012). *Learning the hard way: Masculinity, place and the gender gap in education.* New Brunswick, NJ: Rutgers University Press.

Morris, Paul H., White, Jenny, Morrison, Edward R., Fisher, Kayleigh. (2013). High heels as supernormal stimuli: How wearing high heels affects judgements of female attractiveness. *Evolution & Human Behavior, 34*(3), 176–181.

Moss, Peter, & Deven, Fred. (Eds.). (1999). *Parental leave: Progress or pitfall?* The Hague: Netherlands. Interdisciplinary Demographic Institute.

Moya, Paula M. L. (1997). Postmodernism, "realism," and the politics of identity: Cherríe Moraga and Chicana feminism. In M. Jacqui Alexander & Chandra Talpade Mohanty (Eds.), *Feminist genealogies, colonial legacies, democratic futures* (pp. 125–150). New York, NY: Routledge.

Muehlenhard, Charlene L., & Peterson, Zoë D. (2011). Distinguishing between sex and gender: History, current conceptualizations, and implications. *Sex Roles*, *64*, 791–803. doi:10.1007/s11199-011-9932-5

Mulac, Anthony. (2006). The gender-linked language effect: Do language differences really make a difference? In Katherine Dindia & Dan Canary (Eds.), *Sex differences and similarities in communication: Critical essays and empirical investigations of sex and gender in interaction* (2nd ed., pp. 219–239). Mahwah, NJ: Erlbaum.

Mullany, Louise. (2007). *Gendered discourse in the professional workplace*. Basingstoke, NY: Palgrave Macmillan.

Mulvey, Laura. (1975). Visual pleasure and narrative cinema. *Screen*, *16*(3), 6–18.

Mumby, Dennis K. (2001). Power and politics. In Fredric M. Jablin & Linda L. Putnam (Eds.), *The new handbook of organizational communication: Advances in theory, research, and methods* (pp. 585–623). Newbury Park, CA: Sage.

Murphy, Bren Ortega. (1994). Greeting cards & gender messages. *Women & Language*, *17*(1), 25–29.

Murray, Samantha. (2008). Pathologizing "fatness": Medical authority and popular culture. *Sociology of Sport Journal*, *25*, 7–21.

Muscio, Inga. (2002). *Cunt: A declaration of independence*. New York, NY: Seal Press.

Myers, David G. (2004). *Psychology* (7th ed.). New York, NY: Worth.

Myre, Greg. (2016, August 21). U.S. women are the biggest winners at the Rio Olympics. *NPR The Torch*. Retrieved from http://www.npr.org/sections/thetorch/2016/08/21/490818961/u-s-women-are-the-biggest-winners-in-rio-olympics

Nadeau, Barbie Latza. (2012, April 20). Nuns gone wild! Vatican chastises American sisters. *Daily Beast*. Retrieved from http://www.thedailybeast.com/articles/2012/04/20/nuns-gone-wild-vatican-chastises-american-sisters.html

Nakayama, Thomas K., & Krizek, Robert L. (1999). Whiteness as a strategic rhetoric: In Thomas K. Nakayama & Judith N. Martin (Eds.), *Whiteness: The communication of social identity* (pp. 87–106). Thousand Oaks, CA: Sage.

Narayanan, Vasudha. (2003). Hinduism. In Arvind Sharma & Katherine K. Young (Eds.), *Her voice, her faith: Women speak on world religions* (pp. 11–58). Boulder, CO: Westview Press.

Narula, Svati Kirsten. (2015). Facebook redefines nudity to exclude breastfeeding shots, but rear ends are still off limits. *Quartz*. Retrieved from https://qz.com/363280/facebook-redefines-nudity-to-exclude-breastfeeding-shots-but-rear-ends-are-still-off-limits/

National Alliance on Mental Illness. (2017). Mental health by the numbers. Retrieved from https://www.nami.org/Learn-More/Mental-Health-By-the-Numbers

National Campaign to Prevent Teen and Unplanned Pregnancy. (2008). Sex and tech: Results from a survey of teens and young adults. Retrieved from https://thenationalcampaign.org/resource/sex-and-tech

National Center for Education Statistics. (2013). *School Crime Supplement (SCS) to the National Crime Victimization Survey*. U.S. Department of Justice, Bureau of Justice Statistics. Retrieved from https://nces.ed.gov/programs/crimeindicators/ind_11.asp

National Center for Education Statistics. (2014). Fast facts: Teacher trends. Retrieved from http://nces.ed.gov/fastfacts/display.asp?id=28

National Center for Education Statistics. (2015). *The condition of education 2015*. Washington, DC: U.S. Department of Education. Retrieved from http://nces.ed.gov/pubs2015/2015144.pdf

National Center for Health Statistics. (2015, November 23). National marriage and divorce rate trends. Retrieved from https://www.cdc.gov/nchs/nvss/marriage_divorce_tables.htm

National Coalition Against Domestic Violence. (2015). Domestic violence national statistics. Retrieved from http://www.ncadv.org/images/Domestic%20Violence.pdf

National Eating Disorder Association. (n.d.). Eating disorders in the LBGT populations. Retrieved from https://www.nationaleatingdisorders.org/eating-disorders-lgbt-populations

Negrón-Muntaner, Frances. (2014). The Latino media gap: A report on the state of Latinos in U.S. media. Retrieved from http://www.media-alliance.org/downloads/Latino_Media_Gap_Report.pdf

Nesbit, Jeff. (2015, May 6). Institutional racism is our way of life: Endless studies and reports show that racism exists, whether we want to believe it or not. *US News & World Report*. Retrieved from https://www.usnews.com/news/blogs/at-the-edge/2015/05/06/institutional-racism-is-our-way-of-life

Newman, Michael. (1992). Pronominal disagreements: The stubborn problem of singular epicene antecedents. *Language in Society, 21*, 447–475.

Ng, Sik Hung. (1990). Androcentric coding of *man* and *his* in memory by language users. *Journal of Experimental Social Psychology, 26*, 455–464.

Norton, Robert. (1983). *Communication style: Theory, applications, and measures*. Beverly Hills, CA: Sage.

Norwood, Kristen. (2012). Transitioning meanings? Family members' communicative struggles surrounding transgender identity. *Journal of Family Communication, 12*, 75–92.

NPR. (2015, July 23). From upspeak to vocal fry: Are we "policing" young women's voices? *Fresh Air*. Retrieved from http://www.npr.org/2015/07/23/425608745/from-upspeak-to-vocal-fry-are-we-policing-young-womens-voices

Nunberg, Geoff. (2012, March 13). Slut: The other four letter s-word. *Fresh Air*. Retrieved from http://www.npr.org/2012/03/13/148295582/slut-the-other-four-letter-s-word

Nuns on the Bus. (2012). The Ryan budget. Retrieved from https://networklobby.org/sisters budgetletters/

Obama, Michelle. (2012, September 4). Transcript: Michelle Obama's convention speech. Retrieved from http://www.npr.org/2012/09/04/160578836/transcript-michelle-obamas-convention-speech

O'Brien Hallstein, D. Lynn. (2017). Introduction to mothering rhetorics. *Women's Studies in Communication, 40*(1), 1–10. doi:10.1080/07491409.2017.1280326

Office of Women's Health, U.S. Department of Health and Human Services. (2014). Cyberbullying. Retrieved from https://www.girlshealth.gov/bullying/whatis/cyberbully.html

Oishi, Eve. (2006). Visual perversions: Race, sex, and cinematic pleasure. *Signs, 31*(3), 641–674.

Okimoto, Tyler G., & Brescoll, Victoria L. (2010). The price of power: Power-seeking and backlash against female politicians. *Personality and Social Psychology Bulletin, 36*(7), 923–936.

Oliffe, John L., Han, Christina, Maria, Estephanie Sta., Lohan, Maria, Howard, Terry, Stewart, Donna E., & MacMillan, Harriet. (2014). Gay men and intimate partner violence: A gender analysis. *Sociology of Health & Illness, 36*(4), 564–579.

Olivardia, Roberto. (2000). *Body image and masculinity in college males*. Unpublished doctoral dissertation, University of Massachusetts, Boston.

Olivardia, Roberto. (2001). Why now? How male body image is closely tied to masculinity and changing gender roles. *Society for the Psychological Study of Men and Masculinity Bulletin, 6*(4), 11–12.

Olivardia, Roberto, & Pope, Harrison G., Jr. (1997). Eating disorders in men: Prevalence, recognition, and treatment. *Directions in Psychiatry, 17*, 41–51.

Olivardia, Roberto, Pope, Harrison G., Jr., Borowiecki, John J., III, & Cohane, Geoffrey. (2004). Biceps and body image: The relationship between muscularity and self-esteem and eating disorder symptoms. *Psychology of Men and Masculinity, 5*(2), 112–120.

Olson, Loreen. (2002, Winter). Exploring "common couple violence" in heterosexual romantic relationships. *Western Journal of Communication, 66*(1), 104–129.

Opinions of eminent persons against woman suffrage [Pamphlet]. (1912, October). Massachusetts Association Opposed to the Further Extension of Suffrage to Women, Room 615, Kensington Building, Boston, MA.

Orenstein, Peggy. (2017). *Girls & sex: Navigating the complicated new landscape.* New York, NY: Harper Paperbacks.

Palczewski, Catherine Helen. (1995). Voltairine de Cleyre: Sexual pleasure and sexual slavery in the 19th century. *National Women's Studies Association Journal, 7,* 54–68.

Palczewski, Catherine Helen. (1996). Bodies, borders and letters: Gloria Anzaldúa's "Speaking in tongues: A letter to 3rd world women writers." *Southern Communication Journal, 62,* 1–16.

Palczewski, Catherine Helen. (1998). "Tak[e] the helm," man the ship . . . and I forgot my bikini! Unraveling why women is not considered a verb. *Women and Language, 21*(2), 1–8.

Palczewski, Catherine Helen. (2001, Summer). Contesting pornography: Terministic catharsis and definitional argument. *Argumentation and Advocacy, 38,* 1–17.

Palomares, Nicholas A. (2012). Gender and intergroup communication. In *The handbook of intergroup communication* (pp. 197–210). New York, NY: Routledge.

Paoletti, Jo B. (2012). *Pink and blue: Telling the boys from the girls in America.* Bloomington: Indiana University Press.

Papp, Lauren M., Kouros, Chrystyna D., & Cummings, E. Mark. (2009). Demand-withdraw patterns in marital conflict in the home. *Personal Relationships, 16*(2), 285–300.

Parker, Kim, & Livingston, Gretchen. (2016, June 16). 6 facts about American fathers. Pew Research Center. Retrieved from http://www.pewresearch.org/fact-tank/2016/06/16/fathers-day-facts/

Parker, Patricia S. (2003). Control, resistance, and empowerment in raced, gendered, and classed work contexts: The case of African American women. *Communication Yearbook, 27,* 257–291.

Parker, Patricia S. (2014). Difference and organizing. In Linda L. Putnam and Dennis K. Mumby (Eds.), *The Sage handbook of organizational communication* (pp. 619–643). Thousand Oaks, CA: Sage.

Parker-Pope, Tara. (2008, January 9). School popularity affects girls' weight. *New York Times.* Retrieved from https://well.blogs.nytimes.com/2008/01/09/school-popularity-affects-girls-weights/comment-page-7/?_r=0

Pascoe, C. J. (2011). *Dude, you're a fag: Masculinity and sexuality in high school.* Berkeley: University of California Press.

Pasterski, Vickie, Prentice, Phillippa, & Hughes, Leuan. (2010). Consequences of the Chicago consensus on disorders of sex development (DSD): Current practices in Europe. *Archives of Disease in Childhood, 95*(8), 618–623.

Paterson, Kate. (2014). "It's harder to catch a boy because they're tougher": Using fairytales in the classroom to explore children's understanding of gender. *Alberta Journal of Educational Research 60*(3), 474–490.

Patterson, Charlotte J. (2000). Family relationships of lesbian and gay men. *Journal of Marriage and the Family, 62,* 1052–1069.

Patton, Tracey Owens. (2006). "Hey girl, am I more than my hair?" African American women and their struggles with beauty, body image, and hair. *NWSA, 18*(2), 24–51.

Peck, Emily. (2016, May 13). If high heels are horrible, why do women still wear them? The reasons are as complicated as they are frustrating. *Huffington Post.* Retrieved from http://www.huffingtonpost.com/entry/women-high-heels-at-work_us_5734a3fce4b08f96c1825bbd

Penelope, Julia. (1990). *Speaking freely*. New York, NY: Pergamon Press.

Pennington, Dorothy L. (2003). The discourse of African American women: A case for extended paradigms. In Ronald L. Jackson & Elaine B. Richardson (Eds.), *Understanding African American rhetoric* (pp. 293–307). New York, NY: Routledge.

Peplau, Letitia Anne, & Beals, Kristin P. (2004). The family lives of lesbians and gay men. In Anita L. Vangelisti (Ed.), *Handbook of family communication* (pp. 233–248). Mahwah, NJ: Erlbaum.

Petchesky, Rosalind P. (1997). Spiraling discourses of reproductive and sexual rights: A post-Beijing assessment of international feminist politics. In Cathy J. Cohen, Kathleen B. Jones, & Joan C. Tronto (Eds.), *Women transforming politics* (pp. 569–587). New York: New York University Press.

Petersen, Jennifer L., & Hyde, Janet Shibley. (2010). A meta-analytic review of research on gender differences in sexuality, 1993–2007. *Psychological Bulletin, 136*(1), 21–38.

Peterson, Lori West, & Albrecht, Terrance L. (1999). Where gender/power/politics collide: Deconstructing organizational maternity leave policy. *Journal of Management Inquiry, 8*, 168–181.

Petrecca, Laura. (2012, July 19). Pregnant CEO tests glass ceiling. *USA Today*, p. A1.

Petrow, Steven. (2014, October 27). Gender-neutral pronouns: When "they" doesn't identify as either male or female. *Washington Post*. Retrieved from https://www.washingtonpost.com/lifestyle/style/gender-neutral-pronouns-when-they-doesnt-identify-as-either-male-or-female/2014/10/27/41965f5e-5ac0-11e4-b812-38518ae74c67_story.html?utm_term=.447ce37e1075

Petrow, Steven. (2016, December 19). In 2016, "they" became singular, and everyone learned more about gender. *Washington Post*. Retrieved from https://www.washingtonpost.com/lifestyle/style/in-2016-they-became-singular-and-everyone-learned-more-about-gender/2016/12/16/cabcd846-c3b7-11e6-9578-0054287507db_story.html?utm_term=.e5e57cc8c895

Petrusich, Amanda. (2015, June 9). Free to be Miley. *Paper*. Retrieved from http://www.papermag.com/free-to-be-miley-1427581961.html

Pew Research Center. (2010). Support for same-sex marriage edges upward. Retrieved from http://www.people-press.org/2010/10/06/support-for-same-sex-marriage-edges-upward

Pew Research Center. (2017, January 11). Ownership of other devices. Retrieved from http://www.pewinternet.org/chart/ownership-of-other-devices/

Pheterson, Gail. (Ed.). (1989). *A vindication of the rights of whores*. Seattle, WA: Seal Press.

Piela, Anna. (2013, November). I am just doing my bit to promote modesty: Niqabis' self-portraits on photo-sharing websites. *Feminist Media Studies, 13*(5), 781–790. doi:10.1080/14680777.2013.83835

Piepmeier, Alison. (2004). *Out in public: Configurations of women's bodies in nineteenth-century America*. Chapel Hill: University of North Carolina Press.

Ponterotto, Diane. (2016, January). Resisting the male gaze: Feminist responses to the "normatization" of the female body in western culture. *Journal of International Women's Studies, 17*(1), 133–148.

Pope, Harrison G., Jr., Gruber, Amanda J., Choi, Precilla, Olivardia, Roberto, & Phillips, Katharine A. (1997). Muscle dysphoria: An underrecognized form of body dysmorphic disorder. *Psychosomatics, 38*, 548–557.

Pope, Harrison G., Jr., Olivardia, Roberto, Gruber, Amanda, & Borowiecki, John. (1999). Evolving ideals of male body image as seen through action toys. *International Journal of Eating Disorders, 26*, 65–72.

Pope, Harrison G., Jr., Phillips, Katharine A., & Olivardia, Roberto. (2000). *The Adonis complex: The secret crisis of male body obsession*. New York, NY: Simon & Schuster.

Popenoe, Rebecca. (2004). *Feeding desire: Fatness, beauty and sexuality among a Saharan people*. London, England: Routledge.

Porter, Evan. (2016, September 1). Tired of being humiliated, these girls fought the school dress code. And won. *Upworthy*. Retrieved from http://www.upworthy.com/tired-of-being-humiliated-these-girls-fought-the-school-dress-code-and-won?c=ufb1

Poynter. (2015, December 2). The *Washington Post* changes its style to allow singular "they." *American Press Institute*. Retrieved from https://www.americanpressinstitute.org/need-to-know/shareable/the-washington-post-changes-its-style-to-allow-singular-they/

Presiding bishop. (2012). *The Episcopal Church*. Retrieved from http://www.episcopalchurch.org/page/presiding-bishop

Preston, Cheryl B. (2003, Spring). Women in traditional religions: Refusing to let patriarchy (or feminism) separate us from the source of our liberation. *Mississippi College Law Review, 22*, 185–214.

Price, Janet, & Shildrick, Margrit. (Eds.). (1999). *Feminist theory and the body: A reader*. New York, NY: Routledge.

Putney, Clifford. (2001). *Muscular Christianity: Manhood and sports in Protestant America, 1880–1920*. Cambridge, MA: Harvard University Press.

Quinn, Beth A. (2002, June). Sexual harassment and masculinity: The power and meaning of "girl watching." *Gender & Society, 16*(3), 386–402.

Raby, Rebecca. (2010). "Tank tops are OK but I don't want to see her thong": Girls engagement with secondary school dress codes. *Youth & Society, 41*(3), 333–356.

Rakow, Lana. (1986). Rethinking gender research in communication. *Journal of Communication, 36*, 11–26.

Ramsey, Laura R., & Hoyt, Tiffany. (2014). How being objectified creates sexual pressure for women in heterosexual relationships. *Psychology of Women Quarterly, 38*(2), 151–170. Retrieved from http://journals.sagepub.com/doi/pdf/10.1177/0361684314544679

Rankine, Claudia. (2015, August 25). The meaning of Serena Williams: On tennis and black excellence. *New York Times Magazine*. Retrieved from https://www.nytimes.com/2015/08/30/magazine/the-meaning-of-serena-williams.html?_r=0

Ratzinger, Cardinal Joseph. (2004). Letter to the bishops of the Catholic Church on the collaboration of men and women in the church and in the world. Retrieved from http://archive.wf-f.org/CDF-LetteronCollaboration.html

Rayner, Ju-Anne, Pyett, Priscilla, & Astbury, Jill. (2010). The medicalisation of "tall" girls: A discourse analysis of medical literature on the use of synthetic oestrogen to reduce female height. *Social Science & Medicine, 71*, 1076–1083.

Reiss, David. (2000). *The relationship code: Deciphering genetic and social influences on adolescent development*. Cambridge, MA: Harvard University Press.

Rentschler, Carrie A. (2014). Rape culture and the feminist politics of social media. *Girlhood Studies, 7*(1), 65–82.

Rich, Adrienne. (1976). *Of woman born: Motherhood as experience and institution*. New York, NY: W.W. Norton.

Rich, Adrienne. (1977/2005). Claiming an education. In Chris Anderson & Lex Runciman (Eds.), *Open questions* (pp. 608–613). Boston, MA: Bedford/St. Martin's.

Rich, Adrienne. (1980). Compulsory heterosexuality and lesbian existence. *Signs, 5*, 631–660.

Richardson, Brian K., & Taylor, Juandalynn. (2009). Sexual harassment at the intersection of race and gender: A theoretical model of the sexual harassment experiences of women of color. *Western Journal of Communication, 73*(3), 248–272.

Richardson, Scott. (2015). *Gender lessons: Patriarchy, sextyping & schools*. Rotterdam, Netherlands: Sense.

Rivers, Caryl, & Barnett, Rosalind. (2011). *The truth about girls and boys: Challenging toxic stereotypes about our children*. New York, NY: Columbia University Press.

Robbins, Megan L., Focella, Elizabeth S., Kasle, Shelley, López, Ana Maria, Weihs, Karen L., & Mehl, Matthias R. (2011). Naturalistically observed swearing, emotional support and depressive symptoms in women coping with illness. *Health Psychology, 30*(6), 789–792.

Robnett, Belinda. (1996). African-American women in the civil rights movement, 1954–1965: Gender, leadership, and micromobilization. *American Journal of Sociology, 101*(6), 1661–1693.

Rockmore, Ellen Bresler. (2015, October 21). How Texas teaches history. *New York Times*. Retrieved from http://nyti.ms/1GSGh8H

Rodino-Colocino, Michelle. (2014). The he-cession: Why feminists should rally for the end of white supremacist capitalist patriarchy. *Feminist Media Studies, 14*(2), 343–347.

Roof, Judith, & Weigman, Robyn. (Eds.). (1995). *Who can speak? Authority and critical identity*. Urbana: University of Illinois Press.

Rose, Amanda J., Smith, Rhiannon L., Glick, Gary C., & Schwartz-Mette, Rebecca. (2016). Girls' and boys' problem talk: Implications for emotional closeness in friendship. *Developmental Psychology, 52*(4), 629–639.

Rosen, Christopher. (2017, January 23). Ashley Judd recites powerful "Nasty Woman" poem at Women's March. *Entertainment Weekly*. Retrieved from http://ew.com/news/2017/01/21/womens-march-ashley-judd-nasty-woman-poem/

Rosman, Katherine. (2015, June 5). Me, myself and Mx. *New York Times*. Retrieved from http://www.nytimes.com/2015/06/07/style/me-myself-and-mx.html?_r=2

Ruane, Janet M., & Cerulo, Karen M. (2008). *Second thoughts: Seeing conventional wisdom through the sociological eye* (4th ed.). Thousand Oaks, CA: Pine Forge Press.

Rubin, Gayle. (1984). Thinking sex: Notes for a radical theory of the politics of sexuality. In Carole Vance (Ed.), *Pleasure and danger: Exploring female sexuality* (pp. 267–319). London, England: Victor Gollancz.

Rubinstein, Ruth P. (2001). *Dress code: Meaning and messages in American culture* (2nd ed.). Boulder, CO: Westview Press.

Rudick, Kyle C., & Golsan, Kathryn B. (2016). Difference, accountability, and social justice: Three challenges for instructional communication scholarship. *Communication Education, 65*(1), 110–112.

Ryle, Robyn. (2012). *Questioning gender: A sociological exploration*. Thousand Oaks, CA: Sage.

Sadker, David, & Silber, Ellen S. (Eds.). (2007). *Gender in the classroom: Foundations, skills, methods and strategies across the curriculum*. Mahwah, NJ: Erlbaum.

Sadker, David, & Zittleman, Karen R. (2009). *Still failing at fairness: How gender bias cheats girls and boys in school and what we can do about it*. New York, NY: Schribner.

Salie, Faith. (2013, September 12). On speaking with "vocal fry" with Faith Salie. *BBC*. Retrieved from https://www.youtube.com/watch?v=R6r7LhcHHAc

Sampson, Rana. (2011, August). *Acquaintance rape of college students*. Washington, DC: U.S. Department of Justice. Retrieved from http://www.popcenter.org/problems/pdfs/Acquaintance_Rape_of_College_Students.pdf

Sanger, Kerran L. (1995). Slave resistance and rhetorical self-definition: Spirituals as strategy. *Western Journal of Communication, 59*(3), 177–192.

Sax, Leonard. (2016). *Boys adrift: The five factors driving the growing epidemic of unmotivated boys and underachieving young men* (Rev. & updated ed.). New York, NY: Basic Books.

Scharrón-del Río, María, & Aja, Alan A. (2015, December 5). The case for "Latinx": Why intersectionality is not a choice. *Latino Rebels*. Retrieved from http://www.latinorebels.com/2015/12/05/the-case-for-latinx-why-intersectionality-is-not-a-choice/

Schilt, Kristen. (2011). *Just one of the guys? Transgender men and the persistence of gender inequality*. Chicago, IL: University of Chicago Press.

Schleff, Erik. (2008). Gender and academic discourse: Global restrictions and local possibilities. *Language in Society, 37*, 515–538.

Schram, Sanford F. (1995). *Words of welfare: The poverty of social science and the social science of poverty*. Minneapolis: University of Minnesota Press.

Schulz, Muriel R. (1975). The semantic derogation of woman. In Barrie Thorne & Nancy Henley (Eds.), *Language and sex: Difference and dominance* (pp. 64–75). Chicago, IL: Newbury House.

Schwabe, Franziska, McElvany, Nele, & Trendtel, Matthias. (2015). The school age gender gap in reading achievement: Examining the influences of item format and intrinsic reading motivation. *Reading Research Quarterly, 50*(2), 219–232.

Scott, James C. (1992). *Domination and the arts of resistance: Hidden transcripts*. New Haven, CT: Yale University Press.

Scott, Julie-Ann. (2014). Illuminating the vulnerability of hegemonic masculinity through a performance analysis of physically disabled men's personal narratives. *Disability Studies Quarterly, 34*(1). Retrieved from http://dsq-sds.org/article/view/3570/3526

Segal, Corinne. (2015, May 6). Oxford English Dictionary could soon include gender-neutral title "Mx." *PBS Newshour*. Retrieved from http://www.pbs.org/newshour/rundown/oxford-english-dictionary-soon-include-gender-neutral-title-mx/

Segrin, Chris, & Flora, Jeanne. (2011). *Family communication* (2nd ed.). New York, NY: Routledge.

Sellers, Patricia. (2012, July 16). New Yahoo CEO Mayer is pregnant. *Fortune*. Retrieved from http://fortune.com/2012/07/17/new-yahoo-ceo-mayer-is-pregnant/

Sells, Laura R. (1993). Maria W. Miller Stewart. In Karlyn Kohrs Campbell (Ed.), *Women public speakers in the United States, 1800–1925* (pp. 339–349). Westport, CT: Greenwood Press.

Shapiro, Ari. (2016, December 30). On the men who rattled pop's gender rules—And what it means to lose them now. *All Things Considered*. Retrieved from http://www.npr.org/2016/12/30/507575982/on-the-men-who-rattled-pops-gender-rules-and-what-it-means-to-lose-them-now?utm_source=facebook.com&utm_medium=social&utm_campaign=npr&utm_term=nprnews&utm_content=2058

Shapiro, Eve. (2010). *Gender circuits: Bodies and identities in a technological age*. New York, NY: Routledge.

Sharkey, Linda. (2016, March 7). Zara joins the gender fluid movement with new unisex clothing line. *Independent*. Retrieved from http://www.independent.co.uk/life-style/fashion/news/zara-gender-fluid-agender-unisex-fashion-transgender-ruby-rose-a6917496.html

Shear, Marie. (1986, May/June). Feminism is the radical notion that women are people. *New Directions for Women*.

Shoener, Sara. (2014, June 21). Two-parent households can be lethal. *New York Times*. Retrieved from https://www.nytimes.com/2014/06/22/opinion/sunday/domestic-violence-and-two-parent-households.html

Shome, Raka. (1996, February). Postcolonial interventions in the rhetorical canon: An "other" view. *Communication Theory, 6*(1), 40–59.

Shome, Raka, & Hegde, Radha S. (2002, June). Culture, communication, and the challenge of globalization. *Critical Studies in Media Communication, 19*(2), 72–189.

Sidell, Misty White. (2014, March 11). Target comes under fire for Photoshopping a "square thigh gap" onto young model posing in swimsuits for JUNIORS. *Daily Mail*. Retrieved from http://www.dailymail.co.uk/femail/article-2578406/Target-comes-fire-Photoshopping-square-thigh-gap-young-model-posing-swimsuits-JUNIORS.html#ixzz4VCzmRnkl

Signorielli, Nancy. (2009). Minorities representation in prime time: 2000–2008. *Communication Research Reports*, *26*(4), 323–336.

Silva, Daniella. (2017, March 28). "Stop shaking your head": Sean Spicer lashes out at reporter April Ryan. *NBC News*. Retrieved from http://www.nbcnews.com/politics/politics-news/stop-shaking-your-head-sean-spicer-lashes-out-reporter-april-n739691

Silva, Janelle M., Langhout, Regina Day, Kohfeldt, Danielle, & Gurrola, Edith. (2015). "Good" and "bad" kids? A race and gender analysis of effective behavioral support in an elementary school. *Urban Education*, *50*(7), 787–811.

Sink, Alexander, & Mastro, Dana. (2016). Depictions of gender on primetime television: A quantitative content analysis. *Mass Communication and Society*, *20*(1), 3–22.

Sinozich, Sofi, & Langton, Lynn. (2014, December). Rape and sexual assault victimization among college-age-females, 1995–2013. *Special Report, U.S. Department of Justice*. Retrieved from http://www.bjs.gov/index.cfm?ty=pbdetail&iid=5176

Sipe, Stephanie, Johnson, C. Douglas, & Fisher, Donna K. (2009). University students' perceptions of gender discrimination in the workplace: Reality versus fiction. *Journal of Education for Business*, *84*(6), 339–349.

Sister Marches. (2017). Women's March on Washington. Retrieved from https://www.womensmarch.com/sisters

Slesaransky-Poe, Graciela, & García, Ana María. (2009). Boys with gender-variant behaviors and interests: From theory to practice. *Sex Education*, *9*(2), 201–210.

Sloop, John M. (2004). *Disciplining gender: Rhetorics of sex identity in contemporary U.S. culture*. Amherst: University of Massachusetts Press.

Sloop, John M. (2005, August). In a queer time and place and race: Intersectionality comes of age. *Quarterly Journal of Speech*, *91*(3), 312–326.

Slut Walk NYC. (n.d.). Frequently asked questions. Retrieved from http://slutwalknyc.com/frequently-asked-questions/

Smarick, Andy. (2016, July 7). Guest post: Andy Smarick on the meaning of "they." Retrieved from http://www.justinccohen.com/blog/2016/7/7/guest-post-smarick

Smith, Leann V., & Cokley, Kevin. (2016). Stereotype threat vulnerability: A psychometric investigation of the social identities and attitudes scale. *Measurement and Evaluation in Counseling and Development*, *49*(2), 145–162. doi:10.1177/0748175615625752

Smith, Samuel. (2016, September 11). "Duck Dynasty" star Alan Robertson: I've never seen religious freedom attacked more than it is today. *CP Politics*. Retrieved from http://www.christianpost.com/news/duck-dynasty-star-alan-robertson-ive-never-seen-religious-freedom-attacked-more-than-it-is-today-169406/

Smith, Stacy L., Choueiti, Marc, and Pieper, Katherine. (2014). *Gender inequality in popular films: Examining on screen portrayals and behind-the-scenes employment patterns in motion pictures released between 2007–2013*. Retrieved from http://annenberg.usc.edu/pages/%257E/media/MDSCI/Gender%20Inequality%20in%20Film%202007-2013%20Final%20for%20Publication.ashx

Smith, Stacey L., Choueiti, Marc, & Pieper, Katherine. (2016, February 22). *Inclusion or invisibility: Comprehensive Annenberg Report on Diversity in Entertainment*. Retrieved from http://annenberg.usc.edu/pages/~/media/MDSCI/CARDReport%20FINAL%2022216.ashx

Smith, Stacy L., Pieper, Katherine, & Choueiti, Marc. (2017, February). *Inclusion in the director's chair? Gender, race, and age of film directors across 1,000 films from 2007–2016*. Los Angeles, CA: Annenberg Foundation. Retrieved from http://annenberg.usc.edu/sitecore/shell/Controls/Rich%20Text%20Editor/~/media/C4E24196A17A42649D03B568F1D6F743.ashx

Smyth, Ron, Jacobs, Greg, & Rogers, Henry. (2003). Male voices and perceived sexual orientation: An experimental and theoretical approach. *Language and Gender*, *32*, 329–350.

Solomon, Martha. (1987). *Emma Goldman*. Boston, MA: Twayne.

Sorrells, Kathryn. (2016). *Intercultural communication: Global and social justice* (2nd ed.). Thousand Oaks, CA: Sage.

Spender, Dale. (1985). *Man made language* (2nd ed.). London, England: Routledge & Kegan Paul.

Spitzberg, Brian H. (2011). Intimate partner violence and aggression: Seeing the light in a dark place. In William R. Cupach & Brian H. Spitzberg (Eds.), *The dark side of close relationships II* (327–380). New York, NY: Routledge.

Spivak, Gayatri Chakravorty. (1988). Can the subaltern speak? In Cary Nelson & Lawrence Grossberg (Eds.), *Marxism and the interpretation of culture* (pp. 271–313). Urbana: University of Illinois Press.

Spivak, Gayatri Chakravorty. (1993). *Outside in the teaching machine*. New York, NY: Routledge.

Spivak, Gayatri Chakravorty. (1996). *The Spivak reader* (Donna Landry & Gerald MacLean, Eds.). New York, NY: Routledge.

Spivak, Gayatri Chakravorty. (2004). Terror: A speech after 9-11. *Boundary, 2*(31), 81–111.

Stafford, Sarah L. (2004). Progress toward Title IX compliance: The effect of formal and informal enforcement mechanisms. *Social Science Quarterly, 85*(5), 1469–1486.

Starr, Christine R., & Ferguson, Gail M. (2012). Sexy dolls, sexy grade-schoolers? Media & maternal influences on young girls' self-sexualization. *Sex Roles, 67*(7–8), 463–476.

Statista. (2017). Revenue in the cosmetics and personal care market. Retrieved from https://www.statista.com/outlook/70000000/109/cosmetics-and-personal-care/united-states#

Steele, Claude M., & Aronson, Joshua. (1995). Stereotype threat and the intellectual text performance of African Americans. *Journal of Personality and Social Psychology, 69*(5), 797–811.

Stephens, Mitchell. (1998). *The rise of the image, the fall of the word*. New York, NY: Oxford University Press.

Sterk, Helen M. (1989, September). How rhetoric becomes real: Religious sources of gender identity. *Journal of Communication and Religion, 12*, 24–33.

Sterk, Helen M. (2010, November). Faith, feminism and scholarship: *The Journal of Communication and Religion*, 1999–2009. *Journal of Communication and Religion, 33*(2), 206–216.

Stockman, Dan. (2017, January 12). The "cultural chasm" between American nuns and Vatican is closing. *Huffington Post*. Retrieved from http://www.huffingtonpost.com/entry/the-tensions-between-american-nuns-and-the-vatican-were-due-to-a-cultural-chasm-leader-reports_us_55ccc2c1e4b064d5910ab6b5

Stop Street Harassment. (2011, March 1). Activist interviews: Lani Shotlow-Rincon. Retrieved from http://www.stopstreetharassment.org/2011/03/the-dont-call-me-baby-project

Strasser, Annie-Rose, & Culp-Ressler, Tara. (2013, May 6). How "slut-shaming" has been writing into school dress codes across the country. *Care2*. Retrieved from http://www.care2.com/causes/how-slut-shaming-has-been-written-into-school-dress-codes-across-the-country.html?utm_source=feedburner&utm_medium=feed&utm_campaign=Feed%3A+causes%2Fwomens-rights+%28Causes%3A+Women%27s+Rights%29&utm_content=Google+Reader

Strassner, Elizabeth. (2017). This news proves that Hillary Clinton's loss was about sexism, not her emails. *Bustle*. Retrieved from https://www.bustle.com/p/this-news-proves-that-hillary-clintons-loss-was-about-sexism-not-her-emails-33631?utm_source=facebook&utm_medium=owned&utm_campaign=feminismbustle

Straus, Erwin W. (1966). *Phenomenological psychology*. New York, NY: Basic Books.

Streb, Matthew J., Burrell, Barbara, Frederick, Brian, & Genovese, Michael A. (2008). Social desirability effects and support for a female American president. *Public Opinion Quarterly, 72*(1), 76–89.

Stringer, Jeffrey L., & Hopper, Robert. (1998, May). Generic *he* in conversation. *Quarterly Journal of Speech, 84,* 209–221.

Strong, Bryan, DeVault, Christine, & Sayad, Barbara W. (1999). *Human sexuality: Diversity in contemporary America.* Mountain View, CA: Mayfield.

Stryker, Susan. (2008). *Transgender history.* Berkeley, CA: Seal Press.

Stryker, Susan. (2015). Transing the queer (in)human. *GLQ: A Journal of Lesbian and Gay Studies, 21*(2–3), 227–230.

Stuart, Gregory L., Moore, Todd M., Hellmuth, Julianne C., Ransey, Susan E., & Kahler, Christopher W. (2006). Reasons for intimate partner violence perpetration among arrested women. *Violence Against Women, 12*(7), 609–621.

Subrahmanian, Ramya. (2005). *Promising practices and implications for scaling up girls' education: Report of the UN girls' education initiative South Asia workshop help in Chandigarh, India, 20–22 September 2004.* London, England: Commonwealth Secretariat.

Sue, Derold Wing. (2010). *Microaggressions in everyday life: Race, gender, and sexual orientation.* Hoboken, NJ: John Wiley & Sons.

Summers, Lawrence H. (2005, January 14). *Remarks at NBER conference on diversifying the science & engineering workforce.* Cambridge, MA. Retrieved from http://www.harvard.edu/president/speeches/summers_2005/nber.php

Suter, Elizabeth A., Baxter, Leslie A., Seurer, Leah M., & Thomas, Lindsey J. (2014). Discursive constructions of the meaning of "family" in online narratives of foster adoptive parents. *Communication Monographs, 81*(1), 59–78. doi:10.1080/03637751.2014.880791

Swain, Jon. (2005). Masculinities in education. In Michael S. Kimmel, Jeff Hearn, & R. W. Connell (Eds.), *Handbook of studies on men and masculinities* (pp. 213–229). Thousand Oaks, CA: Sage.

Swain, Scott. (1989). Covert intimacy: Closeness in men's friendships. In B. J. Risman & Pepper Schwartz (Eds.), *Gender and intimate relationships* (pp. 71–86). Belmont, CA: Wadsworth.

Tannen, Deborah. (1990). *You just don't understand: Women and men in conversation.* New York, NY: William Morrow.

Tannen, Deborah. (1994). *Gender and discourse.* New York, NY: Oxford University Press.

Tavris, Carol. (1992). *The mismeasure of woman.* New York, NY: Simon & Schuster.

Taylor, Jessica. (2017, March 29). #BlackWomenAtWork: Women speak out after criticism of journalist, congresswoman. *All Things Considered.* Retrieved from http://www.npr.org/2017/03/29/521954040/-blackwomenatwork-women-speak-out-after-criticism-of-journalist-congresswoman

Teaching tolerance. (n.d.). What is mix it up at lunch day? A project of Southern Poverty Law. Retrieved from http://www.tolerance.org/mix-it-up/what-is-mix

Team USA RIO 2016 Olympic Games. (2016). 2016 U.S. Olympic Team. Retrieved from http://www.teamusa.org/road-to-rio-2016/team-usa/athletes

Tesene, Megan. (2012). Book review: Just one of the guys? Transgender men and the persistence of gender inequality. *Gender & Society, 26,* 676–678.

Teunis, Niels. (2007). Sexual objectification and the construction of whiteness in the gay male community. *Culture, Health & Sexuality: An International Journal for Research, Intervention and Care, 9*(3), 263–275.

Texas Board adopts conservative curriculum. (2010, May 21). *CBS News.* Retrieved from https://www.cbsnews.com/news/texas-board-adopts-conservative-curriculum/

Thébaud, Sarah, & Pedulla, David S. (2016). Masculinity and the stalled revolution: How gender ideologies and norms shape young men's responses to work-family policies. *Gender & Society.* doi:10.1177/0891243216649946

Thie, Marilyn. (1994, Fall). Epilogue: Prolegomenon to future feminist philosophies of religions. *Hypatia*, *9*(4), 229–240.

Thompson, Christie. (2011, Summer). Taking *slut* for a walk. *Ms.*, *21*(3), 14.

Tifferet, Sigel, & Vilnia-Yavetz, Iris. (2014, June). Gender differences in Facebook self-presentation: An international randomized study. *Computers in Human Behavior*, *35*, 388–399.

Tiggermann, Marika, & Slater, Amy. (2013, September 5). Net Girls: The Internet, Facebook, and body: Image concerns in adolescent girls. *International Journal of Eating Disorders*, *46*(6), 630–633.

Tonn, Mari Boor. (1996, February). Militant motherhood: Labor's Mary Harris "Mother" Jones. *Quarterly Journal of Speech*, *82*, 1–21.

Tracy, Karen. (2002). *Everyday talk: Building and reflecting identities*. New York, NY: Guilford Press.

Tracy, Karen, & Robles, Jessica S. (2013). *Everyday talk: Building and reflecting identities* (2nd ed.). New York, NY: Guilford Press.

Traister, Rebecca. (2016). *All the single ladies: Unmarried women and the rise of an independent nation*. New York, NY: Simon & Schuster.

Travis, Cheryl Brown, Meginnis, Kayce L., & Bardari, Kristin M. (2000). Beauty, sexuality and identity: The social control of women. In Cheryl Brown Travis & Jacquelyn W. White (Eds.), *Sexuality, society, and feminism* (pp. 237–272). Washington, DC: American Psychological Association.

Trethewey, Angela. (2001, November). Reproducing and resisting the master narrative of decline: Midlife professional women's experiences of aging. *Management Communication Quarterly*, *15*(2), 183–226.

Trimberger, E. Kay. (2005). *The new single woman*. Boston, MA: Beacon Press.

Trujillo, Nick. (1991). Hegemonic masculinity on the mound: Media representations of Nolan Ryan and American sports culture. *Critical Studies in Mass Communication*, *8*, 290–308.

Truth, Sojourner. (1851). *Aren't I a woman?* Retrieved from http://people.sunyulster.edu/voughth/sojourner_truth.htm

Turner, Jonathan H. (2017). *Theoretical sociology: A concise introduction to twelve sociological theories*. Thousand Oaks, CA: Sage.

Turner, Terisa E., & Brownhill, Leigh S. (2004, January–March). Why women are at war with Chevron: Nigerian subsistence struggles against the international oil industry. *Journal of Asian and African Studies*, *39*(1–2), 63–94.

Understanding Islam and the Muslims. (n.d.). *USC-MSA compendium of Muslim texts*. Retrieved from http://www.usc.edu/dept/MSA/introduction/understandingislam.html

UNESCO. (2013, October). Fact Sheet: Girls-education—The facts. Retrieved from http://en.unesco.org/gem-report/sites/gem-report/files/girls-factsheet-en.pdf

Unger, Rhoda. (1979). Toward a redefinition of sex and gender. *American Psychologist*, *34*, 1085–1094.

Unger, Rhoda, & Crawford, Mary. (1992). *Women and gender: A feminist psychology*. Philadelphia, PA: Temple University Press.

UN High Commissioner for Refugees. (2015, May 4). *Discrimination and violence against individuals based on their sexual orientation and gender identity* [Report]. Retrieved from http://journalistsresource.org/studies/international/human-rights/global-discrimination-against-lgbt-persons-2015-united-nations-report

UNICEF. (2015, July 23). Girls education and gender equity. Retrieved from https://www.unicef.org/education/bege_70640.html

UN Statistics Division. (2015). Chapter 6: Violence against women. *The world's women 2015*. Retrieved from http://unstats.un.org/unsd/gender/chapter6/chapter6.html

UN Women. (2015, April). Facts and figures: Economic empowerment. Retrieved from http://www.unwomen.org/en/what-we-do/economic-empowerment/facts-and-figures#notes

Urban Dictionary. (n.d.). Man-up. Retrieved from http://www.urbandictionary.com/define.php?term=man%20up)

U.S. Census Bureau. (2016, November 17). The majority of children live with two parents, Census Bureau Reports. Retrieved from https://www.census.gov/newsroom/press-releases/2016/cb16-192.html

U.S. Census Bureau. (n.d.). Quick facts. Retrieved from http://www.census.gov/quickfacts/table/RHI125215/00

U.S. Department of Justice. (2012, January 6). An updated definition of rape. Retrieved from http://www.justice.gov/opa/blog/updated-definition-rape

U.S. Department of Justice. (n.d.). Sexual assault. Retrieved from http://www.justice.gov/ovw/sexual-assault

U.S. Equal Opportunity Employment Commission. (2012). Sexual harassment charges EEOC & FEPAs combined: FY 1997–FY2011. Retrieved from http://www.eeoc.gov/eeoc/statistics/enforcement/

U.S. Government Accountability Office. (2010, September 20). *Women in management: Analysis of female manager's representation, characteristics, and pay*. Washington, DC: Author.

Vacek, Edward. (2005, March). Feminism and the Vatican [Electronic version]. *Theological Studies, 66*(1), 159–177.

Vaid, Urvashi. (1995). *Virtual equality*. New York, NY: Anchor Books.

Valdes, Francisco. (1995, January). Queers, sissies, dykes, and tomboys: Deconstructing the conflation of "sex," "gender," and "sexual orientation" in Euro-American law and society. *California Law Review, 83*(1), 3–377.

Valenti, Jessica. (2015, March 30). Social media is protecting men from periods, breast milk and body hair. *The Guardian*. Retrieved from https://www.theguardian.com/commentisfree/2015/mar/30/social-media-protecting-men-periods-breast-milk-body-hair

Valenti, Jessica. (2016). *Sex object: A memoir*. New York, NY: HarperCollins.

Valenti, Miranda. (2013, May 24). What do dress codes say about girls' bodies? *Ms.blog*. Retrieved from http://msmagazine.com/blog/2013/05/24/what-do-dress-codes-say-about-girls-bodies/

Vandenbosch, Laura, & Eggermont, Steven. (2012). Understanding sexual objectification: A comprehensive approach toward media exposure and girls' internalization of beauty ideals, self-objectification, and body surveillance. *Journal of Communication, 62*(5), 869–887.

Vannoy, Dana. (Ed.). (2001). *Gender stratification: Social interaction and structural accounts*. Los Angeles, CA: Roxbury.

Vasquez, Vivian Marie. (2014). *Negotiating critical literacies with young children* (10th ed.). New York, NY: Routledge.

Velez, Brandon, Campos, Irma D., & Moradi, Bonnie. (2015). Relations of sexual objectification and racist discrimination with Latina women's body image and mental health. *Counseling Psychology, 43*(6), 906–935.

Vidal, Catherine. (2011). The sexed brain: Between science and ideology. *Neuroethics*. doi:10.1007/s12152–011–9121–9

Vonnegut, Kristin. (1993). Sarah M. Grimké. In Karlyn Kohrs Campbell (Ed.), *Women public speakers in the United States, 1800–1925* (pp. 216–228). Westport, CT: Greenwood Press.

Voss, Linda D., & Mulligan, Jean. (2000, March 4). Bullying in school: Are short pupils at risk? Questionnaire study in a cohort. *British Medical Journal, 320*(7235), 612–613.

Vuola, Elina. (2002). Remaking universals? Transnational feminism(s) challenging fundamentalist ecumenism. *Theory, Culture and Society, 19*(1–2), 175–195.

"Want Ads." (1958, June 1) *The State*, p. 8D. Newspapers on Microfilm. Published Material Division, South Carolina Library, University of South Carolina, Columbia, South Carolina. Retrieved from http://www.teachingushistory.org/tTrove/wantads.htm

Wainright, Jennifer L., & Patterson, Charlotte J. (2008). Peer relations among adolescents with female same-sex parents. *Developmental Psychology, 44*(1), 117–126.

Walker, Alexis J. (1999). Gender and family relationships. In Marvin Sussman, Suzanne K. Steinmetz, & Gary W. Peterson (Eds.), *Handbook of marriage and the family* (2nd ed., pp. 439–474). New York, NY: Plenum Press.

Walker, Robyn C., & Artiz, Jolanta. (2015). Women doing leadership: Leadership styles and organizational culture. *International Journal of Business Communication, 52*(4), 452–478. doi:10.1177/2329488415598429

Walsh, Froma. (2012). The new normal: Diversity and complexity in 21st-century families. In Froma Walsh (Ed.), *Normal family processes: Growing diversity and complexity* (4th ed., pp. 3–27). New York, NY: Guilford Press.

Walsh, Mary Roth. (1977). *"Doctors wanted, no women need apply": Sexual barriers in the medical profession, 1835–1975*. New Haven, CT: Yale University Press.

Walters, Suzanna Danuta. (1995). *Material girls: Making sense of feminist cultural theory*. Berkeley: University of California Press.

Wang, Yanan. (2015, October 5). "Workers" or slaves? Textbook maker backtracks after mother's online complaint. *Washington Post*. Retrieved from https://www.washingtonpost.com/news/morning-mix/wp/2015/10/05/immigrant-workers-or-slaves-textbook-maker-backtracks-after-mothers-online-complaint/?utm_term=.56468e190d3e

Ware, Susan. (2015, September 1). Title IX's unintended revolution for women's athletes. American Association of University Women. Retrieved from http://www.aauw.org/2015/09/01/title-ix-womens-athletics/

Warner, Michael. (2002). *Publics and counterpublics*. New York, NY: Zone.

Weitz, Rose. (2017). A history of women's bodies. In Bonnie Kime Scott, Susan E. Cayleff, Anne Donadey, & Irene Lara (Eds.), *Women in culture: An intersectional anthology for gender and women's studies* (2nd ed., pp. 248–255). West Sussex, UK: John Wiley & Sons.

Welsh, Sandy, Carr, Jacquie, MacQuarrie, Barbara, & Huntley, Audrey. (2006, February). "I'm not thinking of it as sexual harassment": Understanding harassment across race and citizenship. *Gender & Society, 20*(1), 87–107.

Welter, Barbara. (1976). *Dimity convictions: The American woman in the nineteenth century*. Athens: Ohio University Press.

West, Candace, & Zimmerman, Don H. (1987). Doing gender. *Gender & Society, 1*, 125–151.

West, Candace, & Zimmerman, Don H. (2009). Accounting for doing gender. *Gender & Society, 23*, 112–122.

West, Isaac. (2014). *Transforming citizenship: Transgender articulations of the law*. New York: New York University Press.

West, Richard, & Turner, Lynn H. (2014). *Introducing communication theory: Analysis and application* (5th ed.). Boston, MA: McGraw-Hill.

Westerfelhaus, Robert, & Brookey, Robert Alan. (2004, July/October). At the unlikely confluence of conservative religion and popular culture: *Fight Club* as heteronormative ritual. *Text and Performance Quarterly, 24*(3–4), 302–326.

Westervelt, Eric. (2017, April 17). ACT UP at 30: Reinvigorated for Trump fight. *All Things Considered*. Retrieved from http://www.npr.org/2017/04/17/522726303/act-up-at-30-reinvigorated-for-trump-fight

Weststar, Johanna, & Legault, Marie-Josée. (2015, September 2). Developer satisfaction survey 2015. International Game Developers Association. Retrieved from https://c.ymcdn.com/sites/www.igda.org/resource/collection/CB31CE86-F8EE-4AE3-B46A-148490336605/IGDA%20DSS%202015-SummaryReport_Final_Sept15.pdf

Whipp, Lindsay. (2017, February 3). Made-up men reflect changing 50 billion male grooming industry. *Financial Times*. Retrieved from https://www.ft.com/content/825e520c-c798-11e6-8f29-9445cac8966f

Whitam, Frederick L., Daskalos, Christopher, Sobolewski, Curt G., & Padilla, Peter. (1998). The emergence of lesbian sexuality and identity cross-culturally: Brazil, Peru, the Philippines, and the United States. *Archives of Sexual Behavior*, *27*(1), 31–57.

Whitam, Fredrick L., Diamond, Milton, & Martin, James. (1993). Homosexual orientation in twins: A report on 61 pairs and three triplet sets. *Archives of Sexual Behavior*, *22*(3), 187–207.

Whitehead, Stephen M. (2002). *Men and masculinities: Key themes and new directions*. Cambridge, UK: Basil Blackwell.

Whiteside, Kelly. (2012, July 11). Women majority on Team USA. *USA Today*, p. A1.

Williams, Dmitri, Martins, Nicole, Consalvo, Mia, & Ivory, James D. (2009). The virtual census: Representations of gender, race and age in video games. *New Media & Society*, *11*, 815–834. doi:10.1177/1461444809105354

Wilmot, William W. (1995). *Relational communication*. New York, NY: McGraw-Hill.

Wilson, Elizabeth, & Ng, Sik Hung. (1988). Sex bias in visual images evoked by generics: A New Zealand study. *Sex Roles*, *18*, 159–168.

Wilson, Valerie, & Rodgers, William M., III (2016, September 19). *Black-white wage gaps expand with rising wage inequality*. Washington, DC: Economic Policy Institute. Retrieved from http://www.epi.org/publication/black-white-wage-gaps-expand-with-rising-wage-inequality/

Winfield, Nicole. (2012, June 12). Vatican says U.S. nuns must promote church teachings. *San Francisco Chronicle*. Retrieved from http://www.sfgate.com/cgi-bin/article.cgi?f=/n/a/2012/06/12/international/i071351D11.DTL

Wing, Adrien Katherine. (1997). Brief reflections toward a multiplicative theory of praxis and being. In Adrien Katherine Wing (Ed.), *Critical race feminism: A reader* (pp. 27–34). New York, NY: New York University Press.

Wohn, Donghee Yvette. (2011). Gender and race representation in casual games. *Sex Roles*, *65*, 198–207.

Women's Bureau, U.S. Department of Labor. (2014, August). Pay secrecy [Fact sheet]. Retrieved from https://www.dol.gov/wb/media/pay_secrecy.pdf

Women's Media Center. (2017). *The status of women in the U.S. media 2017*. Retrieved from http://wmc.3cdn.net/10c550d19ef9f3688f_mlbres2jd.pdf

Wood, Jessica L., Heitmiller, Dwayne, Andreasen, Nancy C., & Nopoulos, Peg. (2008). Morphology of the ventral frontal cortex: Relationship to femininity and social cognition. *Cerebral Cortex*, *18*(3), 534–540. doi:10.1093/cercor/bhm079

Wood, Jessica L., Murko, Vesna, & Nopoulos, Peg. (2008). Ventral frontal cortex in children: Morphology, social cognition and femininity/masculinity. *Social Cognitive and Affective Neuroscience*, *3*(2), 168–176.

Wood, Julia. (2001). The normalization of violence in heterosexual romantic relationships: Women's narratives of love and violence. *Journal of Social and Personal Relationships*, *18*(2), 239–261.

Wood, Julia T., & Fixmer-Oraiz, Natalie. (2017). *Gendered lives: Communication, gender and culture* (12th ed.). Boston, MA: Cengage Learning.

World Economic Forum. (2015). It's back to the future as women's pay finally equals men's . . . from 2006. Retrieved from http://reports.weforum.org/global-gender-gap-report-2015/press-releases/

Wright, Paul J., Arroyo, Analisa, & Bae, Soyoung. (2015). An experimental analysis of young women's attitudes toward the male gaze following exposure to centerfold images of varying explicitness. *Communication Reports, 28*(1), 1–11.

Wurtzel, Elizabeth. (1998). *Bitch: In praise of difficult women.* New York, NY: Doubleday.

Wysham, Daphne. (2002, October). Women take on oil companies in Nigeria. *Economic Justice News Online, 5*(3). Retrieved from http://www.50years.org/cms/ejn/story/82

Yang, Li-Shou, Thornton, Arland, & Fricke, Thomas. (2000). Religion and family formation in Taiwan: The decline of ancestral authority. In Sharon K. Houseknecht & Jerry G. Pankhurst (Eds.), *Family, religion, and social change in diverse societies* (pp. 121–146). Cambridge, UK: Oxford University Press.

Yanus, Alixandra B., & O'Connor, Karen. (2016). To comply or not to comply: Evaluating compliance with Title IX of the educational amendments of 1972. *Journal of Women, Politics & Policy, 37*(3), 341–358.

Ye, Zhenzhen, & Palomares, Nicholas A. (2013). Effects of conversation partners' gender-language consistency on references to emotion, tentative language and gender salience. *Journal of Language and Social Psychology, 32*(4), 433–451.

Yep, Gust A. (2003). The violence of heteronormativity in communication studies: Notes on injury, healing, and queer world-making. *Journal of Homosexuality, 45*(2–4), 11–59.

Yesil, Bilge. (2004). "Who said this is a man's war?" Propaganda, advertising discourse and the representation of war worker women during the Second World War. *Media History, 20*(2), 103–117.

Yoon, JeongMee. (n.d.). The pink & blue project. Retrieved from http://www.jeongmeeyoon.com/aw_pinkblue.htm

Young, Iris Marion. (1990). *Throwing like a girl and other essays in feminist philosophy and social theory.* Bloomington: Indiana University Press.

Yousman, Bill. (2003, November). Blackophilia and blackophobia: White youth, the consumption of rap music, and white supremacy. *Communication Theory, 13*(4), 366–391.

Yuasa, Ikuko Patricia. (2008). *Culture and gender of voice pitch: A sociophonetic comparison of the Japanese and Americans.* London, England: Equinox.

Yuval-Davis, Nira. (1997). *Gender and nation.* London, England: Sage.

Yuval-Davis, Nira. (1999). The "multi-layered citizen": Citizenship in the age of "globalization." *International Feminist Journal of Politics, 1*(1), 119–136.

Yuval-Davis, Nira. (2003). Nationalist projects and gender relations. *Narodna Umjetnost, 40*(1), 9–36.

Zack, Naomi. (1998). *Thinking about race.* Belmont, CA: Wadsworth.

Zhao, Shanyang, Grasmuck, Sherri, & Martin, Jason. (2008). Identity construction on Facebook: Digital empowerment in anchored relationships. *Computers in Human Behavior, 24*(5), 1816–1836.

Zimman, Lal. (2012). *Voices in transition: Testosterone, transmasculinity, and the gendered voice among female-to-male transgender people.* Unpublished doctoral dissertation, University of Colorado, Boulder. Retrieved from http://gradworks.umi.com/35/27/3527380.html

Zimman, Lal. (2015). Facebook, the gender binary, and third-person pronouns. In Alice Northover (Ed.), *The OUPblog Tenth Anniversary Book* (pp. 137–142). New York, NY: Oxford University Press.

Zimmer, Ben. (2015, April 11). "'They,' the singular pronoun, gets popular." *Wall Street Journal.* Retrieved from http://www.wsj.com/articles/can-they-be-accepted-as-a-singular-pronoun-1428686651

Zinzlow, Heidi, & Thompson, Martie. (2011). Barriers to reporting sexual victimization: Prevalence and correlates among undergraduate women. *Journal of Aggression, Maltreatment & Trauma, 20*(7), 711–725.

Ziv, Stav, Llyod, Isabel, Westcott, Lucy, Saville, Jordan, Ahmed, Turfayel, Jones, Abigail, . . . & Gidda, Mirren. (2016, December 8). Our favorite TV shows of 2016. *Newsweek.* Retrieved from http://www.newsweek.com/our-favorite-tv-shows-2016-newsweek-staff-picks-529353

Zompetti, Joseph P. (1997). Toward a Gramscian critical rhetoric. *Western Journal of Communication, 61*(1), 66–86.

Zosuls, Kristina M., Miller, Cindy Faith, Ruble, Diane N., Martin, Carol Lynn, & Fabes, Richard A. (2011). Gender development research in sex roles: Historical trends and future directions. *Sex Roles, 64*(11–12), 826–842.

Index

Figures and tables are indicated by *f* or *t* following the page number.

About the Authors

Catherine Helen Palczewski, PhD, is a professor of communication studies, past director of debate, and affiliate faculty in women's and gender studies at the University of Northern Iowa; teaches courses in the rhetoric of social protest, argumentation, gender, and political communication; is a past coeditor of *Argumentation and Advocacy* and director of the 2013 AFA/NCA Biennial Conference on Argumentation held in Alta, Utah; and has received the following awards: the Francine Merritt Award for Outstanding Contributions to the Lives of Women in Communication, the Iowa Regents Award for Faculty Excellence, the University of Northern Iowa College of Humanities and Fine Arts Faculty Excellence Award, the George Ziegelmueller Outstanding Debate Educator Award, and two Rohrer Awards for Outstanding Publication in Argumentation.

Victoria Pruin DeFrancisco, PhD, is a professor of communication studies and affiliate faculty in women's and gender studies at the University of Northern Iowa; studies and teaches courses in gender, intercultural, and interpersonal communication; served as director of the Women's and Gender Studies Program; coordinated the National Coalition Building Institute, a university-wide diversity inclusion program; and has received the following awards: Iowa Regents Award for Faculty Excellence, the UNI Outstanding Graduate Faculty Teaching Award, and the Iowa American Association of University Women Distinguished Faculty Award. Victoria is married and has stepchildren and grandchildren who call her Nana and remind her every day why she wrote this book.

Danielle Dick McGeough, PhD, is an assistant professor of communication studies and affiliate faculty in women's and gender studies at the University of Northern Iowa; teaches and researches how performance is and can be used for collaborative problem solving, community building, and social justice work; and has received the University Book and Supply Award for Outstanding Teaching. Her father taught her compassion, and her mom taught her to believe in people's ability to change.

This book was a truly coauthored endeavor. The fun, sweat, work, and joy were shared.